SCOTTISH SKALDS AND SAGAMEN

SCOTTISH SKALDS AND SAGAMEN

OLD NORSE INFLUENCE ON MODERN SCOTTISH LITERATURE

Julian Meldon D'Arcy

TUCKWELL PRESS

This volume is dedicated to the memory of

George Mackay Brown

(1921–1996)

First published in Great Britain in 1996 by
Tuckwell Press
The Mill House
Phantassie
East Linton
East Lothian EH40 3DG
Scotland

Copyright © Julian Meldon D'Arcy, 1996

The publishers gratefully acknowledge
financial assistance from

towards the publication of this book

ISBN 1 898410 25 9

British Library Cataloguing in Publication Data

A catalogue record for this book is available
on request from the British Library

Typeset by Háskólaútgáfan, University of Iceland Press
Printed and bound by Short Run Press Exeter

CONTENTS

ACKNOWLEDGEMENTS

I would firstly like to acknowledge the generous permission of the following to use copyright material: George Mackay Brown and John Murray (Publishers) Ltd., to quote from the novels and poetry of George Mackay Brown; Dairmid Gunn and the Neil Gunn Literary Estate, to quote from the novels of Neil Gunn; Faber and Faber to quote from Neil Gunn's *Silver Darlings*; Chambers Harrap Publishers Ltd., to quote from Neil Gunn's *Off in a Boat* and *The Lost Glen*; Marjorie Linklater, to quote from the works of Eric Linklater; and Naomi Mitchison, to quote from her novels.

I would also like to express my gratitude to the many institutions which have contributed to the completion of this book: Aberdeen University, for awarding me a bursary from 1985-88; the University of Iceland Research Council, for research grants in 1986, 1987 and 1989; and the Senate of the University of Iceland, for granting me sabbatical leave in 1988. I would like to give thanks to the staffs of the Aberdeen University Library, the National Library of Scotland, the National and University Libraries of Iceland, the Arnamagnaean Institute in Reykjavik, and the Reykjavik City Library, for all their patient assistance. I am also grateful to Mrs Clare Brown of the BBC Archives, Mr. Jonathan Bott, Keeper of Archives and Manuscripts of the University of Reading Library, and Ms Alison Fraser, Orkney Archivist. Special thanks are due to Brian Smith of the Shetland Archives for giving me access to, and copies of, vital material and drawing my attention to previously unknown sources. I am also grateful to Andi Ross, in Orkney, and Val Turner, Shetland Archaeologist, for making my trip to the Northern Isles possible. I would also like to express my gratitude to Mrs Marjorie Linklater and George Mackay Brown for granting me personal interviews whilst I was in Orkney, and for corresponding with me in Iceland. I also wish to thank Naomi Mitchison for writing to me and answering so many of my questions.

Whilst writing the original version of this book as a doctoral thesis at the University of Aberdeen I had help from many members of the English Department, especially David Hewitt and J. Graeme Roberts; special thanks are due to J. Derrick McClure for the loan of rare David Lindsay novels and for advice and discussion on this novelist. In Iceland I would first of all like to express my gratitude to all my colleagues in the English Department at the University of Iceland for their patience and encouragement. Special thanks are due to Pétur Knútsson Ridgewell, Marijane Osborn and Terry Gunnell for reading over and making valuable comments on both early and final drafts. I am also grateful to Andrew Wawn of Leeds University for comments and advice on the first three chapters.

I am especially grateful to Kirsten Wolf, Professor of Icelandic at the University of Manitoba, Winnipeg, Canada, for initially encouraging me to embark on this project; to Professor Douglas Gifford of the Department of Scottish Literature at the University of Glasgow, for his steadfast support in promoting the publication of this book; and to John Tuckwell for his enthusiasm and determination in bringing this about.

Finally, I owe an enormous debt of gratitude to two people: Isobel Murray, my academic supervisor at Aberdeen University, and her husband Bob Tait. Bob has given me much wonderful hospitality and many insights into Scottish literary history and society, and Isobel has been of incalculable help with her knowledge of modern Scottish literature, a stern correcting eye, her sense of humour, and her persistent faith in my ability.

INTRODUCTION

Old Norse literature is the literature of the Scandinavian peoples, written in the Old Norse language (Old Icelandic), mostly in Iceland, from the twelfth to the fifteenth centuries. In its entirety it is a massive collection of myths, legends, poetry, fiction, history, law-books, and hagiography. The core of Old Norse literature, however, the literature which is the most read and which has influenced British writers over the last two hundred and fifty years, can be classified in four main groups: the *Eddas*, skaldic poetry, the sagas, and *Heimskringla*.

Snorri Sturluson's *Prose Edda* (c.1220) and the anonymous *Poetic Edda* (composed between 800 and 1200) contain in poetry and prose most of the myths and legends comprising ancient Scandinavian cosmology, centred on Yggdrasil, or the Tree of Life. The *Eddas* are the most important sources for Old Norse philosophy and the stories of Odin, Thor, and many other gods, and how they and the giants and monsters finally destroy each other at Ragnarök (The Twilight of the Gods).

Skaldic poetry comprises the odes and verses of (mostly) historically recorded and named individual court poets of the kings and nobles of medieval Scandinavia. In very complex, rhythmical patterns of alliteration and kennings (highly elaborate and often obscure metaphors), they eulogise their benefactors' generosity and wisdom, battles and victories – as well as their dignity and fortitude in defeat and death.

The Icelandic or Family Sagas from the thirteenth century are the magnificent prose accounts of many larger-than-life Norse settlers of ninth-, tenth-, and eleventh-century Iceland. Mostly anonymous, part history and part fiction, they immortalise such marvellous stories as those of Njal and his sons and Gunnar of Hlidarend (*Njal's*

Saga), the imperious Gudrun Osvifsdottir and her ill-fated lover Kjartan Olafsson (*Laxdaela Saga*), the poet and berserker Egil Skalla-grimsson (*Egil's Saga*), and the incredibly strong and indomitable outlaw, Grettir Asmundsson (*Grettir's Saga*).

Snorri Sturluson's *Heimskringla* is a long and detailed history of the Norwegian kings, from the mists of legendary antiquity until shortly before the author's death in 1241. Full of colourful character descriptions and anecdotes, it is one of the most vital and powerful sources of early Scandinavian history. Altogether then, these four categories of Old Norse literature, the *Eddas*, skaldic poetry, the sagas, and the *Heimskringla*, comprise one of the finest achieve-ments of early medieval European literature – and have proved to be a creative inspiration to many British, and in particular Scottish writers, from the eighteenth century onwards.

English interest in Old Norse literature first became notable with the publication of Thomas Percy's *Five Pieces of Runic Poetry* (1763) and Thomas Gray's two poems, 'The Descent of Odin' and 'The Fatal Sisters' (1768). From then on until the early nineteenth centu-ry there was a growing vogue for 'Runic' or 'Gothic' poetry (i.e. supposed imitations of Old Norse skaldic verses) which influenced even such well-known poets as Blake. Interest in Old Norse litera-ture waned somewhat after the Napoleonic War, but revived in the middle of the nineteenth century and reached its peak in late Victorian Britain with the poems, stories and saga translations of William Morris and the Viking novels of H. Rider Haggard and W.G. Collingwood. In the twentieth century, however, Old Norse influ-ence on English literature seems to have become restricted to fantasy novels, such as those by J.R.R. Tolkien, and some poems and transla-tions by W.H. Auden. Old Norse history and literature has since had little influence on mainstream, contemporary literature in England.

In direct contrast to this, however, is the fact that Old Norse his-tory and literature have had a far greater influence on modern Scottish literature. Indeed historically, Scottish interest in Old Norse subjects began much earlier than in England – a point often overlooked by scholars dealing with the subject of Old Norse liter-ature in Britain as a whole. Lady Elizabeth Wardlaw's ballad *Hardyknute* (1719), Dr John Campbell's *A Polite Correspondence* (1741), and James Macpherson's 'The Highlander' (1758) all contain

Norse material and thus predate the works of Percy and Gray. There has been a continuing Old Norse influence on Scottish literature ever since and, in direct contrast to English literature, this influence is most notable in the present century. There are two striking features of this influence. Firstly, Scottish writers have made valuable but usually unnoted contributions to the dissemination of Old Norse literature in the eighteenth and nineteenth centuries: the first prose translations into English of saga episodes (by James Johnstone), the first saga redaction (by Walter Scott), the first translation of *Heimskringla* (by Samuel Laing), and the first Viking novel (by R.M. Ballantyne) were thus executed by Scotsmen, not Englishmen. And secondly, again in interesting contrast with English literature, Old Norse influence can be traced in many of the major writers of Scottish literature. Apart from Scott and Ballantyne mentioned above, the list also includes John Galt, James Hogg, Thomas Carlyle, Robert Louis Stevenson, Andrew Lang, R.B. Cunninghame Graham, and 'Fiona Macleod' (William Sharp).

The pervasiveness of Old Norse influence among major Scottish writers becomes even more apparent in the twentieth century. Lewis Grassic Gibbon's prejudiced views of the Vikings mark his books and articles on exploration and Scottish history as well as the characterisation of his novel *The Lost Trumpet*. Hugh MacDiarmid has a very pertinent use for Old Norse mythology in his poetry, and his interest in L.A. Waddell's theories on the *Edda* (1930) had some effect on his Pan-Celtic ideas. Neil Gunn's fascination with the early medieval confrontation of Norseman and Celt in Caithness inspired his interesting early novel *Sun Circle*, and three of his best-known and most successsful novels, *Morning Tide, Highland River*, and *The Silver Darlings*, are to a very real extent based on his atavistic perception of the Norse heritage in Scotland. The character and ethos of John Buchan's secret agents owe much to the actions and beliefs of the warriors of the Old Icelandic sagas. A knowledge of Old Norse mythology is essential for a full understanding of some of David Lindsay's metaphysical novels as Old Norse cosmology provides such works as *A Voyage to Arcturus, Devil's Tor* and *The Witch* with intelligible mythical and metaphorical structures for his otherwise highly esoteric theories. Old Norse history appears in some of the early short stories of Naomi Mitchison, and her novel

The Land the Ravens Found makes an indirect but important plea for
the assimilation of the Norse and Celtic heritages in Scotland; the
framework for her popular fantasy novel, *Travel Light*, is almost
exclusively the world of Old Norse mythology. Eric Linklater's lifelong love of Old Norse literature strongly influenced much of his
work, both fictional and non-fictional, and his concept of the Norse
ethos may well have affected his personal life as well as his art; his
novel *The Men of Ness* is beyond doubt the finest imitation of a saga
yet written. George Mackay Brown's lyrical portraits of the Orkney
earls and saints, Rognvald and Magnus, the wide variety of Viking
characters in his stories and poems, and his Norse-influenced narrative voice and style, play a dominant role in his poetry and fiction. Indeed so pervasive is this Old Norse element that it is virtually impossible to imagine Mackay Brown's art without it.

As this survey of twentieth-century writers indicates, one wave
of Old Norse influence in Scottish literature is contemporary with
the so-called Scottish Renaissance (especially the years 1920 to
1960), and, as this book will suggest, this is by no means a coincidence. Indeed this influence on specifically Scottish literature has
not had the attention it deserves. There has, of course, been some
research published on Old Norse influence on such individual
Scottish writers as Scott, Carlyle and Mackay Brown, but these usually fail to treat this influence from a specifically Scottish perspective, either literary or historical. A fresh and comprehensive study
of Old Norse influence on modern Scottish literature thus seems
desirable, and this book is an attempt to provide such a study. It
aims to show not only how, from the very beginning, Scottish writers have made a distinct and important contribution to the dissemination of Old Norse history and literature in Britain (playing a significant role in the creation of the notion of a Norse ethos), but also
how a consciousness of a literary and historical Norse heritage in
Scotland has influenced the eight major Scottish writers of this century listed above. The main questions addressed include how and
why these authors became influenced by Old Norse history and literature, what sources they used, and what specific effect this has
had on their work.

Some important points should be noted here about the content
and terminology of the book. Firstly, the Scottish literature referred

to throughout the book is that written in English and Scots, for as
the author has very little Gaelic, a detailed study of Old Norse
influence on Gaelic literature lies, regrettably, outside the scope of
this work.

Secondly, within this definition of Scottish literature, the list of
authors studied is not exhaustive. Each author or poet has been
selected either because of Old Norse influence in several of his or
her works, or because Old Norse influence has had some significant
effect on his or her style, subject matter or point of view. There are
other modern Scottish writers apart from those dealt with here who
have also used Old Norse material, but as this is evident only in single works or has had an insignificant effect on their work as a whole
(to date), they have been excluded. Examples of such are the novelists Nigel Tranter (*Macbeth the King*, 1978; *Lord of the Isles*, 1983),
Dorothy Dunnett (*King Hereafter*, 1982), Colin Mackay (*The Song of
the Forest*, 1986), Christopher Rush (*Into the Ebb*, 1989), Sian Hayton
(in her predominantly Celtic trilogy *Cells of Knowledge*, 1989; *Hidden
Daughters*, 1992; *The Last Flight*, 1994), and Margaret Elphinstone
(*Islanders*, 1995).

Thirdly, the phrases Norse, Old Norse, Viking, and early
medieval Scandinavian are used synonymously throughout the
book. On all occasions they relate to the conceptions of the language, history, culture and values of the people of Nordic origin
who lived in or settled in what are now Iceland, Norway, Sweden,
Denmark, the Faroes, and various parts of the British Isles between
the eighth and thirteenth centuries.

Fourthly, there is no standardised method for anglicising Old
Norse proper names and place-names, but the spelling of these in
the book is based on the conventions adopted by Magnus
Magnusson and Hermann Pálsson for their saga translations in the
Penguin Classics series. Thus all accents are dropped, the letters ð
and þ are transliterated d and th respectively, and personal names
are without the nominatival endings of strong nouns: hence Olaf
and not Ólafur.[1] Any variations from this are due to other well-
established spelling conventions (e.g. Balder for Baldur) or the use
of direct quotations and titles of works by writers using a different
system of spelling (e.g. Eric for Eirik) which will be noted in the
text.

Finally, all the major Old Norse works referred to in the book, and which have influenced the writers under discussion, had been translated into English by the early twentieth century. For the sake of convenience, however, only the most recent or readily available translations are quoted in the text, except where an earlier edition is specifically used by a particular author (e.g. George Mackay Brown's versions of A.B. Taylor's translations [1938] of the skaldic verse in *Orkneyinga Saga*). Similarly, wherever possible, references to the works of the Scottish authors discussed will be to the most recent or easily available editions.

NOTES

1   See Magnus Magnusson's and Hermann Pálsson's notes to their translation
    of *Njal's Saga* (Harmondsworth, 1960), pp.33-34.

1. SCOTLAND AND THE VIKINGS:
THE HISTORICAL AND LINGUISTIC BACKGROUND

The Norse Invasions

The ninth to eleventh centuries are often referred to in European history as the Viking Age, the period which saw the remarkable overseas expansion of the warbands, armies, pirates, traders, explorers and settlers from Scandinavia. For more than three hundred years the Danes, Norwegians and Swedes, collectively known as Vikings, Northmen or Norsemen, terrorised or conquered peoples and kingdoms all over Europe, from Russia in the east, to Sicily in the south, and Spain in the west. In the far north they discovered and settled Iceland and Greenland, and historical evidence points to the Norsemen as being the first Europeans to set foot in America.

The British Isles were no exception to this Norse expansion, and various parts of England, Scotland, Ireland and Wales were harried, conquered or settled by the aggressive and acquisitive men from Scandinavia.[1] English historians tend to mark the end of the Viking Age in Britain with the Battle of Stamford Bridge in 1066 when Harald Hardrada, the Norwegian claimant to the Anglo-Saxon throne, was defeated and killed by Harold Godwinsson just prior to the latter's own defeat and death at the Battle of Hastings a fortnight later. In terms of the history of the British Isles as a whole, however, this date is clearly too early, for in 1263 the medieval kingdom of Scotland was still being threatened by a Norwegian monarch, Hakon, and despite his lack of success at the Battle of Largs the Northern Isles of Scotland were to remain under Norwegian and later Danish sovereignty for a further two hundred years. Indeed it can be argued that the Viking settlements in Scotland were to have much longer and more far-reaching effects on the history, language and culture of this nation than they had in any other part of the British Isles.

In terms of recorded history, the Norse presence in Scotland can be dated from 795 A.D. with the pillaging of Skye and Iona, until 1468-69 when the Orkney and Shetland Isles were mortgaged to the Scottish crown in lieu of a dowry for Princess Margaret of Denmark on her betrothal to King James III of Scotland. Thus for more than six hundred years there was a continuous Scandinavian presence in parts of Scotland.[2] The extent of this Norse domain varied, sometimes considerably, but as the place-name, archaeological and literary evidence reveals, the Norsemen settled, ruled, or indirectly controlled an area stretching from the Shetland Isles to Galloway, including the Orkney Isles, parts of Sutherland and Caithness, the western littoral, and all of the Hebrides. These areas were ruled (either together or separately) by various Norwegian monarchs, Orcadian earls, Irish and Manx petty-kings, and even individual Viking chieftains. The height of Norse rule was probably achieved by Earl Thorfinn the Mighty (c.1020-65) who, according to *Orkneyinga Saga*, not only ruled over the entire area mentioned above but also 'nine Scottish earldoms' (though which earldoms these were has never been established) and 'a considerable part of Ireland'.[3] After Thorfinn's death this maritime empire gradually disintegrated. A Gaelic resurgence slowly undermined and finally replaced the Norse linguistic and political hold on the Hebrides, and they were finally ceded to the Scottish crown by the Treaty of Perth in 1266. In the fourteenth and fifteenth centuries the influence of Scottish language, society and politics gradually eroded the Norse domination of the Northern Isles, the two groups finally coming under Scottish sovereignty in 1468 and 1469. Nonetheless, four to six centuries of Norse rule over western and insular Scotland have left their mark politically, socially, toponymically, linguistically and culturally.

Political and Social Influence

Perhaps the single most important result of the Norse invasions of western Scotland in the ninth century was the ascendancy of the Scots of Dalriada under Kenneth MacAlpin. The invasions cut off the Dalriadic Scots from their Irish base and 'promoted a growing

"Scottish" self-awareness' among them.[4] The Norse pressure on northern and eastern Scotland also enabled Kenneth MacAlpin to defeat the Picts and establish his rule over much of eastern, central and southern Scotland. Thus as Barbara Crawford has suggested:

> If his [Kenneth MacAlpin's] emergence really can be directly linked to Norse activity, then we may attribute to the Vikings a decisive role in the creation of a Scottish kingdom.[5]

Furthermore, the gradually mixed Norse-Celtic population of the Western Isles and littoral (called Gall-Gaels in Gaelic, i.e. 'foreign Gaels'; hence Galloway) created a cultural unity in the area distinct from that of the Gaelic highlands and Scots lowlands.[6] It can be no coincidence, therefore, that the later medieval Lordship of the Isles created by Somerled, a Gael of Norse descent, comprised virtually the same area as the original Norse settlements, a fact strikingly noticeable in a comparison of historical maps of the territories of thirteenth century Inse Gall ('islands of the foreigners') and the subsequent Lordship of the Isles.[7] The historian Hugh Kearney has even suggested that the famous military traditions of the Highlanders derive not from their Irish ancestors but from the Vikings, and that some of the later clan feuding (e.g. between the Campbells and MacDonalds) could also be attributed to a legacy from the Norsemen.[8]

Another notable and enduring Norse influence in Scotland can be found in the former Dano-Norwegian colonies of Orkney and Shetland. As previously mentioned, these territories only finally came under Scottish rule in the fifteenth century, with the result that in terms of language, and legal and social organisation (e.g administrative areas for taxation and udal system of land-ownership) the isles remained distinct from mainland Scotland until quite recent times.[9] Indeed Orcadians and Shetlanders often persist in maintaining a nostalgic regard for their Norse origins and even cultivate a sense of a 'Scandinavian' as opposed to 'Scottish' identity. This has had repercussions even in present-day politics as the appeal by the Orkney Movement to the Danish government in 1986 (the 'Declaration of Wyre') over the Dounreay power-station has shown. Moreover it was the Dano-Norwegian connection with the

Northern Isles which later fostered the long-lasting commercial links between Scotland and Scandinavia and the tradition of Scottish soldiers serving in the Baltic, especially in the Danish and Swedish armies.[10]

The Norse legacy in the Northern and Western Isles and littoral can also be found in various aspects of daily life quite distinct from those in other parts of Scotland, including not only methods and terminology in house- and boat-building, fishing, fowling, farming and peat-cutting, but also in local customs, folklore and superstitions. All of this reveals the continuing existence of a North Atlantic seaboard culture which the Northern and Western Isles share with the Faroes, Norway and Iceland.[11]

One interesting aspect of Norse influence on modern Scotland is in its legal system, for as Barbara Crawford claims, it was the Norseman's concern with 'the processes of law' which was:

> ... one of the most valuable contributions made by the Norwegians and Danes to the cultures of the countries they settled in, and it is likely that Scotland was no exception in benefitting from these peoples' flair for judicial organisation.[12]

Early medieval Scottish 'burlaw courts' were probably Norse inspired, for example, and to this day there are specific aspects of Scots law which are Norse both in origin and terminology.[13] Moreover Norse laws continued to be applied in Shetland for many years after it came under Scottish sovereignty, and the existence of these laws still leads to complex legal disputes. One such 'cause célèbre' was the case in 1963 between the Lord Advocate and the University of Aberdeen over the St. Ninian's Isle treasure. The university disputed the Crown's claim to the treasure trove on the grounds that the udal law of King Magnus the Lawmender in 1274 had precedence over the later feudal law of the Scottish kingdom.[14] Although the university lost the case, this did not deter the Shetland Salmon Fishers' Association and the Lerwick Harbour Trust from later considering legal action against the Crown Estate Commission over offshore rents, once again claiming that under Shetland udal law from Norse times the Crown has no jurisdiction over the Shetland sea-bed.[15]

Language, Place-Names and Personal Names

The influence of the Norse settlements on the languages of Scotland is considerable, perhaps more than is generally realised. The separation of the Dalriadic Scots from Ireland had more than just political repercussions, for as Magnus Maclean has claimed: 'The Norse invasions were thus directly responsible for the rise of Scottish Gaelic and our native vernacular literature as distinct from the Irish'.[16] John Geipel has noted that Carl Marstrander was the first scholar to suggest the possibility that 'Scandinavian speech habits may be ultimately responsible for certain traits in the pronunciation of Scots Gaelic', and more recent research has confirmed this, especially in connection with preaspiration of stops and in pitch patterns. Certain aspects of the tone and modulation of the Gaelic spoken on Lewis, for example, are different from the Gaelic spoken elsewhere in Scotland and have striking resemblances to those of the Gudbrandsdal dialect of Norwegian.[17] There are also around 400-500 Norse loanwords in Scottish Gaelic, mostly connected with agriculture, fishing, boat-building and navigation, as might be expected.[18] Although outside the scope of this book, it is also worth noting that the Viking raids on the western isles have also left an indelible mark on Gaelic literature, especially in the development of Finn MacCoul legends, the Manus ballads, the poetry of William Livingstone and oral folklore still extant in the twentieth century.[19]

The Norse influence on the Scots language has also perhaps been underestimated. Old Norse and Scots were both originally Germanic languages, of course, but it was the Viking invasions and settlements of Northern England and Scotland which led to the intensification of the Norse elements in the local dialects and the eventual distinction between English and Scots, the latter retaining elements of Norse grammar, phonology and vocabulary which were gradually discarded in English. When beginning his research for his Scottish dictionary, for example, John Jamieson was astonished to find in the county of Angus 'a vast number of words', many of which were 'classical terms in the languages of Iceland, Sweden and Denmark'.[20] George T. Flom has listed over 500 Scots loanwords from Old Norse and has traced Scandinavian elements in Barbour's *Bruce*, Blind Harry's *The Wallace*, and the poetry of Dunbar.[21] Geipel also claims that 'Scandinavian expressions sprout thickly' in the Scots sketches and dialogues of Scott, Stevenson, MacDonald, Barrie and Crockett.[22] Many distinct features of the pronunciation of Scots consonants, vowels and diphthongs are also directly attributable to Norse influence. Indeed, David Murison argues that 'the legacy of the Norsemen can hardly be overestimated in modern Scots and it is in the main their contribution that differentiates our speech from the standard English'.[23] Orkney and Shetland, of course, have a very special place in any consideration of the languages of Scotland, for a form of Norse was spoken there until well into the eighteenth century. The modern dialects of Orkney and Shetland thus have hundreds of Norse phrases and lexical items in addition to those of mainland Scots. The two dialects were painstakingly recorded by Jakob Jakobsen in *An Etymological Dictionary of the Norn Language in Shetland* (1928-32), and Hugh Marwick in *The Orkney Norn* (1929). The general view has been that the Norse elements in the two dialects are gradually disappearing, but recent research suggests that Shetland Norn died out much later than hitherto supposed, especially as, according to Svavar Sigmundsson, Jakobsen and Marwick had failed to detect some Norse elements in the dialects because they had been so badly corrupted by Scots and English.[24] Thus, as Michael Barnes states: 'the modern dialects of both Orkney and Shetland still contain a sizeable body of words of Norn origin'. Indeed Swedish scholars have been recently doing more research on this aspect of modern Shetlandic.[25] As this brief survey would indicate, therefore, the Vikings have been very influential indeed in the formation and development of the Scottish languages and dialects.

The linguistic influence of the Norse settlements is most clearly evident, however, in the toponymy of insular and west coast Scotland, for as Crawford states:

> The place-name maps of northern and western Scotland are a permanent memorial to the thousands of nameless men and women who moved into these areas from across the North Sea and made the oceanic fringes of Scotland their own domain.[26]

The coastal features of Scotland (headlands, bays, coves, beaches, landing-places, sea-lochs, firths, rivers, islands, reefs) and the inland topography of the main settlement areas (valleys, hills, farmsteads, waterfalls, shielings) all have a predominantly Norse nomenclature, indeed in the cases of Orkney, Shetland and Lewis almost exclusively so. Some of the most obvious farm names are those with endings in -ster and -bost (from ON 'staðir' or 'ból-staðir'), and other easily identifiable Norse place-name endings are -ay (island), -nes, -nish (peninsula), -sker, -sgeir (skerry), and -dal (valley, dale).[27] The Norse dominance of the sea even outside their settlement areas is clearly indicated by the fact that all the major inlets on the east coast of Scotland, where Norse influence was minimal, are nonetheless known as firths (from ON 'fjörður').

A further enduring feature of Norse linguistic influence in modern Scotland is in the large number of family and clan names, traditionally Scottish and yet in fact Norse in origin. Some of these names are (Norse originals in brackets): MacLeod (Ljot), MacAuley (Olaf), Ranald (Rognvald), McManus (Magnus), McIver (Ævar), MacCrimmon (Hrjomund), MacAskill (Asketill). MacDougal is also Norse inspired, although Gaelic in language: MacDubhgall–'son of the dark foreigner'.[28]

In 1971, the archaeologist and historian David M. Wilson claimed that Scottish place-names and loanwords were 'the only real survivals of the Viking Age' and that anyone 'who would argue to the contrary can only be accused of romanticism'.[29] As the above evidence shows, however, this seems to be an oversimplification of the facts. Although it is hardly possible to claim that a Norse influence in modern Scotland is still pervasive, it has nonetheless played a small but significant part in the creation of the nation's culture and society. A present-day Scotsman called MacAuley living in Inverness would have a different surname, a differently named hometown, and would speak a different form of Scots, Gaelic or English, were it not for the Viking invasions of so long ago. Much of the Viking legacy in Scotland has been so well assimilated or transformed that it is virtually unnoticed in everyday life, but a careful analysis of this legacy shows a deep-lying Norse influence on various aspects of Scottish language, toponymy and nomenclature, and in insular Scotland especially, a lasting effect on local dialect, custom, ways of living and folklore. As Magnus Maclean has expressed it: 'The Norseman is still with us in hidden and often unknown corners of our life, our literature, and our history'.[30]

This point has been most noted and appreciated by creative artists who have found a continuing inspiration in Scotland's Norse heritage and, as this book aims to show, many of Scotland's foremost writers from the eighteenth century onwards have turned, in varying degrees, to their Norse past for themes, subject matter, stylistic and structural models, and, not least, a sense of identity.

NOTES

[1] For good surveys of Viking history, see Gwyn Jones, *History of the Vikings*, 2nd rev. edn. (Oxford, 1984); P.G. Foote and D.M. Wilson, *The Viking Achievement* (London, 1971); H.R. Loyn, *The Vikings in Britain* (New York, 1977); Else Roesdahl, *The Vikings*, trans. Susan M. Margeson and Kirsten Williams (Harmondsworth, 1991).

[2] For details, see Barbara E. Crawford, *Scandinavian Scotland* (Leicester, 1987), esp. pp.39-79; Anna Ritchie, *Viking Scotland* (London, 1993); Gordon Donaldson, *A Northern Commonwealth: Scotland and Norway* (Edinburgh, 1990); A.W. Brøgger, *Ancient Emigrants: A History of the Norse Settlements of Scotland* (Oxford, 1929); F.T. Wainwright, ed., *The Northern Isles* (Edinburgh & London, 1962), pp.117-62; Loyn, pp.45-51, 108-112.

[3] *Orkneyinga Saga: The History of the Earls of Orkney*, trans. Hermann Pálsson and Paul Edwards (Harmondsworth, 1981), Ch.32, p.75.

[4] Alfred P. Smyth, *Warlords and Holy Men: Scotland AD 80-1000*, The New History of Scotland, Vol.I (London, 1984), p.178.

[5] Crawford, *Scandinavian Scotland*, p.48. Smyth, pp.189-92, and Loyn, pp.35, 39-40, make the same point, as does Robert Locke Bremner in *The Norsemen in Alban* (Glasgow, 1923), pp.13-15.

[6] Crawford, *Scandinavian Scotland*, p.25.

[7] Peter McNeill and Ranald Nicholson, *An Historical Atlas of Scotland c.400-c.1600* (St. Andrews, 1975), pp.161, 176.

[8] Hugh Kearney, *The British Isles: A History of Four Nations* (Cambridge, 1989), p.58.

[9] Crawford, *Scandinavian Scotland*, pp.82-86.

[10] Barbara E. Crawford, 'Scotland's Foreign Relations: Scandinavia', in *Scottish Society in the Fifteenth Century*, ed. Jennifer M. Brown (London, 1977), pp.85-100.

[11] For an overview of this subject, see Reidar Th. Christiansen, 'Scotsmen and Norsemen: Cultural Relations in the North Sea Area', *Scottish Studies* 1 (1957), 15-57. The bibliography of Crawford's *Scandinavian Scotland* also contains many titles of detailed studies of various aspects of Old Norse influence on Scottish agriculture, fishing and folklore.

12   Crawford, *Scandinavian Scotland*, p.209.

13   Archibald A. M. Duncan, *Scotland: The Making of the Kingdom*, Edinburgh History of Scotland, Vol.I (Edinburgh, 1975), pp.349-60; W. Croft Dickinson, 'Some Scandinavian Influences in Scottish Legal Procedure?' *Arv* 15 (1959), 155-59.

14   *Session Cases 1963*, ed. M.G. Fisher (Edinburgh, 1963), pp.533-64; see also Knut Robberstad, 'Udal Law', in *Shetland and the Outside World 1469 - 1969*, ed. Donald J. Withrington (Oxford, 1983), pp.49-68; Gordon Donaldson, 'Problems of Sovereignty and Law in Orkney and Shetland' in *Stair Society Miscellany Two* (1984), pp.13-40.

15   *Shetland Times*, 11 March 1988, p.1.

16   Magnus Maclean, *The Literature of the Celts* (Glasgow & Dublin, 1902), p.209.

17   John Geipel, *The Viking Legacy: The Scandinavian Influence on the English and Gaelic Languages* (Newton Abbot, 1971), p.83. Carl Hj. Borgstrøm, 'On the Influence of Norse on Scottish Gaelic; Preaspiration of Stops and Pitch Patterns', *Norsk Tidsskrift for Sprogvidenskap* 11 (*Lochlann* 6) (1974), 91-103.

18   For more details of Norse influence on Gaelic, see George Henderson, *The Norse Influence on Celtic Scotland* (Glasgow, 1910), pp.108-218; Magne Oftedal, 'Gaelic: Norse influence', in *The Companion to Gaelic Scotland*, ed. Derick S. Thomson (Oxford, 1983), pp.98-99; Geipel, pp.81-85;

19   For details, see Reidar Th. Christiansen, *The Vikings and the Viking Wars in Irish and Gaelic Tradition* (Oslo, 1931); Proinsias Mac Cana, 'The influence of the Vikings on Celtic literature', in *Proceedings of the International Congress of Celtic Studies 1959*, ed. Brian Ó'Cúív (Dublin, 1962), pp.78-118; Rev. Allan MacDonald, 'The Norsemen in Uist Folklore', *Saga-Book* 3 (1901-03), 413-33; Donald A. MacDonald, 'The Vikings in Gaelic Oral Tradition', in *The Northern and Western Isles in the Viking World*, ed. Alexander Fenton and Hermann Pálsson (Edinburgh, 1984), pp.265-79; Maclean, pp.198-216. The Gaelic poet William Livingstone (Uilleam Mac Dhunleibhe) wrote two epics on the Norse invasion of the Western Isles: 'Na Lochlannaich an Ile' ['The Norsemen in Islay'] and 'Blàr Shunadail' ['The Battle of Sunadale'] in *Duain agus Orain* (Glasgow, 1882), pp.1-36 and 61-100. See also Sorley Maclean, 'The Poetry of William Livingstone', *Transactions of the Gaelic Society of Inverness* 39-40 (1942-50), 1-19.

20   John Jamieson, Preface to *An Etymological Dictionary of the Scottish Language*, (Edinburgh, 1808), p.vi.

21   George T. Flom, *Scandinavian Influence on Southern Lowland Scotch* (New York, 1900), pp.24-74.

22   Geipel, p.75.

23   David Murison, 'Norse Influence on Scots', *Lallans* 13 (1979), p.34; see also Geipel, pp.19-23; Flom, pp.9-17.

24   Laurits Rendboe, 'How "worn out" or "corrupted" was Shetland Norn in its final stage?', *North-Western European Language Evolution* 3 (1984), 53-88; Svavar Sigmundsson, 'A Critical Review of the Work of Jakob Jakobsen and Hugh Marwick', in *The Northern and Western Isles*, ed. Fenton and Pálsson (Edinburgh, 1984), pp.280-91.

25 Michael Barnes, 'Orkney and Shetland Norn', in *Language in the British Isles*, ed. Peter Trudgill (Cambridge, 1984), p.365; G. Melchers, 'Narrowing and Extension of Meaning in the Scandinavian-based Vocabulary of Shetland Dialect', *Scottish Language* 5 (1986), 110-119.

26 Crawford, *Scandinavian Scotland*, p.221.

27 For a detailed survey of Norse toponymy in Scotland, see W.F.H. Nicolaisen, *Scottish Place-Names: Their Study and Significance* (London, 1976), pp.84-120; see also Crawford, *Scandinavian Scotland*, pp.103-115, and Geipel, pp.140-51.

28 For further examples, see Henderson, pp.49-65, and Geipel, pp.179-81. The Gaels distinguished between 'dark' Danes and 'fair' Norwegians.

29 David M. Wilson, 'The Norsemen', in *Who are the Scots?*, ed. Gordon Menzies (London, 1971), p.113.

30 Maclean, p.215.

2. SCOTLAND AND OLD NORSE LITERATURE: THE EIGHTEENTH AND NINETEENTH CENTURIES

One of the most interesting features of Old Norse influence on Scottish literature is that it has been so surprisingly underestimated or even ignored. This is also true of the important Scottish contribution to the acquisition and dissemination of knowledge on ancient Scandinavian subjects. As Edward J. Cowan has pointed out:

> Most commentators have overlooked the distinctively Scottish interest in Icelandic literature, concentrating mainly on England, although Scotland's links with the Northern countries were both stronger and more numerous than those of her southern neighbour.[1]

This oversight can mostly be attributed to the simple fact that many scholars, both American and British, tend to regard anyone in the British Isles who writes in English as *being* English. Nonetheless, a study of translators, poets, critics, historians and philosophers involved in developing a general interest in Old Norse literature and history reveals that many of them were indeed Scotsmen and that their contribution was often essential and far-reaching.

Old Norse Influence in Scotland 1719-1815

Apart from very occasional use of ancient Scandinavian folklore and legend by Shakespeare, Temple, Pope and Dryden, the standard view in British literary history is that Old Norse influence on English literature only really began in the 1760s with the publication of Thomas Percy's *Five Pieces of Runic Poetry* (1763) and Thomas Gray's poems 'The Descent of Odin' and 'The Fatal Sisters' (1768). Percy's work contained translations (from Latin) of five Old Norse poems, many of which were to become popular enough to be retranslated several times. Gray's more renowned poems were paraphrased translations (of ON 'Baldr's Draumar' and 'Darraðar-ljóð') and their impact cannot be underestimated, for over the next fifty years they led to a proliferation of 'Runic', 'Gothic', or 'Danish' odes by many minor poets and even some of the better known Romantic poets such as Southey, Landor and Blake. These often crude and ludicrous attempts to reproduce the ancient poetry of Scandinavia were also stimulated by a revival of interest in Celtic literature and the eighteenth century intellectual fascination with Primitivism and the Noble Savage.[2]

What no scholar or critic appears to have noted in this context, however, is the publication in 1719 in Edinburgh of *Hardyknute: A Fragment*, an ancient ballad purportedly found by Lady Elizabeth Wardlaw in a vault in Dunfermline. This ballad was immensely popular in the eighteenth century and went through many editions, but was later discovered to be the work of Lady Wardlaw herself.[3] What is important here is that the ballad's subject is a Scottish hero's defeat of a Norse invader. Lady Wardlaw's ballad is thus apparently the first ever original work in English based on Viking history – and it appeared in Scotland more than forty years earlier than the poems of Percy or Gray.

Another Scot ahead of Percy and Gray was Dr John Campbell who (together with William Oldys) produced in 1741 *A Polite Correspondence: Or Rational Amusement* which has translations (from the Latin of Ole Worm and Saxo Grammaticus) of two Old Norse poems: 'An Ancient Danish Ode' and 'Another on Victory'. Furthermore, in Part IV of this collection of fictional epistles a certain 'Leander' writes a letter containing a highly idealised and romantic discussion of the ancient Norsemen's mythology, reverence for poetry, and way of life which, according to A.D. McKillop, 'deserves to be called a landmark in the development of the Scandinavian theme in English literature'.[4]

A more important landmark, perhaps, was the publication of James Macpherson's 'The Highlander' in 1758. This epic poem tells the story of a young Scottish chieftain, Albin, who joins his countrymen in successfully repelling an invasion of Danes and Norwegians led by King Sueno [Sveinn]. The verse is very banal and uninspiring, but the subject, a Norse invasion of Scotland, is clearly based on historical legend and the Gaelic *Magnus (Manus) Ballads* which are believed to have originated in the twelfth century and refer to the harassment of the Western Isles by Magnus Barelegs, King of Norway. More importantly, this Norse element of Macpherson's early and rather poor epic is later transformed into the central plot of his Ossianic poem, *Fingal* (1762), Sueno and his Norsemen being Gaelicised into Swaran and the men of Lochlin. The original Norse influence is still discernible, however, as critics have since noted.[5] Furthermore, not only did 'The Highlander' and *Fingal* precede Percy's Norse odes, they were also their direct inspiration. Percy specifically stated that 'this attempt [the *Five Runic Pieces*] is owing to the success of the ERSE fragments' of Macpherson,[6] and he had added the Old Norse texts of his poems precisely to verify them as genuine translations and avoid a controversy similar to the one concerning the sources of Macpherson's purportedly English versions of Gaelic poems. Macpherson's role as a purveyor of Norse literature to the British reading public has thus often been overlooked, but as Margaret Omberg has argued, 'Macpherson's poems were instrumental in the awakening of interest in ancient Scandinavia' and were 'the first in English poetry to portray the Scandinavian North to any appreciable extent'.[7]

Scottish men of letters also produced versions of 'Runic' poems no less than their English counterparts. Henry Mackenzie was so impressed by Gray's odes, for example, that he produced his own 'Introduction to the Fatal Sisters', and *The Edinburgh Magazine* and *Scots Magazine* sometimes published translations of Old Norse poems (e.g. by John Leyden).[8] In April 1803 and January 1804 the *Scots Magazine* published two cantos of a projected epic called 'The Battle of Largs' (dealing with King Hakon's futile invasion of Scotland in 1263) by the young John Galt. The poem was never completed as Galt was clearly mature enough to sense it was not an impressive piece of work; other less than successful attempts by Scotsmen to introduce Norse or Scandinavian material into their work include John Home's play *Alfred* (1778), William Richardson's *The Maid of Lochlin* (1801) and Sir George Mackenzie's play *Helga* which was jeered off the stage on its opening night in Edinburgh, 22 January 1812.[9]

A more interesting and successful contribution to Scottish/ Scandinavian literary relations in this period, however, was Robert Jamieson's *Popular Ballads and Songs* (1806) which made a number of Danish ballads available to readers of English and also drew attention to linguistic similarities between Scots and other Scandinavian languages. Furthermore, in the second volume of this work, Jamieson argued that 'Gothic Scalds', as he termed them, in northern England and Scotland had survived French influence after the Norman invasion, and that many Scottish ballads had been original compositions of these 'skalds' and not later medieval minstrels. Jamieson was thus claiming a direct link between Old Norse and Scottish literature. This claim had been put forward earlier by John Pinkerton in 1786, and more recent research has confirmed Scandinavian influence on the ballads of north-east Scotland in particular.[10]

The most important Scottish author of this period, however, is undoubtedly Sir Walter Scott. Scott's interest in Old Norse literature and history is a well-known fact and frequently commented upon, to a greater or lesser extent, by many scholars and critics. Scott had clearly developed this enthusiasm by the time he was a student in Edinburgh, for by 1791 he had presented papers on Icelandic lore and Scandinavian mythology to the Literary and Speculative Societies in Edinburgh, and in the autumn of 1792 he claimed to be spending his evenings poring over Bartholin's book on Danish antiquities.[11] Scott later became a friend of the Icelandic scholar G.J. Thorkelin (see below) and a subscriber to the Arnamagnaean editions of Old Norse works published in Copenhagen from 1770 onwards. Scott's interest in ancient Scandinavia is evident in background material in his earlier narrative poems such as *The Lay of the Last Minstrel* (1805), *Marmion* (1808), and *Rokeby* (1813), and in 1814 he published a redaction (from the Latin) of *Eyrbyggja Saga*.[12]

Scottish literary critics and philosophers were also active in the promotion of Old Norse history and culture, especially through the theories of Primitivism as expounded by Hugh Blair, Henry Home (Lord Kames), and James Beattie. Blair has a long discussion of the ancient Scandinavians in his *Critical Dissertation on the Poems of Ossian* (1763), and Henry Home also discusses Old Norse literature and manners in some detail in the second volume of his *Sketches of the History of Man* (1774) including many long quotations from Latin versions of *Heimskringla* and *Hávamál*.[13]

A great stimulus to Scottish antiquarians was the visit, in the 1780s, of the highly respected Old Norse scholar G.J. Thorkelin, whose stay with George Dempster at Dunnichen 'led to an acquaintance with many of the foremost Scottish intellects of the day'.[14] Thorkelin was certainly very active in promoting knowledge of ancient Scandinavia whilst in Scotland for it was there he wrote his *Fragments of English and Irish History in the Ninth and Tenth Century* (1788). This once again underlined the importance of Old Norse sources for the history of the British Isles, and his essay on the Slave Trade (1788) included the first English translation of a section of *Laxdaela Saga* (dealing with the high-born, Irish slave Melkorka). Thorkelin's special and lasting contribution to Scottish culture, however, was his vital role in prompting John Jamieson to begin work on his monumental *An Etymological Dictionary of the Scottish Language* (1808).[15]

Thorkelin gave many books to the Scottish Society of Antiquarians and procured many more for them once he had returned to Denmark. But Scottish historians themselves were also active in collecting Old Norse texts. James Johnstone was sending Scandinavian MSS to Scotland from Copenhagen, and after Johnstone's death, J.C Walker attempted to purchase his collection for John Pinkerton.[16] In 1799 William Laing arranged for all the publications of Det Kongelige Bibliotek in Copenhagen to be bought by the Advocates' Library in Edinburgh; indeed by the beginning of the nineteenth century the Advocates' Library had one of the finest collections of Scandinavian and Old Norse books available in the British Isles.

Scotsmen also provided important background information about Iceland, the home of the Old Norse sagas. This is perhaps fairly natural, for as Cowan has pointed out:

> The geographic circumstance that ports on the Firth of Forth such as Leith or Grangemouth were the natural points of embarkation for Iceland meant that a number of Scotsmen pioneered the Icelandic guide book industry.[17]

In 1811 the Scotsman Sir George Mackenzie published his celebrated *Travels in the Island of Iceland During the Summer of the Year 1810*
which contained chapters on Iceland's politics and commerce,
fauna and flora, and other interesting scientific phenomena.
Another zealous Scot, Ebenezer Henderson, also wrote an account
of his stay in Iceland in 1814 and 1815 (on behalf of the British and
Foreign Bible Society) which perhaps became as well known as
Mackenzie's book and, according to Sally Magnusson, is still
respected in Iceland today for 'its sympathetic and scholarly
account of Iceland's life and culture, past and present'.[18]

Further important Scottish contributions to the diffusion of
knowledge of Old Norse history and literature included the publication of James Johnstone's *Anecdotes of Olave the Black* (1780), *The
Norwegian Account of King Haco's Expedition Against Scotland
A.D.1263* (1782), and *Antiquitates Celto-Scandicae* (1786). These not
only provided the first English translations of selected passages
from Old Norse prose works (including the *Heimskringla,
Landnámabók, Egil's Saga, Njal's Saga*, and *Orkneyinga Saga*), but also
made available to a wider reading public essential sources of early
Scottish history. A further Scottish contribution to the knowledge of
the history and culture of ancient Scandinavia was Weber's and
Jamieson's *Illustrations of Northern Antiquities* (Edinburgh, 1814)
which also included the first ever abstract in English of an Old
Norse saga, Sir Walter Scott's version of *Eyrbyggja Saga*.

The Early Nineteenth Century 1815-1861

Between the end of the Napoleonic Wars and the mid-nineteenth
century there was a general decline in the interest in 'Runic' or
Norse-inspired poems even though several important works relating to Old Norse and Scandinavian studies were published in
Britain during this period.[19] The influence of these on English literature remained slight, however, and was chiefly limited to some
translations of Norse poetry by George Borrow (unpublished in his
lifetime), Edward Bulwer Lytton's novel *Harold: The Last of the Saxon
Kings* (1848), and Matthew Arnold's uninspiring 'Balder Dead'
(1855).[20]

In Scotland, on the other hand, Old Norse literature and history
continued to exert much greater influence on poets and writers

between 1815 and 1861. The Viking raids on Scotland, for example, provided the inspiration for two long narrative poems, William Tennant's *Thane of Fife* (1822), and James Hogg's *Queen Hynde* (1825). William Motherwell, a collector of ballads and a friend of both Scott and Hogg, also produced three long poems on Old Norse subjects.[21] The major Scottish author to be influenced by Old Norse literature and history during this period continued to be Sir Walter Scott. As mentioned above, Scott's interest in Old Norse culture had begun in the late eighteenth century and had influenced many of his narrative poems, the last, and most Norse-inspired, being *Harold the Dauntless* (1817). Scott's enthusiasm for ancient Scandinavia has been traced and examined in great detail elsewhere (especially by Paul Robert Lieder, Edith Batho, and John Simpson)[22] and from his knowledge of this subject he drew much incidental material for his poems and novels (often as explanatory footnotes), particularly references to Valkyries, spaewives, magic swords, werewolves, dragons, dwarves, berserkers, and runic spells and inscriptions. Nor was this influence restricted to his early narrative poems and the English abstract of *Eyrbyggja Saga*, for after the publication of *Waverley* in 1814 he continued to use ancient Scandinavian material in his novels, for example *The Antiquary* (1816), *Ivanhoe* (1819), and *The Pirate* (1822). This last named novel, set in Shetland around 1700, is the work most obviously influenced by Scott's knowledge of Old Norse literature, with its melodramatic spaewife, Norna, and plot elements borrowed from *Eyrbyggja Saga* and *Eirik's Saga*.[23] Even as late as 1832, the year he died, Scott used his knowledge of the Vikings for background detail in his description of the Varangian Guard in Constantinople in his novel *Count Robert of Paris*.[24]

A more renowned Scottish historian and novelist to be influenced by Old Norse literature was Thomas Carlyle. There is some slight evidence of Old Norse elements in his *Sartor Resartus*,[25] but without doubt one of his most important works influenced by his knowledge of ancient Scandinavia was his lecture on 'The Hero as Divinity', a discussion of Odin and Scandinavian paganism, later published as the first part of *On Heroes, Hero-Worship, and the Heroic in History* (1840). This influence is especially evident in his pervasive symbolical use throughout the book of Yggdrasil, the Norse

Tree of Life, and his good knowledge of Old Norse mythology and its sources. It is not Old Norse mythology in itself which was of primary interest to Carlyle, however, so much as its anthropological and historical implications, for to him this mythology was not, as in the eighteenth century, a colourful and dramatic background cosmogony for 'sublime' poetic effects, but a fully meaningful, historical, and influential system of belief. His treatment of Odin provided the first serious attempt to discern the essence of the human and historical truth behind the mists of legend and mythology. As Conrad Nordby stated in 1901: 'The grouty old Scotchman of Craigenputtoch ... saw far more deeply into the heart of Icelandic literature than anybody before him.'[26] Carlyle was certainly responsible for a more balanced view of the Vikings, seeing them as explorers, pioneers, and settlers as well as pirates and poets: 'Even Thor himself', Carlyle argued, 'engages in all manner of rough manual work'.[27] Carlyle thus considerably improved the image of the Viking in the eyes of Victorian Britain and made a distinct contribution to the upsurge of interest in Old Norse literature in the latter half of the century. As Cowan has claimed:

> His achievement is to replace the Valholl-seeking Viking of the eighteenth century, who drank beer from the skulls of his enemies, with the pioneer settler communing with nature.[28]

Another important contribution to the knowledge of Old Norse history came in 1844 with the Orcadian Samuel Laing's entire translation (from Swedish and Danish versions) of Snorri Sturluson's vital historical source, *Heimskringla; or the Chronicle of the Kings of Norway*. According to Ralph Berger Allen, 'much of the subsequent interest of readers and writers in Icelandic literature can be attributed to the man who made this veritable storehouse of history and general information of primitive Teutonic times accessible to them'.[29]

The Advocates' Library in Edinburgh continued to collect books and manuscripts on Old Norse and Scandinavian subjects in the early nineteenth century, and in 1819 David Laing, an Edinburgh bookseller, spent three weeks in Copenhagen purchasing some 2,000 printed items from Thorkelin's personal library, most of which were later presented to the Faculty of Advocates. Indeed the

Scandinavian section of the Advocates' Library became so large that it was renamed the Thorkelin Collection and had a full-time custodian, the Icelandic scholar Thorleif Repp, appointed to it.[30] Scots also continued to enlighten the British public on Iceland, the home of the sagas.[31] The publication and success of Lord Dufferin's *Letters from High Latitudes* (1857), however, marked the first of a series of successful English travelogues on Iceland which were to replace the works of Mackenzie and Henderson in both popularity and esteem.[32]

An important but sometimes neglected contribution to Old Norse studies in nineteenth century Britain was that made by the Scottish publisher David Douglas of the Edinburgh firm of Douglas and Edmonston, especially in connection with the publications of Sir George Webbe Dasent. Dasent, already renowned for his translations of the *Younger Edda* and Rask's *Grammar of the Icelandic or Old Norse Tongue*, became very keen to publish a translation of Asbjörnsen and Moe's Norwegian folktales in Scotland, as he felt a Scottish audience would be more appreciative of Norse folklore than an English one. *Popular Tales from the Norse* was thus published in Edinburgh in 1859 and Dasent's supposition proved highly accurate, the book selling a thousand copies in three months.[33] The success of this venture encouraged Dasent to entrust Douglas with his next project: the first English translation of an entire Icelandic Family Saga, in this instance the one often regarded as the greatest, *Njal's Saga*. The result was a beautifully illustrated and bound work, including a cover designed by James Drummond RSA, and a map of Thingvellir drawn by Captain Forbes and prepared by Bartholomews of Edinburgh. Thus whilst Dasent's *The Story of Burnt Njal* is the work of an Englishman, its actual publication reflects another wholly Scottish contribution to a renewed interest in Old Norse literature in mid-Victorian Britain.

The Scottish Contribution 1861-1905

From the appearance of Dasent's *The Story of Burnt Njal* onwards, the translation of important Old Norse sagas and texts increasingly gained momentum as late Victorian Britain saw a remarkable growth of interest in Norse literature.[34] The years 1861 to 1905 also saw the appearance of literally dozens of articles on Old Norse or

related subjects in Victorian journals and the publication of many
historical and scholarly works on ancient Scandinavia. As Karl
Litzenberg summarises:

> By 1870 both Eddas, the *Heimskringla*, three of the five Great Sagas,
> the *Völsunga Saga*, and a considerable body of legends and tradi-
> tional stories had been either translated into or paraphrased in
> English. By 1905 English versions of *virtually all* the Old Norse
> documents which might be of general interest had been pub-
> lished.[35]

The year 1905 then, can be seen as the end of late Victorian British
interest in Norse-inspired literature, for this was not only the year
of Vigfusson and Powell's last major publication (*Origines
Islandicae*), but also the year of Morris and Magnússon's last translation (Vol.VI) in the *Saga Library* series.

The period in question was also notable for its Norse-inspired literature. Two English writers of the time who were highly influenced by Old Norse literature were Charles Kingsley and Edmund
Gosse,[36] and the latter half of the nineteenth century also saw the
emergence of the Viking novel as a genre, the most successful (and
still very readable) being Rider Haggard's *Eric Brighteyes* (1891).[37]
One man dominates Norse-related literature in this period, however: William Morris. Not only was he one of the most renowned saga
translators of the period (with Eiríkr Magnússon), but also the poet
and novelist most influenced by Old Norse material, as is reflected
in a large number of his own poems, stories and novels, many of
which are still popular to this day.[38]

Alongside much English activity in this field, spearheaded by
Morris, there was a continuing and important Scottish contribution
to Norse-inspired literature between 1861 and 1905. Thomas
Carlyle published his *Early Kings of Norway* in 1875, but this para-
phrase of the *Heimskringla* was of a wholly different nature than his
Odin lectures from thirty-five years previously. It is badly written,
with idiosyncratic digressions, and the occasional serious error.[39]
Two other Scottish writers of the late nineteenth century who pro-
duced Norse-inspired works were Robert Louis Stevenson and
R.M. Ballantyne. Stevenson's short story 'The Waif Woman', even-

tually published in *Scribner's Magazine*, December 1914,[40] is a retelling of an incident in *Eyrbyggja Saga* involving the mysterious death of a Hebridean woman in the west of Iceland (a passage much relished by Scott in his *Abstract* of 1814). R.M. Ballantyne wrote two juvenile novels on Norse themes during this period: *Erling the Bold* (1869) and *The Norsemen in the West or America Before Columbus* (1872). The former is especially interesting for two main reasons; it appears to be the first Viking novel to appear in English,[41] and, to provide it with some sense of authenticity, Ballantyne cleverly adapts and integrates sections of the *Heimskringla* into his story.[42] This 'mosaic' approach to the creation of 'sagas' influenced other writers and was later adopted by Rider Haggard, John Buchan, Eric Linklater and George Mackay Brown. Ballantyne's second Viking novel, however, is very misleading and disappointing, and as Ralph Berger Allen expresses it, 'both the longest and the dullest' book on the Norse discovery of America.[43] In terms of good narrative, Robert Leighton's *The Thirsty Sword* (1892), a story of the Battle of Largs between Hakon and the Scots in 1263, and *Olaf the Glorious*, based on the life of King Olaf Tryggvason, are for more readable novels for juveniles.[44] The Shetlander J.J. Haldane Burgess's *The Viking Path* (1894) and the Orcadian J. Storer Clouston's *Vandrad the Viking* (1898) will be considered in a later chapter. An interesting contrast to the above writers' enthusiasm for Old Norse history is R.B. Cunninghame Graham's satirical short story 'Snaekoll's Saga', which humorously ridicules what Cunninghame Graham saw as pretentious, contemporary conceptions of saga heroism.[45]

Another Scotsman who made use of Old Norse and Scandinavian material was Robert Williams Buchanan who produced *Ballad Stories of the Affections from the Scandinavian* (1866) and the epic poem 'Balder the Beautiful'.[46] However, perhaps the most surprising addition to the list of nineteenth-century Scottish writers influenced by Old Norse themes is William Sharp. Either under his own name or his feminine pseudonym, 'Fiona Macleod', Sharp is best known for his stories and poems on Celtic subjects. Nonetheless, it is an apparently little known fact that he was also extremely interested in Old Norse material. Tall and fair-haired, Sharp was always proud of his Nordo-Celtic descent and Viking

bearing, and writing as 'Fiona Macleod', he presented many of his
Celtic heroes as similarly Norse in looks. He also wrote several
short stories on the often brutal ninth- and tenth-century clashes
between Viking and Gael in the Western Isles and a long and appreciative article on Old Norse literature for an American publication.[47]

Scottish no less than English literary journals also played a part
in disseminating knowledge of Old Norse history and culture.
Fraser's Magazine, Blackwood's and the *Scottish Review* published
work on Old Norse topics (e.g. a translation of *The Saga of the Faroe
Isles* in *Blackwood's*, 1869). *The North British Review*, edited by David
Douglas, carried pieces by G.W. Dasent and also the highly influential 'On the Character of Old Northern Poetry' (March, 1867) by
the well-known Icelandic scholar Grim Thomsen.[48] Thomsen had
followed in Thorkelin's footsteps by cultivating strong Scottish
links. Scottish historians were rendered a further valuable service
in 1873 with the publication of Gilbert Goudie's and Jón Hjaltalín's
first English translation of the *Orkneyinga Saga*, and Orcadians and
Shetlanders living in London formed a Viking Club in 1892 which
later became the Viking Society for Northern Research and pub-
lishes to this day one of the most highly respected academic journals on Old Norse subjects.[49]

Scots also continued to produce travelogues on Iceland in the
late nineteenth century,[50] and Scottish academics and men of letters
made significant use of Old Norse literature and mythology. Sir
James Frazer, the famous anthropologist, for example, had two volumes of his monumental work *The Golden Bough* (1890-1915) centred on the Balder myth, and tried to encourage his amanuensis to
continue a detailed study of Scandinavian mythology.[51] Another
Scottish anthropologist, Andrew Lang, also made scattered references to Scandinavian mythology in his works on primitive customs and religions. Lang, however, was also a poet and literary critic who loved Old Norse literature for its own sake. He avidly read
the translations of Dasent and Morris, wrote an enthusiastic appreciation of Old Norse prose narrative, and compared Old Norse and
Greek history and mythology in his books on Homer. Moreover
Lang, as an editor, used incidents from the sagas for his collections
of fairy tales and legends: 'The Story of Sigurd' from *Volsunga Saga*,

'The story of Glam' from *Grettir's Saga*, and 'The Marvels at Fróðá' from *Eyrbyggja Saga*.[52] This last story (translated by William Craigie) is yet another adaptation of the Frod River episode which so attracted Scott and Stevenson. Perhaps Lang's most important contribution to Norse-inspired literature, however, was simply the fact that it was he who encouraged Rider Haggard to write his saga-novel *Eric Brighteyes*, reading over and commenting on the first drafts of the novel before they were sent to the printers.[53]

Two outstanding Scottish scholars, William Craigie and W.P. Ker, made valuable contributions to the study of Old Norse literature at the turn of the century. W.P. Ker held highly influential views on the sagas and Eddic poetry in *Epic and Romance* (1897) and *The Dark Ages* (1904), which stressed the values of what he saw as the purely Germanic concepts of courage and honour. Perhaps his greatest achievement was the establishment of the Department of Scandinavian Studies at University College London in 1917. Craigie first began making a name for himself as an Old Norse and Modern Icelandic specialist at the turn of the century with articles in the *Scottish Review* and his books *Scandinavian Folk-lore* (1896) and *The Religion of Ancient Scandinavia* (1906). In academic terms, as C. B. Burchardt has claimed (with a regrettable use of 'English' for 'British'), the works of Professors Ker and Craigie have provided 'the chief contributions to English knowledge of Northern literature during the latter half of the nineteenth century and have secured a permanent place for old Scandinavian literature in England'.[54]

The Scottish Achievement

The Scottish contribution towards the knowledge and appreciation of Old Norse culture in eighteenth- and nineteenth-century Britain is thus a considerable and impressive achievement. It is an achievement not always acknowledged, however, which is surprising when it is realised just how important the Scottish contribution to Old Norse knowledge has been, and how many of Scotland's foremost men of letters were involved. James Macpherson, Henry Mackenzie, John Galt, James Hogg, Sir Walter Scott, Thomas Carlyle, R.M. Ballantyne, R.L. Stevenson, and Andrew Lang (to mention but the best known) have all, to a greater or lesser extent, translated, retold or been inspired by Old Norse poems, sagas and legends. The use made of Old Norse material by these authors varied markedly in both quantity and quality, so that it would perhaps be unwise to talk about a Scottish tradition in Norse-inspired literature; but as the above list indicates, there existed a substantial awareness and appreciation of Old Norse literature amongst Scottish men of letters between 1719 and 1905, and this prevailing awareness was to provide a solid background and example for twentieth-century Scottish writers.

There are two features specially worth noting about the Scottish involvement with Old Norse literature. Firstly, whereas English poets from Gray onwards tended to find inspiration in the Eddic poetry (i.e. in Old Norse *mythology*), Scottish writers seemed to seek their material in the *Heimskringla* and Family Sagas (i.e. Old Norse *history*). This is not, of course, a hard and fast rule (the poetry of Leyden and Buchanan are exceptions), but as most of the evidence seems to indicate, such a general distinction does exist. Indeed this is not entirely unnatural or surprising when it is borne in mind that Old Norse sagas are considered vital historical sources for early medieval Scotland, in some cases being virtually the only sources available (e.g. for the Northern Isles, Caithness and Moray). Any Scotsman seriously interested in the early history of his country simply could not avoid becoming acquainted with Old Norse literature. This emphasis on the historical rather than the mythical has remained a feature of Scottish writers' interpretation and application of Old Norse culture until the present day.

Secondly, and as a corollary to this, Scottish interest in Old Norse history and literature was not always simply antiquarian or aesthetic, but also sometimes racial and political. The increasing fascination with Viking history in late Victorian Britain ran parallel to, or in conjunction with, the growing belief in an Aryan or Nordic supremacy. In a country like Scotland, where a national identity was already compromised by geopolitical, linguistic, and religious divisions (particularly after the Union with England), such racial attitudes were to have an important influence on the way Scotland's Norse heritage was to be perceived and interpreted. Before embarking on detailed studies of Old Norse influence on individual twentieth-century Scottish writers, therefore, the evolution of the Nordic ideal and some of its effects in Scotland must first be examined. For this reason the following chapter will deal with the phenomena of the Norse/Celtic debate in Scotland between 1880 and 1940 and its influence on Scottish attitudes to identity and Scottish literature.

NOTES

1   Edward J. Cowan, *Icelandic Studies in Eighteenth and Nineteenth Century Scotland*, Studia Islandica 31 (1972), p.109.

2   For details on how British writers and historians became acquainted with and interpreted Old Norse history and literature, see Frank Edgar Farley, *Scandinavian Influences in the English Romantic Movement* (Boston, 1903); C.H. Herford, 'Norse Myth in English Poetry', *Bulletin of the John Rylands Library* 5 (1919), 75-98; Theodore T. Stenberg, 'Blake's Indebtedness to the Eddas', *Modern Language Review* 18 (1923), 204-6; Ethel Seaton, *Literary Relations of England and Scandinavia in the Seventeenth Century* (Oxford, 1935); and Margaret Omberg, *Scandinavian Themes in English Poetry 1760-1800*, Studia Anglistica Upsaliensia 29 (Uppsala, 1976). For details of the Celtic interest, see Edward D. Snyder, *The Celtic Revival in English Literature 1760-1800* (Gloucester, Mass., 1965). For Primitivist interest in ancient poetry, see F.N. Fairchild, *The Noble Savage: A Study in Romantic Naturalism* (New York, 1928), pp.444-55.

3   Norval Clyne, *The Romantic Scottish Ballads and the Lady Wardlaw Heresy* (Aberdeen, 1859), p.7; Sigurd Bernhard Hustvedt, *Ballad Criticism in Scandinavia and Great Britain during the Eighteenth Century* (New York, 1916), pp.87-88. 'Hardyknute' has most recently been reprinted in *Longer Scottish Poems Vol.II: 1650-1830*, ed. Thomas Crawford, David Hewitt and Alexander Law (Edinburgh, 1987), pp.7-14.

4   A.D. McKillop, 'A Critic of 1741 on Early Poetry', *Studies in Philology* 30 (1933), p.513. As McKillop points out (pp.515-18), the two odes were later plagiarised in Michael Bruce's *Poems on Several Occasions* (1770).

5   'The Highlander' appears in *The Poetical Works of James Macpherson* (Edinburgh, 1802), pp.15-98. For further details on the Norse background to Macpherson's poetry, see Alexander MacBain, 'Macpherson's *Ossian*', *Celtic Magazine* 12 (1887), 193-201; Magnus Maclean, *The Literature of the Highlands* (Glasgow & London, 1903), p.85; Derick S. Thomson, *The Gaelic Sources of Macpherson's Ossian* (Edinburgh & London, 1952), pp.11-21; Omberg, pp.26-33; and Fiona Stafford, *The Sublime Savage: A Study of James Macpherson and the Poems of Ossian* (Edinburgh, 1988), pp.61-76.

6   Quoted in Farley, p.30.

7   Omberg, p.26.

8   *The Works of Henry Mackenzie, Esq.*, 8 vols (Edinburgh, 1808), VIII, 63-67. Leyden's poems in the *Edinburgh Magazine* were: 'Danish Ode', 5 (April, 1795), 301-02; 'The Descent of Odin', 6 (Sept. 1795), 222; 'The Incantation of Hervor', 6 (Nov. 1795), 382-83.

9   'The Battle of Largs' appears in *Scots Magazine* 65 (1803), 272-74; 66 (1804), 57, and *The Collected Poems of John Galt 1779-1839*, ed. Hamilton Baird Timothy, 2 vols (London, Ontario, 1969), I, 2-28. For Galt's later more positive assessment of the poem, see his *The Literary Life and Miscellanies of John Galt*, 3 vols (Edinburgh, 1834), I, 41-53; a more recent review can be found in Ruth I. Aldrich, *John Galt*, Twayne's English Authors 231 (Boston, 1978), p.21. For details of Mackenzie's *Helga*, see Andrew Wawn, '*Gunnlaugs saga Ormstunga* and the Theatre Royal, Edinburgh 1812: Melodrama, Mineralogy and Sir George Mackenzie', *Scandinavica* 21 (1982), 139-51.

10   Robert Jamieson, *Popular Ballads and Songs*, 2 vols (Edinburgh, 1806); John Pinkerton, 'An Essay on the Origins of Scotish [sic] Poetry', in *Ancient Scotish Poems*, [sic] 2 vols (London, 1786), I, lxv-lxvi; David Buchan, *The Ballad and the Folk* (London, 1972), pp.7-11.

11   John G. Lockhart, *Memoirs of the Life of Sir Walter Scott*, 7 vols (Edinburgh & London, 1837-38), I, 173, 176; Edgar Johnson, *Sir Walter Scott: The Great Unknown*, 2 vols (London, 1970), I, 90.

12   For a detailed analysis of this work, see Julian M. D'Arcy and Kirsten Wolf, 'Sir Walter Scott and *Eyrbyggja Saga*', *Studies in Scottish Literature* 22 (1987), 30-43.

13   For details of Scottish Primitivists, see Lois Whitney, 'English Primitivistic Theories of Epic Origins', *Modern Philology* 21 (1924), esp. 338-53.

14   Cowan, p.115.

15   For details of Thorkelin's work and sojourn in Scotland and his role in inspiring Jamieson, see *Thorkelin and Scotland*, ed. W.T. Johnson, Sgann Microfilms (Edinburgh, 1982) and John Longmuir's 'Memoir of Dr. Jamieson', *Jamieson's Dictionary of the Scottish Language*, rev. and ed. John Longmuir (Paisley, 1912), p.xv.

16   Farley, pp.205, 206, n.2; Cowan, p.117.

17   Cowan, pp.129-30.

18   Sally Magnusson, 'The Victorian and the Norseman', *Northern Studies* 12 (1978), 4.

19   E.g. Henry Wheaton, *History of the Northmen* (1831); Joseph Bosworth, *Scandinavian Literature* (1839); Benjamin Thorpe, *Northern Mythology* (1851); Sir George Webbe Dasent's translation of the *Younger Edda* (1842). The first volume of William and Mary Howitt's *The Literature and Romance of Northern Europe*, 2 vols (London, 1852) contained a detailed survey of Old Norse literature with copious passages from Eddic and skaldic poetry (I, Chs.2-5, pp.15-219).

20   Borrow's Old Norse material can be found in Vols VII, VIII, IX, XV and XVI of *The Works of George Borrow*, 16 vols, ed. Clement Shorter (London, 1923-24). Lytton used *Heimskringla* as his source for the Battle of Stamford Bridge

in *Harold: The Last of the Saxon Kings* (1848), Everyman's Library 15 (London, 1970), pp.361-87. Sydney Dobell's *Balder* (1854) has no Norse material whatsoever.

21   For comment on Tennant's grotesque descriptions of the Norse gods in *Thane of Fife*, see Alexander Scott and Maurice Lindsay, Introduction to *The Comic Poems of William Tennant* (Edinburgh, 1989), pp.ix-xvi. Hogg claimed his *Queen Hynde* to be 'the best epic poem that had ever been produced in Scotland', in James Hogg, *Memoirs of the Author's Life and Familiar Anecdotes of Sir Walter Scott*, ed. Douglas S. Mack (Edinburgh & London, 1972), p.41. Edith Batho, however, in *The Ettrick Shepherd* (New York, 1969), p.76, sees the poem as boring; for a more charitable view, see Douglas Gifford, *James Hogg* (Edinburgh, 1976), p.221. Motherwell's poems are: 'The Battle Flag of Sigurd', 'The Wooing Song of Jarl Egill Skallagrim', and 'The Sword Chant of Thorstein Raudi', in *The Poetical Works of William Motherwell* (1832), ed. William Kennedy, 3rd edn. (Glasgow, 1849), pp.1-16. In comparison with Tennant's and Hogg's poems, they are still very readable today.

22   Paul Robert Lieder, 'Scott and Scandinavian Literature', *Smith College Studies in Modern Languages* I, No.2 (1920), 8-57; Edith Batho, 'Scott as Mediaevalist', in *Sir Walter Scott Today*, ed. H.C. Grierson (London, 1932), pp.133-57, and 'Sir Walter Scott and the Sagas: Some Notes', *Modern Language Review* 24 (1929), 409-15; John Simpson, 'Scott and Old Norse Literature', in *Scott Bicentenary Essays*, ed. Alan Bell (London & Edinburgh, 1973), pp.300-13.

23   For details of Norse influence on *The Pirate*, see Andrew Wawn, 'Shrieks at the Stones: The Vikings, the Orkneys and the Scottish Enlightenment', in *The Viking Age in Caithness, Orkney and the North Atlantic*, ed. Colleen E. Batey, Judith Jesch and Christopher D. Morris (Edinburgh, 1995), pp.415-18.

24   A point apparently overlooked by Lieder, Batho, and Simpson. The Varangian Guard was the Byzantine Emperor's personal bodyguard. Originally Norse in composition it later recruited mercenaries from all over northern and western Europe. The most famous Varangian leader, prior to his becoming King of Norway, was Harald Hardrada.

25   Joseph Sigman, 'Adam-Kadmon, Nifl, Muspel, and the Biblical Symbolism of *Sartor Resartus*', *English Literary History* 41 (1974), 252.

26   Conrad Nordby, *The Influence of Old Norse Literature upon English Literature* (New York, 1901), p.26.

27   Thomas Carlyle, *Sartor Resartus* and *On Heroes and Hero-Worship*, Everyman's Library 278 (London, 1967), p.271. For further comment on Carlyle's treatment of Old Norse material in his essay on Odin, see Robert W. Kusch, 'Pattern and Paradox in *Heroes and Hero-Worship*', *Studies in Scottish Literature* 6 (1969), 146-55; Charles H. Haws, 'Carlyle's Concept of History in *Heroes and Hero-Worship*', in *Thomas Carlyle 1981*, ed. Horst Drescher, Scottish Studies Vol.1 (Frankfurt am Main, 1983), p.154; and Walter Waring, *Thomas Carlyle*, Twayne's English Authors 238 (Boston, 1978), p.93.

28   Cowan, p.126.
29   Ralph Berger Allen, *Old Icelandic Sources in the English Novel* (Philadelphia, 1933), p.18.
30   For further details on the Thorkelin Collection, see A.A. Calderwood, 'Danish Libraries in Britain', *Denmark* (June, 1948), 8-9, (July, 1948), 13-14, and D. Wyn Evans, 'A Note on the Content of the Thorkelin Collection in the National Library of Scotland', *The Bibliotheck* 4 (1963), 79-80. For details of Repp's contribution to Norse studies, see Andrew Wawn, *The Anglo Man: Þorleifur Repp, Philology and Nineteenth-Century Britain*, Studia Islandica 49 (Reykjavik, 1991).
31   E.g. Robert Chambers, *Tracings of Iceland and the Faröe Islands* (1856), and Andrew Symington, *Pen and Pencil Sketches of Faröe and Iceland* (1862).
32   E.g. Sabine Baring-Gould's *Iceland: Its Scenes and Sagas* (1863), Richard F. Burton's *Ultima Thule* (1875), C.G.W. Lock's *The Home of the Eddas* (1879), John Coles's *Summer Travelling in Iceland* (1882), and W.G. Collingwood's and Jón Stefánsson's *A Pilgrimage to the Saga-Steads of Iceland* (1899).
33   Cowan, p.15.
34   E.g. *Viga Glum's Saga* (Sir Edmund Head, 1866), *Grettir's Saga* (William Morris and Eiríkr Magnússon, 1869), *Völsunga Saga* (Morris and Magnússon, 1870), *Orkneyinga Saga* (Jón Hjaltalín and Gilbert Goudie, 1873), *Eyrbyggja Saga* (Morris and Magnússon, 1892), *Egil's Saga* (W.C. Green, 1893), *Laxdaela Saga* (Muriel C. Press, 1899).
35   Karl Litzenberg, *The Victorians and the Vikings*, University of Michigan Contributions in Modern Philology 3 (Ann Arbor, 1947), p.14.
36   Especially notable for Old Norse influences are Kingsley's *Hereward the Wake* (1866), and Gosse's *King Erik: a Tragedy* (1876) and *Studies in the Literature of Northern Europe* (1879), a standard work for many years.
37   For details of these novels and juvenile Viking fiction, see Allen, pp.42-81. For details of around ten American novels on a similar subject, see George Leroy White Jr., *Scandinavian Themes in American Fiction* (Philadelphia, 1937), pp.19-41.
38   For a comprehensive list of Morris's Norse-related literature, see Karl Litzenberg, 'William Morris and Scandinavian Literature: A Bibliographical Essay', *Scandinavian Studies and Notes* 13 (1933-35), 93-105.
39   E.g. naming Eirik the Red as the first discoverer of America: Thomas Carlyle, *The Early Kings of Norway* (London, 1875), p.54; for further background to this work, including the part played by his brother John, an enthusiastic but amateurish scholar of Old Norse, see Edward J. Cowan, 'The Sage and the Sagas: the Brothers Carlyle and *Early Kings'*, *The Bibliotheck* 9 (1978-79), 161-83.
40   Reprinted in *The Strange Case of Dr. Jekyll and Mr. Hyde, Fables and Other Stories and Fragments*, Tusitala edn. Vol.V (London, 1924), pp.159-79.
41   Sabine Baring-Gould's *The Icelander's Sword* was admittedly serialised in twenty parts in the Hurstpierpoint School magazine in the late 1850s, but it was not published in its entirety as a novel until 1894. See Andrew Wawn,

'The Cult of "Stalwart Frith-thjof" in Victorian Britain', in *Northern Antiquity: The Post-Medieval Reception of Edda and Saga*, ed. Andrew Wawn (London, 1994), p.239.

42   E.g the killing of Einar, son of King Thorkel of Denmark, and his comrades in *Erling the Bold* (London, 1869), pp.112-13, is clearly based on Snorri Sturluson's, *Heimskringla*. See *Heimskringla: the History of the Kings of Norway*, trans. Lee M. Hollander (Austin, 1984), p.183. Ulf of Romsdal's speech to King Harald Finehair in the novel (pp.243-44) is based on Asbjorn Medalhus's address to King Hakon the Good (*Heimskringla*, p.109). Ketil Flatnose's story of the use of a fake funeral in order to enter a besieged city (pp.322-23) is taken from Harald Hardrada's ruse to capture a town in Sicily (*Heimskringla*, p.585).

43   Allen, p.70.

44   Allen, pp.46, 64.

45   The story was published in *The Ipané* (London, 1901), pp.204-25. See also Herbert Faulkner West, *A Modern Conquistador: Robert Bontine Cunninghame Graham. His Life and Works* (London, 1932), pp.159-61, 237.

46   Published in three parts in *The Contemporary Review* 29 (1876-77), 691-710; 800-27; 1004-1026. For an evaluation of the poem, see C.H. Herford, 'Norse Myth in English Poetry', p.85

47   For a description of Sharp's pride in his Norse origins, see Elizabeth A. Sharp, *William Sharp (Fiona Macleod): A Memoir*, 2nd edn., 2 vols (London, 1912), I, 3-7. Examples of Celtic heroes with Norse features include Alastair Macleod in *Pharais* and Alan Gilchrist in *The Mountain Lovers*, *The Works of Fiona Macleod*, Uniform edn., 6 vols (London, 1910), I, 47, 214. Fiona Macleod's most notable stories about Vikings can be found in *Barbaric Tales* (London, 1903), pp.15-29, 33-40, 43-48, 51-60, and 181-202. His piece of literary criticism was published under his own name: William Sharp, 'Icelandic Literature', *Library of the World's Best Literature, Ancient and Modern*, ed. Charles Dudley Warner, Vol.XX (New York, 1896-7), 7865-95.

48   G.W. Dasent, 'Harald Hardrada and Magnus the Good', *The North British Review* 39 (1863), 493-537; 'Harald Hardrada', 40 (1864), 93-143; 'England and Norway in the Eleventh Century', 42 (1865), 357-412. Thomsen's then seminal work, 46 (1867), 111-61, has been reprinted in Studia Islandica 31 (1972), 45-105.

49   *Saga-Book of the Viking Society for Northern Research*. For details, see J.A.B. Townsend, 'The Viking Society 1892-1967', *Saga-Book* 17 (1966-69), 102-115.

50   E.g. William Mitchell Banks, *A Narrative of the Voyage of the Argonauts in 1880* (1881); Elizabeth Jane Oswald, *By Fell and Fjord: or Scenes and Studies in Iceland* (1882).

51   J.G. Frazer, *Balder the Beautiful*, 2 vols, Part VII of *The Golden Bough: A Study in Magic and Religion*, 3rd edn. (London, 1913); R. Angus Downie, *Frazer and the Golden Bough* (London, 1970), p.125.

52   For further details, see Roger Lancelyn Green, *Andrew Lang: A Critical Biography* (Leicester, 1946), pp.21, 68, 77; Andrew Lang, 'The Sagas', in

Essays in Little (London, 1891), pp.141-52; *Homer and the Epic* (London, 1893), pp.382-403; *Homer and his Age* (London, 1906), pp.222-28. The Norse-inspired stories are from *The Red Fairy Book* (London, 1890), pp.357-67; *The Book of Dreams and Ghosts*, 2nd edn. (London, 1899), pp.254-69, 273-87.

53   D.S. Higgins, *Rider Haggard: The Great Storyteller* (London, 1981), pp.128-29.

54   C.B. Burchardt, *Norwegian Life and Literature* (London, 1920), p.77.

3. NORSEMAN AND CELT:
THE RACIAL DEBATE IN SCOTLAND 1880-1940

Although it never developed into the horrifying theories and resulting practices of Nazi Germany, a belief in the inherent racial superiority of the Nordic/Aryan peoples was nonetheless common in Britain, especially England, between the years 1880 and 1940. In Scotland, however (as in Ireland and Wales), a rival Celtic movement emerged to challenge the ideas of Nordic supremacy, and the ensuing debate can be traced in many Scottish magazines, journals and books throughout this period. Indeed this confrontation in Scotland of the racial ideals and attributes of Celt and Norseman was to have a distinct influence on certain aspects of modern Scottish literature.

Notions of Nordic Supremacy

Racial interpretations of history had already developed in Europe as early as the sixteenth and seventeenth centuries,[1] and as the detailed studies of Samuel Kliger and John Greenway have shown, Teutonic and Nordic myths were later appropriated by writers and philosophers in northern and western European countries for various social, political, nationalistic or artistic purposes.[2] In eighteenth-century Britain in particular the notion became established that the ancient Goths/Teutons/ Saxons/Norsemen (these terms were then often interchangeable) were the forefathers of the English (and later American) peoples and their ideals of democracy, enterprise and Empire. In the nineteenth century, with increasing historical knowledge, these ideals became more specifically associated with the Anglo-Saxons and Norsemen. Once again, however, these terms were often interchangeable, the choice often being a slight difference of perspective. The Anglo-Saxons, especially the Jutes from Denmark, were sometimes simply regarded as early Norsemen, or, conversely, the Viking settlers were seen as a northern branch and second wave of the original Saxon race. Nonetheless there were some writers and historians who strictly distinguished between the two races, in particular as they saw the Norsemen as mentally, morally and physically superior to the Anglo-Saxons. According to Henry Wheaton, for example, the Viking invasions of England were necessary in order to revitalise a nation suffering from the 'rapid degeneracy' of the Saxons, a view also held by the Howitts and G.W. Dasent.[3] A typically emphatic statement on this belief was made by the Orcadian Samuel Laing:

> Our civil, religious, and political rights, the principles, spirit, and forms of legislation through which they work in our social union, are the legitimate offspring of the Things of the Northmen, not of the Wittenagemoth of the Anglo-Saxons – of the independent Norse viking, not the abject Saxon monk.[4]

The above writers and many others thus believed that the British Constitution, trial by jury, freedom of the press, and even the Reformation, could be traced to the Norse settlement of Britain. These sentiments are most graphically illustrated in the American Ralph Waldo Emerson's image of Norse gods transmogrified into British politicians, civil servants and industrialists in his *English Traits* (1856):

> Scandinavian Thor, who once forged his bolts in icy Hecla and built galleys by lonely fiords, in England has advanced with the times, has shorn his beard, enters Parliament, sits down at a desk in the India House and lends Miöllnir to Birmingham for a steam-hammer.[5]

A racial view of Britain's industrial and colonial successes gained even greater credence and respectability with the publication of Gobineau's *Essai sur l'Inégalité des Races Humaines* (1853-55), often regarded as the seminal work of modern racism, which particularly exalted the Scandinavian element of the Germanic races.[6] Charles Darwin's *Origin of Species* (1859) and *The Descent of Man* (1871) were also of great significance, for the proposed theories of

natural selection were used to justify claims for superior races and
the necessity of racial discrimination.[7] Indeed by the mid-nineteenth century it had become commonplace to interpret the history
and progress of mankind in terms of the rise and fall of various
races. As Kliger has commented:

> Carlyle, Kingsley, J.R. Green, Creighton, Froude, Kemble, Bulwer-
> Lytton, Meredith, Matthew Arnold – the list of those who start
> from racial assumptions could be made to include nearly every
> writer of the period.[8]

Indeed, as the Empire expanded, racial views became increasingly
xenophobic, aggressive and intolerant. Charles Kingsley, for example, argued strongly that the fair-haired races could say to the
brown-haired ones: '"The blood of the Asas is in my veins. Do you
not see it? Am I not wiser, stronger, more virtuous, more beautiful
than you? You must obey me, and be my man, and follow me to the
death"'. Furthermore the enslaved race 'was thereby not degraded,
but raised out of selfish savagery and brute independence into loyalty, usefulness, and self-respect'.[9] It is easy to see how such views
could lead to Houston Stewart Chamberlain's demand for Teutonic
control of the world, and the ultimate insanity and horror of the
Third Reich.[10]

The popularity of the Morris and Magnússon saga translations
and the great Victorian interest in Norse history can now be seen in
another perspective. The blond, blue-eyed Viking of great strength,
good looks and daring who carried all before him in battle, conquering peoples, founding kingdoms and dynasties, and discovering and settling new lands, was a perfect historical and literary
symbol for the English colonist and American frontiersman. As
Malcolm Elwin states, writing of the year 1887:

> Beards and moustaches were the fashion, because they were the
> emblem of man's physical superiority, and the heroes of fiction
> were ... hirsute he-men, bred in the Kingsley school of muscular
> Christianity, like ... Rider Haggard's Viking-like adventurers.[11]

By the end of the nineteenth century, therefore, a very positive
notion of a Norse ethos had become established which viewed the

Norsemen as brave and resourceful warriors, afraid more of dis-
honour than death, who were intrepid sailors, explorers and
colonists and defenders of individual freedom and the rule of law.
There are some elements of truth in this conception of the Norse
ethos, but it overlooked some of the less appealing aspects of the
Vikings: their paganism, use of slaves, tendency towards violence
for the sake of violence, and their occasionally pragmatic views of
loyalty. These aspects were either ignored or tacitly accepted in
more palatable forms. Thus the fact that most Vikings were pagan
until the eleventh century, for example, did not ruffle the
Victorians' normally stern moral conscience. This was partly
because of a slowly diminishing belief in Christianity and partly
because of what might be termed an ingenious sleight of mind by
many writers and historians in northern Europe. These writers saw
the ancient Scandinavians' view of Odin as 'Allfather' and Balder as
his son, who rose from the dead after Ragnarök, as adumbrating
the Almighty and Jesus Christ. This was interpreted as clear evidence of the Norsemen's 'innate concept of monotheism'[12] if not a
precognitive understanding of Christianity. Thus, early in the nineteenth century, in Denmark, Oehlenschläger could wish for a fusion
of cross and hammer, and Grundtvig address Christ and Odin as
'sons of Allfather'.[13] Later, in Germany, Richard Wagner 'identified
Christ with Wotan [i.e. Odin]' and at the end of the century in
Britain the Scot Robert Williams Buchanan could unblushingly end
his poem 'Balder the Beautiful' with Jesus Christ and Balder quite
literally holding hands.[14] Alternatively, of course, novelists, poets
and historians could emphasise the lives of the Vikings who
attempted to Christianise the north such as the Norwegian kings
Olaf Tryggvason (995-1000) and King Olaf the Saint (1025-30).
These monarchs' brutal methods of converting people were usually excused or overlooked by many Victorians, and their deaths in
battle usually interpreted as martyrdom in spite of the obvious
political and dynastic reasons for their aggressive policies and ultimate military defeat.[15]

Such a deliberate effort to glamorise the Norsemen in late
Victorian Britain could lead to abysmal if not absurd literature, as
in the following passage taken from Paul du Chaillu's *Ivar the
Viking* describing a gathering of Vikings for athletic games:

What superb specimens of manhood they were! The finest the
world could show! Spartan-like in appearance, for all the weak at
their birth had not been allowed to live. What splendid proportions their bodies had! What strong chests and powerful frames!
What muscles![16]

The eponymous hero is naturally the best runner, jumper, swimmer
and wrestler at the meeting and is, of course, quite unbeatable in
single combat. The novel ends with his marriage to Scandinavia's
most beautiful maiden, charming companion and wonderful wife.
Du Chaillu's novel is thus full of the clichés of Nordic supremacy
and tiresomely replete with superlatives whenever the hero
appears. It is an excellent example of how an uncritical and slavish
adulation of the Nordic racial myth can help to prevent a novel
from having any credibility or literary merit whatsoever.

The Celtic Response

Eighteenth-century antiquarians and men of letters were not only
fascinated by Britain's Old Norse (and Anglo-Saxon) heritage, but
also its Celtic past. The publication of Macpherson's Ossianic
poems (1760-63) marked the beginning of intensive interest and
research in the Celtic languages and literatures which led to the
appearance of many important books on these subjects over the
next one hundred years.[17] In the middle of the nineteenth century,
Celtic studies were further boosted by Matthew Arnold's famous
essay 'On the Study of Celtic Literature' (1862) with its call for a
professorship in Celtic studies at the University of Oxford and its
sympathetic view of Celtic influences on English literature. The
academic study of the Celtic cultures also continued apace with distinguished contributions from John Rhys in Britain, Douglas Hyde
in Ireland, Ernest Renan in France and Kuno Meyer in Germany, all
of whom added greatly to the knowledge of Celtic languages and literatures.[18] As Anne Saddlemeyer has stated, 'by the end of the century innumerable scholars, organisations and periodicals were devoted to the recovery of the Celt'.[19] The period was also marked by the
flowering of the so-called 'Celtic Twilight' including Elizabeth Sharp's
Lyra Celtica (1896), the works of Yeats and Synge in Ireland, and the
Scottish novels of 'Fiona Macleod', William Black, and Neil Munro.[20]

This Celtic revival in the latter half of the nineteenth century clearly emerged as a form of cultural self-defence in the face of the increasingly hostile attitudes of the supporters, especially English ones, of the notion of Aryan or Nordic supremacy. Indeed over the centuries the English have been accused of looking down upon their Celtic neighbours as defeated peoples with barbaric languages and a predilection for non-Anglican religions: Catholicism in Ireland, Presbyterianism in Scotland, and Methodism in Wales. Edward D. Snyder has shown, for example, that anti-Celtic prejudice has been common in English literature since the twelfth century, from Gerald Cambrensis through Shakespeare, Dryden and Dr Johnson. Moreover he claims that this 'universal contempt' for the Welsh, Irish and Scots 'is a tradition so powerful that at times it seems to have had considerable importance in influencing the history of literature'.[21] Anti-Celtic prejudice in England increased significantly in the late eighteenth and early nineteenth century as a result of Scottish Jacobitism, Irish nationalist rebellions (1798, 1803, 1848), and large-scale Irish immigration. As 'Goronva Camlann' wrote in 1846:

> In whichever of the three kingdoms a poor Celt may have been born, he can scarcely take up an English newspaper, but he finds himself and his birth and kin either disparaged, or by implication, annihilated.[22]

Matthew Arnold made a sincere effort to reconcile the two races with his 'On the Study of Celtic Literature' in which he heartily condemns all English arrogance and insensitivity towards the Celtic peoples. He especially points out that the Celts are also members of the Indo-European race and that their culture has helped infuse the English tradition with a sense of spiritual beauty, the mystery of life, and a vivacious use of colour and rhythm, without which English literature would be greatly impoverished. The Celtic imaginative flair was a necessary antidote to Saxon dullness and regularity; Arnold even argues that the superiority of Old Norse over early Germanic poetry is probably due to Celtic influence.[23] Unfortunately, however, despite his good intentions, Arnold's essay only seems to have exacerbated the racial debate, partly because of his undisguised contempt for the actual Celtic languages (especially Welsh), and partly because his general claims for Celtic attributes merely reinforced previously held convictions about racial stereotypes. Thus the Celt was more than ever seen as indolent, irresponsible, garrulous, mystical and passionate with a prediliction for alcohol, music and lost causes, whereas the Norseman/Saxon was seen as industrious, responsible, taciturn, pragmatic and phlegmatic with a predilection for sobriety, statistics and success. The second half of the nineteenth century thus saw an increasing racial differentiation between Celt and Norseman or Saxon, as Curtis has noted:

> The cult of Anglo-Saxon virtues and the explicit or implied condemnation of Celtic vices constitutes one of the more persistent themes in Victorian novels, poems, and plays, autobiographies, periodicals, and cartoons.[24]

Some Celts, exasperated perhaps by the volume of the literature extolling the wonders of the Nordic blood of the English, began to produce their own grossly exaggerated claims for the racial purity and/or supremacy of the Celts, using sometimes tortuous and dubious theories to substantiate them. Thus Luke Owen Pike tried to prove that the English were not a Teutonic race but a Cymric division of the Celts, and Joseph Fisher attempted to show that the Saxons were Scandinavians from the Baltic who were originally an offshoot of the Celts.[25] Yet others tried to show that the Celtic languages were the purest and most enduring forms of the original Indo-European or Aryan language.[26]

Norseman and Celt in Scotland

The Norse/Celtic debate also took place in Scotland, especially in the years 1880 until 1940, but with a very important difference. In England the literary confrontation between Norseman and Celt had helped unify English Imperialists and nationalists by instilling in them a strong Teutonic identity hostile to the Celtic element of the United Kingdom. In Scotland, however, the debate became a divisive and acrimonious domestic dispute over racial origins. This stirred up many old Scottish antagonisms of the Highland versus

Lowland type, and was perhaps one of the factors which helped prevent twentieth-century Scottish nationalism from presenting a united front.[27] On the one hand were Scots who could only see an independent Scotland as essentially Celtic in culture, and preferably language, whilst on the other were Scots who, perhaps overwhelmed by the anti-Celtic diatribes in English language journals, preferred to adopt a Norse identity. This allowed them to disassociate themselves from the apparently undesirable attributes of the Celt and yet made it possible for them to claim all the virtues of the Teuton without being identified too closely with the Saxon English.

The question of the racial identity of the Scots has a long history. The first major discussion of the subject was probably John Pinkerton's *An Enquiry into the History of Scotland* (1789) in which he argued that the original Caledonians and contemporary inhabitants of Scotland were not the Dalriadic Scots from Ireland, but the ancient Picts, a Scythian or Germanic race which had come from Scandinavia via Shetland and Orkney. Thus only twenty-five per cent of the population were Celtic:

> These Gaël [sic] are most slavish and poor, natural effects of their indolence. The better ranks in the Highlands and Western Isles are almost all of Norwegian race, which is in fact the very same with the Pikish [sic].[28]

This argument was later disputed by the historian W.F. Skene in his *The Highlanders of Scotland* (1837) in which, although agreeing with Pinkerton on the Dalriadic Scots, he stoutly maintained the original Scottish races were Celtic and not Germanic. E. William Robertson, in his *Scotland under her Early Kings* (1862), also later argued for the Celtic origins of the peoples of the Scottish Lowlands. Thus by the mid-nineteenth century the battle lines were drawn, especially with the publication of *The Races of Men* (1850-62) by the Edinburgh anatomist Robert Knox in which he argued that there was a mutual and inherent antagonism between the Nordic and Celtic races.[29]

These differences of opinion continued well into the twentieth century. Supplementing W.F. Skene's and James Logan's earlier detailed histories of Celtic civilisation in Scotland, 'Fiona Macleod' and Neil Munro eulogised the Gael in their English language nov-

els and short stories. Ruaridh Erskine pleaded the cause of the
Gaelic language and culture in the pages of the *Scots Magazine* and
founded Gaelic journals and societies. Thomas D. MacDonald,
under the pseudonym Fionn Mac Colla, made perhaps the most
exaggerated (if not eccentric) claims for Gaelic civilisation as the
purest and finest in human history.[30] Meanwhile, the Norse heritage in Scotland was vigorously propounded by James
Cruickshank Roger with his *Celticism a Myth* (1884), George
Henderson with his *Norse Influence on Celtic Scotland* (1910) and
Robert L. Bremner in *The Norsemen in Alban* (1923). Important journalists and literary critics such as Andrew Lang, Sir William Craigie
and William Power likewise scarcely veiled their admiration for the
Norse ethos and contempt for most things Celtic.[31]

All the various aspects, both positive and negative, of the Nordic
and Celtic races were continuously debated in Scottish journals
throughout the late nineteenth and early twentieth centuries. Some
journals presented both sides of the argument, for example *The
Scottish Review*; although it published many articles on Old Norse
subjects, it also contained the six Rhind lectures on Celtic history by
the renowned Celtic scholar John Rhys, and R. Erskine's views on
the supremacy of Gaelic culture.[32] *Blackwood's Magazine*, however,
tended to be anti-Celtic throughout the period, and was especially
hostile to Irish Home Rule or the regeneration of the Celtic languages. *The Edinburgh Review* also tended to be strongly Nordic in
its sympathies.[33]

A good example of how virulently and intransigently many
Scots could argue over this issue can be found in the pages of the
Scottish Educational Journal between July 1925 and February 1926.
During these seven months a tremendous battle raged in pen and
ink between half a dozen contributors under a variety of headings,
'Nordic Origin of the Scots', 'Celt and Teuton', 'A Celt's Reply', etc.,
in which the whole gamut of passions and prejudices on the subject
were uninhibitedly aired. The exchange began innocuously enough
with a claim by R.L. Cassie, an author from north-east Scotland,
that the dialects of northern Scotland should provide the basis of a
revitalised Scots language as these were the purest and most
Nordic forms (17.7.25, p.10).[34] Hugh MacDiarmid (writing under
his own name, C.M. Grieve) was naturally very quick to give a con-

temptuous reply to this attack on his own claims to lingusitic authority on Scots matters (24.7.25, pp.12-13). Robert W. Tait, however, argued that 'overwhelming claims can be put forward for the Nordic origin of the great majority of Scotsmen' (2.10.25, p.43) and that 'nothing could ever be half so ridiculous as the pan-Celtic doctrines supplied to us in our school-books for generations' (25.12.25, p.73). A correspondent calling himself 'Buchan' wholeheartedly rejected this 'ridiculous "Nordic" theory' (20.11.25, p.60) and urged writers to 'devote more time and attention to Gaelic matters, and less to "side-shows" like Braid Scots and the perpetuation of Scandinavian and Germanic influences in Scotland' (5.2.26, p.85). Donald A. Mackenzie was likewise very angry with the way many critics considered Scottish virtues as 'Teutonic' and all Scottish failings as Celtic, especially as it was the Celts who saved the Anglo-Saxons from 'Paganism and a low code of morals' (15.1.26, pp.77-78). Despite his Celtic sympathies Mackenzie had very personal views on language and poetry and attacked both C.M. Grieve's Scots and Erskine's Gaelic movement (20.11.25, p.60). Finally, R.L. Cassie returned to the fray to declare himself a Celt, but supported the idea of the more 'virile and Germanic' Scots displacing Gaelic as it was likely 'to infuse more of action and achievement into the Celtic contemplation and dreaminess' (8.1.26, p.76).

Another brief exchange took place in the pages of the *Scots Magazine* early in 1931. The January edition carried an article by Alexander Urquhart, 'Celt and Norseman: A Contrast',[35] which compared the Norse Faroe and Lofoten Isles with the Celtic Hebrides and delivered the by then pro-Nordic standard judgement of 'a picture of energy and vitality on the one hand and of lethargy and slackness on the other' (p.248). Urquhart blames the poverty and decline of the Western Isles not on the Celtic race, for the Hebrideans 'share the blood of the Norse peoples with whom to-day they contrast so amazingly' (p.249), but on the Celtic language and culture which has turned them into dreamers. In the very next edition appeared the article 'The Gael Will Come Again' by Neil M. Gunn (writing under his pseudonym of Dane McNeil)[36] which vigorously rejects Urquhart's findings, blaming the poor economy of the Hebrides on the post-1745 brutality of the English government, especially the Clearances, by which any Gaels who were not 'hunted and dragooned, or shipped abroad like cattle,' having been 'cowed into a mood of utter subjection, were by the most subtle and insidious means, religious and educational, made to despise their language and tradition' (p.326). Gunn ends by pointing out that the 'Saxon ideal of the go-getter' had not 'landed the world in a golden age completely devoid of poverty and squalor' (p.327), and that the values and humanity of the Gaelic way of life may well be needed once more.

A final example of this debate can be found in the pages of *The Scotsman* between October and December 1935. On 16 October the paper reported on Lord Salvesen's address to the Scottish Anthropological Society on 'Scandinavian Influence on the Population and Languages of Scotland' which stressed the vital importance of the country's Norse heritage. The following day, an indignant letter appeared in the paper, under the name 'North Highlander', refuting Salvesen's claims and arguing that 'the pagan Scandinavians of the Viking Age were on a very much lower stage of culture and civilisation than Christian Scotland' (17.10.35, p.13). Thus began a fractious correspondence between many contributors, including Lord Salvesen himself, which only finally petered out just before Christmas of that year.[37] Salvesen received stout support, for example, from Frank Maitland, who argued that Scotland was not a Gaelic civilisation (30.10.35, p.15), and Alexander Thomson, who insisted that 'all patriotic Scots ought to be intensely proud ... of their ancient Nordic race' (3.12.35, p.11). On the opposing side, 'North Highlander' received firm support from, amongst others, a certain MacLabhran, who claimed 'the Teuton was always a barbarian' until he came under the influence of Celtic civilisation (18.11.335, p.13), and D. Murray Rose, who insisted that the Norse sagas and fables had 'polluted Scots history to an incredible extent' (19.11.35, p.11). Only one correspondent, 'K.H.', made any attempt to reconcile the two sides through irony and humour:

> When the Aberdonian, in his pride of caste, repudiates all connection with the Celt, he is actually a Celt speaking an English language inflicting chastisement upon a Viking who speaks Gaelic! I am proud to be able to speak the language of Columba, Gaelic, but I can trace my descent to the Kings of Norway. And the whole

thing is so very amusing that we should have enough to keep us
from bad tempers. (29.11.35, p.13)

These exchanges in the *Scottish Educational Journal*, the *Scots Magazine*
and *The Scotsman* thus reveal many of the typical arguments used in
support of either the Nordic or Celtic race. Racial views are notoriously illogical and emotional and, as some of the above examples
illustrate, many of them are clearly based on debatable and prejudiced evidence and are highly personal and subjective opinions
rather than realistic or verifiable facts. Nonetheless these journalistic
debates present a fairly good picture of the various attitudes and
positions adopted towards the racial and linguistic issues surrounding the question of Scottish identity in the early twentieth century.

Literary Significance

But what exactly is the literary significance of this Norse/Celtic
debate between 1880 and 1940? Broadly speaking it had three main
consequences for modern Scottish literature. Firstly, it illustrates
that most Scottish writers of the twentieth century have had a very
distinct sense of their country's racial and linguistic history. In the
works of Gibbon, Gunn and Linklater, just to mention three of the
best known writers of the post-1920 Scottish renaissance, there are
constant references to Scotland's early history and an underlying
sense of the importance and relevance of racial consciousness and
atavism in the character and behaviour of modern man. As Kurt
Wittig has argued, this is perhaps one of the most distinctive features of Scottish literature during this period:

> This harking back to the primordial beginnings of the race strikes
> a keynote for modern Scottish fiction, in which the dim ages of
> history often throw their shadow across the path of modern man.
> Man is no longer seen as a being living on the level of the present;
> he carries his ancestors on his back, and whether he realises it or
> not his values and reactions are largely determined by his ances-
> tral past.[38]

Secondly, the frequent reiterations of the positive and negative
aspects of Norseman and Celt could, and unfortunately often did,

lead to the promotion of racial stereotypes, both Nordic and Gaelic, in Scottish literature, especially, for example, the Nordic heroes of Buchan and Linklater and the Celtic heroes of Gunn (points to be discussed in the relevant chapters). Indeed Malcolm Chapman has persuasively argued that the post-Arnold 'ethnological typecasting' of the 'idealist Celt' has become deeply rooted in the Scottish consciousness right up until the present. Gaelic culture has become so 'folklorised' that the Celt is always 'located in some kind of opposition to the modern world'. In some Scottish bookshops, for example, Celtic books, including Iain Crichton Smith's contemporary Gaelic prose, can be found shelved in the prehistory section 'only inches away from stone circles, druids and speculations on the exact location of Atlantis'.[39]

Thirdly, and perhaps inevitably, the ongoing Norse/Celtic debate and its animosities naturally led to Scottish writers taking specific sides or adopting varying racial identities or postures which, as the following chapters of this book will show, were to affect both the style and subject matter of their work. In *Scottish Country* (1935), for example, Neil Gunn, in his article on 'Caithness and Sutherland', relates the story of the arranged battle between Clan Gunn and Clan Keith in which both parties agreed on a specific number of horses. The Clan Keith chieftain was cautious or treacherous enough to have two men on each horse, however, and so won the battle. In the very next chapter in the same book, Eric Linklater, writing on Orkney, has exactly the same plot, only this time a version from *Orkneyinga Saga* in which the protagonists are Earl Sigurd the Norseman and the Celtic chieftain Maelbrigta, the Orkney earl winning the battle with his extra men.[40] As with all such legendary tales shared by two cultures it is virtually impossible to determine the exact ethnic origin of the story. This is irrelevant in this instance, for what is much more revealing here is the indicative choice each author makes: Linklater unhesitatingly relates a Norse version – and Gunn a Celtic one. The lines are not always so clearly drawn, but many Scottish writers in the twentieth century have seemingly felt obliged at one time or another to state their (occasionally varying) position on the subject. The Norse/Celtic debate has indeed prompted a wide spectrum of sometimes surprising and idiosyncratic literary responses.

As these last three chapters have shown, the Viking invasions and settlements of so long ago have made a long-lasting impression on Scottish history, language and culture. Though often hidden or unrecognised, there is quite a significant Norse heritage in Scotland, a heritage which has provided an example, a style, subject matter, a voice, and a sense of purpose or identity to many of Scotland's best known poets and novelists. The notable increase in Norse-inspired literature in Scotland, especially between 1920 and 1940 (involving such writers as Buchan, MacDiarmid, Gunn, Mitchison, Lindsay, and Linklater), is thus no sudden or inexplicable phenomenon but the continuing development and exploration of literary and historical themes which had already inspired Scottish authors for more than two hundred years.

NOTES

[1]   Léon Poliakov, *The Aryan Myth: A History of Racist and Nationalist Ideas in Europe* (London, 1974).

[2]   Samuel Kliger, *The Goths in England: A Study in Seventeenth and Eighteenth Century Thought* (Cambridge, Mass., 1952), esp. pp.7-33, 72-209; John L. Greenway, *The Golden Horns: Mythic Imagination and the Nordic Past* (Athens, Georgia, 1977), esp. pp.60-82, 119-68.

[3]   Henry Wheaton, *History of the Northmen* (London, 1831), p.319; Howitt, I, 3, 5; G.W. Dasent, Introduction to *The Story of Burnt Njal*, (Edinburgh, 1861), p.x.

[4]   Samuel Laing, 'Preliminary Dissertation' to his translation of Snorri Sturluson's *Heimskringla* (London, 1844), pp.106-7.

[5]   *The Selected Writings of Ralph Waldo Emerson*, ed. Brooks Atkinson, 2nd edn. (New York, 1950), p.609.

[6]   For details, see Michael D. Biddiss, *Father of Racist Ideology: The Social and Political Thought of Count Gobineau* (New York, 1970), esp. Ch.5, 'The Viking Inheritance', pp.225-33.

[7]   For further details on racial thinking in the nineteenth century, see Hannah Arendt, *The Origins of Totalitarianism* (London, 1958), pp.158-221. On Aryanism in Britain, see L.P. Curtis, *Anglo-Saxons and Celts: A Study of Anti-Irish Prejudice in Victorian England* (Bridgeport, Mass., 1968), pp.36-48, 66-89, and Frederic E. Faverty, *Matthew Arnold the Ethnologist* (Evanston, 1951), pp.13-40.

[8]   Kliger, p.104.

[9]   *The Roman and the Teuton*, Works of Charles Kingsley Vol.X (London, 1879), p.49.

10 Houston Stewart Chamberlain, *The Foundations of the Nineteenth Century,*
    trans. John Lees, 2 vols (London, 1911) II, 222-29. For a horrifying account
    of how Old Norse literature was used in the Third Reich, see Christa
    Kamenetsky, *Children's Literature in Hitler's Germany: The Cultural Policy of
    National Socialism* (Athens, Ohio, 1984), pp.85-118.

11 Malcolm Elwin, *Old Gods Falling* (London, 1938), p.23. Quoted in Wendy R.
    Katz, *Rider Haggard and the Fiction of Empire* (Cambridge, 1987), p.59.

12 Greenway, p.95.

13 Greenway, pp.159, 161.

14 Poliakov, p.311; Buchanan, *The Contemporary Review* 29 (1876-77), p.1026.

15 E.g. Carlyle on Olaf Tryggvason, *Early Kings of Norway*, pp.56-85.

16 Paul du Chaillu, *Ivar the Viking* (London, 1893), p.238.

17 E.g. Evan Evans, *Specimens of the Poetry of the Antient Welsh Bards* (1764);
    Charlotte Brooke, *Reliques of Irish Poetry* (1789); Lady Guest's translation of
    The Mabinogion (1838-49); Thomas Stephens, *The Literature of the Kymry*
    (1849); John Francis Campbell, *Popular Tales of the West Highlands* (1860-62).

18 For further details, see Snyder, *The Celtic Revival in English Literature 1760-*
    1800; Curtis, pp.108-16; Faverty, pp.111-61.

19 Ann Saddlemeyer, 'The Cult of the Celt: Pan-Celticism in the Nineties', in
    The World of W.B. Yeats: Essays in Perspective, ed. Ann Saddlemeyer and
    Robin Skelton (Dublin, 1965), p.20.

20 For further details, see Seamus Deane, *A Short History of Irish Literature*
    (London, 1986), pp.60-89; Richard Fallis, *The Irish Renaissance: An
    Introduction to Anglo-Irish Literature* (Dublin, 1978), pp.30-70; Francis Russell
    Hart, *The Scottish Novel: From Smollett to Spark* (Cambridge, Mass., 1978),
    pp.164-69, 340-47; Roderick Watson, *The Literature of Scotland*
    (London,1984), pp.311-14, 339-40.

21 Edward D. Snyder, 'The Wild Irish: A Study of Some English Satires
    Against the Irish, Scots, and Welsh', *Modern Philology* 17, No.12 (April
    1920), p.147.

22 Preface to *Lays from the Cimbric Lyre*, quoted in Roland Mathias, *Anglo-Welsh
    Literature: An Illustrated History* (Bridgend, 1987), p.53.

23 'On the Study of Celtic Literature', *The Complete Prose Works of Matthew
    Arnold*, Vol.III, *Lectures and Essays in Criticism*, ed. R.H. Super (Ann Arbor,
    1962), pp.291-395.

24 Curtis, p.33.

25 See Faverty, p.34.

26 Rev. U.J. Bourke, *The Aryan Origin of the Gaelic Race and Language* (London, 1875).

27 See Colin Kidd, 'Teutonist Ethnology and Scottish Nationalist Inhibition
    1780-1880', *The Scottish Historical Review* Vol.LXXIV 1: No.197 (1995), 45-68.

28 John Pinkerton, *An Enquiry into the History of Scotland Preceeding the Reign of
    Malcolm III or the Year 1056*, 2nd edn., 2 vols (Edinburgh, 1814), I, 349-50.

29 See Curtis, p.70.

30 Fionn Mac Colla, *At the Sign of the Clenched Fist* (Edinburgh, 1967), pp.44-48,
    189-204; *Too Long in this Condition* (Thurso, 1975), pp.20-57 and *passim*.

31   See, for example, Andrew Lang, 'The Celtic Renascence', *Blackwood's*
     Magazine 161 (1897), 181-91; William Craigie, 'Gaelic Historical Songs',
     Scottish Review 18 (1891), 301-41; William Power, *Scotland and the Scots*
     (Edinburgh & London, 1934), pp.106-7.

32   *Scottish Review* 15 (April 1890), 233-52; 16 (July 1890), 30-47; 16 (Oct. 1890),
     240-56; 17 (Jan. 1891), 60-82; 17 (April 1891), 332-49;18 (July 1891), 120-43. R.
     Erskine, 'The Two Cultures', 37 No.74 (1914), 283-306; 'Celt, Slav, Hun, and
     Teuton', 37 No.75 (1914), 315-25.

33   For examples from *Blackwood's Magazine*, see: 154 (Aug. 1893), 264-71; 192
     (Aug. 1912), 153-59; 193 (Jan. 1913), 30-48, 115-27; 193 (Feb. 1913), 245-53;
     216 (Sept. 1924), 372-84. For examples from *The Edinburgh Review*, see: 196
     (1902), 120; 229 (1919), 209-31.

34   Dates refer to the original editions of the *Scottish Educational Journal*; page
     references are to *Contemporary Scottish Studies*, ed. Hugh MacDiarmid, 2nd
     rev. edn. (Edinburgh, 1976).

35   *Scots Magazine* 14 (Jan. 1931), 246-51.

36   *Scots Magazine* 14 (Feb. 1931), 324-27; rpt. in *Landscape and Light: Essays by*
     Neil M. Gunn, ed. Alistair McCleery (Aberdeen, 1987), pp.166-69.

37   There are 24 letters in all, appearing in the 'Points of View' column of *The*
     Scotsman, usually under the sub-heading 'Scandinavian Influence'. The last
     one was published on 13 December 1935 (p.13). I am grateful to Brian
     Smith, Shetland Archivist, for drawing my attention to this source.

38   Kurt Wittig, *The Scottish Tradition in Literature* (Edinburgh & London, 1958),
     p.326.

39   Malcolm Chapman, *The Gaelic. Vision in Scottish Culture* (London &
     Montreal, 1978), pp.94, 129, 131.

40   Neil Gunn, 'Caithness and Sutherland', p.66; Eric Linklater, 'Orkney', p.91;
     both in *Scottish Country*, ed. George Scott-Moncrieff (London, 1935). See
     also *Orkneyinga Saga*, Ch.5 pp.30-31.

4. LEWIS GRASSIC GIBBON

The first modern Scottish author to be examined in this book is ironically the one most hostile in attitude towards Old Norse history and literature: Lewis Grassic Gibbon (1901-35). Born James Leslie Mitchell in Aberdeenshire, he spent his childhood and youth in the north-eastern part of Scotland known as the Mearns before joining the armed forces and travelling extensively for many years, mostly in the Middle East. When finally demobilised he settled in Welwyn Garden City in England where he became a professional writer and novelist under his own name. Between 1932 and 1934, however, he published his trilogy, *A Scots Quair*, and a collection of polemical essays with Hugh MacDiarmid, *Scottish Scene*, under his pseudonym Lewis Grassic Gibbon. It was under this name that he gained a permanent place in Scottish literary history as a major novelist and an instigator of the twentieth-century Scottish Renaissance. Rather paradoxically, however, Gibbon himself, as a convinced communist, adopted a somewhat aggressive and ambivalent stance towards both Scottish nationalism and Scottish literature, perhaps his most famous outburst being in his article 'Glasgow' in which he very stridently proclaims:

> I would welcome the end of Braid Scots and Gaelic, our culture, our history, our nationhood under the heels of a Chinese army of occupation if it could cleanse the Glasgow slums, give a surety of food and play – the elementary right of every human being – to those people of the abyss.[1]

But this was only Gibbon the political idealist, for as William Malcolm has pointed out, Gibbon the man was deeply involved with Scottish language and culture and 'never ceased to feel emotionally and romantically attached to his native land'.[2] His stylistic innovations in *A Scots Quair* proved that Scots language and grammar could be used effectively in fiction, and his magnificent creations of Chris Guthrie and the towns and villages of Kinraddie, Segget and Duncairn revealed that a Scottish character and setting could provide as vivid and moving a base for literary genius as any such local colour south of the border. Thus Gibbon's art seems to contradict his political beliefs, and vice versa, for as Ian Campbell has noted:

> Gibbon finds himself torn between the desire to maintain a distinct Scottishness in life and literature, and an inability to subscribe to the political manifestation of Scottish nationalism.[3]

This dichotomy in Gibbon's thinking is reflected in other aspects of his life and art. He always remained ambivalent in his attitude towards country life, loving its beauty, permanence and sense of purpose, but loathing its drudgery, squalor, and the conservative, narrow-minded forms of society it tended to create. A basically fastidious and shy person, Gibbon nonetheless remained in the army, imposing on himself years of the crowding and discomfort of military barracks. Following the example of 'Fiona Macleod' and Hugh MacDiarmid, he created a persona as well as a pseudonym in the name Lewis Grassic Gibbon, sometimes referring to his 'cousin' James Leslie Mitchell, and even reviewing the work of one persona under the name of the other. It might be too glib to talk about the Caledonian Antisyzygy, but it is very tempting to view some aspects of Gibbon's life in the light of this concept.

Diffusionism and the Picts

Whatever stance Gibbon adopted he tended to do it pugnaciously, and his response to the Norse/Celtic debate was no exception. Of all the Scottish writers in the first half of the twentieth century, Gibbon was perhaps the most qualified in a certain sense to comment on the racial history of Scotland in that he made a life-long study of archaeology and anthropology, becoming friends with some of the leading academics in these fields (e.g. Professor G. Elliot Smith) and publishing articles on these subjects in highly reputable journals.[4] Moreover many of his characters in his 'English' novels (i.e. written under his own name, James Leslie Mitchell) are archaeologists or anthropologists.

Gibbon's greatest passion in this field was a belief in Diffusionism, the idea that an original Golden Age of mankind of nomadic hunters was destroyed by the spreading out (diffusion) from the Nile Delta of a static agricultural-based form of society which developed concepts of land ownership, the division of labour, and ultimately everything loosely included in the term 'civilisation'. In Gibbon's view, therefore, the primitive hunters of aeons ago were the only true and civilised people and 'progress' and 'civilisation' had only led to the degradations of urban life, a class society, and the horrors of mechanised warfare.[5] In effect, Diffusionism is a reworking of the Noble Savage ideal using more recent anthropological and archaelogical data and terminology. Naturally such a view of history completely contradicted the pre-vailing Whig tradition (from Macaulay onwards) of continual progress and the triumph of democracy, and implied a complete revaluation of the historical process. The history of Gibbon's native country was no exception to this: 'Few things cry so urgently for rewriting as does Scots history, in few aspects of her bastardized culture has Scotland been so ill-served as by her historians'.[6]

Given the racial debates so prevalent during the 1920s and 30s, it is no surprise that Gibbon's Diffusionist view of Scotland is expressed in racial terms. This view is most succinctly put forward in his essay 'The Antique Scene'; his main premise in this essay is that the Golden Age hunters who first occupied Scotland were 'perhaps mainly of Maglemosian stock, dark and sinewy and agile', and he identifies these hunters as the ancient Picts.[7] Gibbon indeed always prides himself on being 'a good Venriconian Pict',[8] and 'The Antique Scene' reveals his belief that the Picts are the true enduring race of Scotland. It is they who heroically and defiantly withstand the incursions of other races who bring with them such curses of civilisation as feudalism and industrialism. Gibbon is particularly hostile towards the Celts, whom he sees as being the first race to shatter the primitive but idyllic lifestyle of the Maglemosian Picts. The Celtic invaders from Europe were thus 'one of the greatest curses of the Scottish scene, quick, avaricious, unintelligent, quar-relsome, cultureless and uncivilizable'.[9] Indeed Gibbon has rarely anything good to say of the Celts in any of his works. As Malcolm has pointed out, Gibbon clearly brands them as the prehistoric villains of the piece, as 'the Pictish and Celtic races are both glibly apprehended as the antagonists in the historical conflict between slave and oppressor'.[10] In Gibbon's defence, Campbell has argued that 'Gibbon's scathing contempt for the Kelt [sic] is probably overemphasised in deliberate hostility to what he saw as the romanticised view of Scotland's history in the Gaelic revivals of his own time'.[11] Nonetheless, this contempt is strong enough for Gibbon to ignore generally accepted historical facts and dogmatically maintain that the Celts were only a 'conquering military caste' who merely 'imposed their language and their social organisation' on the Picts and thus, in modern Scotland, are only 'a thin strand in the Scottish population' and of 'a strain quite alien to the indubitable and original Scot'. Gibbon ends his diatribe against the Celts with an extraordinarily biased, if not bigotted comment:

> It is one of the strangest jests of history that they should have given their name to so much that is fine and noble, the singing of poets and the fighting of great fights, in which their own actual part has been that of gaping, unintelligent audition or mere carrion-bird raiding.[12]

The poets and soldiers of the true Scottish race, however, were finally defeated in the twentieth century. In his lyrical and poignant novel *Sunset Song*, Gibbon presents what Douglas Young describes as 'the story of the last few years of the genuine Pictish folk of the Mearns and their final defeat by the forces of civilisation'.[13] *Sunset Song* is an evocative portrayal of the crofters of Kinraddie, the 'dour folk of the old Pict stock',[14] as their society and way of life is destroyed by the effects of the Great War. Robert Colquohoun's moving tribute to the Kinraddie war dead at the end of the novel is also Gibbon's eulogy for a passing race, *'the Last of the Peasants, the last of the Old Scots folk'*.[15]

Gibbon and the Norsemen

Gibbon's contempt for the Celts does not mean that he has any sympathy for the Norsemen. On the contrary, Gibbon maintains that if 'the Kelts [sic] were the first great curse of Scotland, the Norse were assuredly the second', and he goes on to affirm that the 'dull, dyspeptic whey-faced' Norseman 'brought nothing of any permanence to Scotland other than his characteristic gastritis'.[16] Gibbon thus detests the Norsemen even more than the Celts, and his antagonism towards them can be traced throughout his works, both fictional and non-fictional. He harshly criticises the Viking novels of Linklater and Gunn, and in his iconoclastic article on Ramsay MacDonald, he obviously intends an insult by stating that the former Prime Minister was probably of Norse blood.[17] In his fiction any references to Norse mythology or characteristics usually have negative overtones. Malcolm Maudslay's father, in *The Thirteenth Disciple*, has the 'oddly owlish' looks of the Norse, and Maudslay prefers the attractions of Domina Riddoch, who is of Maglemosian stock, to those of Jean Stanley, the 'flaming Nord'. In the same novel is an unsympathetic, if not anti-semitic, portrayal of the Jewish archaeologist, Newman, who had 'ratted to the Nords', especially by trying to associate himself with 'the Nordic destiny'.[18] One curious exception to the rule is that of Long Rob of the Mill, one of the heroes of *Sunset Song*, who is twice referred to as Viking-like in appearance due to his fair hair and long moustache.[19]

The Lost Trumpet

The most obviously Norse-inspired character in Gibbon's fiction is Aslaug Simonssen, a character in one of the sub-plots of *The Lost Trumpet*. The novel is mostly concerned with an archaeological dig by Huebsch and Marrot for the Lost Trumpet of Jericho, and the love-affair between the guide Colonel Anton Saloney and Pelagueya Bourrin. Aslaug Simonssen, of Scoto-Norwegian parentage, arrives in Cairo to try and track down the murderer of her brother Carl. She is described as tall and blonde and very cool and frigid; frequent references to her as a 'Valkyr' and 'sagawoman' indicate her determination to seek vengeance in blood. As Douglas F. Young has commented:

> Aslaug Simonssen is in unrelenting pursuit of revenge, and in her obsessive drive we are asked to see the combined result of her Scottish and Norwegian background, all the cruelty and ruthless-

ness of the Norseman, and all the moral austerity and rigour of the Calvinist.[20]

Such is her cold-bloodedness that she agrees to sacrifice her virginity to the dissolute and alcoholic novelist Esdras Quaritch in return for his bringing to her Huth Rizq, Carl's blind prostitute mistress. Huth freely confesses to the murder of Carl, but it is made clear that he was a thoroughly bad character and deserved his fate. Aslaug and Quaritch are ultimately united by mutual desire and not their cynical agreement, but only after the Lost Trumpet (symbolically 'the trumpet voice of human sanity') has been blown.[21] It also transpires that Quaritch had been a Good Samaritan to the prostitutes of Cairo and not their pimp, so that Aslaug's emotional future is not so bleak as at first appears, though Quaritch's alcoholism will presumably remain a problem. In all events Gibbon's portrayal of Quaritch's vicious anti-semitism and Aslaug Simonssen's ice-cold Nordic will make them the least attractive characters in the novel.

Leif Eiriksson and 'Wineland the Good'

Malcolm Maudslay, the hero of Gibbon's *The Thirteenth Disciple*, 'read translated sagas of Morris and Magnusson' and 'became a champion of the Norsemen as the discoverers of America'.[22] This is the only reference in Gibbon's fiction to the one aspect of Norse history which had truly interested him as he researched this subject in some detail for the chapter on Leif Eiriksson for his book on exploration, *Nine Against the Unknown* (1934). This chapter will be dealt with in some detail, as it is especially revealing of Gibbon's prejudiced if not perverse view of Norse history. Gibbon's thesis in his book is a clearly Diffusionist one, with 'civilised' Western European peoples discovering and settling new lands in North and South America and consequently destroying the primitive and admirable Golden Age cultures of the native populations. According to Gibbon, these European explorers are primarily motivated by the medieval legend of the Fortunate Isles, a land of treasure and beauty beyond the western seas. This idea is well-documented in Fridtjof Nansen's *In Northern Mists*, one of Gibbon's main sources for his book.[23] After an introductory chapter on this theme, Gibbon moves on to describe the expedition of Leif Ericsson [Gibbon's spelling], who according to Old Norse sources was the first man to land in, explore, and winter in North America c.1000 A.D.

The two primary sources are *The Greenlanders' Saga* and *Eirik's Saga*, but there are important differences in their presentation of events.[24] According to *The Greenlanders' Saga* Bjarni Herjolfsson is the first to actually sight the North American coast when blown off course en route from Iceland to the Norse settlements in Greenland, but he does not land there. Leif Eiriksson subsequently buys Bjarni's ship and returns to explore and winter on these unknown coasts, giving the country the name of Vinland ('Wineland') because of the discovery of wild grapes there by Leif's German foster-father, Tyrker.[25] In *Eirik's Saga*, however, there is no mention of Bjarni Herjolfsson, and it is Leif himself who sights, lands in, and explores Vinland after being blown off course en route to Greenland. Both sagas mention a later attempt by Leif's brother, Thorstein, which is aborted due to bad weather, before they are at variance once again. In *The Greenlanders' Saga* another brother of Leif's, Thorvald, leads an expedition which remains in Vinland for three years. Their sojourn is ended when they are forced to abandon their settlement after an attack by the local natives, Thorvald dying from his wounds. Thorfinn Karlsefni then leads a third expedition with around 150 people and some livestock which also lasts about three years. The Norsemen trade peacefully with the natives at first, but after a misunderstanding hostilities break out and the Greenlanders prudently decide to return home as they are no match in numbers for the Vinland inhabitants. A fourth expedition by Freydis Eiriksdottir ends in horror and disaster when the Norsemen become divided into two hostile camps and Freydis persuades her husband literally to decimate the other camp, Freydis herself personally killing five women with an axe. Freydis's group returns to Greenland where rumours of the truth gradually leak out and she begins to be shunned by her neighbours. *Eirik's Saga* has no mention of Freydis's expedition, and Thorvald and Thorfinn's trips are conflated into one. Moreover according to this version it is Thorfinn's two Scottish slaves, Haki and Hekja, who find the wild grapes which give the country its name. After initially peaceful trading with the natives, fighting breaks out and Thorfinn and the survivors return to Greenland. Thorvald Eiriksson is killed by a fantastic one-legged creature, a uniped. The sources thus agree only on two basic facts: that Leif Eiriksson was the first Norseman to land and explore in America, without sighting any natives, and Thorfinn Karlsefni's attempt at a settlement was thwarted by the hostile reactions of the natives.

But how does Gibbon present the conflicting versions to his readers? The answer is, unevenly, especially as he seems incapable of overcoming his anti-Norse prejudices to present a balanced and convincing view of the Greenlanders' discovery of America. Gibbon's antipathy to the Norsemen is evident in the very first paragraphs of the chapter where he calls the Vikings 'brutish and implacable bands of pirates' who:

> ... had no native literature, no native culture, no religion, though much brutish superstition; no single thought or impulse to stir our later sympathies. Their sagas tell of a mean and bloody and cowardly life, comrades throat-cutting on minor matters like the stealing of fish or firewood, mean squabbles on little roods of land, clownish cruelties and clownish curiosities in that cruelty.
> (NAU, 21)

Everyone is entitled to their opinion, of course, but it seems clear from the above references that either Gibbon knew very little about ancient Scandinavian culture and society, or else he was indeed extremely biased in his view of it. By the 1930s it was generally accepted that the Old Norse sagas were amongst the finest gems of medieval European literature and that the political and legal organisations of the Vikings were important forerunners of parliamentary democracy and the jury system.

Gibbon's virulent dislike of the Norsemen is also revealed through various snide and unsubstantiated remarks; thus Eric [sic], Leif's father, killed his enemies 'probably very cold-bloodedly' and Eric's father died 'possibly and righteously of a slit throat' (NAU, 23). Gibbon even argues that Eric wanted to colonise Greenland because 'it probably irked him that he had so few companions to dominate and browbeat and fight with' (NAU, 25). Such gratuitous and unhistorical remarks tend to detract from the reader's confidence in Gibbon's knowledge and treatment of his subject matter, especially when he makes such a careless error as to call Eric's father Jaederen [sic], which is in fact the misspelt name of the Norwegian province Eric and his father, Thorvald, came from (NAU, 23).

Gibbon's retelling of the story begins reasonably enough with the *The Greenlanders' Saga* version of Bjarni Herjolfsson's sighting of the American coast. He then turns to *Eirik's Saga* for the account of Leif's love affair in the Hebrides prior to his expedition to Vinland. It is in the description of Leif's journey that Gibbon tries to simplify the story by conflating some of the events of Leif's and Thorfinn's expeditions. Though it is superficially a neat condensation, Gibbon creates problems for himself by thus claiming that Leif took with him all of the recorded finders of the wild grapes, i.e. Tyrker *and* the Scottish slaves. He tries to solve this by having the slaves find the grapes while Tyrker actually sees to their fermentation, in secret, on Rhode Island! After finishing with Leif's expedition, Gibbon then completely edits out those of his brothers Thorstein and Thorvald, and continues with a shortened version of Thorfinn Karlsefni's attempt at a settlement and Freydis's final disastrous and homicidal expedition.

Gibbon's description of the Norse discovery of North America thus has both its good and bad points. It is an imaginative if slightly fanciful conflation of the existing Old Norse sources, and Gibbon's dogmatic and forthright attitude to his subject matter is stimulating for readers who like their history packaged in no uncertain black and white terms and with a breezy disregard for factual or moral subtleties. Moreover Gibbon's inclusion of Leif Eiriksson in a book aimed at the general public was a useful contribution towards establishing the importance and relevance of the Old Norse sources on the Viking discovery of America, for in the 1930s many general history books continued to cite Christopher Columbus as the first European to land in America and not Leif Eiriksson.[26] Less appealing aspects of the work are Gibbon's contemptuous descriptions of the Norsemen and his perhaps misguided attempt to place them in his own preconceived view of Diffusionist history. It seems inconsistent, for example, that after continually emphasising that the Vikings were virtually subhuman morons with a propensity for bloodshed and alcoholism, Gibbon then maintains that they were inspired by such an imaginative and subjective idea as the Fortunate Isles far in the west. Indeed one of the other major sources for his book, Gathorne-Hardy's *The Norse Discoverers of America*, quite specifically states that no such knowledge of the Fortunate Isles was likely to have existed in Iceland or Greenland at that time.[27] From an historical point of view, such inspiration was unnecessary in any case, for as many scholars have noted, once the Vikings had settled in Greenland it was geographically inevitable that they would reach America:

> ... when men climbed the high mountains behind the settlement areas of Greenland ... they would see far in the distance either land itself or the cloud formations they associated with land. At the narrowest point of Davis Strait just two hundred miles separate Cumberland Peninsula from Greenland. It is unthinkable that during the great age of Norse exploration men would not have undertaken so short and challenging a passage.[28]

Gibbon's suggestion that the Vikings were the first in a long line of 'civilised' corruptors of the Golden Age cultures of America also seems unconvincing. Apart from some unscrupulous trading practices by Thorfinn Karlsefni's men (which, curiously enough, Gibbon fails to mention),[29] the Norsemen come off much the worse in hostile clashes with the natives (a great contrast to their successes, even when heavily outnumbered, in Britain and Europe) and are consequently forced to abandon any hopes of a permanent settlement there. Such a negligible result of the brief encounter between native Americans and the Greenlanders bears no comparison whatsoever with the later depredations of the Spanish and Portuguese in South America in the sixteenth century. Nonetheless, Gibbon's presentation can mislead even very recent critics; William Malcolm, for example, relates, without comment, on how Gibbon condemns 'the atrocities carried out in the name of civilisation by such illustrious historical figures as Lief Ericsson [sic], Cabeza de Vala, Magellan and Columbus'.[30] But as a careful reading of the sources reveals, and as even Gibbon himself states, Leif Eiriksson never even sighted any natives, let alone committed atrocities against them. Indeed in terms of the number of victims, the worst atrocity committed by the Norsemen in America was Freydis Eiriksdottir's organisation of the mass murder of another group of Norsemen. Gibbon's views of the role of the Norsemen in America, therefore, seem tenuous and unconvincing, the result of an inflexible application of Diffusionist theory and a biased view of Viking history and achievement.

Gibbon's/Mitchell's presentation of the Picts, Celts and Norsemen in his fictional and non-fictional works is thus a typical example of the effect of the racial debates surrounding the question of Scottish identity in the early twentieth century. On the positive side, Gibbon's racial views of Scottish history and his sense of identity with the Picts provided him with with a powerful, imaginative stimulus for *A Scots Quair*, especially *Sunset Song*. On the negative side, his rigid and biased racial classifications led to the portrayal of stereotyped and unsympathetic characters in his fiction (e.g. Aslaug Simonssen in *The Lost Trumpet*), and crude and dogmatic generalisations in his historical works (e.g. Leif Eiriksson's discovery of America in *Nine Against the Unknown*). Although Old Norse influence on Gibbon's work is thus of a rather vestigial nature, his negative attitude to Viking history and literature is a good illustration of a hostile response to the Norse heritage in Scotland prior to the Second World War.

NOTES

1 'Glasgow', in *Scottish Scene* (London, 1934), p.141; rpt. in *A Scots Hairst* (1967), ed. Ian S. Munro, 3rd edn. (London, 1983), p.87.

2 William K. Malcolm, *A Blasphemer and Reformer: A Study of James Leslie Mitchell (Lewis Grassic Gibbon)* (Aberdeen, 1984), p.8.

3 Ian Campbell, *Lewis Grassic Gibbon*, Scottish Writers Series 6 (Edinburgh, 1985), p.49. See also Keith Dixon, 'Lewis Grassic Gibbon, Scotland and Nationalism', in *Nationalism in Literature*, ed. Horst W. Drescher and Hermann Völkel, Scottish Studies Vol.8 (Frankfurt am Main, 1989), pp.201-12.

4 For details, see Ian S. Munro, *James Leslie Mitchell: Lewis Grassic Gibbon* (Edinburgh & London, 1966), pp.62-66.

5 For a discussion of Gibbon's Diffusionism, see Douglas F. Young, *Beyond the Sunset: A Study of James Leslie Mitchell (Lewis Grassic Gibbon)* (Aberdeen, 1973), pp.9-30.

6   'The Antique Scene', in *Scottish Scene*, p.19; *Scots Hairst*, p.123.
7   'Antique Scene', *Scottish Scene*, p.20; *Scots Hairst*, p.124.
8   'The Land', in *Scottish Scene*, p.294; *Scots Hairst*, p.68.
9   'Antique Scene', *Scottish Scene*, p.22; *Scots Hairst*, p.127.
10 Malcolm, p.15.
11 Campbell, p.45.
12 'Antique Scene', *Scottish Scene*, pp.22-23; *Scots Hairst*, pp.126-27.
13 Young, p.91.
14 Lewis Grassic Gibbon, *Sunset Song* (1932), Canongate Classics 12 (Edinburgh, 1988), p.4.
15 *Sunset Song*, p.256.
16 'Antique Scene', *Scottish Scene*, p.24-25; *Scots Hairst*, p.129.
17 'Literary Lights', in *Scottish Scene*, pp.200, 202-3; *Scots Hairst*, pp.149, 151. 'The Wrecker – James Ramsay MacDonald', in *Scottish Scene*, p.98; *Scots Hairst*, p.111.
18 J. Leslie Mitchell, *The Thirteenth Disciple* (1931), Scottish Fiction Reprint Library (Edinburgh, 1981), pp.19, 43, 269.
19 *Sunset Song*, pp.19, 151.
20 Young, p.53.
21 J. Leslie Mitchell, *The Lost Trumpet* (London, 1932), p.141.
22 *The Thirteenth Disciple*, p.38.
23 Fridtjof Nansen, *In Northern Mists,* 2 vols (London, 1911), I, 348-84.
24 The two sagas can be found in *The Vinland Sagas: The Norse Discovery of America*, trans. Magnus Magnusson and Hermann Pálsson (Harmondsworth, 1965). They can also be found in Gwyn Jones, *The Norse Atlantic Saga*, 2nd rev. edn. (Oxford, 1986), pp.186-232.
25 There has been much scholarly speculation as to the exact location of Leif's landfall. Many suggestions have been put forward ranging from Labrador in the north to New York in the south. Gibbon himself decided on Martha's Vineyard: J. Leslie Mitchell and Lewis Grassic Gibbon, *Nine Against the Unknown* (London, 1934), p.35. All further references are to this edition, abbreviated NAU.
26 There are, of course, also Welsh and Irish traditions regarding the finding of America (e.g. Madoc and Brendan), but these are outside the scope of the present work.
27 G.M. Gathorne-Hardy, *The Norse Discoverers of America* (Oxford, 1921), p.155. Gibbon misquotes the title of this work in his bibliography, NAU, 317.
28 Gwyn Jones, *The Norse Atlantic Saga*, p.116.
29 See *The Vinland Sagas*, p.99.
30 Malcolm, p.20.

5. NEIL M. GUNN

The novelist Neil M. Gunn (1891-1973) may seem an unlikely author to be influenced by Scotland's Old Norse heritage, as his novels, often seen as the finest achievement in prose fiction of the Scottish Renaissance, are mostly renowned for their presentation of the Gaelic world of the Scottish Highlands. Gunn became intimately acquainted with the Highlands through his career as an Excise Officer, for between 1911 and 1921 he was posted to various places all over Scotland, often for months at a time. He finally received a permanent post in Inverness from 1923 until 1937, when the success of *Highland River* encouraged him to become a full-time writer. It was precisely during this period that Inverness was the centre of the revival of interest in Scottish Gaelic culture, and Gunn enthusiastically took lessons in Gaelic and became seriously involved in Scottish nationalist politics.[1] Gunn's motivating idea was the promotion of a sense of a separate Scottish identity – an identity which was essentially Gaelic in attitudes and beliefs, if not in language. It was this feature of his politics and fiction which gained him the friendship and encouragement of Hugh MacDiarmid in the early 1930s, though the two men became sadly estranged in later years. As Margery McCulloch has claimed in a recent study of Gunn:

> ... the theme which predominates throughout the main part of his work is that of the viability and intrinsic worth of the way of life of the Scottish Highland communities.[2]

Gunn's novels, stories and plays are thus permeated with Celtic history, folklore and mythology, and many of his themes, images and symbols are a result of his extensive and familiar knowledge of ancient and modern Celtic literature, gained from reading

Rolleston's *Myths and Legends of the Celtic Race*, Carmichael's *Carmina Gadelica*, Campbell's *Tales of the West Highlands* and the novels and stories of Neil Munro and 'Fiona Macleod'. As Gunn himself once said in the 1960s: 'Whenever I heard or remembered a Gaelic proverb, it led me to visualise a whole story'.[3] Gunn's animism has thus, according to Wittig, 'a consciously Gaelic undertone', and this is supplemented by his good understanding and appreciation of pibroch music, and the rhythms and cadences of the English language as spoken by native Gaelic speakers. Indeed certain passages from his novels reveal a distinct influence of Gaelic on his own prose style.[4] By the time he stopped writing novels, in the 1950s, Gunn had attained a place in the history of Scottish literature as the finest spokesman of the Gaelic consciousness in the English language.

Nonetheless, despite Gunn's emotional and creative sense of identity with Scottish Gaeldom, he was also keenly aware of the importance and relevance of Scotland's Norse heritage. Indeed in the earlier part of his writing career he seemed to see the Norse element of the Scottish character and temperament as compensating for some of the flaws of the Celtic one. Thus in some of his early novels, Gunn seemed to seek ways in which the different aspects of the two races could be reconciled and assimilated within a broader Scottish consciousness.

Caithness and the Norse Heritage

The key to Gunn's interest in Scotland's Norse past is his birthplace, Dunbeath, on the southern coast of Caithness. Apart from Orkney and Shetland, no part of Scotland has as much Norse history as Caithness. As John R. Allan has said, the people from this northernmost county of the British mainland are 'different from any other people in Scotland':

> They are not highland, not Celtic, not Scots. In the great days of the Norse people, Caithness was colonised from Scandinavia and that strain remains, unique.[5]

Caithness was certainly a racial melting pot in early medieval Scottish history. Its first inhabitants, possibly the elusive broch-builders, were conquered or replaced in early Christian times by the Picts, who themselves succumbed to the Celts, who in their turn were defeated and subjugated by Norse invaders, mostly by way of Orkney. According to Mark Rugg Gunn, the Gunns were 'of Nordo-Celtic descent'. The clan originated from Gunni, the grandson of no less than Sweyn [sic] Asleifsson, one of the most renowned Orcadian Vikings of the twelfth century. However, although 'the main stem was Norse, successive generations of intermarriage with their Celtic neighbours produced a race which was more Celtic than Nordic'.[6] Ian Grimble, on the other hand, believes the Clan Gunn is more likely to be a Pictish one which had gradually retreated from a series of aggressors:

> When the Picts were overrun by the Gaelic Scots of Dalriada in the south, and by Vikings from the north, the survivors would naturally have taken refuge in inaccessible hinterlands behind the areas in which such substantial evidence of their presence remains. It is precisely here, in the heights of the Caithness-Sutherland border, that Clann Gunn is to be found.[7]

Gunn was always fascinated by this strange mixture of ethnic origins in Caithness, which is especially noticeable in local place-names. One of the best descriptions of this phenomenon can be found in Gunn's novel *Highland River* in which many of the experiences of the young boy Kenn are obviously autobiographical, the boy's home village being almost certainly based on Gunn's own, Dunbeath:

> On one side of the harbour mouth the place-name was Gaelic, on the other side it was Norse. Where the lower valley broadened out to flat, fertile land the name was Norse, but the braes behind it were Gaelic. A mile up the river where the main stream was joined by its first real tributary, the promontory overlooking the meeting of the waters was crowned by the ruins of a broch that must have been the principal stronghold of the glen when the Picts, or perhaps some earlier people, were in their heyday.[8]

As Gunn himself has asserted: 'No writer can now refer to Caithness without using the word Norse',[9] but he was also aware of the existence of a Norse heritage throughout the rest of Scotland, as many of his comments in *Off in a Boat* reveal:

> A philologist once told me that in Skye for every two place names in Gaelic there are fully three in Norse. Already I had seen more than one mountain-top where a princess of Lochlann had elected to be buried.[10]

Other aesthetic experiences also seemed to underline for him the Nordic elements of Scottish consciousness. Listening to a symphony on the radio by the Finnish composer Sibelius, Gunn relates how he felt as if 'the whole of the Northland of forest and loch and legend came alive before me, evoked out of the blood'. Gunn's only explanation for this 'evocative power' is that it was due to:

> ... some degree of affinity between our Scottish Northland and the Scandinavian, to both a personal and traditional apprehension of these northern lands and seas and the legends or myths bred out of them.[11]

The pseudonym he adopted for some of his nationalist articles, 'Dane McNeil', also seems to reflect his need to represent both the Nordic and Celtic races in Scotland. Like other Scottish nationalists (eg. Hugh MacDiarmid), he also looked to Scandinavia for examples of small nations winning struggles for linguistic and political independence.[12] Most important of all, however, is the effective influence of this Norse heritage on Gunn's own works, especially some of his best known novels such as *Morning Tide*, *Highland River* and *The Silver Darlings*. This influence can be seen in his attempt to present an historical recreation of the first meeting of Celt and Norseman (*Sun Circle*, 1933), in his conception of the racial consciousness of 'the folk', and in his view of skill and heroism at sea as a modern atavistic version of the Norse ethos.

Sun Circle: History and Legend

Sun Circle is one of Gunn's least-known novels, but it is worth considering in some detail in a Norse context, for as an interesting but flawed work it reveals much of his fascination with the racial and

religious confrontations of early medieval Scotland. Gunn graphically describes the inspiration for *Sun Circle* in his 'Portrait Address':

> Briefly, then, down by Dunbeath harbour, there is a long stretch of
> beach on which a whole flotilla of Viking longships could readily
> be hauled up. It's the only beach of its kind in the solid rock wall
> that stretches from Helmsdale to Wick. And that such ships must
> have landed there we know from the place names.... What hap-
> pened when the armed Vikings arrived there so troubled my
> imagination that I tried to get rid of the burden by writing an
> imaginary account of it.[13]

Sun Circle is thus set in ninth-century Caithness and tells the story
of a Picto-Celtic tribe, the Ravens, and its confrontation with two
powerful forces: the internal threat of the growing influence of
Christianity, and the external threat of Viking marauders.
Christianity was beginning to undermine the very foundations of
the Druidic culture of the Celts, and the Viking invasions threatened their physical survival. The tension between these three forces
is reflected in a love triangle: Aniel, the pupil of the Master Druid,
is attracted to two different women, Breeta, the dark-haired pagan
girl from his own tribe, and Nessa, the fair-haired daughter of the
chieftain Drust and his Christian wife Silis who is from another
Celtic tribe from southern Scotland. The dramatic events of the
novel are swift and bloody. The Vikings, under their leader Haakon
[Gunn's spelling of Hakon], destroy the Ravens' army, killing all
their leading men, including Drust the chieftain, and capturing
both Silis and Nessa. The former commits suicide at her husband's
graveside, and the latter falls in love with Haakon, only to die with
him in a climactic forest fire. The novel ends with Aniel, now united with Breeta, setting off for southern Scotland to bring back
Drust's son to be the new leader of the remnants of the Raven tribe
as it resettles the glen. The Celtic tribe has thus survived this particular Viking raid, but its acceptance of Christianity and Norse
immigrants is clearly revealed as inevitable and the only way forward is some kind of compromise and synthesis.

   As this brief survey would suggest, *Sun Circle* is an important
attempt to recreate and analyse a vital period in the history of
Caithness, but how successful is the novel as historical fiction and

as a statement about the impact of Christianity and Norse invasions on the Celtic racial consciousness? In dealing with the historical aspect first, many critics have pointed out that *Sun Circle* is not strictly speaking an historical novel at all. Wittig describes Gunn's novel as 'groping towards a mythology of the events' which created the forefathers of the Scottish race, whilst Hart sees it as a 'philosophical romance rather than novel.' Alexander Reid refers to it as a 'dramatisation of ... psychological conflict', and Richard Price calls it 'an allegorical recreation of the past'.[14] Gunn's main difficulty in writing about this historical period is the simple lack of source material relating to the Picts' and Celts' way of life. Even today little is known with certainty about the beliefs and practices of Druidism, the builders and purposes of the brochs (one of which is obviously the Ravens' fortress), or the exact ethnic and linguistic make-up of the inhabitants of Caithness prior to the coming of the Norsemen.[15] A perusal of Gunn's notebooks (in the National Library of Scotland) reveals that he studied with great interest much of what was available on these subjects at the time, especially sources relating to Saint Columba, the Picts, and early Christianity.[16] His presentation of the Celtic tribe's daily life, Druidic religion, and relations with neighbouring tribes tends to be rather romanticised, however. Throughout the novel Gunn seems anxious to stress the essential innocence of the Ravens:

> They were a pastoral rather than a fighting people. Field sports and hunting and music were their pastimes, not in a spectacular way, but here and there singly or in groups, though sometimes in the shieling season all would find themselves combining on great and memorable days of rivalry and boasting and fighting and roaring fun, yet the typical picture was that of a man fashioning something by himself and whistling a low liquid tune he only half heard, or of women working together, helped by an endless song.[17]

This idealised view of the Celts is clearly based on Gunn's belief in a Golden Age in the Highlands when tribes lived a very simple and natural existence untrammelled by the severer social, economic and moral restraints of civilisation. There are obvious similarities here with Gibbon's views of history, and Gunn later has the hero of

Highland River, Kenn, viewing the Great War as the final horror of Civilisation and leaning towards anthropologists' theories of the Golden Age (HR, 113-14; 205-6). Nonetheless, despite further references to such a Golden Age in recorded conversations and letters,[18] Gunn never formally adhered to such theories as Diffusionism.

Unfortunately, however, no matter how attractive such ideas of a Golden Age might be, they are an indirect cause of one of the major flaws in *Sun Circle*: the unconvincing response of the Ravens to the threatened Norse raid. Gunn presents his tribesmen as being so innocent that they prepare for battle as if it were a sporting contest rather than a grim fight for survival:

> The excitement and mirth of the men in the glen made her [Breeta] feel restless. They were full of fun and jokes, and fights were common among the boys.... For nothing is more thrilling than a fight, and the thought that oneself may be at it any moment keeps the eyes bright and laughing. They measured and admired one another, and life was sweet and expectant. (SC, 120)

Perhaps unwittingly, Gunn undermines the reader's credulity about such an attitude by intermittently introducing evidence which shows that the Ravens could not have been as innocent as they are presented as being. In the first place some of the tribe have experienced Viking raids before. Breeta's mother had once fled from such a raid to give birth to Breeta in the forest and she recalls how there had been "'the fight, the killing, the wrecking of the houses'" (SC, 23). Moreover just prior to the opening of the novel Vikings had attacked another nearby settlement at Harst and, as Breeta reports, they had burnt down the houses and "'killed everyone at the dwellings'" (SC, 65). The chieftain, Drust, meets leaders of other tribes to discuss action against 'the dreaded invasions of the Northmen' (SC, 123) and at a later council of the Ravens comes to the conclusion that, compared to their local rivals, the Logenmen, "'the Northmen would be more terrible fighters and would kill more'" (SC, 138). Molrua, the missionary monk, is also well aware of the horror and destruction of Viking depradations and ends his address to the tribesmen with the cry that resounded throughout ninth-century Europe: "'*A furore Normanorum libera nos,*

Domine"' (SC, 95). The tribesmen's teasing of Garam, one of their number, also reveals their knowledge of the efficacy and skill of the Vikings and their weapons: 'The Northmen, they said, were such experts with their sharp iron axes that in one blow they could split a man in two from the crown of his head to the place between his legs' (SC, 80). It is no surprise, therefore, that Breeta is terrified by the threatened attack: '"If the Northmen come ... we shall all be killed"' (SC, 49).

Despite this knowledge and experience, however, Gunn presents the Ravens as being extraordinarily blasé about the whole affair as 'this very expectancy of the fight excited everyone, but particularly the girls' (SC, 146). This is especially surprising as the Ravens have little or no experience of any kind of warfare for 'a fight against raiders was a rare thing, hardly happening more than once in a generation' (SC, 24). Nonetheless, Breeta's brother Col exultantly boasts that the Ravens will '"smash them to bits"' (SC, 55) and Drust grandiosely plans to defeat both the Vikings *and* the Ravens' local enemies, the Logenmen:

> 'This is what we are going to do. We meet the Northmen as they land and cut them up. Then we set along the coast, head off the Logenmen, slaughter them to a man, and drive back the cattle. The sea fight will only put us in trim for our vengeance. Nor will that be the end of our vengeance, by the blood-gods!' (SC, 144)

Drust's speech is more reminiscent of a Hollywood Western than that of a responsible leader formulating a pragmatic plan of campaign. Once the Vikings have actually arrived on the beach and are face to face with the Ravens, Taran the Bard sees the truth only too clearly:

> But now against these Northmen, famous men of Lochlann, who were in their prime, trained and hardened warriors, experts with the shield, the sword, and the axe, what chance had these home-grown, crude-weaponed bunch of his countrymen, from old men to youths? (SC, 155)

It is a demonstrable historical fact that the Vikings were superior to the Picts and Celts in both weapons and fighting skills. Moreover the internal evidence of the novel (eg. Taran's very remark on the 'famous men of Lochlann') shows that the Ravens themselves must have been aware of the Vikings' superiority. Nonetheless, Gunn presents them as gleefully looking forward to a confrontation with the Norsemen. True, they had foreknowledge of the raid and a certain amount of bravado is natural, but the overall response of the Ravens to the coming of the Vikings is simply unbelievable. McCulloch argues that:

> ... what the book does communicate successfully is the perennial weakness of the Celtic peoples, their inability to work together in the face of danger, their insouciance and lack of planned action when that danger materialises.[19]

This is true up to a point, but the simple fact remains that in his attempt to convince the reader of the Celts' natural innocence and good nature he has made them extremely naive and gullible, and what should stir admiration and sympathy in the reader only succeeds in evoking incredulity and amazement.

Gunn's treatment of the Norsemen becomes relevant here, as this also lacks conviction. His notebooks in the National Library of Scotland show that he did far less research on the Vikings than on the Picts and Celts, and what he did do was mainly confined to the practical aspects of their way of life, in particular weaponry and boat-building. He uses this knowledge to good effect in the vivid battle scene on the beach and in the Norsemen's problems in repairing their longship. There are also frequent stock references to Odin and Valhalla, and Sweyn [sic], Haakon's second-in-command, makes a brief summary of the Vikings' general attitude to life as frequently reiterated in both Saga and Eddic literature: that a man can only rely on his own sword and strength and must seek a glorious death in battle (SC, 290). The detailed and gory description of the carving of the blood-eagle on Drust's back also reveals Gunn's knowledge of certain Viking practices; indeed there is a slight suspicion that this scene is introduced precisely to illustrate this point (SC, 168). Much of Gunn's Norse material thus strikes one as being little more than perfunctory 'scene-setting'. Indeed Gunn makes errors in both his conception and presentation of Norsemen. The first concerns Norse nomenclature. Most of the names Gunn gives his Viking characters are generally accepted variants of anglicised forms of Old Norse names, but the Viking boat-builder is called Sigrid. This is really a schoolboy howler in that Sigrid is a *woman's* name, the correct masculine form being Sigurd. To readers unfamiliar with saga literature this is perhaps an unimportant point, but to those who are familiar with Old Norse or modern Scandinavian culture it has unfortunate consequences. Apart from being rather disconcerting, this error, however unintentional, unavoidably adds a touch of farce to the scenes involving the boatman, and it generally undermines the reader's confidence in Gunn's knowledge and presentation of Vikings.

An error with more far-reaching consequences concerns the conception of the Viking leader Haakon. A tall, fair-haired, broad-shouldered, and bearded man, he is presented as a magnificent and daring warrior who leads his men to victory against the Ravens and then resourcefully captures their stronghold, himself being the first man over the ramparts. His men torment their captives and rape the women and Haakon carves the blood-eagle on Drust's back. When he becomes enamoured of Nessa, Drust's daughter, however, we are suddenly informed of the surprising fact that 'however his men might think, she was to be his first woman' (SC, 333). This is both historically and artistically unconvincing. There is a great deal of historical evidence to show that the Vikings, and in particular their chieftains, often practised polygamy, and were even reported to take their pleasure of female slaves in public.[20] That Haakon would admire and respect Nessa as the daughter of the fallen enemy leader is quite credible (especially as their union could further his own political ends), but that at 25 – the age of a veteran in Viking terms – he would be sexually inexperienced is highly improbable. This is not just to quibble with Gunn's historical accuracy, for within the context of the novel this inexperience is also artistically unconvincing. Haakon has killed many men in battle, indifferently witnessed the tormenting and humiliation of captured women and, with his *bare hands*, has torn out the lungs from Drust's back. It is simply highly incongruous for a man so familiar with such gross physical acts to have had no carnal knowlege of women. It is at this point that Haakon ceases to be a flesh and blood Viking and becomes a symbol, for, as Marie-Hélène Rescanières has pointed out, Gunn intends the coming together of Haakon and Nessa to represent 'the welding of the two peoples who gave birth to Scotland'.[21] Within Gunn's mythology Haakon and Nessa must create a pure, virginal and amoral blending of Norse and Celt:

> Here were the lovers of legend, beyond good and evil, beyond treachery and honesty, beyond the laws of family or tribe, splendid in bearing, alive like fire, selling all the world, father and mother and home and honour, for their love's pleasure. (SC, 333)

Sun Circle: Celtic Consciousness and Celtic Survival

As stated earlier, *Sun Circle* is not purely and simply an historical novel, it is also an exposition of Gunn's beliefs about the integrity and wholeness of the individual and his race, especially the Celt in Scotland. His basic premise, as described by Hart and Pick, is that each person has two separate selves:

> ... a 'first self' responsive and vulnerable to social and institutional influences, and a 'second self' that is free. The first he calls the 'social self', the second 'the inner core of himself'....[22]

The very title of the novel provides a powerful image of this idea: 'As the Sun put a circle round the earth and all that it contained, so a man by his vision put a circle round himself' (SC, 365).

The most important representative of the Celtic consciousness in the novel is that of Aniel, the pupil of the Druid Master, who finds his 'inner self' threatened by outside forces which have already had far-reaching effects on his 'social self' in both religion and love. A pupil of Druidism, he is nonetheless impressed by Molrua and the Christian message; in love he is torn between the elemental Breeta, a woman of his own race with whom he has a deep spiritual rapport, and the beautiful, aristocratic and sexually attractive Nessa. The confusion and disaster brought about by the Viking raid highlight his ambivalence towards his religious belief and the two women in his life. In a trance-like state following the defeat of the Ravens he almost leads Breeta to her death as a desperate sacrifice to propitiate the tribe's gods, and then is later tempted to free the captured Nessa and flee with her to begin a new life elsewhere.

Aniel's nerve fails him, however, when Nessa places her fate in his hands (SC, 351), and she returns to the Viking Haakon. Aniel later rationalises his indecision by a belated realisation that a union between Haakon and Nessa would provide a neat and pragmatic end to future Norse invasions. This is the argument he presents to the Master in an attempt both to save and to vindicate Nessa (SC, 356-57). Gunn seems unduly influenced by the theories of Nordic supremacy here, for he also has Aniel surmising that the strong leadership the Ravens lacked would be supplied by the Vikings, for they 'had that one thing, the supreme thing, that creates the ruler and the conqueror, the maker and the breaker of laws' (SC, 351). The Norsemen 'are of those who make their own decisions. And however we rail against them as transgressors, as betrayers, yet, because they have done what we dared not do, we recognise them as our masters' (SC, 357). Moreover, Aniel detects something else in his earlier vacillation: 'He had avoided decision, avoided action. And he knew that that was the fatal flaw in his make-up, an eternal weakness of will against the supreme moment' (SC, 351).

Gunn is clearly implying here, in 1933, that this failure of nerve is a general weakness of the Celtic race, but one which could be compensated for by a pragmatic harnessing of the strengths of other races, in this case the Nordic one. This is the one glimmer of hope for the Celtic people: their ability to assimilate their 'outer selves' to external circumstances whilst retaining their 'inner selves', their sense of racial identity. This is seen in Aniel, for after the death of Haakon and Nessa he is reunited with Breeta and together they set out southwards to the Broad River to bring back Drust's son to be the Ravens' new leader. They do this despite Aniel's awareness that the son is a Christian and will not help resurrect the tribe's ancient faith now that the Sacred Grove has been destroyed and the Master himself is dead.

> Aniel would bring back the young chief with his Christian religion. But he need not be hopeless about that. At the end of all religions that which is offered is always the same thing. That might be difficult, more difficult than all else to feel and to believe, and impossible for the old. But if Aniel had to satisfy his own people in the old ways, then he would do so, even if he had to do it secret-

> ly. For there was only one law in the end: the spirit has to be satis-
> fied. In the fullness of time the Christian religion might satisfy it,
> for it, too, was based on blood and sacrifice. There were many reli-
> gions in the world and the gods had many names. The rest was
> loyalty. (SC, 388)

Thus Aniel, despite religious and political setbacks in his outer life,
remains true to his own personal inner being, and in doing so is
meant to represent, for modern readers, a hope for survival for the
Celtic peoples. Their outer forms of worship and social structure
may be attacked and destroyed, but if they can preserve their 'inner
selves' and remain true to the deepest elements of their racial consciousness they will survive the calamities of history.

   Despite its daring and imaginative themes, however, the success
of *Sun Circle* as an historical novel and as a statement on Celtic
racial consciousness remains questionable. Personal friends and
some contemporary·reviewers greeted the novel favourably, but
others found it a puzzling work or ignored it altogether. Moreover
the book was a commercial failure.[23] More recent critical responses
have been very divided. Rescanières is 'deeply affected by Gunn's
attempt at a thoroughly artistic and philosophical rendering of the
birth of Scotland' and Gifford sees *Sun Circle* as the first part of a
trilogy (continued with *Butcher's Broom* and *The Silver Darlings*)
which is 'perhaps the greatest, most affirmative, and most artistically effective and coherent contribution to Scottish literature'. He
especially praises Gunn's attempt to explore the 'utterly alien
thought processes' of the ancient Celts and his belief that the 'magical transcendance of tragedy' intimates that 'endurance and
resilience can break the black circle of defeatism'.[24] A possible
weakness in Gifford's interpretation of *Sun Circle* is that it is only
really evaluated within the context of a trilogy – a trilogy which
seems more Gifford's conception than Gunn's. Indeed, contrary to
Gifford, Price sees Gunn's vision of 'hedonistic anti-heroism' in
emphasising 'endurance not aggression' as a return to a tacit acceptance of some of the premises of the despised Celtic Twilight.
Moreover he argues that the Ravens' relationship with other local
tribes (the Finlags and Logenmen) 'hardly amounts to a vision of a
pan-Celtic harmony' and that his historical vagueness can, in fact,

lead to anachronism. McCulloch, too, is unconvinced by Gunn's historical recreation of the daily life of ninth-century Celts and the 'titillating reticence' of his love scenes. She is also critical of Gunn's unsure use of the registers of Scots and English.[25]

On the whole, therefore, *Sun Circle* still remains one of Gunn's less successful works. This is partly due to stylistic weaknesses (coy love scenes and wooden dialogue in particular), but its greatest failure lies in the frequently noted lack of historical conviction. This is particularly evident when *Sun Circle* is compared with *Butcher's Broom* and *The Silver Darlings*, Gunn's two other historical novels, in which careful research into well-established historical facts helped him provide detailed, impressive and totally believable settings. As indicated above, however, the main flaw in *Sun Circle* is Gunn's conception and presentation of the Norsemen and the Picts' and Celts' response to their invasion. There is simply too much myth and legend and not enough convincing historical reality, and as a result Gunn's overriding attempt to present a sound and coherent view of the early contacts between the Nordic and Celtic races lacks a solid and credible basis of fact. Perhaps the strongest evidence for the novel's relative failure is Gunn's own clear dissatisfaction with it, for as his biographers reveal, when enumerating all his works Gunn invariably 'forgot' one of them: *Sun Circle*.[26]

Although this attempt at an historical presentation of racial synthesis was a failure, Gunn was to find a more successful inspiration for his vision of assimilation and harmony in two more intuitive ideas: his atavistic conceptions of 'the folk' and the Norse ethos of courage and seamanship.

Highland River and 'The Folk'

For Neil Gunn there were two kinds of history: the academic study of facts, figures, dates, names and places, i.e. the kind of history taught in schools, and folk history, the largely unrecorded day-to-day life, through the centuries, of ordinary people in small communities. It is this latter form of history which is the true history for Gunn, and one which can only be intuitively sensed and not learned from textbooks. *Highland River* (1937) is perhaps Gunn's finest statement of this idea. Its hero Kenn, as a young boy, is never told much about his local medieval ancestors at school, as the curriculum is mostly concerned with facts and figures about Romans and Saxons (i.e. it is English-orientated rather than Scottish-orientated). Nonetheless, in his own wanderings in the nearby strath the natural surroundings evoke in the boy a consciousness of a different kind of history:

> ... no Gael or Viking or Pict was ever drawn as humanly as Alfred, and Kenn in his boyhood had certainly no glimmering of an idea of how these three had filled his own glen with peaceful and violent history, with cunning tunes for the chanter, with odd laughable twists of thought, with courage for the sea. And yet in some unaccountable way he seemed to be aware of the living essence of this history without having being explicitly taught it ....
>
> And knowing this, he would like to stop the thickening of his mind, to hunt back into that lost land, where Alfred and Nero, for all that they could be understood, were foreigners to his blood. The mind that secretly quickened before a broch, before a little path going up through a birch wood, to presences not looked at over the shoulder, possessed a magic that it seems more than a pity to have lost. For it was never deliberately induced. It was often feared, and sometimes hated. It was intensely real.
> (HR, 53-54)

This is not simply the sensation of a fictional character, for Gunn himself often had similar experiences, as related in his autobiographical works *Off in a Boat* and *The Atom of Delight*:

> Even to this day the scent of a wood fire or of burning heather can do more in the grey realm of thought to dispose me to believe in Freud's 'archaic heritage' or Jung's 'collective unconscious' than any number of analyses.[27]

In the context of the intense racial and nationalist debates of the 1920s and 30s, therefore, Gunn soon blended together his sense of racial identity with Jung's 'collective unconscious' to see all human experience as essentially atavistic. Gifford has succinctly summarised Gunn's views on this subject:

> The 'collective unconscious' in Gunn's communities and individuals is that deep racial memory and instinctive knowledge of tra-

dition which Gunn sees as accumulating through thousands of
years, without being taught or learned, in the individual mind. It
is 'collective' because it has been 'collected' by the race....[28]

As Wittig has expressed it, this is the driving force behind the
actions and beliefs of all Gunn's characters: 'Man is at one with all
his ancestors, he carries his racial past in him'. Stewart Angus has
argued that this is no mere literary device, either: 'These atavistic
references are no affectations or poetic fancies in the case of Gunn;
they are of a piece with his view of man and society'. Indeed, as
Price has stated, 'that the personal and the historical are assumed
inseparable is essential Gunn'.[29] It is this sense of atavism which
provides Gunn with a vision of a possible synthesis of Norseman
and Gael. Throughout *Highland River* Kenn, both as boy and man,
gradually follows his native river right to its source. His many
atavistic experiences along the way (especially in connection with
hunting and fishing) reinforce his adult contempt for the history of
kings and queens, and strengthens his belief that 'all the more subtle elements of human intuitions, the sap and health of life, come
naturally out of his heritage from the folk'. This is a folk with whom
Kenn is only too proud to identify himself (HR, 204-6). Most importantly, on his journey up the river, Kenn passes through areas with
place-names or features associating them with the Pictish, Gaelic and
Nordic past. The final source is a remote loch high up on the moors.
Here Kenn has a vision of himself walking towards the mountain:

> Pict, and Viking too, and Gael; the folk, through immense eras of
> time; sea and river, moor and loch; the abiding land: of which the
> departing figure was a silent emanation, more inevitable than any
> figure in any vision. (HR, 241)

In other words, the individual, like 'the folk', is an accumulation
and combination of many races and pasts, each race and period
contributing to the collective unconscious of the community. This
is, perhaps, a suggestion of the ultimate unity of all peoples in a
common humanity, an implied universal identity of 'the folk'
which looks forward to Naomi Mitchison's belief in the necessity of
extending tribal loyalties to global ones (see Chapter 9).

One final aspect of *Highland River* is worth noting: the fact that Kenn's river and its source are joined invisibly and underground. This is highly symbolic, for the 'subterranean linking of sea and land ... had its own strange potency' for Kenn (HR, 233), as it does for Gunn. It alludes to Gunn's growing association of the Celt with the land and the Norseman with the sea, an association which provides him with one of the important elements of his atavistic conception of the Norse ethos in the lives of Caithness fishermen.

Racial Consciousness and the Norse Ethos

Gunn's belief in 'the folk' and atavism contributed to an imaginative perception of the Norse heritage in Scotland. This perception is based not on Old Norse sagas, mythology, history or legend (as in *Sun Circle*), but on what he sees as two fundamental elements of the Norse racial consciousness: courage and seamanship. Gunn's archetypal Viking in a nineteenth- or twentieth-century context is the cool, brave, expert seaman who will not take stupid risks, but will face unavoidable danger with phlegm and skill.

The first conception of this archetype can be found in his short story 'The Sea', in which a young boy, Hugh, is down by the shore anxiously watching the stormy seas whilst awaiting the return of his father and brother from a fishing trip. The boy's courage is kept up by Ould John, the ancient and bearded harbour master:

> His breezy old voice was warm with admiration, and the warmth went about Hugh's heart. The whiskers swept Hugh's face as the antique head went erect. Hugh had a sudden strange intuition of being admitted to the valhallas of men.[30]

Gunn's use of Valhalla in this context clearly shows his association of bravery at sea with a Viking ethos. This ethos, and its accompanying archetypal character, is enlarged in his second novel *Morning Tide*, which both incorporates and expands the scene referred to above in 'The Sea'. In the great storm scene in *Morning Tide* the little boy anxiously awaiting the return of his father and brother is again named Hugh, but the character previously called Ould John has now become an even greater figure of knowledge, experience and stoicism. He is the oldest and most respected man in the community and is always simply referred to as 'the Viking':

> Though eighty years of age, the Viking was a great upstanding
> man, with a broad chest under a blue guernsey and no jacket. As
> skipper-owner of the *Viking*, he had been in his day one of the
> finest seamen on the coast. Too big a man for a sarcasm, he was
> kindly and just. His uplifted head carried the seaman's look. The
> blue eyes gazed at you in the first moment; then they looked past
> you. Afterwards you would remember their colour, but be puz-
> zled to describe its sea-tone.[31]

During the tremendous storm which ravages the village, many of
its inhabitants go down to the shore to see the fate of two boats running for the harbour. As the boats come into view everyone is agi-
tated except, of course, the Viking, who stoically stands erect, waiting. As the boats crash either into the quay or onto the shore it is the
Viking who shouts instructions and encouragement as well as taking a vital part in the rescuing of the crews. The final boat, with
Hugh's father at the tiller, safely makes the harbour through a brilliant and daring piece of seamanship. Hugh is esctatic with relief
and pride:

> Managed it! Managed it!! He turned from the woman, his soul a
> flame. 'Oh, Father!' sang the flame to generations of Norsemen
> and Gael.[32]

This reference to the Nordic and Celtic components of the people's
character appears again in Gunn's next novel, *The Lost Glen*, with its
'land of the Gael, the shore-haunts of the Norseman'. Ewan
Macleod's father, though of 'the old Celtic stock that is of the land
rather than the sea', turns from crofting to fishing because his spirit has 'that something extra of the moving deeps', and he dies
bravely and dramatically in a storm at sea.[33] It is also interesting to
note that Ewan Macleod has a Gaelic Christian name but Gaelicised
Norse surname.

The Silver Darlings

By far the most imaginative of all Gunn's explorations of the Nordic
and Celtic racial consciousnesses is the novel many critics regard as

his masterpiece: *The Silver Darlings*. This novel is Gunn's tribute to the courage and tenacity of the Caithness people trying desperately to build a new life on the shores of the Moray Firth in the early nineteenth century, after having been cruelly dispossessed of their homes in the inland straths during the infamous Clearances. Set in the small community of Helmsdale, the novel tells the story of the birth of the herring boom during the Napoleonic Wars, and of the lives of three main characters: Catrine, her son Finn (by her first husband, Tormad), and Roddie Sinclair, who patiently courts Catrine for twenty years before winning her hand. The main reason for this long courtship is simply that although Catrine senses her husband is dead she has to wait many years for confirmation of this fact before she can accept Roddie. Thus throughout the novel there is a touching contest for Catrine's love between the living and vital Roddie and the dead but ever-present and cherished spirit of Tormad.

Gunn's greatest and most obvious celebration of the Norse spirit in northern Scottish seamen is the character of Roddie Sinclair, the daring and resourceful fisherman of Helmsdale. As Hart has argued, Roddie is 'as fine a male figure as Gunn has drawn'[34] and many critics have commented on his portrayal as a modern-day Viking. Gifford compares him to one of the 'great heroes of Icelandic saga', especially commenting on his crew's 'Viking spirit of understated humour and loyalty' on their epic voyage when blown off course into the Atlantic. Isobel Murray and Bob Tait also see Roddie and his crew as 'reincarnations of the Vikings' and McCulloch underlines the significance of Roddie's Norse ancestry as, 'part living character and part symbol', he helps establish the successful herring industry in north-east Scotland in the early nineteenth century.[35] Gunn clearly intends Roddie to be seen as an archetypal Norse seaman, for in addition to specific references to him as a Viking, his physical characteristics (tall and fair-haired), great strength, skillful seamanship, and coolness and stoicism when in danger, all indicate this. Gunn even has Roddie go 'berserk' in true Viking style in a pub in Stornoway. All this is self-evident, but what is perhaps of greater interest is Roddie's role of Viking within the context of Gunn's belief in the importance of racial atavism.

To begin with, as Gifford has pointed out, Gunn makes a clear contrast between 'Roddie's Sutherland and Viking fairness with [Tormad's] Pictish darkness and heavy breadth'.[36] The relevance of this is simply that Tormad, the Pict of land and strath, lacked the innate knowledge and experience to be a successful fisherman – the only means of a living open to him – and this duly results in his capture and death at the hands of a press-gang. Roddie, on the other hand, with his Norse ancestry and, by implication, innate sea-manship, makes a great success of the herring fishing, helps create a viable and even prosperous community, and finally unites with Catrine, their child symbolically representing the union of Norseman and Gael.

This theme is underlined by the story of Finn, Catrine's son by Tormad. As his name and other allusions imply (e.g. the trumpet he gains at the hill market and the names of his dogs, Bran and Oskar), Finn is meant to be a reincarnation of Finn MacCoul the legendary Gaelic hero and leader. Like the archetypal Celt, Finn is very sensi-tive to artistic beauty. He is deeply moved by music and song and like his legendary counterpart becomes an accomplished story-teller. Moreover he has inherited from his mother the ability to see and feel things which are not of the real world, indicated by his supernatural experiences in the House of Peace and on the Flannan Isles. As a young boy Finn deeply admires Roddie and does his best to emulate him. He becomes a member of Roddie's crew, learns the skills of the sea, and even has his own 'berserk' outburst at a ceilidh. As Finn grows older and becomes aware of the implications of Roddie's interest in his mother, however, his emulation turns to jealousy and rivalry. The two men finally become reconciled when they are called upon to act in unison – Roddie with his great strength and Finn with his head for heights – in a daring sea-cliff rescue of the crew of a foundered boat. By the end of the novel Finn has his own boat and has succeeded Roddie as the leading fisher-man in Helmsdale.

The important point here is that it is Finn the Gael who is now the master of the sea – and the owner of his mother's croft now that she has married Roddie. The reconciliation at the end of the novel is not only between Roddie and Finn, and Finn and Catrine, but also between the world of land and sea, between Norseman and

Gael. As Murray and Tait express it: 'Finn brings Viking and Celt, pagan and Christian, old world and new world together'.[37] Gunn has thus paid his finest tribute to the Norse characteristics of bravery and seamanship, but with the clear suggestion that these attributes can be attained as well as inherited by the Gael. This interpretation is supported by the intriguing point that although *The Silver Darlings* is clearly a paeon of praise to the modern-day Viking, Roddie, it is also his swan-song. By the end of the novel Roddie has settled down as a landsman who is reluctant to leave his wife and child for the sea. In Viking terms he is ready to disgrace himself by living a quiet life and dying by the fireside. It is significant that Finn, who has succeeded him as Helmsdale's leading fisherman, loses some of his respect for his erstwhile skipper and idol:

> And he could afford to smile with contempt at the thought of Roddie, the great seaman, being overcome by his wife; Roddie making excuses – because he must stay at home! ... Things had come to a pretty pass with the great Viking!

Finn is even rather contemptuous of Roddie's sentimentality as a father: 'Roddie, the great seaman, the Viking, carrying on like a silly woman!'[38] Thus, as argued earlier, although *The Silver Darlings* pays homage to the Norse heritage in Caithness and Sutherland, it also clearly indicates that it is the Gael (in this case Finn, born of Pict and Celt) who will both inherit and attain the skill and stoicism necessary to conquer the sea; the Celt had finally absorbed and subjugated the Viking. The day of the Norseman was over. In spite of its Viking theme, therefore, *The Silver Darlings* remains, as Maurice Lindsay comments, 'a magnificent tribute to the indomitable spirit of the Gael'.[39]

Old Norse Influence: Ambivalence and Change

The Silver Darlings was Gunn's last major work to extol the praises of his atavistic interpretation of the Norse ethos. This fact also reveals an intriguing and important aspect of Gunn's interest in Norse history and culture: it was always slightly ambivalent, and did not remain static but underwent a very gradual and definite transformation. Gunn's ambivalence towards Scotland's Norse heritage is notable in that, despite his admiration for the Norse ethos in certain contexts in his earlier works, his references to Vikings and Norse history become increasingly negative. His angry reply to Urquhart's denigrating comments in the *Scots Magazine* in 1931 has already been discussed in Chapter 3. In 1933 the Vikings in *Sun Circle*, despite their qualities of leadership and action, are generally presented as being brutal and callous, and in his article 'Caithness and Sutherland' in 1935 he describes Vikings as essentially little more than robbers 'with the conqueror's technique of spoil-getting and land-grabbing'.[40] By the time he wrote *Off in a Boat* in 1938, he had begun to regard the coming of the Norsemen to the Western Isles as having disastrous consequences on Celtic culture:

> Towards the end of the eighth century Norwegians and Danes started their murderous inroads, and from then on the old sense of peace and security vanished in that lust for landownership and power which is still with us.[41]

After 1941 there are virtually no further references to Vikings or the Norse heritage in Gunn's works, and in post-war years he relished his friend Ian Grimble's efforts 'to prove that the Gunns were not Norse but pre-Celt, or Pictish' and he signed his letters to Grimble as 'Neil Firbolg (remnant of ancient race among mere upstart Gaels and parvenu Norsemen)'.[42]

This gradual change is also evident even in Gunn's attitude towards the Norse ethos in seamanship. In his earlier novels, especially *Morning Tide*, *The Lost Glen*, and *Highland River*, his heroes or father-figures are all uncritically presented as courageous, fearless and skillful fishermen who can usually conquer both the elements and their own fears. This admiration for seamen reaches its climax, as noted above, with the character of Roddie Sinclair in *The Silver Darlings*. Ten years later, however, a much more critical view of the Norse ethos in seamanship can be found in *The Well at the World's End* (1951). The hero of the novel, Peter Munro, becomes involved in many adventures whilst on a walking tour in the Highlands. Staying in a small fishing village, he witnesses a dramatic event during a storm at sea: Old Malcolm, out fishing with Willie and Angus (his son), is caught in a storm and gets into difficulties. The lifeboat, skippered by Norman, comes alongside to help, but Malcolm refuses any assistance, extremely offended that he 'should be caught out in his sea lore, that he should be wounded so deeply in his sea pride, that he should be saved by Norman of all people'.[43] His son Angus, however, suggests that perhaps it would be better to board the lifeboat, but his father gives him such a contemptuous look, clearly believing Angus is afraid, that he desists. Malcolm successfully brings the boat back to harbour, but once ashore he learns that his son is courting Norman's daughter and that the only reason he had wanted to board the lifeboat was so as not to offend his future father-in-law.

> Malcolm stood still for a little; then he sat down as if his legs had weakened; and Willie for the first time in his life saw the forearm that held the tiller shake.[44]

Malcolm and Norman are reconciled with a public handshake, but the incident has been a revealing comment on the nature of pride. As Hart and Pick astutely remark:

> On first reading, this prompted a number of questions: would it not have required more courage for Malcolm to lay aside his pride, avoid risking the lives of his crew, and go aboard the lifeboat? Must a man never, in any circumstances, fail in courage if he is to be acceptable to his father? Are we to see something admirable in the old man's rejection of his son?[45]

Gunn has certainly come a long way from the uncritical and eulogistic descriptions of seamen fighting the sea in his earlier novels. In this, his final 'storm scene' at sea in fiction, he seems to take a more critical look at stoicism and bravery at sea, realising that, in the wrong context, these attributes can so easily become obstinacy and vanity. Gunn seems to be finally admitting that, despite its admirable aspects, the Norse ethos as applied to seamanship could also have its disadvantages.[46]

There are perhaps two main reasons for Gunn's changing attitude to the Norse heritage in Scotland. The first and most logical one is simply his growing sense of identity and commitment to an independent and Gaelic orientated Scotland (in culture if not in lan-

guage). This is supported by McCulloch's thesis that Gunn's creative career can be divided into three main periods: the early novels with their pessimistic 'Celtic Twilight' view of the Highlands
(1926-34); the novels of his middle years which try to come to terms
positively, factually, and optimistically with the problems of the
Gaeltachd (1937-46); and his late novels which deal with important
and wide-ranging social and philosophical themes in which the
values of the Scottish Highland communities are often proffered as
'an opposing cathartic or reconciling vision' to the evils of twentieth-century modes of living (1940s-54).[47] Gunn's most positive
view of the Norse ethos (*The Lost Glen, Morning Tide, Sun Circle*)
appears in the early period when he is most pessimistic about Celtic
life in the Highlands. His literary attempts to absorb the Norse
ethos into the Celtic consciousness (*Highland River, The Silver
Darlings*) come in the second period when his confidence in a Celtic
future is growing. The almost complete lack of Norse references in
the final period matches his total commitment to a Celtic vision for
Scotland. Gunn's shift in orientation is also paralleled by a significant change in the characterisation of his heroes; as already mentioned, in the earlier novels these tend to be associated with the sea,
but after *The Silver Darlings* they are increasingly associated with
the land (and are often academics or intellectuals).[48]

A second possible reason for Gunn's diminishing enthusiasm for
the Norse ethos could have been a gradual realisation of the way in
which Nordic values were being extolled and exploited by Nazism
in the 1930s. Gunn himself is not entirely innocent in this matter. In
Sun Circle Aniel is concerned for the Celts' need for a strong leader
and Gunn apparently approves of the Vikings' practical superiority through the amoral and decisive imposition of their will. This is
all uncomfortably reminiscent of Nietzsche's concept of the 'über-
mensch' and general Nazi views of racism. German Nazis indeed
made discreet approaches to Gunn (hinting that he might be
awarded the Shakespeare Prize from the University of Hamburg)
and Gunn visited Germany in May 1938 and February 1939. As a
mitigating circumstance, his biographers have argued that 'at the
time he failed to realise what monsters moved beneath the surface
life of cafés, streets and the Europa Hotel', but as McCreery has tart-
ly commented: 'unawareness in 1939 will not do'.[49]

But, however misguided or innocent Gunn's visits to Germany may have been, the evidence of his own writing and actions clearly confirm that he had no sympathy whatsoever with any fascist or totalitarian form of government, and indeed the German Nazis soon abandoned their attempts to solicit his support. The only thing which Gunn had in common with Nazism was a belief in racial consciousness, and an unfortunate use and interpretation of the word 'race' which makes modern readers uncomfortable. As McCreery has pointed out in his defence: 'If we do condemn him over this, then we are guilty of a linguistic anachronism and ignorant of the change that took place, largely due to the War, in the acceptability of the term'.[50] As the war progressed there could be no illusions as to the nature of Nazism or its interpretation of racist ideas, and Gunn revealed his detestation of both its creed and practices in his anti-totalitarian fantasy *The Green Isle of the Great Deep* in 1944. In this context it is perhaps highly significant that there is no trace of any Norse influence in Gunn's fiction after 1941. Although it is impossible to prove such speculation, it may not be too fanciful to suggest that, during the war, Gunn became increasingly embarassed by his previous visits to Germany and his semi-fascistic comments in *Sun Circle*. Perhaps this may provide another reason for his 'forgetting' this novel, and one might go further to suppose that this embarassment was what made him avoid any further reference to a Norse spirit or heritage in connection with the Scottish consciousness.

Gunn's attitude to Norse history in a Scottish context may have been ambivalent and shifting over the years, as the evidence in this chapter suggests, but there can be no doubting its importance and relevance to his earlier work. The contrasting Norse and Gaelic place-names of his childhood Dunbeath and his vivid image of the first Viking invasion there provided him with a deep and enduring inspiration for some of his most important novels. Whether in the form of historical fiction, as in *Sun Circle*, or in terms of racial atavism, as in *The Silver Darlings*, Scotland's Norse heritage has had a potent influence on Gunn's vision of the history and culture of the coastline communities of the Scottish Highlands.

NOTES

1   Gunn was never a fluent speaker of Gaelic. In politics he played a vital role
    in the forming of the Scottish National Party; see Francis Russell Hart and
    J.B. Pick, *Neil M. Gunn: A Highland Life* (London, 1981), pp.112-15.
2   Margery McCulloch, *The Novels of Neil M. Gunn: A Critical Study*
    (Edinburgh, 1987), p.4.
3   Hart and Pick, pp.52, 184.
4   Wittig, p.334; James B. Caird, 'Gaelic Elements in Neil Gunn', *Studies in
    Scottish Literature* 15 (1980), 88-94.
5   John R. Allan, *North-East Lowlands of Scotland*, 2nd edn. (London, 1974),
    p.63.
6   Mark Rugg Gunn, *History of the Clan Gunn* (Glasgow, n.d. [1969]), p.9.
7   Ian Grimble, *Scottish Clans and Tartans*, 2nd edn. (London, 1977), p.101.
8   Neil M. Gunn, *Highland River* (1937), Canongate Classics 37 (Edinburgh,
    1991), p.52. All further references are to this edition, abbreviated HR.
9   *Scottish Country*, p.67; *Landscape and Light*, p.29.
10 Neil M. Gunn, *Off in a Boat* (London, 1938), p.55.
11 Neil M. Gunn, 'The Essence of Nationalism', *Scots Magazine* 37 (1942),
    p.171; rpt. in *Landscape and Light*, p.143.
12 See Neil M. Gunn, 'A Visitor from Denmark', *Scots Magazine* 27 (1937), 96-
    101; also in *Landscape and Light*, pp.170-74.
13 Quoted in Hart and Pick, p.32.
14 Wittig, p.326; Francis Russell Hart, 'Beyond History and Tragedy: Neil
    Gunn's Early Fiction', in *Essays on Neil M. Gunn*, ed. David Morrison
    (Thurso, 1971), p.65; Alexander Reid, 'Neil Gunn's Mysticism', in *Neil M.
    Gunn: The Man and the Writer*, ed. Alexander Scott and Douglas Gifford
    (Edinburgh, 1973), p.350; Richard Price, *The Fabulous Matter of Fact: The
    Poetics of Neil M Gunn* (Edinburgh, 1991), p.50.
15 See, for example, Robert B. Gourlay, 'Before the Vikings: The Pre-Norse
    Background in Caithness', in *The Viking Age in Caithness, Orkney and the
    North Atlantic*, ed. C. Batey *et al.* (Edinburgh, 1993), pp.111-19.
16 National Library of Scotland. Dep. 209, Boxes 1 and 10.
17 Neil M. Gunn, *Sun Circle* (1933), Souvenir Press edn. (London, 1983), p.323.
    All further references are to this edition, abbreviated SC.
18 Hart and Pick, pp.96-97; letter from Neil Gunn to Gordon Bottomley
    (27.3.35), NLS Dep. 209, Box 17. McCleery points out, in his Introduction to
    Landscape and Light, that this is an important element of Gunn's use of hunt-
    ing and poaching themes (pp.4-5).
19 McCulloch, p.47.
20 See Ibn Fadlan's reports in Johannes Brøndsted, *The Vikings* (1960), trans.
    Kalle Skow (Harmondsworth, 1965), p.265.
21 Marie-Hélène Rescanières, 'Scottish Saga: *Sun Circle* and *Butcher's Broom*', in
    Neil M. Gunn: The Man and the Writer, p.92.
22 Hart and Pick, p.22.

23   For a favourable contemporary review, see Frank Kendon's in *John O'London's Weekly*, 3 June 1933, p.309; on the commercial aspect, see Hart and Pick, p.102.
24   Rescanières, p.88; Douglas Gifford, 'Neil Gunn and the Mythic Regeneration of Scotland: The Two Great Epic Cycles', in *Neil Gunn's Country: Essays in Celebration of Neil Gunn*, ed. Dairmid Gunn and Isobel Murray (Edinburgh, 1991), pp.76, 86, 87.
25   Price, pp.48-51; McCulloch, pp.45-47.
26   Hart and Pick, p.103.
27   Neil M. Gunn, *The Atom of Delight* (1956), Polygon edn. (Edinburgh, 1986), p.114. See also *Off in a Boat*, p.30.
28   Douglas Gifford, *Neil M. Gunn and Lewis Grassic Gibbon* (Edinburgh, 1983), p.128.
29   Wittig, p.336; Stewart Angus, 'The Novels of Neil M. Gunn', *Scottish Periodical* 1:2 (1948), 97; Price, p.53.
30   Neil M. Gunn, 'The Sea', in *Hidden Doors* (Edinburgh, 1929), p.15.
31   Neil M. Gunn, *Morning Tide* (1931), Souvenir Press edn. (London, 1982), p.80.
32   *Morning Tide*, p.101.
33   Neil M. Gunn, *The Lost Glen* (1932), Richard Drew edn. (Glasgow, 1985), pp.47, 62.
34   Hart, *The Scottish Novel*, p.309.
35   Gifford, *Gunn and Gibbon*, pp.126, 139; Isobel Murray and Bob Tait, *Ten Modern Scottish Novels* (Aberdeen, 1984), p.47; McCulloch, p.88.
36   Gifford, *Gunn and Gibbon*, p.119.
37   Murray and Tait, p.49.
38   Neil M. Gunn, *The Silver Darlings* (1941; London, 1978), pp.506, 559.
39   Maurice Lindsay, *History of Scottish Literature* (London, 1977), p.425.
40   *Scottish Country*, p.68; *Landscape and Light*, p.29.
41   *Off in a Boat*, p.145.
42   Hart and Pick, p.264. See also Dairmid Gunn, 'My Uncle and I', in *Neil Gunn's Country*, p.9.
43   Neil M. Gunn, *The Well at the World's End* (1951), Souvenir Press edn. (London, 1985), p.249.
44   *The Well at the World's End*, p.258.
45   Hart and Pick, p.227.
46   The change in Gunn's attitude is even more evident when comparing this incident in *The Well at the World's End* with its original version, the short story 'The Storm' from 1935. In the short story it is the lifeboat captain who is made to look foolish, and the old seaman caught in the storm is seen as heroic. *Scots Magazine* 22 No.5 (Feb. 1935), 349-57; rpt. in Neil M. Gunn, *The Man Who Came Back: Short Stories and Essays*, ed. Margery McCulloch (Edinburgh, 1991), pp.174-84.
47   McCulloch, p.135.
48   In *The Lost Chart* (London, 1949), Dermot Cameron, the hero, is admittedly

an ex-Royal Navy man, and Captain Laird is once described as staring 'like a Viking' (p.137); moreover some of the novel's action takes place on boats. Nonetheless the sea plays only an incidental role in the themes and values Gunn explores in this novel.

49 Hart and Pick, p.163; Alistair McCreery, Introduction to *Landscape and Light* (Aberdeen, 1987), p.12.

50 McCreery, p.13.

6. HUGH MacDIARMID

Hugh MacDiarmid is, in fact, the pseudonym and alter ego of Christopher Murray Grieve (1892-1978), who, as editor of such journals as *Northern Numbers* and *Scottish Chapbook* in the early 1920s, was the driving force behind the modern Scottish Renaissance. MacDiarmid is indeed mostly renowned for his impassioned and importunate determination to replace the Doric of Burns with a new and revitalised Scots as a serious literary language, and in 1926 he produced the first modern classic in the Scots tongue, the epic poem *A Drunk Man Looks at the Thistle*. His sometimes exteme political views on nationalism and communism, and his espousal of somewhat idiosyncratic theories on the Gaelic Idea and the East-West Synthesis, have also ensured him a place in Scottish literary history as the most colourful and memorable writer of this century. Indeed the name of MacDiarmid has almost become synonymous with the Scottish Renaissance itself.

A general reader of MacDiarmid's poetry, criticism and journalism may well be a little sceptical of any suggestion that there is some Old Norse influence in his work, especially as MacDiarmid very vociferously championed the cause of a Gaelic culture for Scotland. Nonetheless, a careful study of his prolific output reveals a slight but very distinct Old Norse influence on some specific works and ideas. He first seems to have become acquainted with Old Norse literature in his early teens when (as recorded in the autobiographical *Lucky Poet*) he spent many a happy day discussing a variety of subjects with a friend, including:

> Icelandic sagas and their bearing
> On the population of the Moray Firth;
> Relics of the Norse language in Lewis speech;

Points of resemblance between *Beowulf* and
the *Grettla* or *Grettis Saga*
William Herbert and his Scandinavian poetry.[1]

Bearing in mind MacDiarmid's reputation for glib exaggerations, one should always take his references and lists of an enormously eclectic reading with some reservations. In this particular instance, however, there seems little reason to doubt his claims as the allusions to Old Norse mythology and literature in his works show that, over the years, he attained a fair knowledge of the subject. As the above quotation reveals, MacDiarmid was also well aware of the existence of an Old Norse heritage in Scotland and its influence on Scottish culture.

MacDiarmid and Old Norse Mythology

The first traces of Old Norse influence on MacDiarmid can be found in his pioneering days in the 1920s as the instigator of the Scottish Renaissance. As one specific and many indirect references in his long epic poem, *A Drunk Man Looks at the Thistle*, indicate, the Thistle, amongst its many other symbolic functions, represents Yggdrasil, the cosmic tree of Old Norse mythology. The roots of Yggdrasil thrust through and beyond the earth and its branches extend beyond heaven; like life itself it is unlimited and unfathomable and subject to all the powers of good and evil.[2] This straightforward reference to the Thistle as the Tree of Life with all its consequent implications has, of course, frequently been noted by critics. Indeed a tree as an organic symbol of the universe is common to the cosmogonies of many cultures. However, an important possible interpretation of the Old Norse form of this symbol, as it appears in *A Drunk Man*, seems to have been overlooked. Within MacDiarmid's poem there are references to crucifixion (ll.1191-1218, pp.94-96) and the identification of the poet with Christ himself (ll.1665-70, p.124). Moreover the poet must suffer in order to gain 'The secret that I'd fain find oot / O' this bricht hive, this sorry weed,/ The tree that fills the Universe ...' (ll.1347-49, p.104). This is a task even more difficult for a poet in Scotland and is almost certain to end in failure:

A Scottish poet maun assume
The burden o' his people's doom,
And dee to brak' their livin' tomb.
Mony ha'e tried, but a' ha'e failed.
Their sacrifice has nocht availed.
Upon the thistle they're impaled. (ll.2638-43, p.190)

The important point here is the implied image of a god sacrificed
on the tree/thistle, and this image gains immediate significance for
the reader aware that, in Old Norse mythology, Odin hung for nine
days on Yggdrasil, exposed to hunger and the wind, his side
pierced by a spear. This was a personal sacrifice to gain knowledge
of the runes, the magic of written signs.[3] This idea is never overtly
stated by MacDiarmid in the poem, indeed he may well have been
unaware of this aspect of the mythology concerning Odin and
Yggdrasil. Nonetheless, as W.N Herbert has noted, the symbols of
A Drunk Man can operate on two different levels, one of which
being 'a darker, more ambiguous level, at which symbols exert a
power the poet doesn't fully analyse....'[4] Thus, whether consciously intended or not, MacDiarmid's use of this aspect of the Yggdrasil
myth has very apt and powerful references to his own self-sacrific-
ing struggle to establish the Scots language as a medium for the
Scottish Renaissance.

A further interesting application of Old Norse mythology can be
found in MacDiarmid's second epic poem *To Circumjack Cencrastus*.
Basically a vehicle for proclaiming his new Gaelic Idea, the intended unifying symbol of the poem is, as the title indicates, the curly
sea-serpent, a symbol of knowledge and eternity in Celtic mythology. As MacDiarmid's earlier poem 'The Sea-Serpent' (I, 48-51)
reveals, the creature is also, in the words of Kenneth Buthlay, 'conceived to be the original manifestation of the life force which
emanated from the divine creative power'.[5] Thus throughout the
poem we have the image of the poet as fisherman, desperately trying to catch the serpent of wisdom and the imagination: 'Flashing,
wise, sinuous, dangerous creature, / Offspring of mystery and the
world without end' (I, 285). In Old Norse mythology, the Norse
Midgard Serpent encircling the world, Jormungand, is also a dangerous and elusive creature; indeed Thor, on a fishing trip with the

giant Hymir, almost catches it in a tremendous duel of strength. The monster is actually being drawn on board when the terrified Hymir cuts Thor's line at the gunwale and so lets the serpent escape. The important point here is that in fact Thor *may not* capture the Midgard Serpent as they are destined to destroy each other at Ragnarök – the end of the world in Old Norse mythology.[6] Again, whether consciously used or not, in the context of *To Circumjack Cencrastus* this myth gives added significance to MacDiarmid's own never-ending struggle with the sea-serpent of poetic imagination. He may always struggle desperately with the monster, but he must never actually land it, for to do so would signify the poet's doom as well as the serpent's.

Norwegian *Landsmaal* and Synthetic Scots

A more indirect Old Norse influence on MacDiarmid's early work can be found in his interest in the *Landsmaal* ('National Language') movement in Norway to revive an older and purer form of Norwegian. MacDiarmid probably learned of this movement from a lecture delivered by W.A. Craigie to the Vernacular Circle of the London Burns Club in 1921 in which he suggested that this movement could provide an example for a revival of the Scots language.[7] MacDiarmid's interest in this idea can be seen in his references to the Norwegian poet Henrik Wergeland in his poems 'Gairmscoile' (I, 73) and *To Circumjack Cencrastus* (I, 208). Wergeland was the first Norwegian poet who attempted to break away from the Danish literary language then in use in Norway (which had been under the Danish crown 1349-1814) by bringing into his poems words and rhythms from the Norwegian spoken dialects, especially when he considered they represented the oldest and purest extant forms of the original Old Norse language.

There is an obvious parallel here with what MacDiarmid was trying to do with Scots poetry in the 1920s, and it is thus not surprising that he would see Wergeland as a model and inspiration, not least as Wergeland's mother was of Scottish extraction. Wergeland's pioneering efforts were later reinforced by the work of the linguist and grammarian Ivar Aasen who produced a grammar and dictionary of a new language based on the synthesis of the dialects which soon became known in Norway as the *Landsmaal*.

The literary possibilities of this new 'Synthetic Norwegian' were revealed by the novelist Arne Garborg in the late nineteenth century, and the language is now codified as a legal language of Norway: Nynorsk or 'New Norwegian'. Later references to Aasen ('In Memoriam James Joyce', II, 741) and his obituary on Garborg[8] reveal that MacDiarmid was clearly aware of the history of the *Landsmaal* movement in Norway – especially its successful acceptance in the twentieth century – and it must have been an inspiring example to him in his attempt to revitalise and revivify Lallans in Scotland.

Although MacDiarmid was willing to accept the importance of Old Norse in the creation of what was, in effect, a 'Synthetic Norwegian', he at first totally refused to accept that it had any relevance to the history of Scots. This is most evident in the discussions of the Nordic origin of the Scots in the *Scottish Educational Journal* between 1925 and 1926 (discussed in Chapter 3). In the debate over the linguistic origins of the Scots language, R.L. Cassie argued that the northern dialect should provide the basis of a new revitalised Scots, mostly because its original form 'is the primitive Norse (urnordisk) of the Jutish and Anglian colonists of Northumbria, between the Forth and Humber'. This was then later 'reinforced by the distinctive Norse of the Vikings, and gradually assimilated many Gaelic words and idioms'.[9] MacDiarmid (writing under his own name, Grieve) harshly rejected such ideas, however, as he believed the dialects of the north of Scotland to be too contaminated by foreign influence:

> But however large the accession of Norse and Gaelic terms in Northern Scots, its interest so far as a movement for the revival of the Scots vernacular is concerned, must surely depend not upon its differences from – but upon its connections with – Scots in other districts.[10]

Apart from MacDiarmid's understandably parochial bias in favour of his own Border dialect and his determination to be the general law-giver as to what constituted Scots, his position vis-a-vis Old Norse is not really tenable. As more recent research has suggested, it is precisely the Old Norse element in Scots which helps marked-

ly differentiate it from English.[11] Moreover, ironically, the dictionary on which MacDiarmid based so much of his early poetry was
Jamieson's *Etymological Dictionary*. MacDiarmid seemed unaware,
or did not wish to acknowledge the fact, that Jamieson's dictionary
was inspired (as noted in Chapter 2) by G.J. Thorkelin's collection
of the many Scots words of Old Norse origin. Thus although
MacDiarmid recognised the importance of Old Norse as a source
for a new and purer Norwegian, he was less willing to accept the
existence of an Old Norse element in the Scots tongue. This attitude
towards Old Norse language, literature and history, underwent a
distinct change after 1930, however, for two main reasons: firstly,
his adoption of the Gaelic Idea and the theories of the amateur historian L.A. Waddell; and secondly, his living on Whalsay, Shetland,
from 1933-42 which brought him into contact with Shetland Norn
and Scandinavia.

The Gaelic Idea and *The British Edda*

The Gaelic idea was first announced in MacDiarmid's poetry in *To
Circumjack Cencrastus* in 1930, by which time he had come to believe
that 'the main hope of a Scottish revival' lay not in Lowland
Scotland, but 'in the Gaelic heritage which Scotland shared with the
other Celtic countries, most notably Ireland'. Thus 'Scottish
Scotland must be a Gaelic Scotland' and MacDiarmid increasingly
championed Gaelic culture and language.[12]

   In the context of the Norse/Celtic debate in the 1930s, one would
have assumed that the Gaelic Idea would have ruled out any further interest in Old Norse history or culture. That this was not so
was due to MacDiarmid's naive and enthusiastic acceptance of the
theories of the amateur historian L.A. Waddell as published in *The
British Edda* (1930). Waddell's thesis is an amazing pot-pourri of
theories and legends in a fantastic attempt to link together all the
myths of Thor and Odin, Cain and Abel, Adam and Eve, King
Arthur and the Round Table, the Search for the Grail, and St.
George and the Dragon. Waddell's main thesis, however, as the title
of his book implies, is that:

> The translators [of the *Edda*] have totally failed to recognize that
> the Edda is *not* at all a medley of disjointed Scandinavian mytho-

logical tales of gods as has been imagined; but that it forms one
great coherent epic of historical human heroes and their exploits,
based upon genuine hoary tradition; that it is an ancient British
epic poem written with lurid realism in the ancient British language.[13]

This thesis cannot be supported by any serious linguistic, literary,
or historical study of the *Edda*, but MacDiarmid apparently accepted it quite unquestioningly, as quotations from his poems illustrate,
e.g. 'Ceol Mor':

> Remembering how the 'Norse' epics of Thor (Icelandic)
> Were compiled in the British Isles
> And were known to the Ancient Britons
> Whose traditional hero, Arthur,
> Is the Icelandic 'Her Thor'
> Ultimately identifiable by his exploits
> With the Sumerian King, Dur. (I, 682)

A further example can be found in his 'Cornish Heroic Song for
Valda Trevlyn':

> And I know King Arthur – pace Layamon,
> Chaucer, Malory, Spenser, Dryden, Wordsworth,
> Tennyson, and all the rest of the romancing bards –
> Is none other than Thor, Her-Thor, Ar-Thur,
> Thor Eindri of the Edda, the Indian Indra ... (I, 708)

In other words, Old Norse history and mythology were really
Celtic and the Norsemen perhaps a 'lost tribe' of Gaeldom. From
his reading of Waddell's book and L. Albert's *Six Thousand Years of
Gaelic Grandeur Unearthed* (1936), MacDiarmid frequently maintained that the Celtic people had originated in Georgia and gradually moved westward. This enabled MacDiarmid to incorporate
two of his greatest passions, the Celtic and Russian cultures, in a
bizarre East-West Synthesis.[14] Moreover this idea also implied that
the Celts embraced all the main Aryan cultures of Europe and that
the 'the original impetus to civilisation was an Ur-Gaelic initiative'.[15] Many critics have found MacDiarmid's extraordinary ideas

hard to accept. Bold refers to his belief in the Ur-Gaelic theory as 'obvious eccentricity' and an 'idiosyncratic obsession'. Alexander Scott, however, is much more forthright, saying that MacDiarmid's 'haverings on Celtic subjects, where he accepted forgeries as gospel and reiterated the inaccuracies of unreliable scholars as if they were novel revelations, are embarrassingly awful'.[16] In a letter to D.G. Bridson in 1956, however, MacDiarmid openly admits that Waddell's ideas on the *Edda* are 'in some respects quite heretical'. Nonetheless he is impressed by Waddell's 'quality of imagination' and that 'waiving the question of scholarly accuracy altogether, elements could be drawn from him which could be worked up in verse-drama form very effectively'.[17] MacDiarmid was thus admitting that he was less concerned with the accuracy or otherwise of Waddell's theory than with its inspiring vision. It was MacDiarmid's acceptance of this vision, which included a place for Old Norse history *within* the Celtic genius, which later had an undoubted influence on his attitudes to the Old Norse heritage in Scotland.

Shetland Norn and World Language

MacDiarmid's changing attitude to Old Norse language and history became increasingly apparent after he moved to Shetland, arguably the most Norse part of Scotland, from 1933 until 1942. Living on Whalsay, MacDiarmid soon came into contact with the local dialect and its remnants of the Shetland Norn.[18] An inveterate ransacker and hoarder of new words, he clearly enjoyed delving into the dialect and its vocabulary as recorded in Jakobsen's *An Etymological Dictionary of the Norn Language in Shetland* and *The Dialect and Place Names of Shetland*, a 1926 reissue of two lectures published in 1897. MacDiarmid savoured the harsh-sounding words of the Norn and used a list of them in his perhaps most famous Shetland poem, 'On a Raised Beach' (I, 427), and also later in 'In Memoriam James Joyce' (II, 764).[19] His increasing fascination with Gaelic and his contact with the Shetland dialect made him increasingly sensitive to language as a whole and finally led him to:

> The painful and ecstatic awareness
> Of language as the central mystery

Of the intellectual life, the great obsession
With language and the point of consciousness.
('In Memoriam James Joyce', II, 763).

MacDiarmid's study of languages thus became as eclectic as his reading of literature: 'There is no language in the world / That has not yielded me delight' ('In Memoriam James Joyce', II, 818), and with Joyce as his inspiration he began to search for new modes of linguistic expression which would cross all national, geographical, and lexical boundaries. This new aim for an international language was a logical development from his earlier theories, MacDiarmid claimed, and not a divergence from them:

> ... for a world language which isn't an esperanto but an interpenetration of all languages, accommodates as far as I am concerned the Lallans movement and similar movements in various European countries. I'm looking for a diversity in unity, not for a unification of languages.[20]

This attitude obviously included a reappraisal of Old Norse, both as a language for a new Scotland: 'We must have Gaelic and Old Norse and Latin and much else', and as part of a world language:

> A Joycean amalgam of Scots, Gaelic, and English, plus Gothic, Sanskrit, Old Norse, seems to me a medium through which a great deal could be done to advance this world-wide experimentation and bring language abreast of modern psychological requirements.[21]

Shetland and Scandinavia

Living in Shetland, MacDiarmid could not avoid its more obvious Scandinavian links, both past and present. Moreover soon after he moved to Whalsay he spent a week in the Faroe Isles and was very impressed with everything he saw there, especially the Faroese determination to maintain their own language.[22] MacDiarmid had previously written rather disparagingly of the Shetlanders' 'vague notion of their connection with the Viking period',[23] but now inspired by his close contact with the islanders and his impressions of the Faroese, his views on Shetland's Norse past changed markedly. In his book *The Islands of Scotland* he makes frequent comparisons between the situation of the Shetlanders and that of the Faroese, especially how the latter had used their Norse heritage to maintain a degree of linguistic and cultural independence from Denmark. Thus, MacDiarmid argues:

> ... the insistence that the Shetlanders are Scandinavians is stirring and presents a tendency which I think ought to be encouraged by all possible means, and especially by a recovery of the old Norn tongue, and an effort to build up a vigorous cultural movement on that basis, since that can only help them to preserve and develop a distinctive life.... [24]

So impressed was MacDiarmid by all the new cultural and linguistic experiences in Shetland and the Faroe Isles, that he began to seek ways of expanding his Gaelic Idea into a more comprehensive union of all the North Atlantic seaboard cultures. As he later claimed in his autobiographical *Lucky Poet*, it was whilst working on his book about the Scottish islands that he first developed his view of:

> ... the ancient Thulean continent, and coastal connexions between Scandinavia, Iceland, the Faroes, the Orkneys, Shetlands, Hebrides, Island of Man, Wales, Cornwall, and Ireland – a framework for all my chief enthusiasms and my sense of the inter-relationships, the underlying design, of all these. (p.60)

In other words, MacDiarmid's Pan-Celtic idea seems to have become a Pan-Northern or Pan-Nordo-Celtic one. This is also supported by the fact that there are a growing number of Old Norse references in his work and a greater appreciation of Old Norse literature. Comments in *The Islands of Scotland* (pp.99-100) show that he was familiar with *Orkneyinga Saga* and *Njal's Saga*, and he had clearly been interested in the many theories as to the origin of kennings, the difficult and obscure metaphors of skaldic poetry. MacDiarmid agreed with an unnamed critic of Axel Olrik's *Viking Civilisation* that these kennings were most likely based on the noa-words of seamen:

... verbal ingenuities sprang far more probably from that practical
habit of the fisher-folk which in the Shetland Islands, as in
Norway and the Faroes and elsewhere, led, and still leads, to the
use of 'lucky words'.[25]

Bearing in mind MacDiarmid's own preference for writing long
poems and having, many would argue, a tendency to prolixity, it is
also surprising to read of his admiration for the terse and succinct
style of the Old Norse sagas in 'My Heart Always Goes Back to the
North' (II, 1347). Another poem, 'A Skald's Death', as both the title
and a reference to the midnight sun would suggest, is also clearly
influenced by his Norse reading in Shetland. It is particularly interesting to note that in this poem MacDiarmid refers to himself as a
'skald', the court poet of the Norsemen, and not a 'filí', the bard of
the ancient Gaels.

The Final Synthesis: 'Audh [sic] the Deep-Minded'

During his stay in Shetland in the 1930s, therefore, MacDiarmid
was influenced by many new ideas and experiences. Most interesting of all, he had adopted a much more receptive attitude to both
Old Norse language and literature, even, to a certain extent, incor-
porating them into his Pan-Celtic world view. The extraordinary
way in which MacDiarmid could synthesise his interpretations of
Waddell's theory, his perception of Shetland, and his concern for a
world language, is perhaps encapsulated in the following unex-
pected declaration in *The Islands of Scotland* (pp.41-42):

> The Muse with whom I am concerned in this book – since it deals
> not only with the Hebrides but with the Scottish Islands as a
> whole – is not Deirdre, but (one of the greatest, yet least-known,
> women in Scottish History) Audh, the 'deep-minded,' wife and
> mother of chieftains, Gaelic and Scandinavian, who, at the end,
> left the Hebrides and voyaged, via the Faroes, where she landed
> to see some of her grandchildren, to Iceland, where she died and
> lies buried in one of its cold *jokulls*.[26]

For MacDiarmid, Audh the Deep-Minded is thus a perfect representative of his Pan-Northern cosmogony: a woman of Norse origins who lived in Norway, Orkney, Caithness, the Hebrides and

Iceland, and who married and gave birth to Nordic and Celtic
chieftains, and who freed and gave land to Celtic slaves in Iceland.
One of the most famous women in Old Norse history, her strong
links with Scotland were also to inspire Naomi Mitchison, as we
shall see. A long and detailed footnote in *Lucky Poet* reveals
MacDiarmid's careful research into her history, referring to editions
of *Laxdaela Saga*, *Eyrbyggja Saga*, and *Heimskringla*. MacDiarmid
goes on to reiterate the importance of Audh as his muse and as an
inspiring example for a Scottish revival: 'Audh gives us to drink a
mead not unlike that the young woman gave in a cuach of white silver to Fionn....'[27] MacDiarmid wrote two poems on Audh, 'Choice'
(II, 1340), a very short and rather rude jibe at W.H. Auden (possibly
indicating MacDiarmid had read his *Letters from Iceland*), and
'Audh and Cunaide', a poem in praise of Audh's inspiring propensity for life:

> Oh, the cry might be found even yet
> To bring Audh back to life again,
> To quicken that resourceful heroic old body
> Lying there like a cameo under glass.
> A cry might be found to bring back
> Audh, wife and mother, whose intrepid blood
> Still runs in far generations
> Of her children's children. (II, 1047-48)

MacDiarmid's more reserved attitude to Old Norse language and
mythology in the 1920s had thus become a more positive and fruit-
ful inspiration in the following decades. The amount of Old Norse
influence on MacDiarmid's work is in some cases indirect, but as
the evidence of this chapter suggests, it was very specific and of
some importance. Old Norse mythology provided very effective
and subtle motifs in two of his early epic poems, and the use of Old
Norse language in the Norwegian *Landsmaal* provided a model for
MacDiarmid's attempts to revitalise Scots by going back to its earliest roots and forms. His exposure to Shetland and its dialect and
his incorporation of Waddell's theories on the *Edda* led him to be
more appreciative of Old Norse literature and to refer to it positively, if sporadically, in his later works. This in turn encouraged
him to expand his Gaelic Idea into a broader Pan-Northern ideal

and led him to his espousal of Audh the Deep-Minded, a famous woman in Old Norse history, as his muse. Like Neil M. Gunn, MacDiarmid had gradually shifted his ground in the Norse/Celtic polarisation of the time, but in the opposite direction. Whereas Gunn's interest in Scotland's Norse heritage faded throughout the 1930s and 40s, MacDiarmid's correspondingly increased and became more inspirational. It is therefore perhaps fitting that it is MacDiarmid, the poet who always strove to be 'whaur extremes meet', who suggests the most intriguing and idiosyncratic synthesis as a possible compromise in the divisive feuding over the Nordic and Celtic origins of the Scottish people.

NOTES

1   Hugh MacDiarmid, *Lucky Poet* (London, 1943), p.328.
2   Hugh MacDiarmid, *A Drunk Man Looks at the Thistle*, ed. Kenneth Buthlay (Edinburgh, 1987), ll.477-512, pp.40-42; ll.1348-49, p.104; ll.1451-1631, pp.110-20; ll.2097-98, p.152. Ygdrasil (MacDiarmid's spelling) is specifically referred to in l.1457, p.110. All further references to *A Drunk Man* are to this edition.
3   For details of Odin's sacrifice, see Kevin Crossley-Holland, *The Norse Myths* (London, 1980), pp.186-88; E.O.G. Turville-Petre, *Myth and Religion of the North* (New York, 1964), pp.48-50; A.G. van Hamel, 'Óðinn Hanging on the Tree', *Acta Philologica Scandinavica* 7 (1932-33), 260-88.
4   W.N. Herbert, *To Circumjack MacDiarmid: The Poetry and Prose of Hugh MacDiarmid* (Oxford, 1992), p.48.
5   *The Complete Poems of Hugh MacDiarmid*, ed. Michael Grieve and W.R. Aitken, 2nd rev. edn., 2 vols (Harmondsworth, 1985). All further references to MacDiarmid's poems (apart from *A Drunk Man*) are to this edition; Buthlay, notes to *A Drunk Man*, p.17.
6   For details of Thor's struggle with Jormungand, see Crossley-Holland, pp.208-10 and Snorri Sturluson, *Edda*, trans. Anthony Faulkes (London, 1987), pp.46-47.
7   Alan Bold, *MacDiarmid: Christopher Murray Grieve. A Critical Biography* (London, 1988), p.125. Craigie's speech was later published in *The Scottish Tongue* (London, 1924), pp.1-46.
8   C.M. Grieve, 'Mannigfaltig', *New Age* 35 (14 August 1924), 185-86. On the history of the *Landsmaal*, see Oscar J. Falnes, *National Romanticism in Norway* (London & New York, 1933), pp.30-34, 289-306; Einar Haugen, *Language Conflict and Language Planning: The Case of Modern Norwegian* (Cambridge, Mass., 1966), pp.27-36.

9   R.L. Cassie, Letter to *Scottish Educational Journal* 17.7.25; rpt. in
      Contemporary Scottish Studies, p.10.
10   C.M. Grieve, Letter to *Scottish Educational Journal* 24.7.25; rpt. in
      Contemporary Scottish Studies, p.13.
11   See David Murison, 'Norse Influence on Scots', *Lallans* 13 (1979), 31-34.
12   Kenneth Buthlay, *Hugh MacDiarmid*, Scottish Writers Series 2 (Edinburgh,
      1982), p.62; *Lucky Poet*, p.201. For an overview of MacDiarmid's Gaelic Idea,
      see Anne Dooley, 'Hugh MacDiarmid and the Gaelic Muse', in *The Celtic
      Consciousness*, ed. Robert O'Driscoll (Edinburgh & Portaloise, 1982), pp.459-
      66.
13   L.A. Waddell, *The British Edda* (London, 1930), p.v.
14   Alan Bold, *Hugh MacDiarmid: The Terrible Crystal* (London, 1983), pp.202,
      222.
15   Hugh MacDiarmid, *The Islands of Scotland* (London, 1939), p.ix.
16   Bold, *MacDiarmid*, p.348; Alexander Scott, review of Alan Bold's *The Terrible
      Crystal*, in *Scottish Review* 32 (November 1983), 34.
17   *The Letters of Hugh MacDiarmid*, ed. Alan Bold (London, 1984), p.657.
18   For details of MacDiarmid's sometimes ambivalent relations with the peo-
      ple of Whalsay, see Brian Smith, 'Stony Limits: the Grieves in Whalsay,
      1933-1942' in *MacDiarmid in Shetland*, ed. Laurence Graham and Brian
      Smith (Lerwick, 1992), pp.42-72.
19   For details of MacDiarmid's use of Jakobsen's works, see Ruth McQuillan,
      'MacDiarmid's Other Dictionary', *Lines Review* 66 (1978), 5-14.
20   'MacDiarmid on MacDiarmid', in *The Uncanny Scot* (London, 1968), p.171.
21   *Lucky Poet*, p.364. 'The Case for Synthetic Scots', in *At the Sign of the Thistle*
      (London, 1934), pp.186-87.
22   Bold, *MacDiarmid*, pp.292-93; in a letter to W.R. Aitken, 21 April 1941,
      MacDiarmid even claimed he was writing a book on the Faroes, but noth-
      ing ever came of this. *Letters of Hugh MacDiarmid*, p.582.
23   'The Sea', in *Scottish Scene* (London, 1934), p.280.
24   *Islands of Scotland*, p.59.
25   *Islands of Scotland*, p.53. These theories have been summarised by Richard
      Perkins in his 'Rowing Chants and the Origins of *Dróttkvæðr Háttr*', *Saga-
      Book* 21 (1984-85), 168-71.
26   Audh is MacDiarmid's spelling of the more usual Aud. She is also known
      as Unn(ur) in some Old Norse sources. Her remarkable story is best record-
      ed in *Laxdaela Saga*, trans. Magnus Magnusson and Hermann Pálsson
      (Harmondsworth, 1969), Chs.4-7, pp.51-59. Curiously enough, in his
      'MacDiarmid's Muses' (in *The Age of MacDiarmid*, ed. P.H. Scott and A.C.
      Davis, Edinburgh, 1980, pp.163-69), Ronald Stevenson fails to mention
      Audh among the nine muses he lists as inspiring MacDiarmid.
27   *Lucky Poet*, pp.394-95.

7. JOHN BUCHAN

John Buchan (1875-1940) is, in terms of sales, undoubtedly the most popular of all the writers considered in this book. A son of the manse who conscientiously worked his way up to Oxford University, the Houses of Parliament, a peerage and, finally, the Governor-Generalship of Canada, Buchan also found time to be a successful journalist and publisher, as well as an author of best-selling thrillers and spy-stories. The adventures of Buchan's heroes Richard Hannay, Edward Leithen, and Dickson McCunn (along with such able helpers as Sandy Arbuthnot, Archie Roylance and Peter Pienaar) have become known and loved by millions of readers in many languages all over the world. *The Thirty-Nine Steps* (1915), perhaps Buchan's most famous novel, has been filmed no fewer than four times, and a television series has been based on its hero, Richard Hannay.

Conversely, however, Buchan's success in book sales has not been matched in terms of critical acclaim. Despite two excellent biographies of Scott and Montrose and a truly fine historical novel, *Witch Wood* (1927), Buchan's reputation has always seemed to rest on his 'shockers', as he called them, and these have usually been dismissed, to some extent rightly, as inferior in literary depth and execution. Though they continue to sell well, these novels have dated badly in terms of Buchan's social and political attitudes. Richard Usborne, for example, has criticised Buchan's 'success ethic', and Gertrude Himmelfarb has condemned in detail his 'unseemly preoccupation with race and class; and a still more unseemly glorification of nation and empire'.[1]

More recently, however, some critics have begun to adjust their evaluations of Buchan's thrillers by regarding their more obvious limitations as regrettably, but unavoidably, symptomatic of the

times and *mores* in which they were written. Despite Buchan's
foibles and prejudices, therefore, there remains much worthy of literary and psychological interest in his undeniably entertaining
adventure stories. Their continuing popularity, at a time when
many of the works of Buchan's contemporary thriller-writers have
long been out of print, also suggests some underlying values still
applicable, or at least appealing, to modern readers. M.R. Ridley,
for example, has claimed that 'there is always apt to be a great deal
more in Buchan than meets the eye', and Jeanne F. Bedell has
argued the importance of Buchan's clear but simple sense of
Christian values. David Stafford has also pointed out that, for historians, 'Buchan's romantic shockers form an important file in the
popular archive of twentieth-century Britain'.[2] Janet Adam Smith
has very definite claims as to what makes Buchan's 'shockers' still
relevant today:

> It is his ability to touch deeper concerns than the triumph of hero
> or the fall of villain. He can convey a sense of the real possibility
> of evil and irrational forces breaking through the facade of civi-
> lized life. Many of the social attitudes of his thrillers are outdated;
> not so their intimations of destruction and disorder, their warning
> that civilization cannot be taken for granted.[3]

Moreover, as his most recent biographer, Andrew Lownie, has
noted, many of Buchan's novels 'have a prophetic strain, anticipat-
ing twentieth century dictatorship, black power and child kidnap-
ping and he was one of the first writers to put cars and planes at the
centre of his books'.[4] As far as this present work is concerned, however, there is yet another aspect of Buchan's thrillers which justifies
a fresh look at his fiction: his use of Old Norse material, a feature
which has been given no critical attention. In the only full-length
study of Buchan's works, David Daniell has suggested that the
main sources for the style and content of Buchan's novels are the
Bible, Bunyan's *The Pilgrim's Progress*, the classical authors and
Celtic mythology, but Hart, probably with more insight, states that
Buchan's vision 'combined fairy tale and Norse myth with 'the old
Calvinistic discipline'.[5] Hart, however, makes no further reference
to this Old Norse element, and Daniell ignores it completely. This is

a surprising omission, for a careful reading of Buchan's thrillers and historical novels reveals a deep-lying influence of Old Norse history and mythology on his fiction and values.

Buchan's Knowledge of Old Norse Literature

Buchan first discovered Old Norse mythology as a young boy in *Heroes of Asgard*, by Annie and Eliza Keary, in his father's library when the family were living on the Fife coast. This book clearly made a vivid impression on his young imagination, as he recalls in his autobiography: 'Norns and Valkyries got into the gales that blew up the Firth, and blasting from a distant quarry was the thud of Thor's hammer'.[6] Buchan learned more of Old Norse literature at Glasgow University, where he read William Morris's translation of the *Volsunga Saga*, and in the summer vacation of 1894 he became 'enthusiastic about the Icelandic sagas' and even taught himself enough Old Norse 'to read them with some difficulty in the original'.[7] When he later moved to Oxford, Buchan maintained his Scandinavian interests by helping to found the Ibsen Society and presenting a paper to Brasenose College literary society, The Ingoldsby, on 'Our Debt to the North', which 'involved reading much Celtic and Norse poetry'.[8]

Buchan's most surprising statement on this subject, however, came in a speech made as Governor-General of Canada in September 1936 to Icelandic immigrants at Gimli, Manitoba, in which he actually claims that his family was of Norse descent.[9] It is quite possible, of course, that as a politician and diplomat Buchan is slightly exaggerating his national origins in order to please his audience. Nonetheless, it reveals quite clearly Buchan's continuing fascination and somewhat romantic identification with the Old Norse heritage in both Scotland and Canada. Indeed, a careful survey of his fiction will reveal that, although they are not a dominating feature of his work, Buchan makes many both explicit and implicit allusions to Old Norse literature and history. These have had an interesting and important influence on his work and can be seen in three main aspects of his fiction: firstly, in providing general plots and backgrounds; secondly, as a means of presenting character and temperament; thirdly, and perhaps most important of all, in presenting a conception of heroism partly modelled on the Norse ethos. All of these elements can be found in detail in his final thriller *The Island of Sheep* (1936).

Old Norse Backgrounds

The Icelandic sagas occasionally provided Buchan with useful ideas for stories or settings. He makes references to *Jarla Saga* (an alternative name for *Orkneyinga Saga*) in his story 'Skule Skerry' so as to create a sense of authenticity for this short story concerning a reputedly haunted 'ultima insula' to the north of Scotland.[10] In '"Divus" Johnson' he may well have taken the plot from an incident in *Eyrbyggja Saga* (available to Buchan in Morris and Magnússon's *Saga Library*) in which an Icelander is shipwrecked in America and finds that the chieftain of the local tribe of Indians to be another Icelander, Bjorn Asbrandsson the Breidavik-Champion, who had been forced into exile many years previously and believed lost at sea. The chieftain asks many pertinent questions about his former neighbours on the Snaefellsness peninsula in Iceland before arranging for the shipwrecked men to depart in peace with gifts to take back for the chieftain's former lover and his illegitimate son.[11] In Buchan's short story, set in the twentieth century, Captain Peter Thomson is the only survivor of a shipwreck in south-east Asia and the local natives take him to their temple to be interviewed by their god. Rather disconcertingly, the god's first words are: '"Godsake, Peter, is that you? And how did ye leave them a' at Maryhill?"'[12] The 'god' turns out to be 'Divus' Johnson who himself had been shipwrecked years before and had cowed, impressed, and finally gained the worship of the island's inhabitants by means of his red hair and great strength. Both men eventually return safely to Scotland. Buchan later claimed that the story had been told to him 'by a man, who had it from a man, who had it from the man to whom it happened'.[13] Nonetheless, 'Divus' Johnson's situation is curiously and undeniably similar to that of Bjorn Asbrandsson's in the Icelandic saga.

The Norse discovery of America has inspired Buchan with plot elements in more than one story. In *John Macnab* the American archaeologist Mr Acheson Bandicott excavates the howe of Harald Blacktooth[14] and in addition to a gold hoard finds some bracelets and a necklace made from shells, artifacts hitherto found only in the graves of North American Indians.

'It follows that Harald Blacktooth obtained them from the only place he could obtain them, the other side of the Atlantic. There is historical warrant for believing that he voyaged to Greenland; and now we know that he landed upon the main North American continent. The legends of Eric the Red and Leif the Lucky are verified by archaeology.'[15]

The Norsemen who originally discovered America were in fact forced to abandon their settlements and return to Greenland or Iceland because of the increasing hostility of the natives as we have seen (Chapter 4).

In *The Path of the King* (fourteen separate but interlinked stories), however, Buchan whimsically creates a fictional twist to this historical fact. The first story is set in Hightown under Sunfell, a Viking settlement in Norland (in this instance clearly Norway) and tells of Biorn Thorwaldson [sic] the son of the mighty king Thorwald Ironbeard. In his eleventh year Biorn goes to a weird-wife, Katla, who makes the following prophecy: '"His thread runs westward – beyond the Far Isles ... not he but the seed of his loins shall win great kingdoms ... beyond the sea-walls"'. The old sailor Othere Crainsfoot also tells him how he had heard stories in Iceland of 'a fine land beyond the sunset',[16] and these stories, together with the prophecy, give rise to Biorn's dream of finding the country across the Atlantic. His dream does not come true, of course, for, as with Moses and the Promised Land, it is not he who will reap the benefit of the prophecy, but his offspring. At twelve years of age Biorn goes on a Viking raid to France which ends in complete disaster and his father and most of the Hightown Norsemen are slain in battle. Biorn is left, a defeated and destitute boy in a Frankish hut. The rest of *The Path of the King* relates the story of Biorn's descendants as their fortunes fluctuate throughout the centuries in various places: France, the Netherlands, England, Scotland, and America. Biorn's final descendant turns out to be no less a man than President Abraham Lincoln. In fictional terms at least, therefore, Buchan has a man of Norse blood, however greatly diluted, as bringing about the unification of the United States of America. However unlikely this may be in fact, it still reveals Buchan's interest in the idea, fostered throughout the nineteenth century, that the

Norsemen were the original bearers of the spirit of freedom and democracy.

Hightown under Sunfell is in fact used once more by Buchan in one of his final works of fiction *The Long Traverse*, a children's book and a tribute to the history of Canada, of which Buchan was Governor-General for the last five years of his life (1935-40). *The Long Traverse* is the story of a young Canadian boy, Donald, who goes on fishing trips with the Indian Negog. On several occasions Negog, through the use of hallucinogenic fumes, induces a trance in Donald who then 'sees' into the past, in each case an important or illustrative incident involving the early pioneers and settlers of Canada. Donald's first 'vision' involves the story of Hallward [sic] Skullsplitter, from Hightown under Sunfell, who leads a band of Norsemen on an expedition, via Greenland, to a settlement he has already established near the Great Lakes in North America. The journey takes them to Hudson's Bay, up the Albany River, and across land to Lake Nipigon, Buchan seemingly relishing the opportunity to describe the lush scenery and abundant wildlife of Canada. The trip has been so uneventful, however, that the Norsemen are less vigilant than they should be and are suddenly attacked by a band of Indians. The attackers are successfully driven off, but not before Hallward, the original explorer and leader of the band, has been killed by an arrow in his eye. He is buried in a howe which is later excavated in the twentieth century.[17]

Although all the events in these three books are totally fictitious, they reveal Buchan's knowledge of *Greenlanders' Saga* and *Eirik's Saga* and are clearly an attempt to draw the reader's attention to this evidence and reiterate that it was indeed the Norsemen who discovered the American continent and not Christopher Columbus as so many history books then asserted. Furthermore the Viking sections of *The Path of the King* and *The Long Traverse* suggest Buchan's deep admiration for the early exploring and pioneering aspects of the Norsemen, a feature of the Norse ethos first noted by Carlyle. Indeed, as with many previous writers of Victorian Britain, and especially after his own experiences in South Africa (1903-4), Buchan clearly saw the Viking discoverers of Iceland, Greenland and America as worthy examples for the vision and endeavour of the colonial settlers of the British Empire.

Character and Temperament: Norseman and Celt

The subject matter of many of his novels – eighteenth-century Jacobite plots or twentieth-century espionage in Europe and many other parts of the world – would hardly seem to lend itself to Old Norse references. Nonetheless a careful search through Buchan's fiction reveals several Old Norse allusions for purposes of describing character and temperament. Prince John of Evallonia in *Castle Gay*, for example, is of Scandinavian descent and thus an 'elegant Viking'. Dickson McCunn, on setting out to explore Galloway (in *Huntingtower*), is somewhat humorously compared to the coloniser of Greenland, Eirik the Red.[18] There are, of course, many references to the Danes Marius and Valdemar Haraldsen as Vikings and berserkers in *The Island of Sheep*, a novel which will be dealt with in greater detail below. The women of Old Norse literature clearly made a vivid impression on Buchan, and on more than one occasion provide models for formidable and dangerous female characters in his own stories. In *The House of the Four Winds* the beautiful but aggressive and ambitious Countess Araminta Troyos is described as a Valkyrie and in *Greenmantle* we are told the renowned and ruthless German spy Hilda von Einem, 'with her bright hair and the long exquisite oval of her face ... looked like some destroying fury of a Norse legend'. Even the less glamorous but firmly resolute Mrs Catterick, jailer of the newspaper magnate Craw at Back House of the Garroch, is 'built like a heroine of the Sagas, deep-bosomed, massive, straight as a grenadier'.[19] It is also interesting to note that the wives of Buchan's heroes, like the heroines of the sagas, are made of stern stuff. They not only approve of their men taking dangerous action, they sometimes participate in it themselves: Mary Hannay in *The Three Hostages*, Janet Roylance in *The House of the Four Winds*, and Barbara Dasent (later Arbuthnot) in *The Courts of the Morning*.

More interesting than these basically incidental allusions is the way Buchan presented some of his characters as actually having, like himself, a knowledge of and interest in Old Norse literature and mythology. Lewis Haystoun, hero of *The Half-Hearted*, has one or two volumes of Morris and Magnússon's *Saga Library* and Powell and Vigfusson's *Corpus Poeticum Boreale* on his bookshelves. The learned scholar Mr Graves of St. Chad's, in the short story 'No

Man's Land', learned Gaelic and Icelandic, wrote 'a monograph on the probable Celtic elements in the Eddic songs' and became deputy-professor of Northern Antiquities before his melodramatic and fatal confrontation with subterranean Picts in the Galloway Hills. Valdemar Haraldsen, in *The Island of Sheep*, has similar scholarly interests, working on 'an inquiry into the interaction of the old Norse and Celtic peoples'.[20] Even some of Buchan's more accomplished secret agents have also read the Old Norse classics. Adam Melfort, the well-trained and dedicated officer of *A Prince of the Captivity*, had, like Buchan himself, 'in his youth learned enough Icelandic to read the Sagas', and could successfully hold his own in an impromptu conversation with a country parson who had 'engaged him in a discussion on Norse remains in Britain'.[21] Sandy Arbuthnot, Lord Clanroyden, perhaps Buchan's most daring spy and master of disguises, captured the confidence of Marius Haraldsen because he 'knew all about his blessed Sagas,' and presumably knew something of the Old Norse language itself, for Anna Haraldsen later reports him (disguised as Martel) as being fluent in Norland (IS, 39, 204).

The most interesting character in this category, however, is Richard Hannay, hero of four adventures. In his third appearance, in *The Three Hostages*, Hannay informs us that his family originally came from Norse stock and that he 'had once taken an interest in Norse mythology'. Indeed such was his interest that when faced with the last two lines of a riddle (sent by a gang of international kidnappers): 'Where beside the sacred tree / Spins the seer who cannot see', he immediately associates them with the Old Norse tree of life, Yggdrasil, and the Norns.[22] The answer to the riddle, in fact, is a far more prosaic word play: a blind Gaelic weaver who lives in Gospel Oak. In *The Island of Sheep*, however, Hannay is openly irritated by Valdemar Haraldsen's frequent allusions to Old Norse classics and seems to know little about them. He does indeed read one or two sagas on the advice of Sandy Arbuthnot, but finds them 'gloomy anecdotes' and their heroes 'a whirl of outlandish names'. He remembers vaguely 'that Balder was some sort of Norse god,' but has no idea what the *Hávamál* is (IS, 147, 148, 153). Such complete ignorance of one of the most well-known poems of the *Edda* seems amazing for a man who had once tried to solve a riddle

in terms of Yggdrasil and the Norns! Although most of Buchan's plots
and characters are wildly improbable they do generally have a certain
coherence and continuity; thus Hannay's knowledge of Old Norse –
or rather lack of it – is an unusual error on the part of the author, for
it is clearly Buchan's memory which has lapsed and not Hannay's.

Apart from this minor error, there is one notable feature of the
use of these Old Norse allusions in describing character: they are
almost always meant to reflect positively on the character's temperament, even when referring to such an enemy as Hilda von
Einem. This becomes even clearer with a comparison of Buchan's
Celtic allusions, for as Smith has pointed out, although he was fond
of Celtic legend he was irritated by 'the waywardness and whimsy
of the Celt' and was out of patience with a people who seemed to
be forever harping on old wrongs.[23] This apparent lack of sympathy for Highlanders is especially revealed in his regarding them as
'foreign people' and in a harsh article published in *The Spectator* in
which he claims that Highland society is essentially parasitic, has
never had a Golden Age, and, despite some local hardships, had
benefitted enormously from the Clearances.[24] In another article, on
ancient Irish literature, Buchan shows he holds many of the stereotyped opinions on the Celt listed in Chapter 3: the Irish are so 'sensitive and imaginative' that 'reality could not be kept separate from
dreams'; they are 'a fairy folk who dwell in a world where effects
never follow causes'. In literary terms, too, their sagas and folklore
are inferior to the Old Norse and Greek epics.[25] Buchan's seeming
contempt for the Irish may also be reflected in the comments of
many of the characters in his thrillers. John Heritage and Dickson
McCunn make derogatory remarks about the Irish in *Huntingtower*,
and so do Dr. Greenslade, MacGillivray and Sandy Arbuthnot in
The Three Hostages. Indeed it is precisely the Irish blood in the latter
novel's evil villain, Dominick Medina, which reputedly brings
about his downfall as this 'freakish element' makes him eccentric,
arrogant and careless in leaving vital clues.[26]

In his two Jacobite novels, it is again the impulsiveness of the
Scottish Highland heroes which brings about the defeat of their
cause. Daniell writes of Francis Burkinshaw, in *A Lost Lady of Old
Years*, that 'his enemy is his own shifting nature, capable of betrayal even when inspired by visionary loyalty'. In *Midwinter*, Alastair

Maclean whimsically chooses to defend the illusions of a woman married to a traitor instead of travelling to the Prince's camp with vital information which may prevent his turning back at Derby.[27] The Celtic temperament, Buchan seems to be implying, is impractical and unreliable. Buchan also seems to suggest, in Hannay's response to the 'antediluvian' woes of the old crofters near Skye, in *Mr Standfast,* and Janet Raden's speech, on holding property as a 'perpetual challenge', in *John Macnab,* that the particular failure of the Celt in the Scottish Highlands is a kind of racial decadence, a failure of conviction and adaptability.[28] A possible answer to the problem is presented by another of the characters in *John Macnab,* Professor Babwater:

> 'The Celt,' he said, 'has always sought his adventures in a fairy world. The Northman was a realist, and looked to tangible things like land and cattle. Therefore he was a conqueror and a discoverer on the terrestial globe, while the Celt explored the mysteries of the spirit. Those who like you, sir' – he bowed to Colonel Raden – 'have both strains in their ancestry, should have successes in both worlds.'[29]

It is also notable that the eponymous hero of the novel, 'John Macnab', is deliberately referred to as the successor to Harald Blacktooth, the daring Viking who had sailed to America and back and whose burial mound was being excavated in the Radens' land.[30] The inference here is clear: an infusion of the bravery and initiative of the Norsemen is needed in the Highlands. Despite the obvious falsity of the 'poaching' involved, 'John Macnab's' adventure has brought life, excitement, and a sense of purpose, however briefly, to a moribund Scottish glen. Within the context of the ongoing Norse/Celtic debate between the two World Wars, Buchan thus clearly values the Norse spirit as a more seemly one for his leading characters than its Celtic counterpart. This identity with a Norse ethos becomes even more evident in a study of his conception and presentation of heroism.

Buchan, Christianity and the Norse Ethos

The typical Buchan heroes (Hannay, Leithen, McCunn, *et al.*) have many things in common: a stiff upper-lip, great physical stamina, apparently unlimited courage, and an unwavering belief in the British Constitution, the Empire, and decent Christian values. Bedell has illustrated in detail how Buchan 'fuses romance with protestant morality' in his espionage novels. Indeed many of them are 'linked structurally and linguistically with *The Pilgrim's Progress* and the Christian's journey towards salvation', and Buchan's villains are presented as 'embodiments of evil and as agents of the devil'. The plot of *Pilgrim's Progress* is, of course, 'modified and adapted ... to write a secular adventure story', but the way in which such novels as *The Thirty-Nine Steps*, *Greenmantle*, and *Mr Standfast* are closely modelled on the classic of Protestant literature is often both ingenious and illuminating. Other Buchan thrillers emphasise such Christian values as redemption (*A Prince of the Captivity*) or Christian duty (*The Three Hostages*, *The Island of Sheep*). In all instances, Bedell argues, Buchan stresses that 'the good life must be earned and civilisation protected from those who would destroy its foundations'.[31]

This image of Buchan's essentially Christian hero is fairly self-evident and readily acceptable, but some discerning readers may be disturbed by other characteristics of his heroes which bear little resemblance to Christian teachings: their eagerness for and acceptance of physical action and violence, and their occasional emphasis on vengeance as a motive in itself. It is precisely these elements of Buchan's conception of his heroes which seem to be derived from the Old Norse ethos.

The apparent dichotomy of Christian values and the pagan Norse ethos has often been noted. R.D. Fulk has commented that 'real Christian virtues are not simply absent from the saga world, but are actually inimical to it', and Christa Kamenetsky has pointed out that 'what Christian ethics and Roman laws would have condemned, the Nordic Germanic laws seemed to support and even sanction'.[32] Paradoxically, however, it is precisely this non-Mediterranean, non-Christian element which is part of the attraction of the Norse ethos. W.P. Ker (a personal friend of Buchan's), for example, argued that the Icelandic sagas 'are the last and also finest expression and record of the spirit and the ideas belonging properly to the Germanic race in its own right, and not derived from Rome or Christendom'. In the Norse world in particular, these common

Germanic ideas were developed to produce 'a code of honour, a consciousness of duty, and a strength of will' unknown to earlier German nations confronted by the power of Rome.[33] A further distinguishing feature of Old Norse paganism, he points out, is the fact that the gods are actually doomed to be defeated at Ragnarök. Thus, as Ker claims, the Norse 'intensity of courage' is an 'assertion of the individual freedom against all the terrors and temptations of the world. It is absolute resistance, perfect because *without hope*' [my emphasis].[34] In the modern, acquisitive world this selfless defiance of fate can be interpreted by Buchan as meaning that 'truth and righteousness must be followed for their own sake, quite independent of any material rewards'.[35] Thus Buchan, the son of a Presbyterian minister and the High Commissioner of the General Assembly of the Church of Scotland in 1933 and 1934, can unabashedly state in his speech in 1936 to the Icelandic settlers of Canada:

> Odin was the first of the gods, the personification of all manly virtues. But in their strange belief some day Odin was destined to be defeated; some day the powers of evil would triumph and Odin and his bright company would disappear into the dark. Yes, but that did not weaken the prestige of Odin, even though some day he was destined to fall. It was better to fall with Odin than to survive with the powers of evil.
>
> That is the only true and manly morality.... It was the creed of your forefathers. It is the creed of Christianity. It is the only creed which can put salt and iron and vigour into human life.[36]

As we can see, this is very much in the tradition of seeing the Norse myths as a precognitive understanding of Christianity; it also has some similarities with Eric Linklater's concept of the 'aesthetic motivation' of the Norsemen (to be discussed in Chapter 11). A further important aspect of Buchan's statement is his emphasis on atavism ('It was the creed of our forefathers'), for it implies that these values are a deep-rooted and vital element of the racial consciousness. Old Norse creeds were perhaps crude and unsophisticated, but before the light of Chistianity entered the Dark Ages, they provided some kind of moral code of conduct in the face of a frequently hostile and meaningless world. In the horror and apparent futility of the First World War trenches, for example, where all

Christian virtues appeared to have disappeared, the Norse insistence on meeting death, however pointless, with defiance and dignity, must have seemed a very ancient and appropriate moral code to fall back on. This indeed seems to be the implication in the startling assertion by Naomi Mitchison that 'the ethos of the sagas helped my brother to deal with what happened during the first war'.[37] It may certainly explain why Buchan could unself-consciously blend together Christianity and Old Norse mythology, both in fiction and biography. In *Mr Standfast*, Buchan has Peter Pienaar, a brave and loyal friend of Hannay's, die a hero's death in an aerial dogfight in the Great War. Hannay witnesses his death on his knees and in tears, and the book ends with Pienaar's epitaph which is a long quotation from *Pilgrim's Progress*; indeed Pienaar was clearly meant to be the *Mr Standfast* of the title. In *The Island of Sheep*, however, Sandy Arbuthnot refers to Pienaar as having 'long ago entered Valhalla' (IS, 66). Even more illuminating, perhaps, is a passage from Buchan's autobiography in which he describes his last ever meeting with his closest friend Bron Herbert during the Great War. It is October 1916 and the two men are standing by the trenches in Picardy when they are confronted by the rather eerie sight of a band of stray horses led by a white stallion: 'It seemed to me that I was looking at a ride of Valkyries, the Shield Maids of Odin hasting eastward to the battle front to choose the dead for Valhalla'.[38] Two days later Bron Herbert went missing. That Buchan should turn to Old Norse mythology to describe such a poignant and memorable moment must be a sure sign of his sincere respect for the 'grave dignity and moral profundity of the Norse Valhalla'.[39] The Norse ethos is seen as complementing, not contradicting, Christian ethics, and as providing an ancient but vigorous ally in the constant fight to preserve civilisation.

The Buchan Hero and the Norse Ethos

Most of the Norse-inspired characteristics of Buchan's heroes can be found in his first espionage thriller *The Half-Hearted* (1900), whose hero, Lewis Haystoun, is stirred by a speech from Wratislaw:

> 'There are a certain number of things in the world to be done, and we have got to do them. We may fail – it doesn't in the least mat-

ter. We may get killed in the attempt – it matters still less. The
things may not altogether be worth doing – it is of very little
importance. It is ourselves we have got to judge by. If we are playing our part well, and know it, then we can thank God and go on.
That is what I call happiness.'

Haystoun willingly accepts this creed that 'you strive to strive, not
to attain'. Having lost the girl he loves after a diffident courtship, he
seizes the chance to do dangerous espionage work on the Russo-
Indian border: 'It was a chance of high adventure, a great mission,
a limitless future'.[40] Moreover Haystoun had always prayed for an
active death, possibly on the hunting field, but dying alone, defending the Nazri pass against a Russian invasion, he ecstatically wel-
comes as a valiant death 'beyond his dreams'.[41] Haystoun indeed has
many of the virtues of the saga hero: he is contemptuous of sedentary
life, seeks glory in action, even though it may serve no purpose, and
dies valiantly, heavily outnumbered, in an impossible position.

    As Ker has pointed out, this is the death of many famous saga
heroes: Kjartan in *Laxdaela Saga*, Gunnar of Hlidarendi in *Njal's
Saga*, and Grettir and Gisli in their respective sagas.[42] Haystoun is
thus the model of most of Buchan's heroes, especially Richard
Hannay. 'If my neck's safety was to hang on my own wits I was prepared to be cheerful about it', says Hannay at the beginning of *The
Thirty-Nine Steps*. After a rigorous chase by the police across difficult terrain he later adds: 'The exercise had warmed my blood, and
I was begining to enjoy myself amazingly'.[43] This borders danger-
ously on the ludicrous, but Buchan's heroes are never happier than
when pursued into a tight corner. John Heritage 'must glut his
appetite for the heroic' by defending Huntingtower alone against a
gang of Bolsheviks, and Adam Melfort dies at the hands of Fascist
thugs whilst covering Creevy's retreat in the Swiss mountains.
Hannay and Arbuthnot defend apparently hopeless positions both
in Turkey and the Norlands.[44] The list is endless. Similarly, for
Buchan as well as the medieval saga audience, a good intellect or
knowledge of foreign countries and languages are considered as
much requisite for a hero as the martial arts and physical
endurance. Thus, just as famous Norsemen like Harald Hardrada,
Egil Skallagrimsson and Snorri Sturluson were renowned as poets

and authors as well as soldiers and statesmen, so are Buchan's major heroes well-read men or scholars who have travelled widely and are often multilingual.

There are three further and important features which Buchan's leading characters have in common with saga heroes. Firstly, their sense of honour and dignity dictates that they never shirk a violent confrontation. There are untold examples of this throughout the thrillers. That this is a true test of heroism for a Buchan character is made very clear in *Mr Standfast*, in which Buchan draws a sympathetic portrait of a conscientious objector in the Great War, Launcelot Wake. Wake redeems himself in Hannay's (and Buchan's) eyes by dying bravely as a non-combatant messenger at the front. Wake may have moral objections to war, but he is *not* a coward. Conversely, in the same novel, Buchan's final pitiful portrait of the evil German agent Moxon Ivery is as a terrified, weeping and trembling wreck when under fire. He is finally mown down by his own side.[45]

Secondly, not only do Buchan's heroes never shirk confrontation, they often actively seek it. Indeed it is often considered an antidote for boredom. At the beginning of all his adventures, for example, Hannay is usually depicted as being dispirited by his lack of fitness, an unexciting business career, cosy domesticity and general lassitude. He is saved from this *ennui* by being offered secret and dangerous missions wherein he must risk his life. The apotheosis of this kind of hero is in *John Macnab* in which three highly respectable men (a lawyer, a banker and a politician) risk ruining their reputations by embarking on a poaching expedition in a desperate attempt to enliven the tedium of everyday existence. Like Vikings of old, nothing seems so disreputable to a Buchan hero as inaction and a peaceful middle-age by the fireside.

Finally, as in the sagas, vengeance for previous offences or defeats is a very clear motive for some of Buchan's heroes. Hannay's pursuit of Ivery in *Mr Standfast*, and Medina in *The Three Hostages*, and Sandy Arbuthnot's determination to defeat D'Ingraville in *The Island of Sheep*, are inspired by personal vendettas as well as a sense of justice. Indeed Hannay's insistence on placing the terrified Ivery in the front line smacks of a sadistic sense of revenge. As with Viking chieftains, the Buchan hero will brook no insult to his honour or sense of fair play and will not rest until his adversary is finally vanquished, preferably in single combat.

Many of the features mentioned above are not exclusive to the Old Norse ethos, of course, but within the context of Buchan's thrillers, they do seem almost certainly influenced by his reading of the sagas and Eddic poetry. This is particularly supported by the fact that, as noted above, all of Buchan's most daring agents, Hannay, Arbuthnot, Melfort and Haystoun, are presented as familiar with Old Norse language and literature, if not of Nordic racial descent themselves.[46] The best evidence of all, however, is Buchan's final thriller, *The Island of Sheep* (1936), for this not only contains all the elements mentioned above, but is also quite clearly his personal tribute to his lifelong love of Old Norse history and literature. It is a tribute worthy of a closer study.[47]

The Island of Sheep: the Viking Heroes

The Island of Sheep is the story of Marius and Valdemar Haraldsen (father and son), two wealthy and eccentric Danes who are both successively threatened and attacked by Aylmer Troth and, later, his son Lancelot. In both instances the Haraldsens are rescued by Richard Hannay (ex-secret-service agent) and his friend Lombard, with the assistance of Peter Pienaar in South Africa and Sandy Arbuthnot, Lord Clanroyden, in the Norlands. Both Marius and Valdemar Haraldsen are described as very large men with fair hair and Nordic features and are frequently referred to as Vikings. Marius Haraldsen, the elder of the two, is a mineralogist and poet fired by a dream that 'the Northern culture was as great a contribution to civilization as the Greek and Roman, and that the Scandinavian peoples were destined to be the true leaders of Europe'. Haraldsen is not seeking military or political hegemony, however, but simply 'a revival of the Northern mind, a sort of Northern Renaissance' (IS, 38). In order to bring this about he needs a fortune and becomes a gold prospector in South Africa, finally having some success in the Rand gold rush. This success attracts the attention of unscrupulous men, led by Aylmer Troth, who besiege Haraldsen at Mafudi's kraal in Rhodesia. As luck would have it, Hannay, Lombard and Pienaar are also there and decide to help him. They retreat to a holy Kaffir fortress, surrounded by a

scherm of a five-foot hedge and a big fence of stakes on the Hill of
the Blue Leopard, confident of holding out until police reinforcements arrive. Troth's gang set fire to the *scherm*, however, and in
this desperate situation, Haraldsen refuses a rifle but takes instead
an axe which he swung round his head, 'looking like some old
Viking' (IS, 63), and charges through the flames to sink it into the
skull of one of his enemies. The local Kaffirs, enraged at Troth's
wanton destruction of their sanctuary, come to Haraldsen's aid and,
using only knobkerries and axes, totally rout the besieging villains.
Haraldsen is so grateful to Hannay, Lombard and Pienaar that he
persuades them all to swear to a blood-brotherhood pact which will
also extend to their offspring.

Marius Haraldsen's son Valdemar, however, apart from his looks
and size, is a much more shy and introspective person with no
grandiose ambitions. Despite his father's rigorous and comprehensive education programme he is totally uninterested in a Northern
Renaissance, and 'the future of the Northern races was no more to
him than a half-forgotten fairy tale' (IS, 74). Living off his father's
wealth (invested in stocks and shares) he lives modestly on a
remote island in the Norlands where he mostly indulges in scholarly research on Old Norse and Celtic history. Twenty years after
the South African affair, Lancelot Troth, Aylmer Troth's son, together with an odd assortment of shady lawyers and business men,
begins to harass Haraldsen with pseudo-legal claims on Marius
Haraldsen's estate. This clear attempt at blackmail becomes more
threatening and frightening when Troth is joined by a vicious and
unscrupulous criminal, D'Ingraville. Haraldsen immediately goes
into hiding, placing his daughter Anna in an English boarding
school under an assumed name. Finding a record of the blood-
brotherhood pact in his father's papers he also calls on Hannay and
Lombard for assistance (Pienaar has died in the First World War).
Hannay and Lombard, both highly successful middle-aged men
bored by the routine of life, accept the challenge as it promises
adventure and excitement and, with Sandy Arbuthnot, help to hide
Haraldsen in England and Scotland before deciding to retreat to
Haraldsen's island in the Norlands, the Island of Sheep, to make a
last stand. The South African adventure is virtually repeated all
over again: Haraldsen and his allies are besieged, Haraldsen in a

special hideaway, an old Irish monk's cell with a thatched roof –
once again a religious sanctuary. This is discovered and set ablaze
and Haraldsen, like his father before him, goes berserk, rushes out
of the burning cell and, before anyone can stop him, seizes
D'Ingraville and hurls him off the top of a cliff. At the same
moment Anna, his daughter, and Peter John, Hannay's son, arrive
on the scene with a large gang of *grind* fishermen who, covered in
whale blood and armed only with spears, soon overpower the
remainder of D'Ingraville's thugs. Troth, Barralty and Albinus, the
minor villains and pawns in D'Ingraville's plans, are treated magnanimously by Haraldsen and Arbuthnot. Instead of being charged
with serious offences they are presented with the inscribed piece of
jade on which they had all placed their avaricious hopes. Its inscrip-
tion did not reveal the whereabouts of buried treasure, as they supposed, but a list of the twelve major virtues and the ninety-nine
names of God!

This synopsis of *The Island of Sheep* has already revealed most of
the obvious influences of Buchan's reading of Old Norse literature.
The very way the narrative is presented is reminiscent of an Old
Norse saga. A quarter of the novel is devoted to Hannay's chance
meetings with Lombard and the younger Haraldsen and a résumé
of the South African attempt on Haraldsen the elder before the central drama unfolds in Britain and the Norlands. This reflects the
long, and often apparently irrelevant, introductory geneological
and anecdotal chapters of many sagas through which characters
and their intricate relationships are established before the major
action takes place. Forms of medieval Icelandic warfare are also literally employed in the novel's twentieth-century context: axes and
spears are commonly used as weapons, both Haraldsens go berserk
in true saga fashion, and in both major confrontations the defensive
positions are fired. This was a recognised form of attack in Old
Norse sagas, though significantly enough it was not always considered an honourable way of defeating one's enemies. Moreover it
was not uncommon for a saga hero to make a daring escape from a
burning building.[48] The swearing of blood-brotherhood and all its
implications of trust, honour, loyalty and duty, and the passing on
of a feud from one generation to the next are also important themes
in many Old Norse sagas.

One obvious aspect of Old Norse influence on *The Island of Sheep* is the characterisation of Marius and Valdemar Haraldsen (and the latter's daughter, Anna), for they are clearly modelled on Buchan's general conception of Viking heroes. Their physical appearance has already been commented on (both are referred to as 'giants') and they both have a similar temperament in that although highly cultivated and intellectual men (the elder is a poet, the younger a scholar) they can become physically very aggressive, indeed homicidal, when necessity demands it. Although as intelligent and humane men they try to avoid conflict wherever possible, they will not shirk a final confrontation; Marius Haraldsen, for example, could easily have escaped on horseback from Mafudi's kraal before Troth's gang had arrived, but this he totally refused to do: '"If I flee," he said, "they will find me later and I shall live with a menace over my head. That I will not face. Better to meet them here and have done with it"' (IS, 57).

Valdemar Haraldsen, although he runs away from his enemies at first, finally determines on a showdown in the Norlands; when there he could have remained safely hidden in the monk's cell, but instead deliberately draws attention to himself at a critical moment. Buchan makes it clear that the motivating force behind the Haraldsens' final determination to face their enemies is a typical form of northern fatalism: '"We Norlanders get tied up in a skein of fate from which there is no escape. Read in the Sagas, and you will see how relentless is the wheel"'(IS, 148). Such a belief in fate can encourage superstition; certain events and dreams can be important omens in the Old Norse sagas and even the sturdiest warrior would take them seriously.[49] Valdemar Haraldsen also interprets natural phenomena as having a personal message for him. He is very moved, for example, by an exciting duel in the sky between a falcon and a white-fronted goose, the latter escaping into the shelter of a wood: '"It is safe because it was humble," he cried. "It flew near the ground. It was humble and lowly, as I am. It is a message from Heaven"' (IS, 34).[50] Later, at Laverlaw, Sandy Arbuthnot's estate in Scotland, Haraldsen sees an old red sheep dog, Yarrow, cornered by a pack of other dogs, suddenly retaliate by savagely turning on them. Again Haraldsen is quick to see this as an omen: '"It is a message to me," he croaked. "That dog is like Samr [sic], who died with Gunnar of Lithend [sic]. He reminds me of what I had forgotten"' (IS, 152). This reference to the famous warrior and his dog from *Njal's Saga* reveals another aspect of Buchan's characterisation of Haraldsen: the use of allusions and quotations from Old Norse literature. This is, of course, an obvious method of establishing the Viking aspect of Haraldsen's personality, but an essential and effective one nevertheless, for it convincingly presents the reader with the character of a man steeped in, and ultimately ruled by, his knowledge and belief in his ancient culture. For those familiar with Old Norse literature, many of the quotations and allusions from the sagas and the *Edda* are indeed very apt and illuminating, for example when Haraldsen realises he must no longer stay at Laverlaw he quotes the following proverb from the *Hávamál*: "'Stay not in the same house long, but go; for love turns to loathing if a man stays long on another's floor"' (IS, 153).[51]

For the most part Buchan is also accurate in certain factual details; Haraldsen's collapsing and falling asleep immediately after having hurled D'Ingraville from the cliff may seem extraordinary if not melodramatic, but there are references in the sagas to the fact that berserkers became extremely weak and tired once their tremendous outpouring of rage had abated.[52] There are, however, two interesting features of Buchan's use of Old Norse history and mythology. The first is an error of little importance and could even be a slip of the pen when Buchan has Haraldsen referring to the sea-goddess Ran as 'stoking *his* ovens' (IS, 186). More interesting is Buchan's version of the blood-brotherhood ceremony which Haraldsen employs:

> 'We took his right hand in turn in ours and put it to our foreheads, and then we raised our right arms and repeated a mad formula about dew and fire and running water.' (IS, 66)

This is not in accordance with the specific descriptions of such a ceremony as recorded in the Icelandic sagas which in all instances involve the walking under a raised sod of earth, the shaking of hands, and the mixing of all the participants' blood in the soil.[53] Buchan is not ignorant or squeamish about this ceremony, for in the Viking section of *The Path of the King* the berserkers (or Bearsarks as

Buchan calls them) swear brotherhood in battle with 'the mixing of blood in the same footprint', and when the longships are launched live goats are tied to the rollers so that 'the keels slid blood-stained into the sea'.[54] So why does he abandon the known and recorded Viking formula for a blood-brotherhood ceremony, when he has hitherto consistently and accurately used the sagas and Eddic poetry for his themes and allusions? The answer may lie in the fact that Buchan's ceremony is very reminiscent of the oath of truce found in *The Story of the Heath-Slayings* (which Buchan would have read in the Morris translation). The oath is recited by Thorgisl to Snorri the Priest and has some poetic turns of phrase involving rivers and the sea. Moreover it ends by stating that the oath is binding for 'heirs born and unborn, begotten and unbegotten, named and unnamed'.[55] This final element, very pertinent to the plot of *The Island of Sheep*, may well have influenced Buchan to use poetic license and change the oath of truce into a blood-brotherhood ritual.

A further aspect of *The Island of Sheep* worth commenting on is Buchan's suggestion that the two Haraldsens behave like Vikings not only because they are well-read and enthusiastic about Old Norse sagas, but also because they actually have Viking blood in them. Their attitudes to life are thus a racial as well a literary inheritance. When besieged in the Norlands Hannay comments on Haraldsen as having 'reverted to some wild ancestral type' (IS, 170) and indeed Haraldsen seems more than just a general reincarnation of a Viking and berserker, for he quite literally relives one of the Norland sagas: the pirate Hallward Skullsplitter was thrown off the Foulness cliff by the natives of the Island of Sheep, and this is precisely how Haraldsen disposes of D'Ingraville.[56] Moreover it is not only Haraldsen who atavistically reverts to Viking behaviour, but also the Norland whalers who raise his daughter Anna on a platform of arms so as to hear her plea for help:

> She stood on a human platform, like a Viking girl in the Shield-ring, the wind plucking at her skirts and hair, her figure braced against it, her voice shrill and commanding. Something had been re-born in her out of the ages, some ancient power of domination; and something too had been re-born in her hearers, an ancestral response to her call. (IS, 217)

The whalers immediately rush to Haraldsen's assistance and armed
like a Viking horde with spears and knives soon overpower the
remainder of D'Ingraville's gang:

> I doubt if the Norlanders knew what they were doing. Like
> Haraldsen they had gone back to type – they were their forbears of
> a thousand years ago making short work of a pirate crew. (IS, 239)

This atavism is important because it bestows a final confirmation of
rightness on Haraldsen's, Anna's, and the fishermen's actions.
They had not only a moral and legal right to defend themselves, but
also an ancestral need and conviction to assert their defiance and
freedom in the face of danger.

The Island of Sheep: the Buchan Heroes

The Haraldsens, father and son, are thus presented as essentially
Vikings in a twentieth-century context. But *The Island of Sheep* also
reveals the importance of the Norse ethos to Buchan's non-Viking
heroes: Hannay, Lombard and Arbuthnot. Throughout the novel
they reveal all the Norse elements of character and behaviour listed earlier in this chapter. At the beginning of the story Hannay is
restless and bad-tempered because he does not have 'the grit to
grow old cheerfully' (IS, 20), and Lombard is also anxious to prove
that, although 'flabby and out of training', he could take on any
challenge (IS, 72). This enthusiasm for action, even dangerous
action, also applies to Mary Hannay who, like a true saga heroine,
sends her son Peter John into the fray rather than see him fret at
home (IS, 171-72). The key to Hannay's and Lombard's involvement in Marius Haraldsen's affair in South Africa is a sense of honour and fair play. Peter Pienaar asks them for help to protect
Haraldsen until police reinforcements arrive and they consider it
churlish to refuse, especially as the Troth gang planned to murder
Haraldsen and they felt they 'couldn't allow that' (IS, 63). The second involvement, with Valdemar Haraldsen, is based on their loyalty to the blood-brotherhood oath to his father. Lombard claims:
'"I've never gone back on my word or funked a duty"', and Hannay
calls it '"a solid obligation of honour"' (IS, 72, 83). In true Norse
fashion, they embark on their alliance without any certainty of suc-

cess. As with his earlier Imperial enthusiasm, Lombard 'might fail, but he would fail superbly', and, as in the first trouble in South Africa, all Hannay can hope for is 'a good scrap and a quick death' (IS, 16, 63). True to form as Buchan heroes, their loyalty ensures they do not shrink from a final almost suicidal confrontation, heavily outnumbered, on a remote and indefensible island. The fortuitous arrival of the *grind* fishermen saves the day, but had they been defeated they would have accepted their fate, as any Viking hero, with sword in hand, faithful to their honour, their oath, and their sense of justice.

Sandy Arbuthnot's concern with the younger Haraldsen's affair is based more on a personal vendetta with one of Haraldsen's enemies than any sense of obligation to Haraldsen himself. Two years previously, Arbuthnot had been involved in destroying a gang of criminals in Olifa, South America (recorded in *The Courts of the Morning*, [1929]), including the particularly vicious Jacques D'Ingraville. The latter was presumed dead, but his sudden reappearance as the leader of Haraldsen's enemies prompts Arbuthnot to announce to Hannay and Lombard: '"He's too dangerous a lad to be left at large. I haven't finished my Olifa job till I have settled with him. The time, I think, has come for me to take a hand"' (IS, 97). Arbuthnot immediately tests his opponent's nerve by making himself D'Ingraville's guest for a night in D'Ingraville's personal lair in the Swiss mountains. Arbuthnot knows he is perfectly safe, for D'Ingraville is of Norman (i.e. partly Norse) blood and in the Old Norse ethos hospitality is sacred: no man may murder his guest.[57] Moreover, in D'Ingraville's lair the struggle takes on a different complexion, as Arbuthnot reports to his friends: '"The main quarrel now is not between Haraldsen and the Pack, but between D'Ingraville and me. He challenged me, and I accepted the challenge"' (IS, 166, 167). Arbuthnot's motivation is no longer simply justice, but personal pride and a sense of vengeance on the man who had eluded him two years before. Their final confrontation is fittingly on a small island, an apt translocation of the Old Norse 'holmgang', or duel, which takes place in a strictly defined and limited area, traditionally an islet.

The Island of Sheep ends with the forces of evil defeated and justice triumphant. As in most of Buchan's thrillers, however, victory is a near thing, and Buchan once again underlines how civilisation, even in a remote corner of the Norlands, is always 'on a razor's edge' (IS, 182). Nonetheless, with a Christian sense of faith and righteousness, and a Norse ethic of courage and defiance, goodness may still succeed – provided it is always ready for the 'holmgang' when the next challenge is made.

As mentioned at the beginning of this chapter, the Bible, *The Pilgrim's Progress,* and Buchan's views on class and Empire have had a powerful influence on his style and subject matter. As this study of aspects of *The Island of Sheep* and other thrillers has shown, however, Old Norse literature and mythology have played a more important role in the forming of Buchan's concepts and stories than has hitherto been noted. Buchan's lifelong love of the sagas has provided him with material for themes, plots and characters within a wide spectrum of his fiction: thrillers, historical novels, short stories and children's books. Most important of all, his reading of Old Norse literature helped shape Buchan's heroic ideals and values, especially as revealed in his thrillers. His interpretation of the saga ethics may be considered fanciful and possibly even anachronistic in twentieth-century espionage novels, but however one regards their successes or failures, there can be no denying that Buchan's sincere espousal of the Norse ethos has had an important and stimulating influence on his life and fiction.

NOTES

1   Richard Usborne, *Clubland Heroes* (London, 1953), pp.92-95; Gertrude Himmelfarb, *Victorian Minds* (London, 1968), p.271.
2   M.R. Ridley, *Second Thoughts* (London, 1965), p.23; Jeanne F. Bedell, 'Romance and Moral Certainty: The Espionage Fiction of John Buchan', *Midwest Quarterly* 22:3 (1981), 230-41; David Stafford, 'John Buchan's Tales of Espionage: A Popular Archive of British History', *Canadian Journal of History* 18:1 (1983), 21.
3   Janet Adam Smith, *John Buchan and his World* (London, 1979), p.78.
4   Andrew Lownie, *John Buchan: The Presbyterian Cavalier* (London, 1995), p.14.
5   David Daniell, *The Interpreter's House: A Critical Assessment of John Buchan* (London, 1975), p.27; Hart, *The Scottish Novel*, p.171.
6   John Buchan, *Memory Hold-the-Door* (London, 1940), p.15.

7   Janet Adam Smith, *John Buchan* (London, 1965), p.36; John Buchan, 'The Iceland Colony', in *Canadian Occasions* (London, 1940), p.30.

8   Smith, *John Buchan*, p.57; Lownie, p.41.

9   'Iceland Colony', p.30.

10   John Buchan, *The Runagates Club* (1928; London, 1954), pp.241-62.

11   *Eyrbyggja Saga*, trans. Hermann Pálsson and Paul Edwards (1972), rev. edn. (Harmondsworth, 1989), Ch.64, pp.161-63.

12   '"Divus" Johnson', *The Runagates Club*, p.164.

13   John Buchan, 'Some Scottish Characteristics', in *The Scottish Tongue* (London, 1924), p.79.

14   Buchan probably coined the name from Harald *Blue*tooth, a tenth-century king of Denmark.

15   *John Macnab* (1925), OUP World's Classics edn. (Oxford, 1994), pp.86-7.

16   John Buchan, *The Path of the King* (London, 1921), pp.12, 13. There is a sorceress called Katla in *Eyrbyggja Saga*, Ch.20, pp.60-63; a Norse explorer called Othere visited the court of Alfred the Great, see Eleanor Shipley Duckett, *Alfred the Great* (London & Chicago, 1956), pp.162-67.

17   John Buchan, *The Long Traverse*, (London, 1941), Ch.3, pp.65-90.

18   John Buchan, *The Adventures of Dickson McCunn*, Penguin Omnibus edn. of *Huntingtower* (1922), *Castle Gay* (1930) and *The House of the Four Winds* (1937), (Harmondsworth, 1994), pp.23, 411.

19   *The Adventures of Dickson McCunn* pp.274, 676; *Greenmantle* (1916), OUP World's Classics edn. (Oxford, 1993), p.179.

20   John Buchan, *The Half-Hearted* (1900; London, 1922), p.101; 'No Man's Land', in *The Watcher by the Threshold* (1902; London, 1951), p.12; *The Island of Sheep* (1936), Penguin edn. (Harmondsworth, 1975), p.75. All further references are to this edition, abbreviated IS.

21   *A Prince of the Captivity* (1933), Hamlyn edn. (London, 1981), pp.23, 28.

22   *The Three Hostages* (1924), OUP World's Classics edn. (Oxford, 1995), pp.35, 145.

23   Smith, *John Buchan*, p.185.

24   'Some Scottish Characteristics', p.52; 'The Highland Clearances', *The Spectator* Vol.112 (6 June 1914), 955-57.

25   John Buchan, 'The Heroic Age of Ireland', in *Some Eighteenth Century Byways* (London, 1908), pp.302, 305.

26   *The Adventures of Dickson McCunn*, pp.35, 120; *Three Hostages*, pp.13, 24, 50, 139-40. Juanita Kruse has commented on Buchan's anti-Irish sentiments in her *John Buchan (1875-1940) and the Idea of Empire* (Lampeter, 1989), pp. 125, 126; Christopher Harvie has also noted Buchan's 'distrust' of Gaelic Scotland and the Irish in his 'Second Thoughts of a Scotsman on the Make: Politics, Nationalism and Myth in John Buchan', in *Nationalism in Literature*, Scottish Studies Vol.8, ed. Horst Drescher and Hermann Völkel (Frankfurt am Main, 1989), pp.220-21.

27   Daniell, p.67; *Midwinter* (1923), B&W edn. (Edinburgh, 1993), pp.203-28.

28   *Mr Standfast* (1919), OUP World's Classics edn. (Oxford, 1993), p.89; *John Macnab*, pp.125-26.

29   *John Macnab*, p.103
30   *John Macnab*, p.134. 'John Macnab' is the *nom de guerre* of three adventurers,
     poaching to relieve the *ennui* of city life: Palliser-Yeates, Lord Lamancha
     and Edward Leithen.
31   Bedell, pp.231, 236, 237, 239.
32   R.D. Fulk, 'The Moral System of *Hrafnkels Saga Freysgoða*', *Saga-Book* 22
     (1986-89), 3; Kamenetsky, p.103.
33   W.P. Ker, *Epic and Romance* (1897; London, 1926), pp.57-58.
34   W.P. Ker, *The Dark Ages* (London, 1904), p.57.
35   'Iceland Colony', p.30.
36   'Iceland Colony', p.30.
37   Letter to present writer from Naomi Mitchison postmarked 18.8.88.
38   *Memory Hold-the-Door*, p.73.
39   'The Heroic Age of Ireland', p.302.
40   *The Half-Hearted*, pp.208, 216.
41   *The Half-Hearted*, pp.216, 376.
42   Ker, *Epic and Romance*, p.5.
43   John Buchan, *The Thirty-Nine Steps* (1915), OUP World's Classics edn.
     (Oxford, 1993), pp.21, 58.
44   *The Adventures of Dickson McCunn*, p.179; *Prince of the Captivity*, pp.268-71;
     Greenmantle, pp.257-70; IS, 219-38.
45   *Mr Standfast*, pp.305-6, 316-17.
46   Janet Raden, Archie Roylance's wife, is also of Nordic descent (*John Macnab*,
     p.56), as is Prince John of Evallonia (*Adventures of Dickson McCunn*, p.400).
47   *Sick Heart River* (1941), Buchan's last novel, is much more an adventure
     story than a 'shocker'.
48   Gizur the White refuses to burn Gunnar of Hlidarend to death even though
     he thus risks defeat; see *Njal's Saga*, Ch.77, p.170; Kari Solmundarson and
     Earl Thorfinn of Orkney made notable escapes from burning buildings
     (*Njal's Saga*, Ch.129, pp.268-89; *Orkneyinga Saga*, Ch.28, p.66).
49   Gunnar of Hlidarend falls off his horse when riding into exile and thus
     decides to return home even though he knows it will mean almost certain
     death; see *Njal's Saga* Ch.75, p.166.
50   Note the prophetic dream involving birds at the beginning of *The Saga of
     Gunnlaug Snake-Tongue*, trans. Alan Boucher (Reykjavik, 1983), pp.23-24.
51   *The Poetic Edda*, trans. Lee M. Hollander, 2nd rev. edn. (Austin, 1986), Verse
     35, pp.19-20.
52   See, for example, *Eyrbyggja Saga*, Ch.28, p.79.
53   The best example is in *The Saga of Gisli*, trans. George Johnston (1963), rev.
     edn. (London, 1987), Ch.6, pp.7-8.
54   *The Path of the King*, pp.16,18.
55   *The Story of the Ere-Dwellers and The Story of the Heath-Slayings*, trans.
     William Morris and Eiríkr Magnússon [sic], The Saga Library Vol.II
     (London, 1892), p.246.
56   Buchan has almost certainly borrowed this incident from a similar event in

The Saga of the Faroe Islanders, trans. Muriel C. Press (London, 1934), p.82.
Buchan uses the name Hallward Skullsplitter again in *The Long Traverse.*
57   Shipwrecked in bad weather, Kari Solmundarson confidently seeks refuge
      at Svinafell, the homestead of his sworn enemy, Flosi (*Njal's Saga,* Ch.159,
      p.354).

8. DAVID LINDSAY

The esoteric fantasy novelist David Lindsay (1876-1945), is probably the most unusual and least-known author dealt with in this
book. Born of a Scottish father who later abandoned his wife and
children and emigrated to Canada, Lindsay was brought up and
later lived and worked in London until his marriage in 1916 when
he and his wife moved to Cornwall and Lindsay became a full-time
writer. In 1929 the Lindsays moved to Ferring in Sussex and in 1938
to Hove near Brighton where Lindsay lived until his death in 1945
from an abscess of the jaw for which he refused all treatment. Thus
although classified as a Scottish writer in many critical works dealing with Scottish literature, Lindsay's Scottishness is, in a geographical sense, rather tenuous and limited to long summer holi-
days with relations near Jedburgh. However slight, Lindsay's
Scottish connections were nonetheless very real and in a note to his
publishers he claimed to trace his family 'to the main stem of the
Lindsays, whose history is in any book of Scottish families'.[1] Furthermore he was apparently distantly related to Thomas Carlyle and even
facially resembled him.[2] Though living in London, his childhood was
also rather Scottish in that he was brought up in a strict Calvinist faith
(going to church three times on Sundays) and this was to have a lifelong influence on his writings, for his novels, according to J.B. Pick,
are 'in the Scottish metaphysical tradition of James Hogg's *Confessions
of a Justified Sinner* and George Macdonald's *Lilith*'.[3]

   Lindsay published only five novels in his lifetime, *A Voyage to
Arcturus* (1920), *The Haunted Woman* (1922), *The Sphinx* (1923), *The
Adventures of M. de Mailly* (1926) and *Devil's Tor* (1932), but his reputation rests most firmly on his first novel, the science fiction/fan-
tasy *A Voyage to Arcturus*, which Alan Bold describes as 'an extraordinarily inventive allegory on the basis of Calvinist theology'.[4] In

this novel Lindsay investigates the duality of human experience through an allegorical exploration of Tormance, a planet of the star Arcturus. The first edition only sold 596 copies (a further 834 were remaindered), but, as Roderick Watson states, the novel's 'conceptual originality' was clearly noted and Lindsay's reputation slowly grew by word of mouth. With the reissue of *A Voyage to Arcturus* in 1963, he 'achieved a serious critical reputation', even becoming, in the words of Bold, the 'object of undergraduate veneration' on university campuses in the United States.[5] This growing interest in Lindsay's work is also shown in the posthumous publication of one unrevised and one incomplete novel, *The Violet Apple* and *The Witch* (1976), several articles in Scottish and Science Fiction/Fantasy journals, a book of criticism (*The Strange Genius*), and a critical biography by Bernard Sellin.[6]

Old Norse Literature and Mythology

An important and apparently underestimated aspect of Lindsay's character and work concerns his belief in his Nordic origins and his lifelong fascination with Old Norse literature and mythology. Lindsay even claimed Norse descent, for in the note to his publishers on his family origins, he asserts that 'Ivar, Jarl of the Norse Uplanders, is said to have been the original ancestor'.[7] Lindsay's love of Old Norse literature was not simply literary, either, for as Sellin relates: 'He was never closer to his children than when telling them, on their return from school, of the adventures of Grettir the Strong, or of Odin in the Land of the Giants'. He was also fond of walking in the rain and mists of the Scottish hills or on Dartmoor, 'a convenient substitute for distant Scandinavia'.[8] His 'Sketch Notes for a New System of Philosophy', written over several years, have references to *Laxdaela Saga* (No.147), *Njal's Saga* (No.234) and *Grettir's Saga* (No.297), and frequent references to Muspel of Sturluson's *The Prose Edda* (Nos. 471, 493, 498, 501, 534, 545).[9] Particularly revealing are notes 235 and 278 dealing with the Old Norse concepts of luck and fate and the Norsemen's stern defiance in the face of adversity. As Sellin comments:

> Lindsay admires the Viking spirit, and the ease with which these
> Scandinavian warriors treated death, pain, work and anxiety. He

recognises in them a detachment which he immediately adopts as
being the best means of confronting the world.[10]

Sellin indeed frequently refers to Lindsay's admiration of the Old
Norse ethos and points out many instances of its influence on individual novels, especially *A Voyage to Arcturus* and *Devil's Tor*;
nonetheless, his examples are far from exhaustive and his comments
tend to summarise Lindsay's application of Old Norse mythology
rather than provide a detailed analysis of how effectively the Old
Norse sources are used in Lindsay's work as a whole.[11] Apart from
Sellin, other critics of Lindsay's fiction have paid curiously little
attention to Lindsay's use of Old Norse material. In a review of *The
Strange Genius*, for example, Jack Schofield points out that none of its
three authors say much about 'the enormous background (so well
hidden in *A Voyage*, so obtrusive in *Devil's Tor*) of Icelandic and all
northern literature'. Colin Manlove makes a very brief reference to it,
Eric Rabkin has one paragraph on the subject, as does Gary K. Wolfe,
and Katharyn Hume, in a long and detailed discussion of Lindsay's
allegorical technique, mentions Old Norse influence in just two short
sentences.[12] This is surprising, for Lindsay's knowledge of Old
Norse literature and mythology is clearly evident throughout his
works and philosophical notes, as both Sellin and Schofield have
noted. Furthermore, Old Norse mythology provided Lindsay with
imaginatively powerful images and themes through which he created and exemplified his difficult and intriguing metaphysical interpretations of the human world. Indeed, it could be argued that a
knowledge of Lindsay's use of Old Norse material is essential to a
full understanding of his complex ideas and fantasy worlds.

A Voyage to Arcturus

A Voyage to Arcturus begins in a séance in London in which a supernatural being is brought visibly into the spectators' presence by the
medium only to be killed by a stranger called Krag who has burst in
on the meeting; the apparition dies with a hideous expression on its
face. During the confusion which follows this dramatic end to the
séance, Krag leaves with two other guests, Maskull and Nightspore,
to whom he offers an opportunity for a truly new experience: a journey to Tormance, a planet of the star Arcturus. The two men accept

and a couple of days later they depart with Krag from an abandoned observatory in Starkness, Scotland, in a spaceship propelled by Arcturian back-rays.[13] Landing on Tormance, Maskull finds he is alone, Krag and Nightspore having disappeared; he is found and helped by a female humanoid called Joiwind and then sets off on a journey northwards, guided by a distant drumming sound, in search of Surtur and the source of Muspel-light – two names readers of Old Norse mythology will immediately recognise. Tormance provides Maskull with an extraordinary number of visual experiences including crimson sands, purple trees, and green snow, and multifarious fauna such as giant, flying, lizard-like creatures called shrowks. The planet is inhabited by various kinds of humanoids with extra organs (usually eyes, arms or probosces), many of whom die with the same hideous expression on their faces as the apparition at the séance. It is known as 'Crystalman's grin' throughout the novel. Maskull has many unnerving moral and emotional experiences in each country he visits which force him to reconsider all his previous moral and philosophical values and perceptions. As Hume has stated:

> In each unit, Maskull enters a new region with some strikingly unearthly properties. He grows new sense organs that allow him different modes of perception. He interacts with the inhabitants and is frequently responsible, directly or indirectly, for their deaths. In each of his encounters, he falls under the sway of the local philosophy and then declares it an illusion when he has passed on to the next region, philosophy, and set of acquaintances. This paratactic, repetitive pattern establishes Maskull as trying and rejecting most philosophical approaches to the world as inadequate. Because he falls for most of them at first, so do we.[14]

Maskull eventually meets Krag again only to die and be reborn as Nightspore, now revealed as his alter-ego. He reaches the tower of Muspel and has a final vision of the true realities of life. As Nightspore prepares to return to Earth he has one last enlightening conversation with Krag:

> 'Are you not Surtur, Krag?'
> 'Yes.'
> 'Yes,' said Nightspore in a slow voice, without surprise. 'But what

is your name on Earth?'
'It is Pain.'
'That, too, I must have known.'[15]

The truth gradually revealed to Maskull/Nightspore throughout
his journeys on Tormance is that, as Lindsay describes it in his
philosphical notes: 'One must not regard the world merely as a
home of illusions; but as being *rotten* with illusion from top to bot-
tom'. All earthly pleasures are thus Crystalman's delusions to
ensnare and destroy the pure essence of man's spirit and prevent it
from returning to its original source, 'the real, tremendous, and
awful Muspel-World, which knows neither Will, nor Unity, nor
Individuals!'[16] This parallel world to the human one represents
Lindsay's conception of the Sublime and remains a dominating
theme throughout most of his novels.[17]

As Bold has commented, this metaphysically bracing work is 'a
very Scottish novel in its obsession with morality and duty',[18] and
its debts to certain aspects of Calvinism, especially the idea that
pleasure is intrinsically evil, are self-evident. Nonetheless, some of
the basic ideas on which the novel is structured owe much to Old
Norse cosmogony. This is immediately noticeable in that although
virtually all the names of Lindsay's characters are semantically
intriguing compounds like Maskull, Panawe, Polecrab, Corpang,
Sullenbode, Earthrid, etc., the only two non-original names on
Tormance are Surtur and Muspel, taken directly from the
Gylfaginning section of the *Edda* and the *Völuspá*.[19] According to
the Old Norse cosmogony, there was originally a great void,
Ginnungagap, which was bordered on the north by Niflheim or Hel
(ON 'heimur' = 'world'), a region of freezing mists and ice, and in
the south by Muspelheim, a region of raging heat and flames. The
edges of Niflheim are melted by the heat from Muspelheim and
turn into the giant Ymir and the cow Audhumla who licks a man
out of the ice and whose sons are Odin, Veli and Ve. These three
brothers slay the giant Ymir and create the world out of his body.
Surtur (or Surt) is the guardian of Muspelheim and at Ragnarök he
and his sons will ride across the rainbow bridge Bifröst with blaz-
ing swords and help destroy the gods. Surtur will personally slay
Freyr, the god of fertility, and then set fire to the whole world.

The roles of Surtur and Muspel in Old Norse mythology are thus borrowed almost in their entirety in *A Voyage to Arcturus*; Muspel is the tower of light on Tormance and, as in the myth, it existed before the world began and is a source of its existence. Surtur (Krag) is the guardian of Muspel who leads Maskull towards it and allows him his revealing vision from its tower. Most critics have briefly noted Lindsay's use of Surtur and Muspel from the *Prose Edda*, but Lindsay has adopted more than just the names, for the actual Norse myth of creation itself is used to provide the basic image of Lindsay's view of the human soul. When Maskull lands in the country of Matterplay he finds a valley teeming with life in which all kinds of fauna and flora constantly and instantaneously come into being. He notices that the sources of these are green sparks shooting up from the brook flowing through the centre of the valley. The sparks attempt to reach the upper air but are surrounded and imprisoned by clouds which then suddenly transform themselves into some creature or plant. Maskull then meets a phaen, or humanoid of no gender, which explains this phenomenon to him:

> 'The stream is life, and it is all the time throwing off sparks of life. When these sparks are caught and imprisoned by matter, they become living shapes. The nearer the stream is to its source, the more terrible and vigorous is its life.' (VA, 210)

This is a powerful image for pure human spirit trapped in a prison of flesh and bone. Moreover this basic image of sparks being captured and turned into forms with functions parallels that in the *Prose Edda* where Odin, Vili and Ve,

> … took molten particles and sparks that were flying uncontrolled and had shot out of the world of Muspell [sic] and set them in the middle of the firmament of the sky both above and below to illuminate heaven and earth. They fixed all the lights, some in the sky, some moved in a wandering course beneath the sky, but they appointed them positions and ordained their courses.[20]

In Nightspore's final vision from the tower of Muspel he sees green sparks (pure spirits and the back-rays of Muspel) attempting to

reach their source but being imprisoned in corporeal whirls of
white light, the shadow of Crystalman.

> The spirit-stream from Muspel flashed with complexity and vari-
> ety. It was not below individuality, but above it. It was not the
> One, or the Many, but something else far beyond either. It
> approached Crystalman, and entered his body – if that bright mist
> could be called a body. It passed right through him, and the pas-
> sage caused him the most exquisite pleasure. *The Muspel-stream
> was Crystalman's food....*
>
> The truth forced itself upon him in all its cold, brutal reality.
> Muspel was no all-powerful Universe, tolerating from pure indif-
> ference the existence side by side with it of another false world,
> which had no right to be ... Muspel was fighting for its life ...
> against all that is most shameful and frightful – against sin mas-
> querading as eternal beauty, against baseness masquerading as
> nature, against the Devil masquerading as God.... Now he under-
> stood everything. The moral combat was no mock one, no
> Valhalla, where warriors are cut to pieces by day and feast by
> night; but a grim death-struggle in which what is worse than
> death – namely, spiritual death – inevitably awaited the van-
> quished of Muspel. (VA, 299-301)

This disturbing and thought-provoking view of human existence is
thus in terms of imagery and symbolism firmly rooted in Old Norse
cosmogony. Lindsay thus not only suggests that it is of extreme
antiquity, but also that ancient pagan cultures had a greater insight
into the metaphysical origins of life than modern man floundering
in materialism and hedonism.

There are various other references or echoes from Old Norse
mythology in *A Voyage to Arcturus*. Maskull's description as a
robust giant with full beard and coarse features (VA, 8) has, as
Sellin has pointed out, more than a passing resemblance to the
giants and trolls of the sagas and Scandinavian folklore.[21] Whilst
Joiwind is leading Maskull across the crimson desert they come to
Shaping's Well, an oasis with a large tree in the centre; this well is
held in reverence by the local inhabitants and is full of beneficial
gnawl water (VA, 51); this is clearly reminiscent of the World Tree
Yggdrasil with its roots in the Spring of Mimir, the Spring of

Hvergelmir and the Well of Urd.[22] Maskull's determination to exe-
cute Tydomin in the sunlight and not the darkness of her cave
reflects the Norse differentiation, both legal and linguistic, between
various forms of killing, the worst, and most despised, being done
at night or in darkness (VA, 125). Whilst dying, to be reborn as
Nightspore, Maskull has a vision of the source of the drumbeats he
had been following: Krag beating his heart with a huge hammer
(VA, 290), an image immediately reminiscent of Thor and his hammer Mjölnir. Crystalman has many different shapes and names on
Tormance, as does Odin in the Old Norse world, and in
Crystalman's final manifestation to Maskull as Gangnet he is
dressed in blue with a large slouch hat, a common disguise used by
Odin (VA, 279).[23] Finally, although J. Derrick McClure has persuasively argued against too literal an interpretation of Lindsay's com-
pound names,[24] there does seem to be at least one exception. It is
hard to believe that in naming the abyss on Starkness the Gap of
Sorgie, where Maskull first hears Krag's drumbeats, Lindsay is
unaware that in German, a language he read fluently, 'Sorge' means
'sorrow' (as indeed does 'sorg' in Old Norse).

The Old Norse creation myth, therefore, with its fiery world of
Muspel and its guardian Surtur, has provided Lindsay with powerful images and metaphors for his ideas on the corporeal imprisonment of pure spirit. Lindsay deviates from this myth in one or
two important details, however. In the *Edda*, Muspelheim is in the
south and a region of great heat, but Lindsay, paradoxically, has
Maskull always travelling due *north* to reach Muspel, and the tem-
perature becomes notably cooler as he approaches it. Moreover in
Old Norse mythology Surtur's destruction of the world apparently
includes himself, for he is never mentioned again after Ragnarök.
Lindsay's Surtur would certainly like to destroy the world of
Crystalman, i.e. of human will, but his aim would not seem to
include self-destruction; moreover the final paragraphs of the novel
suggest that Surtur and Nightspore are fighting an almost hopeless
rearguard action, whereas Surtur of the Old Norse myth is fated to
triumph. The association of Krag with Thor (see above) is also confusing as the giant and the god are on opposite sides at Ragnarök.
Perhaps these discrepancies do not really matter, in that Lindsay is
clearly *adapting* the myth to suit his literary and philosophical pur-

poses. Indeed, bearing in mind that one important aim of *A Voyage to Arcturus* is to shock and confuse the reader's sensual and intellectual orientations, Lindsay may well have introduced these changes for precisely this reason.[25] Nevertheless by evoking a particular myth Lindsay also stimulates certain expectations which, if not met, may puzzle or possibly even alienate the knowledgeable reader. Hence although the Old Norse creation myth provides a powerful centre to *A Voyage to Arcturus*, it could also be argued that it is a weakness. For some readers, the difficulty in understanding the novel may be as much a result of confusing inversions of a known myth as the inherent opacity of a very esoteric philosophy.

Although Lindsay's next two novels, *The Haunted Woman* and *The Sphinx*, continue to try and analyse the Sublime, in these instances through supernatural and parapsychological phenomena, he makes them more accessible to the reading public with simple plots and contemporary terrestial settings; with his fourth novel, *The Adventures of M. de Mailly*, he even competently produces a conventional historical romance. In none of these novels does he use any Old Norse material except, very slightly, in *The Haunted Woman* in which there are runes on the beams of Runhill Court, a manor built in Anglo-Saxon times containing a supernatural room called Ulf's Tower, reputedly carried off by trolls.[26] This is an interesting slip on Lindsay's part as trolls are part of Norse and not Anglo-Saxon legend. With *Devil's Tor* (1932), however, Lindsay once more returns to cosmic interpretations of human history with the Old Norse creation myth at its core.

Devil's Tor

Lindsay certainly had high aims for this novel, the themes of which were to be, according to his own account:

> Fate made visible, the Great Mother, the mystic stones belonging to a world of other dimensions, the part of the Northern races in history, the supernatural bringing-together of a chosen pair for the uplifting of humanity, the purpose of the creation of the universes....[27]

Lindsay looked back to a primitive belief in the creator of the world as a Great Mother, an emanation from God. This original creative aspect of femininity had been gradually degraded into sexuality, however,[28] and in order to save the world from what Lindsay saw as sensual and moral decadence, *Devil's Tor* expresses the idea that a new saviour or avatar is necessary and that this new Christ or Buddha should be from the Nordic races. Although the overt racism of *Devil's Tor* makes disturbing reading for today's reader, it must be borne in mind that when the novel was published, in 1932, such racial interpretations were more current and acceptable, as has been discussed in Chapter 3. Indeed, it was perhaps a sign of the times that *Devil's Tor* 'received wider recognition and more attention than any other of his books, and was noted by all the best reviewers of the day'.[29]

As has also been mentioned earlier, a common weakness of novels dealing with racial destinies is the tendency for their authors to rely on racial stereotypes, and Lindsay is no exception to this. Moreover in a writer of Scottish origins these stereotypes assume a familiar pattern, for as Pick notes, 'he makes a mystique of the pure Norse race and its fair, cold, strong-willed, beautiful representative Ingrid, contrasting her with the somehow-to-be-despised Celt, Hugh Drapier'.[30] Red-haired Drapier, a distant relative of Ingrid's, is presented to us as a stereotype Gael who 'fell quickly into the lonely mood of wild musical melancholy bequeathed him by his ancestors of the red-deer hills and rushing torrents and phantom mists'.[31] His ancestors, however, are described as having been 'unbreeched savages' when Kolbiorn [sic], from whom Ingrid is descended, 'was already subduing peoples and framing laws under the great King Olaf Tryggvesson [sic]' (DT, 1-2). Ingrid's great grandfather had indeed 'the fair hair, fair skin, heavy fair moustaches, scowling blue eyes, prodigious stature' (DT, 45-46) of the picture-book Viking, and she herself is 'the pure Nordic type', her complexion 'the fairest and most unblemished ever seen' (DT, 13). She is also very cool and self-possessed, the paragon of all Nordic virtues – and the intended mother of the new avatar.

The plot of *Devil's Tor* is very simple and rather absurd. Two explorers in Tibet, Stephen Arsinal and Henry Saltfleet, find half of a meteoric stone with strange powers and, unable temporarily to leave the country, give it to Hugh Drapier for safe-keeping. Hugh returns to Britain and the house Whitestones on Dartmoor,[32] the home of his cousin Helga Colborne, her brother-in-law Magnus, and daughter, Ingrid. Out walking on the moor, Hugh and Ingrid are caught in a storm and a prominent rocky landmark, Devil's Tor, is split open by a flash of lightning to reveal an ancient tomb in which Ingrid has a vision of a giant female. Hugh returns to the tomb the following day and finds a mysterious stone – the other half to the one found in Tibet. Both halves are now at Whitestones, but because of misunderstandings and a certain fear (those holding the stones are subject to visions of primeval times)[33] they are not immediately joined. Arsinal and Saltfleet appear and demand the halves, and negotiations begin; Hugh has a premonition of death and is duly killed by a falling rock when an earthquake closes the tomb on Devil's Tor. Growing aware of the portentous meaning of the stones, the Colbornes surrender them to Arsinal and Saltfleet. Arsinal is killed by the powerful forces released when he joins the two halves, but with the stone now complete, Ingrid and Saltfleet realise their destiny to be the parents of a new Nordic avatar – Ingrid's earlier suitor, the artist Peter Copping, having withdrawn once he has appreciated his unsuitability to be the husband of a chosen woman.

The story is basically ludicrous, but what makes it interesting is the author's attempt to give it more credence and justification by invoking the Old Norse creation myth as a primitive and garbled version of similar events aeons ago. Arsinal is the main spokesman for this argument in the novel, claiming that a great racial change in the inhabitants of north-western Europe was brought about by chemical emanations from a meteorite which had struck the earth; in the Old Norse myth the sparks from Muspelheim had landed on Niflheim and been licked by the cow Audhumla. Arsinal continues:

> 'Those licked stones, then, were the same dark half-giants of Niflheimr; and that cow was the allegorised figure of the Mother. The stones as well, however, were doubtless the fragments of the aerolith, shattered by its fall to ground, and here the myth must somehow have become corrupted. The father of Odin and his named wife ... were the chosen individuals from a pre-existing barbarous tribal forest-folk. Odin himself was the resulting god-man.' (DT, 331)

Arsinal supports his claim by references to the respect for noble
women in Old Norse culture (DT, 271) and certain racial types in the
sagas: the more troublesome and difficult heroes (e.g. Egil and
Grettir in their eponymous sagas) are often black or red-haired,
whilst the '"favourites of all men, the beloved of all women"' (e.g.
Kjartan in *Laxdaela Saga* and Gunnar of Hlidarend in *Njal's Saga*) are
fair-haired and blue-eyed and '"remained the standard of perfection
of the stock"' (DT, 330). This new Nordic/Aryan stock (Arsinal
includes all Germanic races in his theory) spread all over the world
bringing civilisation and order (DT, 272-73). In common with many
racist theorists of the early twentieth century, Arsinal is appalled by
the gradual miscegenation caused by intermarriage with other races
and the debilitating effects of warmer climates: '"The vigorous
blood, used to cold temperatures, sickened and ceased under with-
ering suns"' (DT, 273). Salvation is at hand, however, for according
to the myth of Ragnarök the present world is to be destroyed by the
flaming sons of Muspel lead by Surtur, and as Arsinal declares:

> 'These fiery golden beings ... may well stand for the archetype of
> the yellow-haired men of the north; and that last destruction of the
> old order should surely be the second coming of the power of the
> lith, raising those yellow-haired ones to new and sublimer and
> final splendours.' (DT, 331)

Lindsay's adaptation of the Old Norse myth is very imaginative
and cleverly based on plausible suppositions. Meteors *have* struck
the earth and, according to some scientists, have brought about
irreparable changes in the earth's ecology (e.g. the extinction of the
dinosaurs) and possibly given rise to ancient legends (e.g. the Flood
and the destruction of Atlantis). Moreover, several years before the
introduction of atomic weapons, Lindsay's story uncannily fore-
casts the now well-established fact of nuclear radiation as a cause
of genetic mutation. Anthropological research in the earlier part of
the century (e.g. Frazer's *Golden Bough*) also adds to the plausibility
of the tale, in that myths are increasingly regarded as elaborate and
ritualised metaphors of momentous prehistoric events.

   Nonetheless, the reader's initial appreciation of Lindsay's inventive adaptation of Old Norse mythology is soon overborne by the

novel's more obvious and serious flaws. Even on a superficial level, Lindsay's style leaves much to be desired; the quality of the writing is uneven and the novel is full of long and tedious cogitations and lengthy, rambling dialogues full of obscure and erudite suppositions. Characterisation is formulaic and perfunctory; Ingrid is far too wooden and unconvincing as a human being, let alone a new Great Mother. Even the Old Norse mythology becomes a weight too burdensome for credibility to bear when Ingrid solemnly warns Hugh not to enter the tomb for '"the monument was struck to nothingness by the hammer of Asa-Thor, hurled in wrath. That hammer was named Mjölnir, and was what we call lightning"' (DT, 33). To use Old Norse mythology for *symbolic* purposes is one thing, but to have twentieth-century characters talk of the Norse gods as if they still exist is quite another and insults the reader's credulity. Lindsay's racial stereotyping, as might be expected, is based on totally erroneous premises. Egil Skallagrimsson (*Egil's Saga*) is quoted by Arsinal as an example of a black-haired, dark complexioned, infamous hero, and Kjartan Olafsson (*Laxdaela Saga*) the typical fair-haired, blue-eyed one; but it is the former who is born and bred in 'Nordic' Norway, whilst the latter's grandmother was an Irish slave and he is named after his Irish great-grandfather.

The novel's major flaw, however, is simply its overt racism, for it demands from the reader a belief in the superiority of the Nordic races and their right to rule the world. Some of Arsinal's remarks on, for example, Jewish, Arabic and Chinese cultures are quite simply offensive and reveal an astonishing degree of bigotry and ignorance.[34] The fact that the novel was written in 1932 might be regarded as a mitigating factor for Lindsay, but it provides no justification for a *present-day* reader's acceptance of the novel's terms of reference. One's final response to Lindsay's *Devil's Tor* must be one of disgust and sadness: disgust at the work's overt racism, and sadness that a writer capable of great literary imagination and daring should apparently endorse 'a belief which contributed to the direst catastrophe of modern times'.[35]

The Witch

Lindsay's final two novels, *The Violet Apple* and *The Witch* were never published during his lifetime, but thirty years after his death they were revised and edited by J.B. Pick and published together in one edition in 1976. Not all critics are entirely pleased with Pick's editing principles or the publisher's standards of printing and proof-reading, but at least the works have been saved from oblivion.[36] Both novels again attempt to analyse the nature of the Sublime and the possibility of its attainment in this world. *The Violet Apple* uses biblical imagery, the fruit of a plant from the Garden of Eden, and does not concern us here. *The Witch*, however, perhaps Lindsay's most ambitious and optimistic treatise on the Sublime, once more turns to Old Norse mythology for its basic symbols and themes.

Even by Lindsay's standards, *The Witch* is an extraordinarily plotless novel, most of the 'action' consisting of journeys between town and country houses and long esoteric discussions on the possible attainment of the Sublime. The two main characters are Ragnar Pole, a writer who is particularly interested in discovering the ultimate meaning of existence, and Faustine Gaspary, who, although interested in magic, is much more worldly than Ragnar and warns him against indulging in mystical experiences. In the early part of the novel Ragnar, through various meetings and dreams, becomes intrigued by three women, Cecilie Toller, Marya Klangst and Urda Noett, and gradually realises that they have the key to the knowledge he seeks, particularly Urda Noett. Furthermore he receives messages and even a letter (which disappears) from a mysterious character called Bluewright, a tall, shadowy man, clearly a personification of Death. After long heart-searching talks with Faustine and his brother Waldo, Ragnar eventually accepts an invitation, with Faustine, to visit Cecilie Toller at her country house, Swayning. Ragnar becomes separated from Faustine during his mystical experiences with Cecilie Toller and Marya Klangst, and is then sent on to the ruins of Morion House to meet Urda Noett and undergo the ultimate experience: a knowledge of the life of the soul after death. As Bernard Sellin explains it:

> *The Witch* traces the steps taken by Ragnar Pole to regain his divine nature, beginning with emancipation from the Earth, on his becoming aware of the world's illusory nature, and proceeding to the annihilation of the self, under the pressure of passionate love,

withdrawal of the soul to itself, and, finally, to fusion with the universal soul, as represented by Urda.[37]

Ragnar himself describes these three stages to Faustine as the three 'musics', a reflection of Lindsay's own belief in music as the most superior art form and the one which is most likely to succeed in expressing the sublime in this world:

'The first music is passion, the second rests on passion, but itself is calmness. The third, I think, is the soul's longest journey through heavens and spaces, to its wisdom of loneliness. The three musics will be the history of our soul after death.'[38]

The novel abruptly ends with Urda's revelations to Ragnar as the remainder of the MS is too confused and incomplete to be edited, but, as Pick comments, what remains of the text indicates 'that Ragnar will return to ordinary life, and to Faustine. At some stage he will encounter Bluewright, as place or person, and Bluewright means his death. More than that cannot be said' (*Witch*, 395).

Although an extremely abstruse novel, for students of Lindsay *The Witch* has two particularly interesting aspects. Firstly, Lindsay seems to have at long last answered the question as to how one can trust any experience in the human or Crystalman's world if everything is illusion. Some human emotions, for example love, *do* have some purpose according to Waldo, Ragnar's brother:

'The spirit of the dawn in love is purest joy. Clearly, love is not worthless. The man in love is prepared to sacrifice his settled course, his money, his convenience; in case of need, his very life; to one who will perhaps betray him in a year or so. Judged by reason, the passion is foolish. It fails to balance values, and gives up worldly advantages which may afterwards be wanted again. Yet as all personality is base, and its surrender always good, love, which is the most joyful and dangerous way to it, can't be bad.' (*Witch*, 327)

In other words, although human emotions can be illusory, they can at least be an attempt to reach beyond physical limitations; they are, as Herdman comments, 'hybrid forms, alloys; speaking of heaven but corrupted by earthly grossness' and as such have some limited value as intuitive yearnings for the sublime.[39] Secondly, having insisted throughout most of his novels on the existence of another world, a Something parallel and superior to this one, Lindsay attempts the impossible in trying to describe this world for us. Ragnar Pole's experience of metaphysical heaven is an extraordinary piece of simple but opaque writing in which the reader is presented with a series of highly esoteric sensory perceptions such as the following:

> Just as a colour of earth, besides its sensible distinction from other colours possessed for perception a mental quality that should have no other ground than its own unsearchable being, so earthly beauty offered, besides its interpretable strangeness, an uninterpretable oneness with the perceiving mind, the ground of which was in nothing real, but in itself. It was the principle of life in beauty. (*Witch*, 392)

Several pages of this sort of writing leave the reader bewildered and very possibly irritated. Lindsay's problem is that, by definition, the other world cannot literally be described; indeed he himself has referred to it as 'inconceivable'.[40] Nonetheless, it could be argued that these abstruse passages of exquisite sophistication and utter mystery do partly succeed in their aim in that although the reader may not *understand* Ragnar's experience, he can still *sense* what an elusive and transcendental experience it was.

The final most interesting feature of Lindsay's metaphysical explorations in *The Witch* is that, as in *A Voyage to Arcturus* and *Devil's Tor*, its symbolism is firmly based on Old Norse mythology. The reader is immediately alerted to this by the hero's obviously Nordic name, Ragnar; the name implies associations with the legendary Viking warrior Ragnar Lodbrok and his contempt for death, and also with Ragnarök itself, with the destruction of the present world and emergence of a new one. Ragnar first becomes acquainted with the three women (Cecilie, Marya and Urda) either personally or in a dream at the house of his friends the Waylands. Once again a simple name has many allegorical associations; Wayland the Smith is a legendary figure common to both Anglo-Saxon and

Old Norse mythology and, according to the 'Lay of Völund' (ON 'Völundr' = 'Wayland'), Wayland and his two brothers meet and fall in love with three swan-maidens with whom they live for seven years. The swan-maidens are in fact three Valkyries in disguise and they leave Wayland and his brothers in the eighth year.[41] The reader is thus warned that the three women entering Ragnar's life are not what they appear to be; after guiding him to an experience of the sublime they will, like the swan-maidens, leave him. The fact that there seems to be some confusion between Valkyries and three Norns is of no consequence, for there is such a confusion in Old Norse mythology itself.[42]

The place of Ragnar's ultimate experience, Morion House, also has strong Old Norse associations. In a conversation with a man called Flint, Ragnar learns that the house's name means 'Sea-Witch-Wood', its etymology from ON 'marr' (poetic), 'sea', and 'Járnviðr', 'Iron Wood' (*Witch*, 317), the home, in Old Norse mythology, of an ancient witch who was the mother of giants and wolves.[43] Even Bluewright has Old Norse associations, for although the name is from the Anglo-Saxon 'Bloodwedswyrth', it is the name of the ground on which Morion House stood and was the place where a small band of Vikings was once decimated. '"I surmise only that Bloodwedswyrth represents the legend, Morion House the personal experience"', is Flint's cryptic summary. Bluewright thus represents death and Morion House – 'unknown to the Post Office' – the other world (*Witch*, 316, 317).

It is indeed in the ruins of Morion House that Ragnar meets the spirit of Urda Noett, the 'Witch' of the novel's title, and experiences the sublime. Once more, Old Norse associations are highly significant. Urd is the name of one of the three Norns who guard the Well of Urd and water the roots of the Tree of Life, Yggdrasil. The well is also sacred in that the gods gather there every day to hold their court of justice.[44] Moreover Urd also exists in Anglo-Saxon mythology as 'Wyrd', fate or destiny, and as such is referred to nine times in *Beowulf* and has survived into modern times in the three *weird* sisters of *Macbeth* and in the Scots phrase 'to dree one's weird'.[45] Thus the Well of Urd is a source of life where fate and justice are decreed by the gods; as the third and final 'Norn', the witch of Morion House, Urda's name is clearly intended to be highly symbolic and meaningful. Furthermore, the surname Noett can be seen as a phonetic presentation of the Modern Danish 'noget' (the 'g' is silent) which means 'something' or 'anything', and as Faustine has told Ragnar: '"Beyond heaven is the Something to which the soul may join itself, and end its loneliness"' (*Witch*, 310).

The Well of Urd and the 'Lay of Völund' have thus provided Lindsay with important symbols and allegories for *The Witch*. Although the latter differs in form and emphasis from the earlier *A Voyage to Arcturus* and *Devil's Tor*, Lindsay's use of Old Norse mythology in these three novels is consistent in purpose. In its most negative form, especially in *Devil's Tor*, it is Lindsay's affirmation of his belief in the destiny of the Nordic race and culture; its more positive application, however, is in providing Lindsay's often abstruse conjectures and theories with more accessible and meaningful symbolic structures and associations. Old Norse myths and legends infuse his novels with a certain sense of authority and antiquity, for they imply a centuries-old and intuitive understanding, in metaphorical forms, of Lindsay's own personal cosmogony. It is, of course, possible to argue over the merits and defects of Lindsay's application of Old Norse material, but what is indisputable is that it provided him with a firm literary and cultural base from which to explore the limits of human experience – and beyond. In terms of Edwin Muir's definitions, one could perhaps describe Lindsay's Norse-inspired novels as an intriguing attempt to use a familiar 'Fable' to write a completely new 'Story'.

NOTES

1   Quoted in J.B. Pick, 'A Sketch of Lindsay's Life as Man and Writer', in J.B. Pick, Colin Wilson and E.H. Visiak, *The Strange Genius of David Lindsay* (London, 1970), p.6. For further details of the relevance and importance of Lindsay's Scottish background, see Bernard Sellin, 'David Lindsay: Scotland and the Northern Connection' in *Studies in Scottish Fiction: Twentieth Century*, Scottish Studies Vol.10, ed. Joachim Schwend and Horst Drescher (Frankfurt am Main, 1990), pp.67-82.

2   E.H. Visiak, 'Lindsay as I Knew Him', *Strange Genius*, p.97.

3   J.B. Pick, Introduction to *The Haunted Woman*, Canongate Classics 9 (Edinburgh, 1987), p.ix.

4   Alan Bold, *Modern Scottish Literature* (London, 1983), p.198.

5   Watson, *The Literature of Scotland*, pp.379, 381; Bold, p.194.
6   Bernard Sellin, *The Life and Works of David Lindsay*, trans. Kenneth Gunnell (Cambridge, 1981).
7   Quoted in Pick, *Strange Genius*, p.6.
8   Sellin, *Life and Works of David Lindsay*, pp.51, 36.
9   NLS, Acc. No.5616. The notes are numbered but not paginated.
10 Sellin, *Life and Works of David Lindsay*, p.189.
11 See for example Sellin, 'David Lindsay: Scotland and the Northern Connection', pp.75-78.
12 Jack Schofield, Review in *Studies in Scottish Literature* 10 (1972), 61; J.B. Pick, *The Great Shadow House: Essays on the Metaphysical Tradition in Scottish Fiction* (Edinburgh, 1993), pp.83, 85; Colin Manlove, *Scottish Fantasy Literature: A Critical Survey* (Edinburgh, 1994), p.163; Eric S. Rabkin, 'Conflation of Genres and Myths in David Lindsay's *A Voyage to Arcturus*', *The Journal of Narrative Technique* 6 (1977), 154; Gary K. Wolfe, *David Lindsay*, Starmont Reader's Guide 9 (Washington, 1982), p.37; Kathryn Hume, 'Visionary Allegory in David Lindsay's *A Voyage to Arcturus*', *Journal of English and German Philology* 77 (1978), 81.
13 As many critics have noted, Lindsay's descriptions of space travel are crude and perfunctory, indeed he is clearly uninterested in the technical aspects of inter-planetary travel; the science fiction genre is simply a literary vehicle for Lindsay's metaphysical allegories.
14 Kathryn Hume, *Fantasy and Mimesis: Responses to Reality in Western Literature* (London & New York, 1984), p.118.
15 David Lindsay, *A Voyage to Arcturus* (1920), Canongate Classics 47 (Edinburgh, 1992), p.302. All further references are to this edition, abbreviated VA.
16 'Sketch Notes', No.534.
17 See J.B. Pick, 'David Lindsay and the Sublime', *Cencrastus* 2 (Spring 1980), 15-17, for a succinct exposition of Lindsay's metaphysical theories.
18 Bold, *Modern Scottish Literature*, p.195.
19 Snorri Sturluson, *Edda*, pp.53-57; Lee M. Hollander (trans.), *The Poetic Edda*, pp.1-13.
20 Sturluson, *Edda*, p.12.
21 Sellin, *Life and Works of David Lindsay*, p.149.
22 Sturluson, *Edda*, p.17; see also Crossley-Holland, *The Norse Myths*, p.xxiii.
23 Crossley-Holland, p.xxvi. Lindsay's 'Gangnet' is similar to 'Ganglari', one of Odin's names; see Sturluson, *Edda*, p.21.
24 J. Derrick McClure, 'Language and Logic in *A Voyage to Arcturus*', *Scottish Literary Journal* 1:1 (1974), 29-38.
25 I am grateful to J. Derrick McClure for this observation.
26 *The Haunted Woman*, p.40.
27 Quoted by Pick, *Strange Genius*, p.28.
28 Colin Wilson, 'Lindsay as Novelist and Mystic', in *Strange Genius*, p.78.
29 Pick, *Strange Genius*, p.27; some of the favourable comments on *Devil's Tor* are recorded in Wolfe, p.10.

30 Pick, *Strange Genius*, p.21.

31 David Lindsay, *Devil's Tor* (London, 1932), p.67. All further references are to this edition, abbreviated DT.

32 In ancient Scandinavia rocks (especially white-coloured) were worshipped or regarded as holy places. See Axel Olrik and Hans Ellekilde, *Nordens Gudeverden*, 2 vols (Copenhagen, 1926-51), I, 339-58.

33 Stones were often used in shamanistic practices in ancient Scandinavia; e.g. the fortune-teller's dress in *Eirik's Saga* Ch.4, in *Vinland Sagas*, pp.81-82.

34 E.g. 'No dark-skinned race has yet achieved a philosophy' (DT, 333).

35 J. Derrick McClure, '*Devil's Tor*: A Rehabilitation of David Lindsay's "Monster"', *Extrapolation* 21:4 (1980), 375.

36 One good example of mixed reactions to this edition can be found in John Herdman, 'The Previously Unpublished Novels of David Lindsay', *Scottish Literary Journal*, Supplement No.3 (1976), 24-25.

37 Sellin, *Life and Works of David Lindsay*, p.227.

38 *The Witch*, in *The Violet Apple* and *The Witch*, ed. J.B. Pick (Chicago, 1976), pp.356-57. All further references in the text are to this edition.

39 Herdman, p.22.

40 'Sketch Notes', No.534.

41 Brian Branston, *Gods of the North*, 2nd rev. edn. (London, 1980), pp.192-93; *Poetic Edda*, pp.159-67.

42 The Valkyries choose those to be slain in battle and then feast in Valhalla; the Norns rule men's fate. It is easy to see, especially in relation to death, how these roles can overlap and be confused. Skuld, for example, is the name of both a Valkyrie and a Norn.

43 Branston, p.71; Sturluson, *Edda*, p.15.

44 Crossley-Holland, p.xxiii.

45 Branston, p.20.

9. NAOMI MITCHISON

Lady Naomi Mitchison (b.1897) is beyond doubt the doyenne of modern Scottish literature. She published her first book in 1923 and, though now in her nineties, she has still been busily producing novels, *The Oath-Takers*, set in ninth-century France, and *Sea-Green Ribbons*, set in the time of Cromwell, both appearing in 1991. Her prodigious output over the last seventy years includes historical and contemporary novels, science fiction and fantasy novels, poems, plays, radio programmes, children's fiction, history books, various articles for newspapers and journals, autobiographical works, and documentary books on a wide range of topics from the Scottish herring fishery to African agriculture, from political philosophy to birth control. No comprehensive bibliography of all her works exists; moreover, as Isobel Murray has commented, it would be 'a stupendous and daunting document' should anyone attempt to produce one.[1]

A major problem with a writer as prolific as Mitchison is simply the difficulty of adequately categorising her works. In her earlier career she was certainly a major historical novelist, her fiction mainly centred on the Roman and Greek worlds in the early centuries of the present millenium. After the Second World War, however, she became a successful writer of children's stories, and in more recent years she has attracted attention with her science fiction and autobiographical works. Her best known and undoubtedly most successful historical novels are *The Corn King and the Spring Queen* (1931) and *The Bull Calves* (1947), the former dealing chiefly with a pre-Christian Black Sea tribe (in contrast to classical Sparta), and the latter with post-Culloden Scotland. *Five Men and a Swan* (1957) and *Beyond This Limit* (1986) contain the best of her short stories, whilst *Travel Light* (1952) and *Solution Three* (1975) are the most interesting of her fantasy and science fiction works. *The Big House* (1950) and *Graeme and the Dragon* (1954) are probably her best known juvenile fiction, the former story being especially popular with Scottish children

Whatever the difficulties in categorising her work, it is notable that within many of the different genres she employs can be traced a small but very distinct Old Norse influence. Like Buchan, Mitchison probably first became acquainted with Old Norse literature as a child when she read Annie and Eliza Keary's *Heroes of Asgard*.[2] As children, she and her brother (later the well-known scientist J.B.S. Haldane) both believed that they were descended from a Viking Halfdan, and the young Naomi fondly imagined herself as a Norse heroine whenever she plaited her long corn-coloured hair.[3] As a teenager she 'thought highly of the Norse pantheon, fed by versions of sagas' and received 'a lovely edition of Leconte de L'Ilsle', whose retelling of the Norse myths, she recalls, 'appealed to me enormously'.[4] By the time she began her literary career in the early 1920s she had a very good general knowledge of Old Norse history and culture and as an historical novelist dealing with the early centuries of the present millenium, it was perhaps inevitable that she would turn to Viking history for some of her plots and material. Her imaginative use of Old Norse sources can be divided into two very distinct periods: 1924-37 when she was almost exclusively an historical novelist; and 1952-57 when she had become interested in fantasy, folklore and children's literature.

Norse-inspired Fiction 1924-37

Between the mid-1920s and mid-1930s, Naomi Mitchison produced at least six short stories and a one-act play based on Old Norse material: the story 'When the Bough Breaks' in the collection of the same name (1924), 'The Konung of White Walls' and 'Oh, Gay are the Garlands' in *Barbarian Stories* (1929), 'The First Breaking of England' in *The Hostages and Other Stories* (1930), 'Spring' in *The Delicate Fire* (1933), 'Brünnhilde's Journey Down the Rhine' in *The Fourth Pig* (1936), and the play 'The Thing That is Plain' in *An End and a Beginning* (1937).

'The First Breaking of England' can be dealt with very briefly, for, apart from being a children's story, its Old Norse element is very slight. The hero of the story is a bitter and broken-hearted Anglo-Saxon youth who, rather than live under the Normans after 1066, leaves England to join the Saxon and Norse Varangian Guard in Constantinople in the hope of being able to strike a blow against the Normans at a later date. 'Spring' is also rather a slight story, relating how a Norse youth comes to manhood through becoming sexually aware and by killing a man on his first Viking raid. The most interesting aspect of the story is that it is Mitchison's only attempt to imitate partially the saga-style of writing, some of the sentences being very short, clipped and laconic. There is also perhaps a little irony in the symbolism of the snow melting and plants blossoming as the boy becomes increasingly interested physically in his young cousin Syrithe (presumably Mitchison's strange anglicisation of Sigrid), for the coming of spring marks not only the arousal of nature but also the preparations for violent death as the longships are cleaned and made ready for the annual Viking raid. The story is ultimately flawed, however, by an inconsistency in the narrative voice. The narrator of the story is the boy himself and whilst wrestling with Syrithe in the forest he describes his sudden physical awareness of her body and the bewilderment as to what this means or what he should do. Later in the story, however, he describes his first Viking raid, which has taken place the *previous* year, and relates how the men, after many days at sea, are 'hungry for she-flesh'; this is glaringly incongruous, for such a worldly knowledge is supposedly unknown to him.[5] As with Neil Gunn's Haakon in *Sun Circle*, it is highly improbable that a youth old enough to go on a Viking raid and kill a man would be totally without knowledge of sex. He might be inexperienced perhaps, but not ignorant.

'Brünnhilde's Journey Down the Rhine' is a curiously slight piece dealing with Brünnhilde's arrival at the court of the Gibichungs to find her beloved Siegfried betrothed to Gutrune.[6] As the German names indicate, Mitchison appears to have based her story on the *Niebelungenlied* version of the Sigurd and Brynhild legend rather than the Old Norse *Volsunga Saga*. The one-act play 'The Thing That is Plain'[7] is a very clichéd and moral tale in which Grep, the slayer of Thorkild's father, is shipwrecked on Thorkild's land and seeks shelter for himself and his men in Thorkild's hall.

Though tempted to kill Grep at first, Thorkild eventually makes peace with him and promises him his younger sister in marriage to seal their newly found peace. The characterisation is both wooden and sentimental and the story unconvincing. Indeed, Thorkild's change of heart is rather trite in the circumstances, for Mitchison seems unaware of the fact that Thorkild would be dishonoured by killing a man who had sought refuge at his home. This one-act play is beyond doubt the poorest of her Norse-inspired works.

'When the Bough Breaks'

The most interesting and successful of Mitchison's early stories inspired by Viking history are 'When the Bough Breaks', 'The Konung of White Walls', and 'Oh, Gay are the Garlands'. The longest of these, 'When the Bough Breaks' from the collection of the same name, is in fact her earliest.[8] The story takes place at the end of the fourth century and the beginning of the fifth and ends with the capture of Rome by the Goths in 410 A.D. The heroine is a young Scandinavian girl, Gersemi, who sets off southwards from Denmark after her father Sämund [sic] Bigmouth and her betrothed, Bodvar the Easterling, have been killed in battle. It is never specifically stated that she is Scandinavian, but many facts indicate this, for example her name (ON 'gersemi' = 'jewel') and those of her father and betrothed; the geographical directions of her journey, east along a seacoast before turning south (WBB, 162-63) also suggest Denmark as her country of origin, and no matter how far south she travels she always remembers to pray to the gods of Asgard, including Odin and Thor (WBB, 164, 168).[9] Finally, apart from Bodvar's sword and her little horse, her most prized possession is a special cloak 'made of a great white bear-pelt from the north, a fairy bear that once had strange dealings with the Finn wizards' (WBB, 162).[10] As Gersemi is big and strong she disguises herself as a man to attract less attention and thus ensure greater safety. After many weeks of travel she reaches the city of Vindabona (modern-day Vienna) where she falls in with a band of Goths and becomes enamoured of their leader, Avilf, though she maintains her masculine disguise. Avilf's band is part of Alaric's huge Gothic army on the march to threaten the Roman Empire. Whilst raiding and looting in Greece, Gersemi captures Innocentia, the young wife

of a Roman governor, Probinus, and protects her from the atten-
tions of other Goths. Gersemi decides to return Innocentia to her
family and claim a ransom, and so, after having revealed the truth
of her sex to Innocentia, they set off for Italy.

After a hazardous journey they finally reach the Roman port of
Colonia Julia where Innocentia carelessly forgets Gersemi's cloak
on board the ship which had brought them there. From then on
Gersemi's fortune declines; having rashly forfeited any claim to a
ransom she becomes dependent on Innocentia's family in a very
unspecified capacity, neither as a slave, nor, since she is not Roman,
as an equal. She is pressured into being baptised and the secret of
her sex is revealed in due course. She falls in love with Innocentia's
brother, Flavius, who is then killed in the fighting with the Goths.
Gersemi then moves to Rome with Innocentia's family and gives
birth to a boy, Flavius's son. She at first names him Sämund, but
later begins to call him by his Gothic name Sunjarith, 'word of
truth'. By this time Gersemi is little more than a servant and she
mixes more with the Goth household slaves Thiudis and her son
Fravitta than with Innocentia and her family. A few years later the
Goths finally storm Rome and Avilf and Gersemi meet again, Avilf
with Gersemi's cloak which he has bought off the sailors who had
found it. Sunjarith has very divided loyalties regarding Alaric's
descent on Rome, for although emotionally sympathetic with their
cause (his mother is Nordic, his friends Goths) he is also proud of
his Roman paternity. When Avilf and Gersemi decide to marry,
however, Sunjarith finally accepts Avilf as his step-father.

The Norse background in 'When the Bough Breaks' is admittedly slight, but nonetheless important as it establishes Gersemi as a
Scandinavian and thus, to a certain extent, neutral in the long war
between the Romans and the Goths. She falls in love with a man of
each race, Flavius and Avilf, and takes enormous risks in saving the
Roman Innocentia from the Goths. Her treatment in Italy, however,
makes her very disillusioned with both Innocentia and the Romans,
and in giving her son a Gothic name and in teaching him all about
the northern gods and her own family (WBB, 250) she finally indicates her ultimate allegiance to her Germanic origins. She thus has
no hesitation in siding with the Goths when they enter Rome, and
when Fravitta is put on trial for raping Innocentia she openly accus-

es the latter of mendacity and secures Fravitta's freedom (WBB, 309-10). Gersemi's bearskin from the north is thus an important symbol for her cultural and racial origins. Whilst she possesses the cloak she maintains a sense of identity and integrity whatever her disguise, but without it she is forced into a different religion and becomes almost a slave. By returning her cloak to her, Avilf is also restoring her freedom, her dignity and her identity.

Vikings in Russia and Constantinople

The stories 'The Konung of White Walls' and 'Oh, Gay are the Garlands' both centre on the Norsemen who raided and settled parts of Russia and the Ukraine and who, in the late ninth to tenth centuries, formed the core of the elite bodyguard of the Byzantine Emperor. 'The Konung of White Walls' tells the story of Sveneld and his Norsemen who take service with Prince Bracislav in Russia.[11] Sveneld is highly attracted to the Prince's wife, the Greek princess Theophano, but establishes a much more sincere and affectionate friendship with the Norse slavegirl Anna Maria, who later turns out to be the long lost daughter of Sveneld's former leader, Ari. Whilst away fighting for the Emperor, Prince Bracislav entrusts his city and wife to Sveneld who, encouraged by a Russian, Yuri, takes the opportunity to seize the city and all its treasures, including Theophano, for himself and his Vikings. For a short while Sveneld enjoys both the Greek princess and the Norse slavegirl and all the wealth White Walls has to offer. With news of the approaching return of Prince Bracislav, however, Sveneld quickly marries Anna Maria and together with his men and much loot, abandons the city and heads north towards Scandinavia.

'Oh, Gay are the Garlands' is based on specific events in the life of Harald Sigurdsson, the chief of the Varangian Guard c.1044, and later better known as Harald Hardrada.[12] Harald asks the Empress Zoe for the hand of her niece, Maria Anastasia, but the aging and extremely vain Empress, incensed that he did not woo her, has him imprisoned. With the help of a Byzantine lady who had been inspired by a vision of St. Olaf (Harald's half-brother), Harald escapes, collects his men, and leaves Constantinople in two longships. As a last gesture of defiance Harald kidnaps Maria Anastasia and, without actually harming her, puts her ashore with a message for the Empress that '"she is an old fool who cannot stop me from doing whatever I choose"'.[13]

These two stories are very lively, interesting and enjoyable. As in so much of her historical fiction, Mitchison brings historical characters to life brilliantly, especially in the latter story. She is especially successful in presenting a much more rounded and less idealistic view of the Norse ethos than some other contemporary novelists. Unlike Buchan and Linklater, for example, she can be scrupulously neutral in revealing both the positive and negative aspects of the Norse character, as represented in these stories by the characters of Sveneld and Harald. On the positive side, the reader is exhilarated by their incorrigible zest for life and their almost childlike pursuit of wealth, sensual pleasure and success. They show great daring, resolution and bravery in their actions, and both are great political opportunists. As their timely retreats also reveal, however, they can be very pragmatic – a feature of the Norse ethos often ignored in more romantic treatments of Viking history (cf. Buchan's heroes' 'last stand' mentality). On the negative side, Mitchison captures well the Vikings' occasional ruthless cynicism and flexible sense of loyalty. Sveneld's betrayal of Prince Bracislav's trust seems especially despicable as it is primarily based on sexual egotism. Pride can indeed be described as a fault in both men. Sveneld's forcing Theophano to submit to him and Harald's humiliating treatment of Maria Anastasia are arrogant gestures of self-esteem and reveal a deep underlying contempt for the feelings of others (though Theophano is admittedly as cynical about the situation as Sveneld himself).

Mitchison is also particularly successful in describing the Norsemen's fascination with women from a different race and culture; but it is only their loins and egos which are fired, their emotions remain basically untouched. Their cold northern curiosity is especially well described in the final confrontation between Harald and Maria Anastasia. The innocent and gullible Maria Anastasia believes she has been abducted for love and with both eagerness and trepidation awaits Harald forcing himself on her; Harald, however, merely plays with her, like a cat with a mouse:

> Harald Hardrada gradually leant all his weight against the girl's shoulders. She lay back on the crimson cushions and at last lifted

her face again to look in his, her lips half parted to the smile of whatever joy she was to get from him at the end of all this trouble. She looked into the queer, distant eyes, as she had often done, and waited for them to come alive and kind and very gentle. He said: 'I have you now,' and she murmured yes, shivering in lovely fear of his cold voice, his strength, his power. She thought he would soon begin to kiss her, she thought he might tear her dress off, gripping the stuff between his two hands; down from her throat she began to be conscious of her body waiting for him under the hot weight of its silk and linen.

He said: 'The Empress of all the Greeks could not even keep her niece from me!' And he laughed and stuck his hand into her hair and shook her head about. She thought only that it would be nice to tell him later that it had hurt. He said: 'They told me that I was a thief – me, Harald Hardrada!'

'I did not call you a thief,' said Anastasia. But she had meant to say it laughingly, and instead her voice had gone thin and little.

'It would not matter much to me if you had.'

He was looking at her, looking at her with those cold eyes, interested but unmoved! The two plaits of his hair rolled down over his shoulders on to her face. He tossed his head and swept them off; they were like snakes. She could not get the eyes to come alive, to be her Harald's eyes! This was the mood in which he had also been interested in death. Now it was she herself who was the curious fact.[14]

Maria Anastasia's later attempts at keeping her dignity as she realises that she is simply a pawn in a spiteful game of revenge are very touching. The whole last section of 'Oh, Gay are the Garlands' is a marvellous set-piece of the confrontation of North and East, man and woman, experience and innocence, politics and humanity, callousness and sensitivity.

Racial Confrontations

All three of these stories, as indeed many of her historical novels in the 1920s and 30s, contain a meeting or confrontation of two very different races, and as such reflect the interest in racial questions so notable in Europe at that time.[15] As already noted, the question of racial origins and loyalties, especially involving Celts and Norsemen or Saxons, was a subject of particular interest to a number of Scottish writers at this time. In this sense Mitchison was very much within a Scottish tradition. However, perhaps because her sense of nationality was more notional than practical at this time of her life,[16] there are two distinct differences in the way she approaches the subject. Firstly, although British and European Celts are featured in her early novels, none of her pre-war historical fiction is set in Scotland, and secondly, in contrast to many other writers of the time, Mitchison never presupposes or maintains that any one race is superior to another; the Celts, Romans, Goths, Norsemen, Greeks, Marobians and Egyptians in her fictional works are all presented as having both good and bad attributes. Throughout her stories and novels different races meet, mingle or clash and then withdraw, the experience usually revealing instructive insights both into their own and others' cultures and values. One of Mitchison's most important suppositions here is that concepts of 'civilisation' and 'culture' are often very superficial, and that so-called barbarian societies or races in fact have very subtle and important contributions to make to human understanding and progress, not least in establishing influential mythical archetypes. This aspect of Mitchison's fiction will be discussed again in another context below.

One important recurring theme of her pre-war fiction, therefore, would seem to be that, however sympathetic and tolerant a person may be towards another race or culture, one's ultimate loyalty lies with one's own people.[17] In the three stories discussed above three characters of Norse origin travel far from their homelands to become intimately involved, both publicly and personally, with a very alien race, language and culture; despite sometimes long-lasting attempts to assimilate or be accepted they remain ultimately despised or feared and thus either return homewards (Sveneld and Harald Hardrada) or throw in their lot with a racially related people (Gersemi and the Goths). This may seem an unduly pessimistic interpretation of human behaviour, but not perhaps a surprising one given the time in which the stories were written.

The general sense of impending catastrophe so prevalent in Europe at that time can indeed be found in Mitchison's poem 'Leaving Denmark', written in the late 1930s, with its references to the 'Fenris Winter' (Ragnarök).[18] The Second World War certainly marks a watershed in Mitchison's work, for after 1945 there is a change of direction as regards the genres she employs and a change of emphasis in her subject matter; as Beth Dickson expresses it, Naomi Mitchison 'went global'.[19]

Norse-inspired Works 1952-57

The second period of Mitchison's Norse-inspired work was almost certainly stimulated by a renewed and intimate contact with Scandinavia. During the 1930s Mitchison had become friends with the Carstensen family in Denmark; contact was naturally broken during the Second World War, but after 1945 the friendship was re-established, especially with the Carstensens' daughter, Sonja Meyer, and Mitchison visited Denmark almost every summer for many years. Her growing knowledge of Danish history and culture naturally revived her former fascination with Old Norse matters, and in the late 1940s and early 1950s she re-read all the Norse myths and sagas with great pleasure. So seriously did she take her research that she went to view the Old Norse MSS preserved in the Royal Library in Copenhagen and actually held the famous Flatey Book in her hands.[20] This personal and well-organised rediscovery of the Old Norse classics had three major consequences. Firstly, it increased her estimation of the literary importance of the sagas, for 'every westerner who cares about good writing should have them as part of his cultural background'.[21] Secondly, it heightened her atavistic awareness of the Old Norse heritage in Scotland, for she herself had done:

> ... so many of the same things that the Norse raiders and settlers did. My farming has been not unlike theirs. I too have sown my corn in small fields by hand and hand-sheared my sheep; I have netted fish as they did; I have felt some of the tide races of the west Highland coast twisting the boat I was trying to steer. I have listened at night for ghosts. And, though our west Highland feuds never quite got as far as murder, that is, after all, only a matter of custom.[22]

Thirdly, it inspired her creatively to write a fantasy novel, *Travel Light* (1952), a history book, *The Swan's Road* (1954), a novel for younger readers, *The Land the Ravens Found* (1955), and two short stories, 'Aud the Deep-Minded' and 'St. Magnus', both in *Five Men and a Swan* (1957).[23]

In considering these works it is perhaps best to begin with a brief appraisal of her non-fictional work *The Swan's Road*. A contemporary critic described it as:

> ... a re-telling of a number of the old Norse sagas, together with a considerable amount of painstaking historical investigation into the origins of these ancient tales and an attempt to put them into some kind of geographical, if not historical, perspective.[24]

The amount of detailed research Mitchison undertook is certainly corroborated by her bibliography at the end of the book where she states her main sources as several of the individual sagas and *Heimskringla* as well as many standard, contemporary works on related subjects, e.g. Kendrick's *History of the Vikings* and Gathorne-Hardy's *The Norse Discoverers of America*. On the whole the book succeeds in its object of presenting a very lively and comprehensive survey of Old Norse history and culture. There are a couple of inaccuracies, but they are of no great significance: Sleipnir, Odin's horse, has eight legs and not six, and, according to all reliable sources, Iceland was fully settled about sixty years after Ingolfur Arnason's landing there (i.e. between c.870 and 930 A.D.) and not ten as Mitchison states.[25] Iain Crawford has also complained about Mitchison's 'jolly school-mistressy style' and 'coy observations',[26] but, although perhaps a little overenthusiastic at times, her obvious enjoyment of the subject matter is generally infectious rather than off-putting.

There is one drawback to the book, however, and that is the inconsistency in the spelling of Old Norse names, mostly due to citations being drawn from a number of different sources. Many of the different anglicised name forms she uses are acceptable variants (e.g. Bjorn or Biorn), but Mitchison appears to use any or all of them indiscriminately without any standardised usage of her own or any explanatory note as to why they vary. This inconsistency is very irritating to a knowledgeable reader, and to one with little or no previous knowlege of the subject, it is possibly even confusing.[27]

Mitchison also sometimes overestimates her readers' linguistic knowledge in her unexplained anglicisation of place-names; not everyone will realise that Streamfirth (p.125) and Straumfiord (p.136) are one and the same place.[28] (For good measure Mitchison also spells fiord as fjord elsewhere in the book!) This criticism may seem petty, but it is sad that such inattention to detail can somewhat mar what is otherwise an enjoyable read.

Whatever the drawbacks to her history book, however, the comprehensive knowledge of Old Norse history and literature Mitchison gained from researching *The Swan's Road*, and her growing awareness of the Norse heritage in Scotland, certainly came to more creative and effective use in her two major Norse-inspired fictional works from this period: *Travel Light* and *The Land the Ravens Found*.

Travel Light

Mitchison's delightful fantasy novel *Travel Light* was first published in 1952.[29] Set in early medieval Scandinavia, Constantinople and Russia, it tells the story of Halla, a young princess who, as a baby, is exposed to die but is rescued by her nurse Matulli who changes into a bear and brings her up in the forest. Halla's inability to hibernate and other bears' gastronomic interest in her eventually make life in the forest unsafe for Halla and Matulli arranges for her to live with the dragon Uggi. Halla is 'fireproofed' to make it possible to live with dragons, all of whom dote on her. Her life is shattered, however, when Uggi is killed by a 'hero' and all his treasure stolen. At this critical point in time All-Father or Odin appears and with the comforting advice to 'travel light' he gives her a magic cloak (TL, 55-57).[30] Halla then sets off southwards and arrives at Micklegard (the Norse name for Constantinople) in the company of three men from Marob (the imaginary ancient kingdom on the Black Sea first created by Mitchison in *The Corn King and the Spring Queen* in 1931). Tarkan Der, Roddin and Kiot are on a secret mission to the Emperor in Micklegard to try and have the governor of Marob recalled as he rules the country through a reign of terror. Halla becomes involved with their efforts to see the Emperor and, through her ability to talk to horses, helps them to win large sums of money on horse-racing. Their renowned success at betting and some subsequently large bribes eventually gain the Marobians an audience with the Emperor who appoints a new governor to Marob. Halla is supposed to remain in Micklegard as part of the deal, but with her magic powers she easily escapes and joins the others on their return to Marob.

Tarkan Der, however, when he hears that his fiancée has been tortured and murdered, decides to head on northwards with Halla to Holmgard (the Norse name for Novgorod). Nearing the town they come across a settlement under attack; Tarkan Der helps beat off the raiders and the 'fireproofed' Halla rescues the headman Modolf from his burning hall. Modolf is a liegeman of the Prince of Holmgard and Tarkan Der takes service with the Prince and marries Modolf's daughter Alfeida. It emerges that Modolf's family had been under a curse for generations ever since a young princess had been exposed to die in the far north. Halla realises she has travelled through time as well as space and that she has fulfilled her purpose in lifting this curse. Her future now lies elsewhere and Steinvor the Valkyrie, who has frequently assisted Halla, makes another timely appearance and again invites Halla to join her. This time Halla accepts the invitation and discarding Odin's cloak she mounts her new steed and rides off with Steinvor to set about collecting heroes for Valhalla.

A careful reading of *Travel Light* will certainly reveal at least two notable aspects: its strong Old Norse ambience and, despite its superficial light-heartedness, its ultimately serious view of human aspirations and motivations. Halla is quite clearly born in Scandinavia, as all the references to fjords, mountains, dragon ships, trolls and giants indicate (TL, 19-22; 28-29).[31] Moreover she is educated in the Norse belief in Odin and Yggdrasil and is indeed given a helping hand more than once by the Valkyrie Steinvor (TL, 30-33; 48-49; 86-89; 113-15; 144-46). Odin appears to Halla as the Wanderer and radically alters her life with his advice and the gift of a magic cloak. In Micklegard there are references to Varangians and by the end of the novel (as the names Modolf, Alfeida and Holmgard indicate) we are once more in Norse territory, at least in terms of language and culture.[32]

There are also many motifs throughout the novel which are clearly Norse-inspired; indeed so many of these motifs exactly parallel similar ones in the *Volsunga Saga* that it is almost certain that this legendary saga had a direct influence on Mitchison's conception of *Travel Light*. In *Volsunga Saga* the two half-brothers Sigmund and Sinfjotli change into wolves to avoid the wrath of King Siggeir, just as Matulli changes into a bear to save Halla.[33] Odin, specifically described as old and one-eyed and dressed in a blue cloak and slouched hat, twice appears to Sigmund, Volsung's son, firstly to provide him with a magic sword, and later to have it destroyed (Ch.3, pp.38-39; Ch.11, pp.52-53). In *Travel Light* Odin, described almost exactly as in the saga, appears to Halla to give her a magic cloak which she eventually discards when Steinvor collects her to join Odin's Valkyries (TL, 55-58; 146-47). In the saga Fafnir, the dragon guarding the Rhine Gold, is described as Regin's *brother*, the clear implication being that Fafnir took on the shape of a dragon because of his greed for gold (Chs.14-18, pp.57-65). In *Travel Light* the Emperor of Micklegard is described as the Great or Master Dragon because he controls so much gold (TL, 45, 61).[34] When Sigurd slays the dragon in the saga he tastes its blood and thus learns the languages of the birds (Ch.19, pp.65-66); in *Travel Light* Halla understood all the languages of humans and animals 'by virtue of dragon's blood or the Wanderer's cloak' (TL, 59). Finally, only Sigurd has the magic power to withstand flames and thus break through the ring of fire to woo Brynhild (Ch.29, pp.80-82); similarly, in the novel, only the 'fireproofed' Halla can brave the flames to rescue Modolf from the burning hall (TL, 131-32).

All this Old Norse mythology is no mere literary decoration, however, but has an important function, for beneath its humorous and fantastic surface, *Travel Light* has quite a serious point to make. Uggi the dragon's complaints over the growing success rate of the 'heroes' against the dragons, mainly due to advancing knowledge in weaponry, may bring a wry smile to the reader's lips, but the wider implications of this ironic viewpoint gradually become apparent. As Halla and her Marobian friends discover in Micklegard, the 'vice of inventiveness' of mankind (TL, 35) can apply to more effective means of political oppression as well as the killing of dragons. Indeed, the negative aspects of so-called human 'progress' have been a frequent subject of Mitchison's historical fiction, usually presented by contrasting barbarian societies with superficially more sophisticated ones. In *Travel Light* the transition from the mythical world of Halla's childhood to the murderous intrigues of Micklegard represents not only a loss of innocence for Halla, but also for mankind. Mitchison has been extremely interested in Jungian theories on the collective unconscious and mythical archetypes, and strongly believes in the importance of ancient myth and symbol in the modern age. She was much influenced on this subject in the 1920s and 30s by the works of Gerald Heard whose ideas she briefly paraphrases in her autobiographical work *You May Well Ask* (p.112):

> The general thesis was the historical growth of the individual out of the soulless mass of very early mankind. Yet the soulless mass seemed to have had a generalised non-individual consciousness and the new individuals lost this and instead developed greed, power and war. Yet as the new individuals grow and achieve more understanding and the more advanced moral sense they can begin to attempt to transcend individualism into something automatically other-regarding (that is loving) because each of us is we. In fact we have to go back to a more primitive social feeling and make it come real in modern terms.

In discussing Mitchison's use of a similar theme in *The Corn King and the Spring Queen*, Isobel Murray neatly summarises this watershed in mankind's past as when 'myth grew into history and man grew into self-consciousness'.[35] Thus Mitchison believes that many of man's psychological problems in the modern world are caused by his blind adherence to scientific formulas and political or religious dogmas and by his ignoring his deeper and more ancient roots within his race, culture and community. As Beth Dickson summarises:

> For Mitchison, mythical archetypes perform two functions; one personal, the other social. They give the individual something to believe in which appeals to the 'otherness' of his humanity and they act as 'social glue' ... binding societies together by giving them common myths through which they can define themselves and their relation to external reality.[36]

As Elizabeth Longford astutely points out in her introduction (p.xiii), there are three main threads interwoven into *Travel Light*: pagan magic, Greek reason and Christian faith, representing the three major motivators of human behaviour: nature, willpower and religion (three forces also perhaps represented in the three cognomens Halla receives: Halla Bearsbairn, Halla Heroesbane, Halla Godsgift). Thus, bearing in mind Mitchison's belief in the enduring importance of primitive myths and values, a particular interpretation of *Travel Light* becomes possible. The sincere but relatively innocent Christian faith of Tarkan Der and his comrades can make little headway against the corrupt world of political will in Micklegard; it requires Halla's mythical and magical talents to secure eventual justice for the Marobians. Even so this justice is shadowed by darker realities: Alexius Argyris only helps the Marobians to gain an interview with the Emperor because he wants to gain Halla's knowledge of which horses would win the races, and the appointment of a new governor comes too late to save Tarkan Der's fiancée from a dreadful death. Halla's success is only a respite; evil will return, but at least there is some vision as to how the struggle must be pursued (cf. Buchan's very different use of the Norse ethos in this context). Human knowledge and political or religious faiths are not always sufficient; the powerful ancient magic of the human spirit, as preserved in archetypal myths and symbols, must also be taken into account, for there are still many powers in this world beyond our ken.

In this context the Old Norse ambience throughout the novel is both justifiable and successful, for it helps create an imaginary but credible fictional world, half historical and half legendary. The application of a well-established pantheon of mythical figures helps sustain an atmosphere of antiquity and authority and places the reader within the bounds of a culturally known time and space. To be convincing as a representative of the powers of myth Halla must exist within a coherent and recognisable mythical environment, and the Old Norse cosmology provides one.

As mentioned above, Mitchison's renewed interest in Old Norse history after the Second World War made her much more aware of the Norse heritage: 'Most of us in this vulnerable island of Great Britain have Norse ancestors if we go back far enough, especially if

we come from the north-east coast of England, the north or east of
Scotland, the Orkneys, the Shetlands or the Hebrides'.[37] For her
final novel of this period, therefore, Mitchison turned to the Norse
settlement of Caithness and the remarkable historical character of
Aud the Deep-Minded (who had also fascinated MacDiarmid). *The
Land the Ravens Found* is officially catalogued as a book for juvenile
readers, but it was certainly not always reviewed as such,[38] and is
a fine and interesting novel for adults as well as children.

The Land the Ravens Found

The history of Aud the Deep-Minded, the Norse noblewoman who
founded dynasties in Ireland, Scotland, Orkney, the Faroes and
Iceland, is recorded in detail in *Laxdaela Saga* and Ari Thorgilsson's
The Book of Settlements. A wife and mother of chieftains, she was a
powerful and wealthy woman who was treated with the greatest
respect and was renowned for her magnanimity. She always maintained her Christian faith and on settling in Iceland she not only
freed most of her slaves but also gave them land and livestock.
Such an active and influential woman was likely to attract the
attention of the socialist and feminist in Mitchison, but there is a
more interesting and important source for her inspiration, as her
biographer, Jill Benton, has noted: '*The Land the Ravens Found* ...
presents an anti-war theme and is a direct result of Naomi's
involvement in the AWPA'.[39] The Authors' World Peace Appeal
(with which Mitchison became involved in the early 1950s) wanted
to create an alternative children's literature to the comics and books
featuring war and violence which US troops had brought into
Britain when they were stationed there during the war. In a letter to
the present writer, however, Mitchison argued that children ought
to have war books, but of a different kind, and that she wrote *The
Land the Ravens Found* to show that a novel with war and violence
could still be a 'moral' book.[40]

The outstanding feature of the novel is indeed the theme of tol-
erance, understanding, forgiveness, and assimilation. The first half
of the book describes in detail the everyday life at the homestead of
Thorstan [sic] the Red, ruler of Sutherland and Caithness. Thorstan
himself is often away campaigning so that it is his mother, the inde-
fatigible Aud, who runs the large household. Aud is Christian and

thus exceptionally considerate to her slaves; a good example of this is the capture of Vivill, the son of a Celtic chieftain slain by Thorstan. He is tied up and injured when presented to Aud, and she immediately loosens his bonds. She further allays his fears by speaking gently to him in his own tongue, Gaelic, by giving him wine to drink, and by assuring him that as the household was Christian he would be well treated.[41] Apart from the obvious humanitarian aspects of her treatment of the slaves, there are also pragmatic reasons for her policy: the slaves become extremely loyal to Aud and do their work conscientiously. Moreover even the war-like Thorstan treats his slaves well since, given the uncertainties of warfare, 'one day he might be taken prisoner himself' (LRF, 15). A slave's loyalty could also pay even greater dividends, for many of Thorstan's free fighters are indeed former Irish thralls. There is very little sentimentality in all this, however, and Mitchison does not gloss over the problems and frictions in Thorstan's hall. Some of the Norsemen regard the Celts with contempt and one in particular, Haurd [sic], is disgusted with the lenient treatment of the slaves. Moreover Haurd and Steinarr [sic] hold with the old faith and despise Christianity as a religion. These conflicts come to a head with the launching of *Safe Farer*, the ship built to take them all from Scotland to Iceland. Aud plans to have the boat blessed by a priest, but Haurd and Steinarr defy her and attempt to have a blood-sacrifice of a Celtic slave's child. They are only prevented from carrying this out at the last moment in an unseemly scuffle.

All the tensions and conflicts inherent in such a society of rulers and slaves of mixed nationality, language and religion, are neatly illustrated in the relationship between Anlaf Feilan (the Celtic form of Olaf the Bullcalf), son of Thorstan, and Vivill, the enslaved son of the defeated Scottish chieftain Niagli. Much of the time the two boys, verging on manhood, are simply friends and companions, hunting, fishing, and practising swordplay together, talking 'a mixture of the two tongues, each learning words from the other without knowing it' (LRF, 34). At other times, however, Anlaf is resentful of the attention Vivill and Yrp (another Scottish slave) receive from Aud, and he becomes more conscious of his position and takes opportunities to play childish pranks to humiliate and annoy them (LRF, 37-38). He also despises them as Celts, but then suffers remorse and embarassment when he remembers that his own great-grandmother was the Irish princess Rafurta (LRF, 36). Vivill, for his part, also has moments of anger and humiliation when he is reminded that he is, after all, still a slave and subject to the whim of his captors (LRF, 32). Vivill's divided loyalties are finally put to the test when, out herding the cattle, he is presented with a chance to exact revenge. A Scot approaches him from the forest wanting to know Thorstan's movements and the strength of his hall. Vivill, with a nod of his head, confirms the destination of Thorstan's war-band, but he steadfastly refuses to betray Aud by guiding the Scots into the hall; indeed he exaggerates the strength of the hall's defences to prevent any attack whatsoever. 'His heart was dark in him; he had spoken and not spoken. Used, and not used, treachery and vengeance. He hated the sounds of the birds singing, since they had no knowledge of good and evil' (LRF, 56). Thorstan is killed in an ambush and Aud and Anlaf prudently decide to retire to Iceland where her brothers have already established themselves. Landfall in Iceland marks a watershed in the relations between the two boys, for on approaching the shore the ship is in danger of foundering on reefs and Haurd attempts to drown Vivill as a belated blood-sacri-fice. Anlaf sees what is happening, saves Vivill, and throws into the sea his arm ring in order to propitiate the gods instead; the ship, though damaged, finally makes the shore. On dry ground, Vivill thanks Anlaf and is told of the other sacrifice:

> 'Your arm ring,' said Vivill and stood silent a moment. Then he said: 'Anlaf Thorstan's son, I must tell you a thing about your arm ring. It was a ring that your father took from my father after he killed him. And whenever I saw that arm ring on you I hated you for it. And now it is gone.'
> 'Into deep sea,' said Anlaf, 'maybe – from us both. So you have no more need to hate me, Vivill.'
> 'No,' said Vivill, 'no more need. We have started fresh.' (LRF, 123)

This is indeed the significance of the new land, for all the faithful slaves are freed and given land; they are no longer Norsemen and Celts, but Icelanders. True to life, not everything runs smoothly; Aud quarrels with Cu-na-Gleinne, one of her freed men, over his treatment of thralls, and Haurd and Vivill continue their feud. On the whole, however, the new settlement of Western Iceland is successful, and the novel ends with Aud's peaceful and dignified death during Anlaf's wedding feast, which then becomes her wake. Her principles and example have shown that with patience, foresight, human kindness and understanding, former enemies can forgive and accept each other, and differences in race, religion and language can be assimilated to form a new sense of identity, unity and pride.

In comparison with her Norse fiction from the 1920s and 30s, therefore, *The Land the Ravens Found* marks a new optimism in Mitchison's view of the future of racial relations. The question of loyalty has always been a key issue in Mitchison's fiction and in an interview with Isobel Murray she once stated: 'One's got a loyalty presumably to one's family to start with, and then it widens out to one's village, one's town, one's country. Perhaps to being a European, and finally, I suppose, to being a human being'.[42] The experience of war proved to Mitchison that it is beyond doubt the loyalty to humanity which is the most important of all if mankind is to survive in the nuclear age. Mitchison has certainly practised what she preaches in that she 'went global', and in many books (especially for children) tried to disseminate knowledge and understanding of the many diverse races and tribes in Africa. In 1963 she even became Tribal Adviser and Mother to the Bakgatla of Botswana. In her Norse fiction the same important extension of her commitment and optimism is apparent. In the pre-war short stories her Norse characters could not ultimately extend their loyalty beyond tribal or racial limits (though Gersemi admittedly assimilated quite well with another Germanic people), but in *The Land the Ravens Found* Aud personally triumphs in her loyalty to mankind by bringing about a general (although realistically shaky) reconciliation between former owners and slaves, Norsemen and Celts in a new settlement in a new land. Mitchison's earlier magnificent postwar novel set in eighteenth-century Scotland, *The Bull Calves* (1947), has exactly the same subject, for as Murray has noted: 'The thematic movement on both national and personal levels is for unity and reconciliation, and against divisiveness: past wounds, however painful, have to be healed and put into the past'.[43] In this sense *The*

Land the Ravens Found is also Scottish in more than just its setting in the early chapters: Aud's aims and actions reveal a very clear model for the future. Just as Norsemen and Celts once settled their differences to create a new nation, Iceland, so could the Norse and Celtic descendants of those who remained behind settle their differences to create another new nation: a united and independent Scotland.

Later Stories

The Land the Ravens Found, however, did not mark Mitchison's final use of Old Norse material in the 1950s, for two Norse-inspired short stories appeared in the collection *Five Men and a Swan* in 1957. 'Aud the Deep-Minded',[44] as the title indicates, is a much shortened version of the story presented in *The Land the Ravens Found*. Although compact and well-written it understandably lacks the emotional tension of the longer work; it is a straightforward retelling of the saga story without any deep analysis of character or motive. The friction and confrontation between the Scots and Norsemen is no longer highlighted and the novel's important and symbolic friendship between Anlaf and Vivill (spelled Vifil in the short story) has been edited out completely. 'Aud the Deep-Minded' thus loses much of the effectiveness of the novel dealing with the same characters and storyline. 'The Story of St. Magnus'[45] is set in early twelfth-century Shetland and tells of a young man's desperate desire to help his wife, Gyrid, who is sick with leprosy. Inspired by the story of St. Magnus's martyrdom and the stories of miracles at his tomb, the young couple make a dangerous journey across the open sea in winter to Orkney to make a nightlong vigil at St. Magnus's tomb on Birsay. Gyrid is miraculously cured, and although this makes a satisfying ending to the story, it is far too slight (less than five pages in total) to make a serious impression on the reader. Even the actual story of St. Magnus is related in just two paragraphs.

Although these two stories were the last fruition of her Norse-inspired work in the 1950s, Mitchison has not totally ignored Old Norse sources since. The short tale 'Orkney Story'[46] is set in the Orkney of Norse times and relates how three women are saved from marauding Vikings by the spirits of the tomb in which they are hiding. This is essentially a ghost story, however, and the Old Norse background is really incidental. Viking warbands are also referred to and appear very briefly in *The Oath-Takers*, but once again they provide only background detail to the political turmoil of the ninth-century Frankish kingdom, the novel's setting.[47] Nonetheless, the publication of this novel means that Viking history and mythology have provided themes and subjects for Mitchison's fiction, in varying forms and degrees, for more than sixty-five years. Thus despite her variety of interests and enormous literary output, she has always maintained a life-long love of Old Norse history and literature. In her pre-war fiction the Vikings' wanderlust provided her with particular historical situations in which to analyse the clashes of races and civilisations and to explore the possible limits of human behaviour and loyalty. Her post-war rediscovery of Old Norse literature enabled her to use the gods and legends of the North to create *Travel Light*, a wonderfully imaginative fantasy novel and a succinct statement of her belief in the present day validity of ancient myth and magic. Finally, her growing sense of both the Nordic and Celtic elements of her Scottish identity and her deeply felt conviction of the need for global understanding, helped her create a deceptively simple but sincere and effective historical novel for readers of all ages, *The Land the Ravens Found*. It would, of course, be a gross exaggeration to claim that Old Norse literature has had an extensive influence on Mitchison's work, but as the above examples demonstrate, it has provided a very distinct and enduring source for her fiction and inspired imaginative themes and backgrounds for some of her profoundest interests and beliefs.

NOTES

1   Isobel Murray, Introduction to *Beyond This Limit: Selected Shorter Fiction of Naomi Mitchison* (Edinburgh, 1986), p.vii.

2   Naomi Mitchison, *Small Talk: Memories of an Edwardian Childhood* (London, 1973), p.52.

3   Letter from Naomi Mitchison postmarked 18.8.88.

4   Naomi Mitchison, *All Change Here: Girlhood and Marriage* (London, 1975), pp.97, 98.

5   'Spring', in *The Delicate Fire: Short Stories and Poems* (London, 1933), pp.323-
    24; 327.
6   'Brünnhilde's Journey Down the Rhine', in *The Fourth Pig: Stories and Verses*
    (London, 1936), pp.243-52.
7   *An End and a Beginning and Other Plays* (London, 1937), pp.82-98.
8   *When the Bough Breaks and Other Stories* (London, 1924), pp.161-314. All fur-
    ther references in the text are to this edition, abbreviated WBB.
9   The story is also dedicated to her Danish friend, Sonja Carstensen (WBB, 160).
10 In the eponymous saga, Viga Glum has three Odinic talismans given to him
    by his grandfather: a sword, a spear and a cloak. Fortune deserts him when
    he gives these away and he is forced off his land. (cf. Gersemi's fate when
    she loses her cloak). *Viga Glums Saga*, trans. John McKinnell (Edinburgh,
    1987), Ch.6, p.62; Ch.25, p.121.
11 *Barbarian Stories* (London, 1929), pp.194-236.
12 *Barbarian Stories*, pp.237-74. Harald Hardrada's life is recorded in
    Heimskringla, but has also been published separately as *King Harald's Saga*,
    trans. Magnus Magnusson and Hermann Pálsson (Harmondsworth, 1966).
    Mitchison bases her story on the events in Chs.13-15, pp.60-63.
13 *Barbarian Stories*, p.270.
14 *Barbarian Stories*, pp.268-69.
15 For a detailed analysis of all of Mitchison's historical fiction from this peri-
    od, see Isobel Murray, 'Human Relations: An Outline of Some Major
    Themes in Naomi Mitchison's Adult Fiction', in *Studies in Scottish Fiction:
    Twentieth Century*, Scottish Studies Vol.10, ed. Joachim Schwend and Horst
    Drescher (Frankfurt am Main, 1990), pp.243-56.
16 *Naomi Mitchison*, Saltire Self-Portraits 2 (Edinburgh, 1986), pp.1-5.
17 Further examples from her novels would include Meromic the Celt's final
    desertion of the Romans in *The Conquered* (1923) and Tarrik and Erif Der's
    return to Marob in *The Corn King and the Spring Queen* (1931).
18 Published in *Chapman* 50-51 (Spring, 1987), 25.
19 Beth Dickson, 'From Personal to Global: The Fiction of Naomi Mitchison',
    Chapman 50-51 (Spring, 1987), 39.
20 Naomi Mitchison, *Mucking Around: Five Continents Over Fifty Years*
    (London, 1981), pp.45-46. *The Swan's Road*, (London, 1954), pp.109, 151; *You
    May Well Ask: A Memoir 1920-1940*, 2nd edn. (London, 1986), p.165. Her vis-
    its to Denmark inspired an historical fiction for children, *Karensgaard: The
    Story of a Danish Farm* (London, 1961) which includes a short section on the
    Viking period of Danish history.
21 *The Swan's Road*, p.27.
22 *The Swan's Road*, p.152.
23 In her letter to the present writer, Mitchison claims to have adapted some
    of the sagas for the radio. Her memory may be at fault here, however, for
    although there are records of her adapting some of her historical fiction for
    the radio, no trace of any Norse-inspired material can be found at the BBC
    Archives.

24 Iain Crawford, review of *The Swan's Road* in *Saltire Review* 1:3 (1954), 93.

25 *The Swan's Road*, pp.15, 63.

26 Iain Crawford, 93.

27 E.g. the Danish King of England is named Cnut on p.36, but Kanute on p.106. The name Svein on p.92 is spelled Svend on p.106, and Thork<u>ill</u> on p.118 becomes Thork<u>el</u> on p.119! Similarly <u>K</u>etil on p.55 becomes <u>C</u>etil on p.57. Earl Ha<u>k</u>on on p.51 becomes Earl Ha<u>c</u>on on p.55 and Helg<u>i</u> Beolan on p.57 becomes Helg<u>e</u> Beolan on p.60. Mitchison uses three variations of the name Bjorn in its various compounds, thus Biorn (p.33), Thorbeorn (p.57), and Gunnbjorn (p.72). Moreover she spells King Olaf's patronymic in no less than three ways: Tryggvasson (p.27), Trygvasson (p.49), and Trigvasson (p.59).

28 *Swan's Road*, pp.125, 136.

29 *Travel Light* (1952), Virago Modern Classics (London, 1985). All further references are to this edition, abbreviated TL.

30 Note the cloak motif from *Viga Glums Saga* already used in 'When the Bough Breaks'.

31 Not Novgorod, as Elizabeth Longford states in her Introduction, p.viii. Modolf's forefathers, i.e. Halla's parents, moved 'south and east' to Novgorod *after* Halla was assumed dead (TL, 139).

32 For historical details of the Norse settlements in Russia and the Ukraine, see Gwyn Jones, *History of the Vikings*, pp.241-68. The Norse settlers were known as 'Rus' to the Slavs, hence 'Russia'.

33 *The Saga of the Volsungs*, trans. Jesse L. Byock (Berkeley & Oxford, 1990), Ch.8, pp.44-45. All further references are to this edition. Meromic, the hero of Mitchison's *The Conquered* also apparently changes into a wolf at the end of the novel. Bjorn Hringsson is turned into a bear by his evil stepmother and King Hrolf's champion, Bothvar, appears as a bear in his final battle in *The Saga of Hrolf Kraki*, trans. Stella M. Mills (Oxford, 1933), Chs.19-20, pp.39-44 and Ch.23, pp.82-87.

34 See also Mitchison's discussion of the dragon/gold symbol in *The Swan's Road*, pp.13-14.

35 Isobel Murray, 'Novelists of the Renaissance', Ch.7 of *The History of Scottish Literature*, Vol.4, ed. Cairns Craig (Aberdeen, 1987), p.104.

36 Beth Dickson, p.35.

37 *The Swan's Road*, p.9.

38 Alexander Scott did not see it as juvenile fiction: 'Related in a pithy prose which enviably combines the ease and unexpectedness of conversation with the formal grace of art, this novel is an achievement of a high order'; *Saltire Review* 3:8 (1956), 66.

39 Jill Benton, *Naomi Mitchison: A Century of Experiment in Life and Letters* (London, 1990), p.142.

40 Letter postmarked 18.8.88.

41 *The Land the Ravens Found* (London, 1955), pp.23-24; all further references are to this edition, abbreviated LRF.

42   Isobel Murray, Introduction to *Beyond This Limit*, p.viii.
43   Isobel Murray, Introduction to *Beyond This Limit*, p.xv.
44   *Five Men and A Swan* (London, 1957), pp.9-23.
45   *Five Men and a Swan*, pp.26-30.
46   *What Do You Think Yourself?* (Edinburgh, 1982), pp.1-9.
47   *The Oath-Takers* (Nairn, 1991). There are references to Viking depredations
     along the Seine (and elsewhere) throughout the novel, but the Vikings
     themselves only actually appear for a brief but bloody skirmish with the
     Franks on pp.71-74.

10. THE NORTHERN ISLES (and EDWIN MUIR)

The Northern Isles of Orkney and Shetland have a special position as regards the Norse history of Scotland, as has already been noted in Chapter 1. The first parts of Britain to be settled by the Vikings (probably as early as the eighth century), Orkney and Shetland were later made the earldom of Orkney c.870-90 A.D. by King Harald Finehair of Norway. For the next three hundred years this earldom (which included Caithness from time to time) was a geopolitical pivotal point in the Norse western world of Scandinavia, Iceland, and the British Isles. In 1195, however, King Sverre detached Shetland from the earldom and placed it directly under the Norwegian crown, and after the defeat of King Hakon at Largs in 1263, the remaining part of the earldom, Orkney, dwindled into international insignificance. Nonetheless, both Orkney and Shetland continued to remain under the Norwegian (and later, Danish) crown until 1469, when the islands finally came under Scottish suzerainty.[1] The Northern Isles, therefore, were under Norse rule longer than any other part of Scotland, and this has naturally had an important influence on the islands' culture, language and literature.

The aim of this chapter is thus to present a general survey of the many Orcadian and Shetlandic writers and poets who have been influenced, over the centuries, by their Norse heritage. It is not intended as an exhaustive study of the subject, but as an explanatory introduction to the pervasive Norse background of the Orcadian authors Eric Linklater and George Mackay Brown, who will be studied in detail in the final two chapters of this book.

The Medieval Literary Heritage

The earldom of Orkney is unique in Scotland and Britain in that its
medieval literature was not simply influenced by Old Norse, it *was*
Old Norse. This fact is reflected in Ernest Marwick's opening selection of skaldic and Eddic poetry (in translation) in his *Anthology of
Orkney Verse* (1949). At least two Orcadian earls, Turf-Einar and
Rognvald Kolsson have left individual strophes to posterity, and
the latter, in collaboration with an Icelandic skald, composed the
Háttalýkill or 'Lay of Metres', 'a kind of metrical key to Old Norse
prosody'.[2] Bjarni Kolbeinsson, Bishop of Orkney 1188-1222, wrote
the *Jómsvíkingadrápa*, or 'Lay of the Jomsvikings', and has also been
credited with the *Málsháttakvæði*, or 'Proverb Poem'. Finally, Arnor
Thordarson, one of the most famous Icelandic skalds, lived for
many years in Orkney, earning himself the sobriquet 'Jarlaskald' or
'Skald of the Earls'.[3] Certain linguistic features in the works of
Bishop Bjarni and Earl Turf-Einar suggest that there was indeed a
distinct form of the Old Norse language developing in the Northern
Isles, and the evolution and use of different skaldic metres, e.g
Bishop Bjarni's use of the 'munnvörp' form and Arnor Thordarson's
memorable 'Hrynhenda', seem to indicate that an original and creative force in Old Norse poetry was centred on Orkney.[4]

Two anonymous classics of Old Norse literature are also associated with Orkney: *Orkneyinga Saga*, written in the thirteenth century, in all probability in Iceland though with the possible assistance
of Bishop Bjarni, and the dramatic 'Darraðarljóð', a Caithness
man's vision of the Norns before the Battle of Clontarf in 1014 (as
preserved in *Njal's Saga*, Ch.157, pp.349-51), and almost certainly
composed within the earldom.[5] The Golden Age of medieval Norse
literature in the Northern Isles had come to an end by the thirteenth
century, however, especially as the earl's court no longer patronised
Norse sagas or poetry. Although Orkney and Shetland remained
politically Norse for a further two centuries, after the death of Earl
Jon Haroldson in 1231, the earls were Scottish in both nationality
and tongue.

Despite being part of the earldom until 1195, Shetland itself has
surprisingly few mentions in *Orkneyinga Saga*. Indeed in direct contrast with Orkney, Shetland seems to play little part in the Norse
history of the time and only 23 Shetlanders have been mentioned in

the entire canon of Old Norse literature, and the majority of these are only listed because they were miraculously cured by St. Magnus.[6] The literary significance of Orkney and Shetland is reversed in late medieval times, however, for unlike Orkney, Shetland has managed to preserve one of its ballads in the Norn language, the so-called *Hildinakvadet* or *Ballad of Hildina*. This was recited to George Low in 1774 by an old farmer on Foula, William Henry, and later published in Barry's *History of the Orkney Isles* (1808) and eventually in Low's own *Tour through the Islands of Orkney and Schetland* [sic] (1879). Low's transcript of the ballad is difficult as he knew no Norn and wrote it down as approximately as he could. A Norwegian scholar, however, has since studied the transcript in detail and presented a 'corrected' version of the ballad in Shetland Norn along with a detailed discussion of its language, style and content.[7] The ballad, clearly based on a legend of the everlasting battle in the prose *Edda*, tells the story of the Norse princess Hildina who is abducted by the Earl of Orkney; the King of Norway pursues them to Orkney where one of his men, Illugi, kills the Earl in battle and receives the princess in marriage as a reward. Hildina takes revenge for her dead lover by having Illugi burned to death on their wedding night. As the only Norn literature extant from the Middle Ages, the ballad is invaluable to Shetland's cultural history and a vital record of its language in the midway stage between Old Norse and the modern dialect.[8]

A further interesting remnant of Shetland's medieval literature are the 'veesiks' and 'goadiks', or fragments of rhymes, riddles and lullabies still extant in print. These are assumed to be Norse in origin, but so many of their words have been corrupted by time and the Scots and English languages that some of them are regrettably quite incomprehensible to modern, even Shetlandic, readers. One of the best preserved and most intelligible, however, is the so-called 'Unst Lay' with its intriguing mixture of Christian and Odinic motifs of the sacrificed god on a tree/crucifix:

Nine lang oors on da rütless Tree,
Hung he der fur au ta see;
Nine lang days in a murky howe
Lay he, we nedder mate or lowe;

Nine lang winters gaed ower his een
Afore he cam till He's ain ageen.[9]

Norse Identity in the Northern Isles

The Northern Isles' magnificent medieval heritage has not been forgotten by modern Orcadians and Shetlanders, and their Norse past
has retained a distinct place in their consciousness. In the nineteenth century there was a growing sense of self-awareness in the
Northern Isles, particularly indicated by the deliberate adoption of
a Norse or Scandinavian identity as opposed to a Scottish one.
Shetlanders were extremely proud and tenacious of their Norse
heritage and by the late nineteenth century the active promulgation
of a Norse racial identity was to have long-lasting political consequences. As in mainland Scotland there was a journalistic debate
over racial origins: were Shetlanders pure Norse or virtually
Scottish and Celtic through immigration and marriage?[10] The interesting point here is that whereas Scots often used a Norse identity
in the cause of Scottish Nationalism, the Shetlanders used it *against*
the Scots. Bronwen Cohen has shown in great detail how Shetland
intellectuals in the nineteenth century deliberately fostered a pride
and consciousness among the islanders of their Scandinavian origin and heritage for political purposes, especially a claim for some
kind of independence from Britain. In the 1830s, for example, the
Shetland Journal 'celebrated Shetland's Norse identity, and attributed the start of Shetland's problems to the advent of Scottish
rule'.[11] This attitude became general in Shetland, as is illustrated in
W. Fordyce Clark's history of the islands, with its chapter on
Shetland's Norse era entitled 'The Heroic Age' and the chapter on
Scottish rule 'The Dark Age'.[12] The Viking spirit was thus associated with a new fight for freedom from overbearing and stultifying
Scottish influences. This emphasis on a Norse identity took several
forms; the windows in the new town hall in Lerwick were adorned
with the heraldic emblems of the Scandinavian countries, many
street names in Lerwick were renamed after famous Norsemen (e.g.
King Harald Street) and, perhaps most inspired and spectacular of
all, the ancient Upp-Helly-Aa ceremony of burning tar-barrels was
completely transformed into a highly organised, colourful parade
of the Guizer Jarl and his squad of Vikings and the dramatic burn-

ing of a Viking longship. The first such event was organised in January 1889 and the festival remains one of the highlights of the Shetland calendar to this day. As Cohen has rightly observed:

> Upp-Helly-Aa was no spontaneous, popular creation, but developed as an orderly and controlled form of celebration that answered the needs of the City Fathers and provided a number of the island's intellectuals with the opportunity to project to a wider audience, and indeed to posterity, the product of their romantic exploration of Shetland's Norse past, conveying to generations of Shetlanders an inescapable sense of their Norse identity.[13]

Orcadians, too, conscientiously explored and glorified their Nordic roots. In the early nineteenth century, for example, the Orcadian poet David Vedder described Orkney as:

> Land of the dark – the Runic rhyme -
> The mystic ring – the cavern hoar;
> The Scandinavian seer – ...
> Land of a thousand Sea-kings' graves.[14]

The strong Norse background to Orkney's culture also led many Orcadians to take a very definite stance in the Norse/Celtic debate. Walter Traill Dennison, for example, is extremely chauvinistic in terms of race in his poem 'The Sons of Orkney', written in rather poor verse:

> Your modern numskull loudly raves
> Of Celt and Saxon – boorish slaves,
> Who safety found but in their graves
>   Before the men of Orkney.
>
> Our fathers found in savage case,
> And conquering, raised the Highland race
> In warfare, to the highest place,
>   And gave them chiefs from Orkney.
>
> The Saxons ne'er in fight could stand
> Nor rule themselves, nor keep their land,
> Till Norsemen took their cause in hand,
>   And gave them kings from Orkney.[15]

A.W. Johnston, however, an Orcadian scholar and one of the founders of the Viking Society, tried to introduce a more balanced view of the racial past of Orkney and Shetland by pointing out that the population of the Northern Isles was in reality very mixed. Indeed Johnston could only trace three earls who were pure-bred Norsemen – all the remainder had Celtic blood to a greater or lesser extent. The islanders' Norse image, he argued, had been created by the Norse author(s) of *Orkneyinga Saga* who had 'exaggerated in their own favour' and wrote disparagingly of Scottish Gaels who settled in the earldom. The existence of a pure 'Nordic' element in Orcadians and Shetlanders was thus a very debateable point.[16]

Racial attitudes towards identity were regrettably common and acceptable between 1880 and 1940, as has been shown in previous chapters. Nonetheless, although the more strident and absurd racial claims have been muted since the last war, the durability of this sense of Norse identity is still evident in more recent political developments. The Orcadian appeal to Denmark in 1986 over the Dounreay power-station and the Shetlanders' insistence on claiming Norse udal law in 1963 and 1988 have already been noted (Chapter 1). In 1977 the Shetland Movement was founded, primarily to concentrate on local politics, but after a meeting in February 1980 it put forward claims for fiscal autonomy or 'Home Rule' for Shetland which should have its own 'Althing' based on the privileges enjoyed by the Faroe Isles and Isle of Man within the Danish and British constitutions. Cartoons in local newspapers have subsequently, and ironically, depicted leaders of the Movement attired in full Viking dress.[17] Certainly some Orcadians and Shetlanders, and undoubtedly many Scots and Britons, may well regard these 'Nordic' separatist aspirations as unrealistic, if not absurd. Nonetheless, there can also be no doubt that for many Northern Islanders their Norse heritage is a vital emotional and psychological aspect of their character and it has had an invigorating influence on their language and literature.

Orkney Norn and Shetland Norn

One of the striking features of the Northern Isles' Norse heritage is the survival of the dialects in Orkney and Shetland based on medieval forms of Old Norse called Orkney Norn and Shetland

Norn. The extent and use of the two dialects has varied considerably in the two groups of islands, however. The influence of Scots on the Orkney language, for example, began much earlier than in Shetland due to trade, politics, and immigration from the south; indeed it is fairly clear that, as Michael Barnes says, 'Scots had replaced Norn as the language of prestige in Orkney before the impignoration'.[18] However, the language was not totally defunct by the late eighteenth century as is proven by the well-known incident (recorded by Walter Scott) of a minister in North Ronaldsay hearing a Norse version of Gray's 'Fatal Sisters', i.e. 'Darraðarljóð'.[19] By the mid-nineteenth century, however, Orkney Norn as an independent language was dead, although its influence on the modern dialect should not be underestimated; Hugh Marwick's *The Orkney Norn* (1929) recorded hundreds of words of Norse origin then still extant in the islanders' vocabulary, and as many other commentators have noted, Norn has had a vital influence on the modern dialect's word-order, use of pronouns, intonation and accent.[20]

Despite all this, very few Orkney writers seem to have availed themselves of such a rich linguistic heritage. Walter Traill Dennison made the first serious attempt at presenting Orkney stories in dialect with his *Orcadian Sketch-Book* (Kirkwall, 1880), but his example inspired few imitations and his book 'remained for three-quarters of a century the only truly authentic collection of Orkney dialect stories' until C.M. Costie's collection of short stories, *Benjie's Bodle*, in 1956.[21] Robert Rendall has also attempted to use the dialect creatively in his poetry, and indeed may have written one of the finest 'Norse' poems in Scottish literature (see below). Rendall's work has been highly praised by fellow Orcadians Edwin Muir and George Mackay Brown, but remains little known outside Orkney.[22] Moreover the three greatest Orcadian writers of this century, Muir, Mackay Brown and Linklater, have all achieved success in an English which 'only now and then is coloured by island speech'.[23]

The situation of the Shetlandic dialect is apparently much better than its Orkney counterpart. This is perhaps partly due to a greater distance from Scots influence in the Middle Ages, and partly due to a powerful resurgence of interest in Shetlandic in the late nineteenth century. Basil Ramsay Anderson's *Broken Lights* (1888), J.J.

Haldane Burgess's *Rasmie's Buddie* (1891) and Laurence J. Nicolson's *Songs of Thule* (1894) established the local popularity of dialect poetry, and further encouragement to use the dialect came with the two-year sojourn in the islands (1893-95) of the Faroese scholar Jakob Jakobsen.[24] His intensive research into the remnants of Shetland Norn and his lectures on this subject were finally published in *The Dialect and Place Names of Shetland* (1897) and later *An Etymological Dictionary of the Norn Language in Shetland* (1928-32). The value of these books should not be underestimated, as they preserve thousands of names and words which might otherwise have disappeared altogether, and, as Jamieson's Scots dictionary succoured Hugh MacDiarmid's attempts to revitalise Scots literature, so did Jakobsen's dictionary inspire Shetlanders to persevere with their own dialect in literary creation.

Since Jakobsen's day there has thus been a flourishing dialect literature in Shetland; the *New Shetlander* magazine has been especially influential, in a twenty-year period, 1962-82, publishing no fewer than 285 poems in Shetlandic by 77 poets.[25] The most recently acclaimed Shetland poets include 'Vagaland' (T.A. Robertson), Rhoda Bulter and Robert Alan Jamieson. 'Vagaland' makes a spirited defence of the use of the dialect in his poems 'Prelude' and 'Shetlanrie' and Jamieson proudly points out that many words in Jakobsen's dictionary are familiar to him through childhood contact with his great-grandmother and that while his 'poems in Norroena/Scots may be artificial, their language is still more natural to my tongue than that of those in English'.[26] Equally important is the fact that the dialect is also used in modern prose fiction. Joseph Gray uses Shetlandic in his stories in *Lowrie* (1933), and Jamieson uses Shetlandic dialogue in his novels *Soor Hearts* (1984) and *Thin Wealth* (1986). Perhaps the most effective use of dialect, however, has been in the crofters' and their families' use of Shetlandic in John J. Graham's *Shadowed Valley* (1987), a beautifully crafted and highly evocative recreation of the Weisdale Clearances of the 1840s. The crofters' dialect reveals their sincerity, simple dignity and strong sense of community, and makes a stark contrast to the calculating and impersonal English used by the minister and the landowners. In linguistic terms, therefore, the Northern Isles' Norse past has had a more enduring influence on Shetland than Orkney.

Vikings in Orkney and Shetland Literature

Another evident feature of Old Norse influence on the literature of the Northern Isles is that of subject matter, whether dealt with in dialect or standard English. Over the last two centuries, Orcadians and Shetlanders have written novels, stories and poems about their Norse forefathers. In the late nineteenth century, for example, Jessie Saxby wrote short stories based on King Harald Finehair's expedition to Orkney and Shetland, and on Norse mythology.[27] The most notable prose fiction of this period, however, are the Viking novels by the Orcadian J. Storer Clouston and the Shetlander J.J. Haldane Burgess.

Burgess's *The Viking Path* (1894) is in many ways typical of romantic Viking novels of the time with its basic plot of treachery, derring-do and revenge, set mostly in Shetland, and it suffers many of the weaknesses of the genre: melodramatic scenes, stilted and archaic language, and poor, anglicised versions of skaldic poetry. The novel's overtly didactic Christian message is also anachronistic, for as one critic for *The Athenaeum* commented (27.7.1895): '... the vein of religious sentiment that runs through the book belongs rather to the nineteenth than the tenth century'.[28] But the novel does have some good points. The story concerning Jarl Alsvid's search for the killers of his brother, his successful revenge and final death opposing King Harald Finehair's subjection of Shetland has a generally credible plot and the battle descriptions are well handled. More interesting is the sub-plot concerning the attempt of a former Viking, Thorvald, now a Christian convert, to persuade Arvak (Jarl Alsvid's chief Viking) to give up his violent life and believe in Christ. As a critic in *The Times* observed (18.12.1894), 'Mr. Burgess strikes a new and original note in analysing the psychological influence of the converted apostles of the White Christ on their heathen comrades'.[29] With reservations about the sentimentality of some of the scenes and their didactic intentions, Burgess's description of Arvak's contempt for Thorvald's pacifism gradually turning into admiration and conviction is quite credible. It is also refreshing, in a late-Victorian context, to see Norsemen presented as thinking beings with a sense of moral values as opposed to the blond-haired, blue-eyed, super-hero stereotype with an axe in his hand and an aphorism on his lips – though some of Burgess's other characters are, unfortunately, much more typical of the conventional literary

Vikings of the time. On the whole, therefore, *The Viking Path* is a flawed but interesting novel.

Storer Clouston's novel *Vandrad the Viking* (1898) is a competent but uninspiring story of a young Norwegian prince, Estein Hakonson [sic], who is attacked by the Vikings Liot and Osmund and shipwrecked on Orkney. He is nursed back to health by Osla, the daughter of a religious recluse, Thord. The latter, as a former Viking, had been responsible for the death of Estein's brother, but Osla's intervention prevents Estein from exacting revenge. Estein's foster-brother comes to Orkney and together they defeat the Vikings, Estein killing Liot in a 'holmgang' or formal duel. Estein returns triumphantly to Norway where he succeeds to his father's throne in Sogn and where Osla duly arrives to become his queen. The story is told in a very straightforward manner, but it lacks the imaginative verve of Rider Haggard's *Eric Brighteyes* or the psychological interest of Haldane Burgess's *The Viking Path*.

In the present century, short stories on Viking themes by various writers can be found in all the main Orkney and Shetland journals. An overemphasis on the Norse past of the Northern Isles, however, can sometimes lead to inappropriateness and the tendency to fall back on racial typecasting mentioned earlier in Chapter 3. An example of inappropriateness can be found in Vivian Bird's short story 'Back Again From the Dark'[30] in which, at a desperate moment during the Second World War, a ghostly Viking longship appears and helps sink a German submarine! An example of racial typecasting can be found in Jack Renwick's short story 'The Shadowed Wave' about four men in an open fishing boat:

> All, with the exception of Andrew, were fair-haired, blue-eyed men, typical products of what had once been a Norse colony. Andrew, by virtue or otherwise of some Celtic ancestor, had acquired high cheek-bones, very dark hair and eyes, and a slighter build than the others. While he was generous to a fault, he was as tempramental as a prima donna, and dangerous in anger as a naked sword.[31]

While they are at sea a raven suddenly, and very unusually, tries to steal their catch; most of the crew see this as a bad omen[32] and want

to cut the line immediately, but first Andrew, who has already upset
the crew by mentioning the name of a suspected witch, Inga, badly
wounds the raven with his gaff.

> 'I throw away fish for no man. You can cut your line now,' Andrew
> said to Magnus and across the centuries Celt and Viking looked at
> each other through the men's eyes.[33]

Needless to say, on coming ashore they find the witch Inga lying
dead on the sand, a huge gash in her thigh. The overt use of racial
stereotypes and a heavy-handed symbolism thus destroys the
story's credibility and virtually reduces it to a narrative formula.
Seamen's superstitions and Celtic and Norse myths can be successfully interwoven for artistic purposes, as we have seen in Neil
Gunn's novel *The Silver Darlings*.

The poets of Orkney and Shetland have also used Norse themes
and subjects, in both English and dialect, over the last two centuries. Vedder's 'To Orkney', from the early nineteenth century, has
already been noted, and the same book also contains a long poem
on a Norse foray in Scotland, 'The Battle of Luncarty'.[34] The two
poems were reprinted, along with two others on Viking themes,
'Hans Snorro' and 'Sigurd Hiort's Death-Chant' in a final collection
of Vedder's poems later in the century.[35] David Balfour saved many
Orcadian songs and ballads from oblivion by recording some from
his own childhood as well as others recited to him later. Two songs
preserved for posterity, 'High as his Glory' and 'Far O'er the Blue
Waters', deal with Earl Sigurd of Orkney and are reputedly Old
Norse in origin. Balfour disarmingly admits, however, that whenever he could not remember the exact words of a song he simply
made them up himself, so that the true provenance of these songs
must be very much in doubt.[36] In the present century the Orcadian
poets Duncan J. Robertson and Robert Rendall have written on
Norse themes, and other poems on Orkney's Norse past by John T.
Wilson, Ann Scott-Moncrieff and the non-Orcadians Sir Edmund
Head and Maurice Lindsay can be found in Marwick's *Anthology*.[37]

In nineteenth-century Shetland, the two poets most concerned
with Norse themes were Basil Ramsay Anderson and J.J. Haldane
Burgess. In Anderson's 'Auld Maunsie's Crö', for example, the

death of Auld Maunsie, clearly a typical Shetlander of the old generation, takes on mythical proportions, especially as the wall of his
crue (a vegetable garden) collapses and kills his colt the very night
he dies. As Rendboe states:

> ... at this stage the Viking symbolism becomes exceedingly vivid,
> because the crue kills its builder's horse at his own death, just as
> the Vikings sacrificed the horse of their chieftain and placed it in
> his grave, to serve him in the after life. Also the foremost bird of
> omen to announce the passing of Old Maunsie's soul is the raven,
> the bird of Odin himself, chief god of the Norsemen. Old Maunsie
> goes in style![38]

J.J. Haldane Burgess later tries to use Old Norse mythology as a
vehicle for promoting some of his socialist ideas. In 'My Trip to
Asgard', Young Rasmie has a vision of flying on the back of
Huginn, Odin's raven, to visit all the realms of the Aesir and Vanir.
Four ships are sighted, Ochlocracy, Autocracy, Democracy and
Ergatocracy, but only the last reaches 'the port of Life'. Thor, we are
informed, campaigns in Midgard for freedom and justice, for
'Workers alone are his delight; / To them he gives his Asa-might',
and eventually all those who take part in the proletarian struggle
will find a place in Gimli, the new and better post-Ragnarök
world.[39] The poetry is not inspiring, however, and Marxism mixes
very uncomfortably with Old Norse mythology; the end result is
not impressive.

More recent and interesting uses of Old Norse mythology in
poetry can be found in William J. Tait's 'A Day Atween Waddirs'
and Stella Sutherland's 'Lament for Balder' and 'Winter Solstice',
which invoke the Balder myth, the first and third of the above mentioned poems once again associating this pagan god with Christ.[40]
John J. Hunter's *Taen wi da Trow* is a long narrative poem in dialect
on Shetland's history and has long sections on the Viking Age and
the Norse myth of creation.[41] However, the material is not presented chronologically, the narrative is somewhat confused and rambling, and the verse rather weak.

The most consistent and successful integration of Old Norse history and mythology and poetry, however, can be found in the

works of probably Shetland's most popular poet, 'Vagaland'. Old
Norse mythology is simply and credibly invoked in such poems as
'Grice Ingans' (p.31),[42] and 'Reflections' (p.158); 'Thus Said
Gunnar' (p.167) is based on a famous incident in *Njal's Saga* (Ch.75,
p.166), whilst 'Aboot da Nicht' (pp.47-48) and 'Da Swan's Gaet'
(pp.26-30) are attempts to recreate Norn riddle-rhymes and a
Hildina-type ballad. Many other poems refer to Shetland's Norse
history, such as 'The Udallers' (p.163), 'Papa Stour' (p.165), 'Viking
Congress 1950' (p.166), and 'The Broch of Mousa' (pp.168-69). The
Norse discovery of America seems to have especially interested
'Vagaland' and he has written three poems on the subject: 'Lamp-
Licht' (p.32-33), 'L'Anse aux Meadows' (pp.118-19) and
'Meadowsweet' (pp.174-75). 'L'Anse aux Meadows' (the title is the
excavated site of a Viking longhouse in Newfoundland) is a beautiful evocation of man's need to push back the boundaries of knowl-
edge and discovery, cleverly comparing Leif Eiriksson's daring and
curiosity with those of modern astronauts (p.119):

> Awa in Göd's grit Universe among da mirds o starns
> Hit's hard to say what windros things may be;
> Wi dir telescopes an space-probes folk can
> learn a grain aboot it,
> Bit a better thing ta dö is geng an see;
> Laek Leif Erikson [sic], dey'll better geng an see.

'Meadowsweet' is a monologue by a young Viking aboard Leif
Eiriksson's longship bound for America; although full of excitement about the new land to be found he is still slightly homesick
and missing his sweetheart. The creation of such a persona, an ordinary Viking taking part in the major events of Norse history, is a
form developed even further, as we shall see, in the Viking poems
of George Mackay Brown. There are further slight references to Old
Norse myths and phrases throughout 'Vagaland's' poetry; suffice it
to say that his work is pervaded by the spirit of Shetland's Norse
past which provides him with many apposite contrasts and symbols.

Perhaps the finest example of a 'Norse' poem would be one com-
bining the Norn-based dialect and/or skaldic poetics with Viking

subject matter. Two good examples of this can be found in the
Northern Isles, Robert Rendall's 'Shore Tullye' and Robert Alan
Jamieson's 'Warld Tell'. Rendall's poem about a Viking raid does
not contain kennings (complicated Old Norse metaphors), but it
does brilliantly recreate, in Orkney dialect, the metrical system of
skaldic verse with its strict patterns of alliteration, internal rhyme
and stressed syllables:

> Crofters few but crafty,
> Krugglan doun b' moonlight,
> Hidan near the headland,
> Hint great congles waited....[43]

Jamieson's 'Warld Tell' cleverly combines the Ragnarök myth,
modern Shetlandic and an abrupt ending in English, to make a very
effective statement on Shetland's cultural fate in the modern world:

> ... At Ragnarok, quhan Fenrir brakks
> Da powre it hads him, quhan
> Wi his brood da lipper wolf
> Raags owre da Ert, dan
> Yggdrasil, midder tree,
> Apo quha aathing rests,
> Will shakk an Odin, wi
> Aa da idder gods'll
> Perish finally.
>
> And a new race will inherit the earth![44]

It must be reiterated at this point that this chapter has by no means
presented an exhaustive study, but a general survey, of the many
writers in Orkney and Shetland who have been influenced by the
Norse element in their own history. As the above examples have
shown, almost all the better-known novelists and poets from the
Northern Isles have been inspired, almost inevitably it would seem,
by their strong sense of a Norse heritage. It is not surprising, therefore, that the two Scottish writers most influenced by Old Norse literature and history, Eric Linklater and George Mackay Brown,
should be Orcadians, and detailed discussions of their works will

be found in the following two chapters. There is one Orcadian, however, who seems an unusual exception in this context. Before embarking on the studies of Linklater and Mackay Brown, therefore, a brief discussion of the intriguing case of Edwin Muir seems appropriate.

Edwin Muir

Edwin Muir is probably the most famous literary son of Orkney, having won a world-wide reputation for his poetry and literary criticism. His early childhood in Orkney is vividly recalled in the first two chapters of his autobiography, and he compares his family's move to Glasgow to a traumatic Fall of Man from the Garden of Eden.[45] This mythopoeic interpretation of life has had a profound influence on all his poetry. Muir never lived permanently in Orkney again, but frequently visited it in later years, especially when he felt a need for spritual or physical rest and renewal.

Muir was immensely proud of his Orcadian origins, and his association with the Northern Isles and their Scandinavian heritage was strongly reinforced by his marriage to Willa Anderson, who was born in Shetland. Despite his Norse cultural background, however, the intriguing feature of Muir's poetry is that there is not one single overt reference to Old Norse history or literature; his symbolism and mythology are predominantly Hellenic. As Margery McCulloch comments:

> It is interesting to speculate why a boy from a non-intellectual farming background, with few books and little formal schooling, brought up in the cultural ambience of Norse-influenced Orkney with its heritage of Viking sagas, should choose the classical severity of Greek myth as his metaphorical medium.[46]

Muir was certainly not ignorant of Old Norse literature, for when he was twelve years old he had read William Morris's *Earthly Paradise* with 'Ogier the Dane and all the Northern heroes and heroines', and much later in life in a paper written for the BBC (but never ultimately broadcast), he reveals an extensive knowledge of *Heimskringla*, *Orkneyinga Saga* and *Njal's Saga*.[47] Muir's notebooks also contain jottings of ideas for future poems based on the latter saga and the legend of Odin hanging on the World Tree for nine days, though nothing ever came of these ideas.[48]

Although there are no overt traces of Old Norse influence in his poetry, in his recent detailed study of Muir's Orkney background, George Marshall has uncovered some well-hidden references to Old Norse history in the poems 'The Mythical Journey' and 'The City'. He very persuasively argues that the journey, in the poems, from 'the North' to what seems almost certainly the Mediterranean Sea and the Holy Land, is based on Earl Rognvald Kolsson's pilgrimage to Jerusalem in the twelfth century (related in *Orkneyinga Saga* Chs.86-89, pp.164-82).[49] Marshall also makes a good case for claiming that Muir's symbolical use of horses could be traced to 'ancient Scandinavian tradition' of the worship of horses, and emphasises the point that the original Norse name of Orkney Mainland was 'Hrossey' or 'Horse Island'. Marshall also traces Norse influence in the poem 'Ballad of the Flood', seeing it as reflecting the Norse legend of the 'Stoor Worm' or Midgard Serpent.[50]

These claims are probably justified, though there are one or two further points to bear in mind. It is true that the Norsemen esteemed horses highly and even sometimes dedicated them to the gods,[51] but the admiration for horses in Orkney could also be associated with the secret society of Horsemen and their Horseman's Word which was widespread in north-east Scotland; indeed the areas most associated with this society are also associated with ancient Pictland, and the Picts were well known for their worship of horses. In other words the folk belief surrounding horses which Muir draws on may conceivably be Pictish in origin rather than specifically Norse. As regards the 'Stoor Worm' legend, there is little doubt that it is of Norse provenance, but the astonishing fact is that Muir seemed unaware of this. Referring to the legend in another context, the formation of Orkney from the sea-dragon's teeth, Muir openly states:

> Who the author of this story was I do not know. It may be an old story, or the recent invention of some enterprising Orkney man; I have never come across it again.[52]

A further surprising omission from his autobiography concerns the island of Wyre on which he spent much of his idyllic childhood. Muir refers to the fact that he often played in the ruins of the near-by castle which had been built by the giant 'Cubby Roo', the Norseman Kolbein Hruga; he curiously neglects to mention that Kolbein's son was Bishop Bjarni, one of Orkney's greatest skaldic poets. The coincidence that two of Orkney's best known poets had been brought up on one small island should surely have been worth some comment. Mackay Brown, for example, wrote a short story based on this very intriguing fact.[53]

All his life Muir was intensely proud of his Orcadian roots and was often homesick for Orkney.[54] He certainly had knowledge of Old Norse history and literature as is shown above, and when he and his wife moved to Swaffham Prior near Cambridge, they had been vaguely pleased

> ... to think that we might be the spearhead of a new Norse inva-sion. What induced us to feel like that was our coming to a ham-let called Quoy, a purely Norse name for a cow-farm that remind-ed us of many Orkney quoys, such as Grimsquoy and Quoydandy.[55]

Indeed, as Heather Hewitt points out, Muir always 'affected to regard himself as a Norseman rather than a Scot',[56] and this enabled him, although involved in the Scottish Nationalist move-ment, to adopt a highly critical but neutral view of Scotland (i.e. non-Scottish and non-English). His *Scott and Scotland* (1936) is a famous attack on MacDiarmid's ambitions for the Scots language and the Scottish Renaissance, and his *Scottish Journey* (1935) pre-sents a grim picture of pre-war Scottish economics and society. He is especially pessimistic as regards the aims of Scottish Nationalism, and very derogatory about the claims for a Golden Age of Celtic civilisation. It eventually comes as no surprise that Muir finds in Orkney the 'only desirable form of life that I found in all my journey through Scotland'.[57]

The question still remains, however, as to why Muir never overt-ly used Orkney or its Old Norse heritage in his own poetry. The full answer to this can now never be known, of course, but some

answers are more possible than others. To begin with, whatever
stance Muir adopted in public, in private he clearly had some reservations about his Norse racial origins. The family name, Muir, is
very Scottish, and despite his idealised presentation of his Orkney
childhood, 'in strictly local terms the Muirs were socially mobile
outsiders'.[58] In a letter to George Thorburn in 1927, he claims: 'I'm
not Scotch, I'm an Orkney man, a good Scandinavian, and my true
country is Norway, or Denmark, or Iceland, or some place like that.'
But he then adds significantly: 'But this is nonsense, I'm afraid,
though there's some sense in it'. In a letter to T.S. Eliot in 1956, nearly thirty years later, Muir admits that 'the Orkney people are a mixture of everything' and that, as regards his own family, 'probably
there was a faint mixture of Vikings somewhere unknown in the
story, but I hope not. What nonsense nice people write'.[59] Despite
his Orkney birth, therefore, Muir became too cosmopolitan or wary
of racial tags to take his possible Scandinavian origins too seriously.

There was one aspect of his Norse Orkney heritage, however,
which was to have a profound influence on him: the Orkney
dialect. Although Muir never wrote in dialect (and only very occasionally in Scots), he had a strong Orkney accent all his life.[60] His
wife's speech also had traces of her Shetland origins and together
they always spoke with the vocabulary and intonation of the
Northern Isles' dialects. Throughout their marriage, for example,
they always addressed each other as 'thu' in private. Moreover, so
strong was Muir's accent that he always found public speaking an
ordeal.[61] His sensitivity over his accent can best be illustrated by an
incident concerning a beautiful cottage called Broad Oaks near
Cambridge. The Muirs would have liked to buy it as a family home,
but they reluctantly refused to do so. Willa instinctively realised
that he wished to avoid a possibly lifelong embarrassment of mentioning the name of the cottage in public, for he would invariably
have transposed the vowel sounds (i.e. 'Brode Awks').[62] Thus
Muir's Norse-based speech provided him *in private* with a highly
personal, indeed unique bond with his wife, but *in public* an
uncomfortable self-consciousness, if not a sense of inadequacy.
Bearing this point in mind, therefore, it might be possible to suggest
a similar psychological inhibition behind his poetry.

As the detailed research of Marshall has shown, Muir's childhood memories of Orkney pervade his poetry, providing many
images and symbols (not least the mythologising of the family's
eviction from Orkney as the Fall from Eden).[63] Moreover Mackay
Brown has claimed that the texture of Muir's verse 'had the grain-
ings of Orkney in it: its shape mirrored the quiet flowing laterals of
the Orkney fields and hills'.[64] Nonetheless, the intriguing fact
remains that not one line of his poetry explicitly mentions Orkney;
Orcadian references and associations can only be deduced from a
knowledge of Muir's childhood and not from the poems themselves (cf. the obvious and frequent Orkney references in the works
of Linklater and Mackay Brown). Lord Grimond has made the
interesting suggestion that Muir 'never felt comfortable with the
real Orkney of his later life ... due to his desire to hold unsullied the
vision of his childhood'.[65] Muir himself certainly seems aware of a
kind of aesthetic sublimation of his childhood experience in his
poetry:

> ... a poem on Achilles pursuing Hector round the walls of Troy
> was really a resuscitation of the afternoon when I ran away, in real
> terror, from another boy as I returned from school. The bare land-
> scape of the little island became, without my knowing it, a uni-
> versal landscape over which Abraham and Moses and Achilles
> and Ulysses and Tristram and all sorts of pilgrims passed.[66]

But the overt references remain consistently biblical or Hellenic,
never Norse. Apart from a few poems referring to Scotland or particular places in Europe, most of Muir's poetical settings 'lack the
specificity of locale', as McCulloch expresses it,[67] and only exist in
an indeterminate or legendary world: 'The Mountains', 'The Hill',
'The Wayside Station', 'The City', 'The Castle', 'The House', or are
based on classical history or mythology: 'Prometheus', 'Oedipus',
'Troy', 'The Labyrinth'.

Margery McCulloch has suggested that when Muir moved from
Orkney to Glasgow 'he found himself a "Displaced Person" psy-
chologically and culturally in the context of mainland Scotland'.[68]
His English poetry, however, with its predominantly Hellenic
imagery and symbolism, gradually placed him well within the

English tradition and gained him a world-wide reputation and a place in the canon of English literature. His translations of novels from the German (especially of Kafka) also gained him critical acclaim and prestige. Moreover for many years Muir lived abroad, working as a teacher and representative of the British Council, thus gaining an international identity not only as a poet and critic, but also as a practitioner and spokesman for the 'Establishment' of English language culture and literature. As a poet and translator in English – for Muir a 'neutral' tongue – he was no longer a 'Displaced Person'. Thus with his poetic voice as with his public speaking voice: Muir did not relish overtly revealing his non-English and parochial cultural origins and thus risk critical isolation or possibly even disdain.

The above theory is pure hypothesis, of course, but it does rest on one important fact: Muir's love of Orkney and some aspects of its Norse heritage is clearly recorded in his private correspondence, biographies (both by himself and his wife) and prose works; the total lack of any specific reference to Orkney within his poetry cannot, therefore, be pure coincidence or forgetfulness. Behind this fact must lie some deep psychological reason, perhaps the one suggested above. So profound and influential was his idealised childhood, so deeply personal and private was Muir's sense of an Orkney identity, that he could only cope with it in his poetry by transmuting it into imaginative symbols or traditional biblical and Hellenic myths in the emotionally neutral language of English.

NOTES

[1]   For details of the Norse history of the Northern Isles, see Crawford, *Scandinavian Scotland*, pp.53-58; Liv Kjørsvik Schei and Gunnie Moberg, *The Orkney Story*, 2nd edn. (London, 1987), pp.45-67; and *The Shetland Story* (London, 1988), pp.33-39.

[2]   Hugh Marwick, *Orkney* (London, 1951), p.68.

[3]   For a general survey of the earldom's Old Norse literature, see Schei and Moberg, *The Orkney Story*, pp.129-33.

[4]   For details, see Anne Holtsmark, 'Bjarne Kolbeinsson og hans forfatterskap', *Edda* 37:1 (1937), 1-17; Magnus Olsen, 'Orknø-Norn og Norrøn Diktning paa Orknøene', *Maal og Minne* (1932), 148-53.

[5]   Anne Holtsmark, 'Bjarne Kolbeinsson', 14-17; 'Vefr Darraðar', *Maal og*

Minne (1939), 96. The arguments for an Orcadian provenance for parts of the saga have been restated by O.D. Macrae Gibson, 'The Other Scottish Language – *Orkneyinga Saga'*, in *Bryght Lanternis: Essays on the Language and Literature of Medieval and Renaissance Scotland*, ed. J. Derrick McClure and Michael G. Spiller (Aberdeen, 1989), pp.420-28.

6   See Appendix to A.B. Taylor, 'Shetland Place-Names in the Sagas', in *The Viking Congress Lerwick 1950*, ed. W. Douglas Simpson (London & Edinburgh, 1954), pp.126-27. For a more radical view of Orkney/Shetland relations, see Brian Smith, 'Shetland in Saga-Time: Rereading the *Orkneyinga Saga'*, *Northern Studies* 25 (1988), 21-41.

7   Marius Hægstad, *Hildinakvadet med utgreiding um det norske maal paa Shetland i eldre tid* (Christiania [Oslo], 1900).

8   'The Ballad of Hildina', trans. W.G. Collingwood, *Orkney and Shetland Miscellany* 1 (1907-08), 211-16. See also Sturluson, *Edda*, pp.122-24.

9   See Jessie M.E. Saxby, *Shetland Traditional Lore* (Edinburgh, 1932), p.59; on the 'Unst Lay', see also *Arthur Laurenson: His Letters and Literary Remains*, ed. Catherine Spence (London, 1901), pp.52-53.

10   See file of newspaper cuttings on this subject in the J.J. Haldane Burgess Papers, Shetland Archives D6/292/4, pp.59-64.

11   Bronwen Cohen, 'Norse Imagery in Shetland: an historical study of intellectuals and their use of the past in the construction of Shetland's identity, with particular reference to the period 1800-1914', unpublished Ph.D thesis, University of Manchester (1983), p.326.

12   W. Fordyce Clark, *The Story of Shetland* (Edinburgh, 1906), pp.37-62; 63-90.

13   Cohen, 'Norse Imagery in Shetland', p.478.

14   David Vedder, 'To Orkney', *Orcadian Sketches* (Edinburgh, 1832), p.10.

15   W. T. Dennison, *The Orcadian Sketch-Book* (Kirkwall, 1880), pp.186-87.

16   A.W. Johnston, 'Orkney and Shetland Folk 880-1350', *Saga-Book* 9 (1920-25), 400.

17   E.g. *Shetland Times*, 8 April 1988, p.2.

18   Barnes, 'Orkney and Shetland Norn', p.354.

19   See Sir Walter Scott, *The Pirate* (1822), Centenary edn. Vol.XIII (Edinburgh, 1886), Note C, pp.460-61.

20   For details, see Hugh Marwick, pp.188-94, and Schei and Moberg, *The Orkney Story*, pp.127-28.

21   Foreword to *The Collected Orkney Dialect Tales of C.M. Costie* (Kirkwall, 1976), n.p.

22   Edwin Muir, *An Autobiography* (1954), 2nd edn. (London, 1987), p.63; George Mackay Brown, *An Orkney Tapestry* (1969), 3rd edn. (London, 1978), pp.179-88.

23   Schei and Moberg, *The Orkney Story*, p.134.

24   For details of Jakobsen's visit to Shetland, see Roy Grønneberg, *Jakobsen and Shetland* (Lerwick, 1981).

25   Laurits Rendboe, *The Shetland Literary Tradition*, 2 vols (Odense, 1986), I, 11. The whole of the first volume, 'An Introduction', contains a good survey of Shetland's dialect literature.

26   *The Collected Poems of Vagaland*, ed. M. Robertson, 2nd edn. (Lerwick, 1980),
     pp.xxx-xxxi; 68-69; Robert Alan Jamieson, *Shoormal* (Edinburgh, 1986), p.18.
     For an invigorating study of the modern Shetland dialect and its literary
     potential, see Brian Smith, 'The Development of the Spoken and Written
     Shetland Dialect: A Historian's View', in *Shetland's Northern Links: Language
     and History*, ed. Doreen Waugh (Lerwick, 1996), pp.31-44.

27   Jessie M.E. Saxby, 'Harold's Grave' and 'Shetland Giants' in *Daala-Mist: or
     Stories of Shetland* (Edinburgh, 1876), pp.138-47; 187-91.

28   File of reviews, J.J.Haldane Burgess papers, Shetland Archives D2/73.

29   Shetland Archives, D2/73.

30   Vivian Bird, 'Back Again From the Dark', *New Shetlander* 43 (1956), 17-19.

31   Jack Renwick, 'The Shadowed Wave', *Scotia Review* 20 (1978), 52.

32   N.B. the raven's associations with Odin and the Valkyries.

33   Renwick, 'The Shadowed Wave', p.55.

34   Vedder, *Orcadian Sketches*, pp.119-27.

35   David Vedder, *Poems, Lyrics, and Sketches*, ed. Rev. George Gilfillan
     (Kirkwall, 1878), pp.1-5; 91-92.

36   David Balfour, Preface to *Ancient Orkney Melodies* (1885), reprinted with a
     Foreword by Howie Firth (Kirkwall, 1985), p.xvii. Songs I and II have no
     pagination.

37   Duncan J. Robertson, *Wraith and Wrack* (London, 1918), pp.60-65; 90-91;
     Robert Rendall, *Orkney Variants and Other Poems* (Kirkwall, 1951), pp.20, 38-
     39, 41, 42, 52. *An Anthology of Orkney Verse*, ed. Ernest Marwick (Kirkwall,
     1949), pp.117, 138-39, 163-64, 175-76.

38   Rendboe, I, 28.

39   J.J. Haldane Burgess, *Young Rasmie's Kit: A Book of Verse* (Lerwick, 1928),
     pp.26-46.

40   William J. Tait, *A Day Between Weathers: Collected Poems 1938-1978*,
     (Edinburgh, 1980), pp.72-76; Stella Sutherland, *Aa My Selves: Poems 1940-
     1980* (Lerwick, 1980), pp.9, 28.

41   John J. Hunter, *Taen wi da Trow* (Lerwick, 1952), pp.23-60, 210-43.

42   *Collected Poems*. All further references to 'Vagaland's' poems are to this edi-
     tion.

43   Rendall, 'Shore Tullye', *Orkney Variants*, p.20.

44   Jamieson, *Shoormal*, pp.56-57.

45   Muir, *An Autobiography*, pp.11-89.

46   Margery McCulloch, 'Edwin Muir and Scotland', *Akros* 16 No.47 (1981), 77.

47   Muir, *An Autobiography*, p.77; 'Returning to Orkney', File of papers in NLS,
     MS.19662, pp.45-61 (especially pp.56-60).

48   Notebook in NLS, MS. 19663; also quoted in P.H. Butter, *Edwin Muir: Man
     and Poet* (Edinburgh & London, 1966), p.289.

49   *The Complete Poems of Edwin Muir*, ed. P.H. Butter (Aberdeen, 1991), pp.69-
     70, 108-9; George Marshall, *In a Distant Isle: The Orkney Background of Edwin
     Muir* (Edinburgh, 1987), pp.19, 28.

50   Marshall, pp.53-54, 65-66.

51   E.g. Hrafnkel Hallfredsson in *Hrafnkel's Saga and Other Stories*, trans.
     Hermann Pálsson (Harmondsworth, 1971), pp.35-71.
52   Muir, *An Autobiography*, p.79.
53   George Mackay Brown, 'The Corn and the Tares', in *The Masked Fisherman
     and Other Stories* (London, 1989), pp.85-104.
54   Marshall, pp.9-10.
55   Willa Muir, *Belonging: A Memoir* (London, 1968), p.307.
56   Heather Hewitt, review of Marshall's *A Distant Isle* in *Scottish Literary
     Journal*, Supplement No.28 (1988), 16.
57   Edwin Muir, *Scottish Journey* (1935; London, 1985), pp.229-34.
58   Hewitt, p.16.
59   *Selected Letters of Edwin Muir*, ed. P.H. Butter (London, 1974), pp.64, 188-89.
60   George Mackay Brown, 'Edwin Muir at Newbattle', *Akros* 16 No.47 (1981),
     8.
61   Willa Muir, *Belonging*, pp.33-34; 48-49.
62   Willa Muir, *Belonging*, p.49.
63   Marshall illustrates in particular the influence of the farm, school, church,
     community and family.
64   Mackay Brown, 'Edwin Muir at Newbattle', p.7.
65   Lord Grimond, Introduction to Edwin Muir's *An Autobiography*, n.p.
66   Muir, *An Autobiography*, p.206.
67   Margery McCulloch, *Edwin Muir: Poet, Critic and Novelist* (Edinburgh,
     1993), p.95.
68   McCulloch, 'Edwin Muir and Scotland', p.67.

11. ERIC LINKLATER

One of Orkney's most famous sons is without doubt the novelist, playwright and historian Eric Linklater (1899-1973). His name has so long been associated with the islands that for many years it was naturally assumed that he was born there, an error in which Linklater acquiesced, and he only publicly corrected this when over seventy years of age.[1] Linklater was in fact born in Penarth, South Wales, and spent the first years of his childhood there. Nonetheless he was of very Orcadian roots: the Linklater name in the Orkneys can be traced back five centuries (it is first recorded in a Norwegian document from 1426) and Linklater's father had only left the islands in pursuit of his career in the Merchant Navy. Linklater's associations with Scandinavia and the sea were strengthened by the fact that his maternal grandfather had been a Swedish sailor, and, as Michael Parnell comments, it was this 'special combination of circumstances that gave him a particularly potent inheritance of Norse blood'.[2] Linklater's mother, though not a native Orcadian, loved the islands deeply, and from 1906 onwards she and her children always spent their summer vacations in Orkney. Linklater's father eventually built a house, Ingleneuk, on Loch Harray, Mainland, and the family moved permanently to Orkney in 1909. Apart from Linklater's school and University days in Aberdeen, his military service in the Great War, his sojourns in India and America in the mid-1920s, and brief spells of journalism in London and Edinburgh, Orkney was to remain Linklater's home base until 1947 when he and his family moved to Easter Ross. Moreover as a youth, when he became old enough to understand such things, Linklater came to realise that, despite his birth in Wales, he had been conceived in Orkney, a fact which never failed to appeal to both his pride and his sense of humour. Thus by blood, temperament, and

many years' residence, Linklater firmly established his claim to be
a true Orcadian.

Linklater's strong sense of his Orcadian identity and the pervasive Norse ambience of the islands' history and culture naturally
led him to take an active interest in Orkney's Golden Age of Viking
earls and saints. At an early age he had soon 'read, and been captured by, the Saga of the Earls of Orkney'[3] and from there it was but
a short step to the major Family Sagas of medieval Iceland, especially *Njal's Saga*, *Laxdaela Saga*, *Egil's Saga*, and *Grettir's Saga*. He
had such a burning interest in Old Norse history and culture that
even at the age of fourteen he was buying and poring over such
academic works as Craigie's *The Icelandic Sagas* and Mawer's *The
Vikings*.[4]

Linklater's fascination with Viking history and culture had a profound influence on his character and imagination. He was especially excited by the historian Storer Clouston's theory that, through
Ingibjorg, the wife of Sigurd of Westness (fl. 1136), the Linklaters
might originally be descended from Earl Thorfinn the Mighty and
King Malcolm II of Scotland.[5] He consciously cultivated his sense
of Orcadian and Norse origins, and in many articles, speeches, and
books he drew attention to the fact that Norse blood and Norse
characteristics were still dominant in the islands. Even in his own
personal life he was fond of making emphatic gestures about his
ancestry; thus he renamed his house the more Norse-sounding
Merkister and gave two of his children the traditional Norse names
of Magnus and Kristin. More dramatically and hilariously, he per-
suaded a group of visiting Norwegians to make a toast to the memory of a totally fictitious Linklater relative, Asgrim Bare-back, who
had supposedly perished at the Battle of Clontarf in 1014![6]

The most important result of Linklater's love of Orkney's Norse
past, however, can be seen in the number of his books so perva-
sively influenced by Old Norse history and culture. Linklater's
Norse-inspired works were published in two distinct periods, 1921-
38 and 1955-68. What is most noteworthy is that they appeared in a
variety of forms: contemporary and historical novels, short stories,
poetry, history books, drama, and journalism, and that some of his
own personal beliefs and values were perhaps moulded by his conception of the Viking ethos.

Nationalist and Novelist 1921-38

Linklater's Norse-inspired work in this period can be divided into two categories: on the one hand poetry, drama, lectures, speeches and an historical novel on Viking history, and on the other, contemporary novels of twentieth-century life in Orkney and Scotland with Old Norse themes and motifs. In order to facilitate a more cohesive critical approach, the works will be studied in these categories rather than in simple chronological order.

His historical works begin in 1921 with a slight but dramatic poem on the Orcadian Viking Sveinn Asleifarson (consistently spelt Sweyn Asleifsson by Linklater)[7] and they end in 1937 with a pageant (co-authored with J. Storer Clouston) to celebrate the eight hundredth anniversary of the founding of St. Magnus Cathedral in Kirkwall. The pageant was performed outdoors in Orkney on 29 July 1937, and was a resounding success involving over 1,200 actors, singers, musicians, helpers, producers, and organisers. Linklater took part in the pageant himself, reading aloud the prologues introducing each scene.[8]

The most strikingly important, Norse-inspired work of this period, however, is *The Men of Ness*, published in 1932, clearly a very personal tribute to the early Vikings of Orkney and the medieval sagas of the Icelanders. Apart from Linklater's need to express imaginatively just how deeply he felt the Norse spirit to be a part of Orkney and himself, there were two other factors which inspired him to create this twentieth-century version of a saga. Firstly, in the early 1930s Linklater had become very involved in Scottish Nationalism and a belief in Scotland's Norse identity. In one of his autobiographic volumes Linklater relates how he passionately discussed with his friend 'Francis Meiklejohn' (Moray McLaren) possible policies for a revitalised Scotland based on 'the Celtic ethos' and the 'Norse propulsion'. Linklater, being more interested in the latter, positively asserted that Scotland could borrow and learn most from Scandinavia. He had been especially impressed by the dictum of the German philosopher Herder ('Study the superstitions and the sagas of the forefathers') and how such a policy had inspired the Irish renaissance and the works of W.B. Yeats, Lady Gregory and Douglas Hyde.[9] Linklater's natural response to this was to write a novel on the Norse ancestors of Orkney. Thus in the

context of the Norse/Celtic debate and the contemporary fascination with historical and racial origins, already noted in the works of
Gibbon, Mitchison and Gunn (in particular the latter's Viking
novel, *Sun Circle*), *The Men of Ness* is not perhaps such an unusual
departure for Linklater as has sometimes been claimed. As a
Scottish novelist and a nationalist he was very much within the tradition of that particular time.

Linklater was certainly determined to 'make Scotland Viking-
conscious', as he expressed it in a letter to Wren Howard.[10] Thus he
was able to use material from his research for his novel to write two
papers on Norse subjects which he read at the Universities of
Glasgow, Aberdeen, and St. Andrews: 'The Story of Kari
Solmundarson' and 'The Unafraid: A General Paper on the Sagas';
he was also asked to broadcast a lecture for the BBC on 'The Norse
Influence in Scotland' in December 1932.[11]

However inspiring this historical motive may have been, there
was a second important influence on Linklater's decision to write a
Viking novel: his personal interest in the Norse ethos and his interpretation of what he believed to be an aesthetic evaluation of action
behind the Viking way of life. In preparing for the novel Linklater
re-read most of the sagas and 'gradually became aware of their
deeper content':

> At work in Viking times – or so I thought – had been a superior
> motive that showed itself in a code of behaviour dominated, not
> primarily by a prospect of material gain, but by wish or determi-
> nation idealistically conceived – by those who later won and
> deserved the saga-writers' regard – to complete an action in accor-
> dance with a pattern that was artistically satisfying.[12]

This theory of an aesthetic appreciation of conduct is vital to an
understanding of Linklater's *The Men of Ness* and was to inspire
much of his historical writing in the 1950s and 60s, as we shall see.

The Men of Ness

The Men of Ness is set in late ninth-century Orkney and is the story
of Kol and Skallagrim, the sons of Thorleif Coalbiter. Thorleif is a
son of the legendary Ragnar Hairybreeks who, on finding a life of

Viking raids distasteful, decides to settle down in Orkney and marry Signy, the divorced wife of his brother, the infamous Ivar the Boneless (the slayer of St. Edmund). Ivar had previously won Signy to wife through the simple expedient of killing her first husband, Bui of Ness, for which he paid her a weregild of a gold armband. On being divorced, however, Signy contemptuously returns the armband and so Bui of Ness becomes once more 'unatoned'. The remainder of the novel describes the growing to manhood of Thorleif's and Signy's two sons, Kol and Skallagrim, their various adventures, both in Orkney and abroad, and their mother's implacable determination that they should one day avenge the death of her first husband. Finally, more than twenty years after Bui's death, Kol and Skallagrim, on a Viking expedition, are ship-wrecked with their men on the coast of Northumbria, near to Ivar's stronghold, and in a bloody and suicidal climax they bring about Ivar's death – and Signy's revenge – but at the cost of their own lives and the lives of all their men bar one. The sole survivor, the comical and cowardly Gauk, an Orkney peasant, eventually returns home with news of the exploit. The novel then ends, somewhat depressingly perhaps, with Signy contemplating revenge for Kol and Skallagrim and 'ever urging all the men in the house to be out-doors and fighting'.[13]

As an historical novel and a recreation of a medieval literary form, Linklater's *The Men of Ness* is quite clearly a *tour de force*. His imitation of the saga style of writing with its austere simplicity, short pithy sentences and blunt dialogue, often with witty and cryptic aphorisms, is by far the most successful of its kind. It avoids the pitfalls of many previous saga-novels of overarchaic language, unbelievable plots and overtly sentimental, laudatory or didactic tones, to present vividly the essence of saga writing: a deceptively simple and bleak prose pregnant with compressed meaning and implication. The basic plot is very credible and convincing (the two supernatural scenes involving ghosts are conventional and accept-able within a saga context) and told in traditional saga manner: Kol's and Skallagrim's family background and early life and adven-tures are developed in detail before they eventually set out on the expedition which ends in the revenge killing of the murderer of their mother's first husband. Some of the incidents may seem irrel-

evant to the main story, but they are in fact essential to a full understanding of Kol's and Skallagrim's personalities and attitudes.

The most effective means by which Linklater creates his saga
ambience, however, is the very imaginative and skillful way in
which he blends historical characters, such as King Harald Finehair
of Norway and Earl Rognvald of More, with many themes and
events borrowed from the Icelandic sagas themselves. Linklater's
later claim that 'no-one – at the time of which I am writing – had
thought of pillaging the Icelandic sagas for such a tale'[14] is not correct, however. R.M. Ballantyne and Rider Haggard had both used a
'mosaic' adaptation of saga incidents as has already been noted.
Furthermore Linklater's own publisher, Jonathan Cape, had recently published E.R. Eddison's *Styrbjorn the Strong* (1926), an imaginative reconstruction of the life of Styrbjorn Olafsson based on various sagas, especially the *Jómsvíkinga Saga*. Linklater may well have
been completely unaware of Eddison's novel, but it is an interesting coincidence nonetheless, particularly bearing in mind that
Linklater himself adapts the decapitation scene from the
Jómsvíkinga Saga for the climax of his own novel. Marjorie
Linklater's claim that the novel is for the most part 'pure Linklater
invention'[15] is thus not really accurate, for many of the characters'
attributes and deeds are borrowed wholesale from the Icelandic
sagas. A careful study of four of the major sagas, *Njal's Saga*,
Laxdaela Saga, *Egil's Saga* and *Grettir's Saga*, reveals just how extensively and cleverly Linklater has 'pillaged' them for his novel.

Perhaps the most important source for *The Men of Ness* is *Njal's
Saga*, not least in that the latter's lawyer and arbitrator, Njal, and his
violent sons, especially Skarphedinn, are clearly models for the
novel's wise counsellor and peace-lover, Thorleif, and his aggressive sons, Skallagrim and Kol. Even more notable is that one of the
novel's important characters, Gauk of Calfskin, is most certainly
based on Bjorn of Mork in *Njal's Saga*; this Bjorn, although clearly a
silly boaster and buffoon, turns out to be of inestimable service to
the saga's avenging hero, Kari Solmundarson, as he protects the latter's back during skirmishes – though careful to take no personal
risks (Chs.148-52, pp.329-39).[16] The parallel to Gauk's relationship
to Kol is evident. Furthermore, the saga's other hero, Gunnar of
Hlidarend, has a faithful guard-dog, Sam, which is probably the

inspiration for Gauk's dog Bran. *Njal's Saga* also provides a model for other minor incidents in *The Men of Ness*; Thjostolf smashes a boat to prevent his being pursued by Thorvald's men (Ch.12, p.60), while in the novel Ivar the Boneless has Signy's boat destroyed so that she has no option but to remain with him and become his wife (MN, 12). In the saga Thrainn Sigfusson divorces his wife at a wedding-feast in order to marry a beautiful young woman (Ch.34, p.96), and in the novel Thorkel Neb does exactly the same at Erling and Hallgerda's wedding (MN, 115-16). The saga's version of the Battle of Clontarf contains the incident when the triumphant victors come across Thorstein Hallsson calmly tying up his shoe thongs. On being asked why he does not flee, he replies: '"I cannot reach home tonight, for my home is out in Iceland"' (Ch.157, p.348). In *The Men of Ness*, Fridleif, one of Kol's crewmen, when offered the chance to try and run from his executioners, replies: '"I am at home out in Birsay, and that is too far for me to run to-day"' (MN, 210). Thorstein is spared in the saga, but Linklater is not so merciful in his novel, and Fridleif is beheaded as are most of the others. This whole scene – the men being questioned and beheaded one by one – is taken directly from the *Jómsvíkinga Saga*.[17] In the saga, too, one of the victims tricks one of his executioners into holding his hair, and when the axe falls pulls his head back sharply so that the axe shears off the hands of the enemy instead of the head of the victim. Linklater has Kol employ the same trick to bring about the death of Ivar the Boneless (MN, 214-15) and so gain Signy's revenge at last.

Two important events in *The Men of Ness* are clearly taken from *Grettir's Saga*: Kol's tricking of the Viking pirate Starkad and his men into entering a warehouse, where they are locked in and later killed by the members of the household as they try to break out (MN, 60-67), closely parallels Grettir's method of disposing of the two villains Thorir Paunch and Ogmund the Bad in the saga (Ch.19, pp.46-54).[18] Moreover Kol's wrestling match with the ghost of Geira (MN, 77-80) and her curse on him as the moon shines on her face – by which he is always overcome with fear in bright moonlight – is based in almost every detail, including the three-night wait, on Grettir's struggle with the monster Glam and the spell the latter casts on him (Ch.35, pp.95-100). There are other echoes, too.

The howe-breaking of Ivar the Boneless (MN, 16-20) is reminiscent of Grettir's incursion into the howe of Kar the Old (Ch.18, pp.42-45). Kol's wounding of Hoskuld of Aikerness during a horse-fight (MN, 50) parallels Grettir's injuring of Odd in similar circumstances (Ch.29, pp.78-80). Kol's and Skallagrim's pranks on the same Hoskuld when they were young (MN, 43-45) also seem reminiscent of Grettir's childish tricks on his father (Ch.14, pp.26-31). Hoskuld's ignominious rout by the mad berserker (MN, 42) is probably modelled on Gisli's hilarious flight from Grettir in the saga (Ch.59, pp.155-60).

The next most important saga as a source for *The Men of Ness* is undoubtedly *Egil's Saga*, not least in that the characters and features of the two brothers, Kol and Skallagrim, (one fair and handsome, the other dark and ugly) seem to be based on the saga's two brothers Egil and Thorolf. Egil's father's name was also Skallagrim (Ch.20, p.56).[19] Egil's grandfather, Kveldulf, was buried at sea, but his coffin floated ashore in Iceland (Ch.27, pp.72-73), an incident which may have inspired Linklater's rather gruesome vision of Reidar of Wasdale's body floating on the surface of the sea and following the *Skua* for a couple of days (MN, 162-63). The *Skua's* shipwreck on the shores of the Humber (MN, 165-70) as a result of winds conjured up by the implacable Signy, mother to Kol and Skallagrim, is quite obviously based on Egil's shipwreck in the same place as a result of the curse laid on him by the vindictive Queen Gunnhild (Ch.59, pp.151-52).

Laxdaela Saga is yet another work which provides Linklater with more minor incidents for his Viking novel. Thorolf's killing of Hall over the division of a catch of fish (Ch.14, pp.69-70)[20] could well have been the source for the murder of Bui of Ness by Ivar the Boneless (MN, 9-10) – the very incident which proves the starting point of the novel's basic story of revenge. The swimming games during which Kol nearly drowns his own serf (MN, 46) are clearly modelled on those of Kjartan Olafsson and King Olaf Tryggvason in the saga (Ch.40, pp.144-45). A merchant called Gilli the Russian makes a brief but vital appearance in the saga (Ch.12, pp.64-65), and Linklater appears to have used his name and profession as the basis for his own Gilli the Chapman in *The Men of Ness*. Finally, the fateful sword 'Legbiter' with which Bolli slays his blood-brother

Kjartan (Ch.49, p.175) is appropriated by Linklater, perhaps with deliberate irony, for his comic character Gauk.

As all the above evidence indicates, therefore, *The Men of Ness* is a magnificent illustration of Linklater's intimate knowledge of the sagas – and the imaginative way he plunders them. The novel was published in November 1932 to a rather cool reception from Linklater's readership, however. The 'blood and guts' adventures of ninth-century Vikings were indeed a far cry from the zany and zestful antics of *Juan in America*, his best-seller from 1931. Not only the subject matter but also the style – the deliberate imitation of an Icelandic saga – was too unusual for modern taste. The novel was enthusiastically received by reviewers in the United States, but as Linklater ruefully reported: 'on the very same day as America went off gold, and nobody bought it'. He also rather peevishly commented that:

> … only five people in the Old World really liked it: Edward Garnett, a professor of English literature, a mountainous warrant officer in the Royal Navy, an Icelandic reviewer, and a schoolboy who for a whole week-end divided his attention between it and stump-cricket.[21]

This is a gross exaggeration of the facts, however. The novel did receive some good contemporary reviews; one very original aspect of the novel was especially singled out: the long and dramatic description of the sea journey of the *Skua* from Orkney to the Humber through a violent storm and days of drifting helplessly in the North Sea. As Linklater has himself remarked, none of the sagas relates such sea-journeys because to the Vikings seafaring 'was what office-life and office-work are to suburbia in our time, and did not call for description'.[22] The physical discomfort of Kol and Skallagrim and their men, their frayed tempers and the series of quarrels, deaths and accidents through desperation and insanity (caused by drinking sea-water) as the *Skua* drifts in the cold and hostile immensity of the North Sea are vividly and memorably portrayed by Linklater. Indeed this part of the novel often recalls to mind Coleridge's 'The Ancient Mariner' and, as Storm Jameson rightly comments, is 'a magnificent piece of writing, and to be added to the great sea-pieces in our literature'.[23] Although *The Men of Ness* was no bestseller on the scale of *Juan in America*, it still sold nine thousand copies within a year and was reissued in 1959 as a paperback. In translation the novel was a great success in Scandinavia and Linklater was visited by many Scandinavian academics in the following years. Indeed the novel also inspired Frans G. Bengtsson, Linklater's Swedish translator, to write his very successful Viking novel *The Long Ships*.[24]

Nonetheless it is true to say that, with a few exceptions, the novel has never received as much critical acclaim as Linklater desired, and this was a great disappointment to him. Some of the reasons for this are not hard to find, for even fifty years after its publication critics still seem somewhat uncertain as to how to approach the work. As F.R. Hart warily comments: 'There is no critical language for the novel applicable to the terse matter-of-factness of *The Men of Ness*'. Other critical interpretations seem to be very general or evasive, and in some instances seem rather contradictory. Thus R. Watson sees the novel as 'a bare saga of Viking fate', whilst Kurt Wittig makes a very general comparison of it with Neil Gunn's *Sun Circle* and then claims: 'Neither is really an historical novel: rather they are both groping towards a mythology of the events which made the forefathers of their race'. According to Hart the novel's motives 'are limited to fame, property, security, and, most of all, atonement', whereas Parnell claims the novel underlines the values of 'love, friendship, companionship and courage'.[25]

All in all, the apparent lack of critical acclaim for *The Men of Ness* is perhaps due to two main factors: the success of Linklater's saga style and the ultimately ambiguous nature of his concept of Norse heroism. That the success of Linklater's imitation of the style of a saga should also be a weakness is a sadly ironic but plausible supposition. For readers of the novel who have no previous knowledge of Old Norse literature it may well be too remote and incomprehensible, especially in contrast to Linklater's very successful use of idiomatic English in *Juan in America*, when dealing with a more familiar subject, Prohibition America in the 1920s. Nonetheless, knowledgeable readers of *The Men of Ness* will certainly admire Linklater's skill in weaving together many saga themes and incidents to create his own 'saga', but this does have one serious drawback: it is almost impossible for them to believe in Kol and Skallagrim as 'real' characters in fictional terms. As shown above, many of their physical attributes, aspects of their characters and most of their deeds are borrowed wholesale from other characters and events in the Icelandic sagas. Thus Kol and Skallagrim are not genuine literary creations but accumulations or summaries of the fictional and imaginative skills of thirteenth-century Icelandic authors/scribes. In this context it is notable that the part of the novel most frequently praised by critics is the sea-journey of the *Skua*, which is Linklater's own original contribution to the story and not based on any saga. A knowledgeable reader's response to the novel may thus be limited to an admiration of Linklater's structural craftmanship in selecting and organising his material. One is not necessarily impressed by any inherent credibility or effectiveness of the novel's characterisation. The success of the form may thus be seen, ironically, as detracting from the integrity of the content.

Linklater himself seems to have come to a similar conclusion when analysing what he sees as the novel's failure nearly forty years later, for he states that the writing of *The Men of Ness* was 'the moment when I forfeited all claim to be recognised as a serious novelist'. He refused to develop a personal style, but instead experimented with many different forms, like the Scottish 'makars' of the sixteenth century who had 'let their subject call the tune, and found words and a style suitable for the music'. With hindsight, Linklater later argued that all true novelists 'shaped and subdued their material to conform with their own temper and understanding ... they set their own mark on what they created'. Linklater's variety of styles, including his brilliant reproduction of a saga, clearly fails to do this. Thus, he maintains, if a true novelist 'is one who imposes himself on all he writes, then I am no novelist'.[26] This may seem unduly harsh self-criticism, depending on whether or not one agrees with Linklater's definition of a novelist, but it certainly corroborates what I have already suggested, that the stylistic success of the novel can also be seen as one of its flaws.

The other major flaw in Linklater's conception of *The Men of Ness* lies in the ambivalence of the novel's ending. Indeed the novel appears to have two endings: a Norse one and a contemporary one. As Linklater later revealed, he intended the novel to be a literary presentation of his theory of the aesthetic appreciation of action as being the driving force behind the Norse ethos.

> Judge conduct by an aesthetic standard – as in the Icelandic sagas it is judged – and heroism becomes life in significant form. The hero is not admirable because he has saved his Colonel's skin, or held the bridge to Rome, but because he has been willing to accept a conclusion to his life that is in conformity with his character or function. He has achieved a pattern.[27]

In Old Norse terms, the climax of the novel is thus the killing of Ivar the Boneless by Kol and Skallagrim. Despite their deaths, the two brothers are clearly the heroes, for they have achieved a pattern by finally avenging Bui of Ness. They never actively sought out Ivar the Boneless in order to exact revenge, but confronted with the opportunity, no matter how hopeless or difficult, there was no way in which they would want to avoid their destiny. Had they not fool-hardily attacked Ivar and his men there would have been no hon-our or glory, no pattern, no story, no *The Men of Ness*.

This Norse interpretation is significantly weakened by two main factors, however. Firstly, Linklater's theory is nowhere explicitly stated within the novel itself but only very obliquely implied; and secondly, there is the more contemporary ending and interpretation of the novel: survival is all that matters. *The Men of Ness* does not actually end with the deaths of Kol and Skallagrim, but with Gauk's returning to Orkney to relate the events. In these final scenes there is a sense of tragic futility. Kol's and Skallagrim's suc-cess in avenging Bui of Ness achieves absolutely nothing in practi-cal terms, indeed their absence from Orkney has led to their family being driven out of Ness altogether. Signy's obsession with the question of who is to avenge Kol and Skallagrim now seems to invite a tiresome cycle of neverending and pointless bloodshed. Moreover the only survivor of Kol's and Skallagrim's expedition is the least heroic character in the novel: Gauk of Calfskin. Many crit-ics have indeed commented on this point. Roderick Watson states that 'it is significant that it is the "little man", Gauk, who survives when grim heroes die at the end', and Isobel Murray also draws attention to 'the anti-hero, the small man, the hen-pecked, artful survivor who returns home when all the heroes are dead'. Marjorie Linklater also refers to Gauk as the anti-hero of the novel who 'possesses essential qualities for survival – endurance and wit', and Francis Hart believes that 'it is on the archaic will to survive that his [Linklater's] notions of heroism ultimately focus'.[28] As a soldier, Gauk is clearly in the tradition of Shakespeare's Falstaff and Scott's Cuddie Headrigg, and is clearly a prototype of Linklater's own contemporary artful survivor: the eponymous Private Angelo. In this sense Gauk is an original character in an Old Norse context whose implications are more far-reaching than those of the original model from *Njal's Saga*, Bjorn of Mork.

If all the above is true, however, it would seem that Linklater's story contradicts his own theory. One alternative interpretation of Gauk's character remains, perhaps. He is not important simply because he *survives*, but because he *survives to tell the story*. In this sense Gauk is fulfilling an important role within Linklater's theory of the aesthetic basis of the Norse ethos, for it is Gauk's telling of the story of Kol's and Skallagrim's deeds which ensures that their honour and valour will survive for posterity and that they have gained a Noreseman's finest achievement: membership of Valhalla and a 'place in the story'. Nonetheless, this interpretation is perhaps too esoteric, especially for a twentieth-century audience. The contrast between the brave but doomed heroes and the cowardly but cunning survivor can, of course, be seen as a highly ironic comment on the realities of existence. But it is perhaps Linklater's lack of an unambiguous answer to his own complex question of conduct which has prevented *The Men of Ness* from earning any lasting critical acclaim.

'Wineland'

A literary by-product of Linklater's *The Men of Ness* is the short story 'Wineland'[29] retelling the story of the Norse discovery of America and the first attempts at a settlement there. As mentioned earlier, in connection with Lewis Grassic Gibbon's treatment of the same subject, there are two major and sometimes contradictory sources for these events: *The Greenlanders' Saga* and *Eirik's Saga*. In 'Wineland' Linklater presents a very interesting and streamlined version of the sagas by relying almost entirely on *The Greenlanders'*

Saga. The first part of the story is thus a straightforward retelling of the saga with an additional and more detailed description of the German Dirk (spelled Tyrker in the saga), who discovers the grapes in America ('Wineland', pp.62-63).

The final two parts of the story present a very interesting and imaginative conflation of the two sagas. *The Greenlanders' Saga* has two final expeditions to Vinland as previously noted: one by Thorfinn Karlsefni and his wife Gudrid (on which their son was born), and one by Freydis, Leif's sister, and two brothers, Helgi and Finnbogi, which ends in the massacre of the brothers and their men on the orders of Freydis. *Eirik's Saga*, however, states that Thorfinn's expedition was the last one and that Freydis also took part in it, but there is no reference to Helgi and Finnbogi or any massacre. Linklater merges these two traditions in his story, i.e. Freydis *and the brothers* accompany Thorfinn and the massacre takes place once Thorfinn and Gudrid have returned to Greenland leaving the others behind. Linklater indeed presents the dissension amongst the Norsemen as being caused by the rivalry between Gudrid and Freydis; the former has been prophesied a very noble and illustrious future, and the latter is the sister of Leif, the very man who first landed in America. They both thus see themselves as the 'First Lady' of the new settlement. When it becomes clear that Thorfinn and Gudrid intend returning to Greenland, Linklater has Freydis accuse them of weakening the defences of the settlement against the Skraelings, the hostile native inhabitants. Finbow (Linklater's anglicisation of Finnbogi) agrees with Freydis, '"for if we were all friendly together, and made common cause, we would have nothing to fear from the Skraelings"' ('Wineland', p.74). But he refuses to help Freydis prevent Thorfinn's and Gudrid's departure by the brutal expedient of murdering them. Freydis is incensed by this refusal, and once Thorfinn and his group have left, she vindictively plots against Helgi and Finbow and eventually encourages her husband to murder them and all their men as in *The Greenlanders' Saga*.

Linklater's conflation of the endings of the two sagas has no basis in historical sources, but does present a clever and intriguing hypothesis as to the reason for the suicidal dissension amongst the Norse settlers. Some readers may well be offended by Linklater's apparent misogyny in putting the blame on female jealousy, but murderous female rivalry is not an unusual element in the sagas,[30] and in *The Greenlanders' Saga* Freydis is indeed responsible for the heinous crime of mass murder. Apart from sheer perversity, there seems to be no real motivation behind these killings, and it is this which Linklater tries to provide through the use of artistic license. To the bare bones of the sagas Linklater has thus 'added a flavour uniquely his own, exemplified in his management of the confused details of the originals'.[31] His version of the attempted settlement of America may or may not be historically accurate, but it certainly presents an artistically unified, coherent and explicable series of events which leaves the reader pondering over the vicissitudes of human behaviour and the loss of opportunity. In this sense Linklater's 'Wineland' is much more satisfying than Grassic Gibbon's version of the story in *Nine Against the Unknown*. In addition, Linklater's thesis is narratively presented in a detached style, whereas Gibbon's is put forward in a blatantly biased manner and arbitrarily shaped to comply with his Diffusionist ideas and pre-conceived views of Norse history.

It is only fair to note, however, that there may well be at least one ulterior motive behind Linklater's version of the story. 'Wineland' is clearly meant to suggest that it was dissension, treachery and racial fratricide which brought about the end of the Norse settlement in America and not simply the threat from the native inhabitants. The very next story after 'Wineland' in *God Likes Them Plain* is the magnificent 'The Duke', Linklater's brilliant and caustic condemnation of the Highland Clearances, and in particular the part played by the clan leaders in betraying their own people. It must be borne in mind that these stories were written in the 1930s when the Norse/Celtic debate and the wrangling between various factions of the Scottish Nationalist movement were at their height. In this context it could well be, therefore, that 'Wineland' was not simply a piece of Norse-inspired historical fiction, but also an oblique comment on some of the possible causes of Scotland's lack of political and racial unity in the mid-1930s.

As mentioned above, a further important feature of Linklater's Norse-inspired works are his contemporary novels with Old Norse themes or motifs. These are especially notable in two of his early novels dealing with Orkney: *White-maa's Saga* (1929) and *Magnus Merriman* (1934). Indeed a comparison of these two novels reveals some interesting contrasts and changes in Linklater's use of Norse themes which reflect changes in the author's own attitudes towards the world and his art.

White-maa's Saga

Like many a first novel, *White-maa's Saga* is based on the author's own experience and background. The hero, Peter Flett, is an Orcadian who, after serving in France in the Great War, returns to Inverdoon (a fictional Aberdeen) and medical studies at the University – all exactly as Linklater himself had done. Many obvious features of the novel draw attention to its 'Norse' inspiration, not least its very title as a saga. Peter Flett is presented to us as very much a modern-day Viking: tall, blond with an almost white moustache, powerfully built (cf. Linklater's own appearance), and generally placid if not melancholic, but with a tendency to go 'berserk' on occasion (either in the boxing-ring or at a brawl at the County Fair) and with an impulsive and reckless attraction for women. To make sure that no one can possibly miss the point, Linklater has Flett's friend Mackay specifically address him as a Viking on several occasions. Flett himself, of course, is very conscious of his Norse inheritance which seems to have a very direct influence on his character and fate. His love for the sea is very clearly meant to be the very kernel of his Norse heritage, as is revealed in a lyrical decription he gives Patricia of the pleasures of fishing and as emphasised by Linklater's personal panegyric to the ocean, 'the mother and mistress of earth', and to the Norsemen who traversed it (WMS, 43, 77-78).[32] Flett's fate seems even more pronounced by the fact that his father, grandfather, and great-grandfather all died at sea in various parts of the world: the Arctic Circle, Mauritius, and the Skaggerak (WMS, 33). Like many a self-respecting Viking they had roamed the oceans and not died of old-age in bed. Going to sea is thus in Flett's blood and all his early plans, including his medical studies, are centred on eventually living an easy life at sea (WMS, 34).

Flett's conscious identification with his Norse ancestry is in itself an important aspect of his character, for in moments of depression, anger, or elation he often thinks back to his Viking forefathers in search of some comfort, guidance or inspiration. In a euphoric and magnanimous mood after losing a boxing bout to a Hebridean in an inter-varsity match, for example, he finds solace and enjoyment in a good-humoured and enthusiastic discussion of their respective Orcadian and Hebridean ancestors with his erstwhile opponent (WMS, 50). It is noteworthy, however, that his opponent is 'a genial natural fighter' from Lewis (WMS, 47) whose name, MacSween, is of Norse origins ('Son of Sveinn'). In a more petulant and alcoholic frame of mind Flett's views on Norse and Celtic history can give way to more aggressive thoughts and emotional prejudices, as at the Celtic Society Dinner in Inverdoon, where his pride in his Norse ancestry turns into contempt for Celtic attitudes and culture. As we shall see, Linklater himself was prone to this prejudiced view of Scotland's Gaelic-speaking community, and one suspects that many of Flett's thoughts on the Celts are also Linklater's own:

> These Celts took themselves too seriously, both drunk and sober. You had to be of their mood, whether tearful or hilarious, or they quarrelled with you. Someone was singing a wailing song of the Hebrides now. Oh, damn their Celtic twilight, Peter thought. Thank God, I'm Norse. We knocked the stuffing out of them pretty thoroughly in the Viking years. They were probably boasting a Celtic renascence then, and the Vikings, not liking their poetry, went to tell them so. (WMS, 175)

The evening ends with Flett insulting two Highlanders (WMS, 177) and thus indirectly causing a brawl during which he and his friends slip away.

Even when courting Flett expresses his feelings and desires in terms of his Viking ancestry. In a playful and romantic mood with Patricia Geddes, he once jokingly remarks that '"if this had been a few hundred years ago I should have picked you up and thrown you into a boat without worrying ... and followed the sun"' (WMS, 65). Ironically enough, this is exactly what he does do with his second love, Norna Sabiston. After killing Isaac Skea in self-defence, he picks up Norna and carries her to the boat where they make love and then sail towards the newly rising sun – and, eventually, a new life in Canada (WMS, 280-84).

Perhaps Flett's supreme moment of identification with his Norse forefathers comes with the slightly improbable but nonetheless eerie scene at the Viking Stone late at night on his native Orcadian isle. This stone had once had a cross carved on it by marauding Vikings many centuries before, but during a recent thunderstorm it had been struck by lightning and the cross partly defaced. The superstitious local people, including Flett's sister, Martin, had been disturbed by this portent and their fears had soon been realised when the bloody carcasses of lambs, their throats cut, had been found mysteriously dumped at the foot of the stone. Late one night, Flett is walking past the Standing Stones when his dog Pickles disturbs Daft Sammy, the local half-wit, performing the grotesque ritual slaughter of a lamb in front of the Viking Stone. The poor half-wit flees in terror and Flett is left with the unenviable task of disposing of the lamb's carcass and revealing the truth to the local community. Flett quickly realises, however, that he cannot expose Daft Sammy's moonlight madness as it would only lead to the half-wit being ostracised and becoming even more deeply and lastingly insane and finally incarcered in an institution. Sammy has to be prevented from repeating his disgusting activities, nonetheless. It was at this crisis point that Flett has a brilliant inspiration:

> An idea, like a flicker of moonlight, came to him. Superstition had given birth to madness and fear; superstition might kill them. The Vikings' symbol that had quietened the Vikings' fear was easy to draw. He felt the knife in his pocket and turned back to the Stone Circle. (WMS, 269)

Exactly as a Norseman had done centuries before – and for exactly the same reasons – Flett carves a cross into the pagan stone.

It is not only the characterisation of Peter Flett which reveals Old Norse influences on Linklater's fiction, however, for as Parnell states, the very title of the novel 'necessitated the provision and extension of saga elements',[33] and this can be traced in various aspects of the structure of *White-maa's Saga*. As for many a former Viking, Orkney provides a safe haven for Flett after adventures and defeats in the outside world. His fighting at political meetings and at the County Fair reveal a Viking propensity to go 'berserk', whilst his boxing matches are an updated and stylised version of the Norse 'holmgangs' or man-to-man duels within a specifically limited territory. Flett's experiences at the Viking Stone (described above) are clearly meant to be the 'supernatural' element of the novel paralleling those of the Icelandic sagas. Moreover, as with the heroes in sagas, Flett's life is bound up with a prophecy. In the Icelandic sagas prophecies were often presented in dreams which a person with the requisite skill would interpret, sometimes rather cryptically. In *White-maa's Saga* Linklater modernises this medieval convention by making his spaewife a typical gypsy-like fortune-teller, Nelly Macafie, who will read one's palm for the traditional silver coin. Nelly reads Flett's palm at the County Fair and foresees death 'and a fine white girl beside him, and the running sea and a dark sky' (WMS, 103). Despite Nelly's unprepossessing character and appearance, her predictions turn out to be true and help form a neat conclusion to the novel, for the prophecy having been fulfilled, Flett is freed from the spaewife's 'fate' to pursue his other one – a life with Norna Sabiston.

This Orkney girl who finally captivates Flett is clearly named after the Norns of Old Norse mythology (the three virgin goddesses of fate who predestine the lives of both gods and mortals) and is obviously meant to be Flett's 'fate'. Moreover Norna's character seems partly based on the fierce and haughty heroines of some Icelandic sagas: she is handsome, quick-tempered, and very proud, or 'maist aaful bigsy' as her neighbours put it (WMS, 80). Like many of her saga counterparts she has many would-be suitors who, in a twentieth-century context, come 'running in the night', or wooing by moonlight with the aid of a ladder at the young woman's bedroom window. All who attempt such activities are scornfully rejected by Norna, and Flett, too, receives short shrift when he climbs through her bedroom window late at night (WMS, 111-13). Like many a saga hero, Flett has to prove his worth to the heroine before she will give herself to him.

In *White-maa's Saga* this climax is reached when Flett rescues Norna from rape at the hands of Skea and kills the latter in the ensuing fight. He then carries Norna to the safety of his boat where he claims, and receives, his reward: '"You're mine," he said huskily. "I want you. I've fought for you; killed for you. Norna, you're mine"' (WMS, 282). This may well be intended as a true Viking sentiment, but in this rather melodramatic context Flett's importunate statement smacks more of a crude caveman-like chauvinism. The fight between Flett and Skea, with its descriptions of the bright moonlight, Skea's huge size, and the way Flett falls on top of him, is very reminiscent of the fatal struggle between Grettir and Glam in *Grettir's Saga*. So as to 'justify' Flett's killing of Skea (apart from self-defence), Linklater has, earlier in the novel, rather disingenuously made it clear that Skea is himself a murderer, being responsible, during the war, for the death of one Tommy Bruce (WMS, 130). His own death at the hands of Flett is thus rather crudely presented as a kind of divine retribution.

White-maa's Saga, as a first novel, has its obvious faults, not least its rather contrived and melodramatic ending and occasional anti-Celtic and male chauvinist elements. Nonetheless it also has an attractive exuberance and optimism which, in many ways, Linklater was never to recapture. The recreation of the life of medical students in Inverdoon (Aberdeen) and the descriptions of life in Orkney (especially the County Fair and the wedding) are lively, convincing and memorable. The application of saga motifs helps give the novel a more solidified and coherent structure and prevents it from becoming merely picaresque. Furthermore there are even early traces of Linklater's theory of the Vikings' aesthetic appreciation of conduct: Flett's deliberate sacrifice of his medical career for a day of pleasure with Patricia is indeed a grand gesture without any thought of practical or material gain (Patricia was going to marry someone else). Flett's attitude to boxing is also in keeping with an artistic conception of life. As Flett's friend Mackay comments:

> 'He's too intelligent not to see the idiocy of boxing, of duelling without danger or provocation, and as he isn't a sadist he can't like getting hurt. But he enjoys boxing because his subconscious mind is full of Tom Sayers and Cribb and Mendoza; he reads Borrow.' (WMS, 39)

White-maa's Saga is still worth reading today, both as Linklater's first novel and for its interesting application of Old Norse motifs. This

latter aspect of the novel becomes even more interesting when compared with similar motifs in his second semi-autobiographical
novel, *Magnus Merriman.*

Magnus Merriman

Published in 1934, *Magnus Merriman* tells the story of the epony-
mous hero, an Orcadian who returns from the Great War to study
English Literature at Inverdoon University, and, after receiving a
Second Class Honours degree, becomes a lecturer at the United
Churches' College in Bombay. After three years in India he travels
back to Britain via the Middle-East and writes a book of his adventures which becomes a best-seller. After a failed love-affair in
London he goes to Edinburgh where he becomes involved in the
Scottish Nationalist Movement and even stands for the party in a
parliamentary by-election, only to lose disastrously. Another tem-
pestuous love-affair with an American girl leads ominously
towards marriage, and so to escape from both the aforementioned
girl, Frieda, and the aftermath of his humiliation in politics he
returns to his birthplace and his sister's home in Orkney. There he
vainly attempts to write a long narrative poem on the resurgence of
Scotland – and has a brief romantic interlude with Rose, the very
young daughter of a neighbouring farmer. Disappointed by the
failure to complete his new poem, he is tempted back to London by
an offer to become a journalist, but is again quickly disillusioned by
the cynical expediency of the newspaper world. A letter from Rose,
informing him that she is pregnant, persuades him to return and
settle down in Orkney as a rather inefficient farmer who is almost
completely under the thumb of his surprisingly resourceful and
manipulating young wife.

The resemblance of the plot to some of the events of Linklater's
own life (studying English at Aberdeen, working in Bombay, writing a best-selling novel and standing for election to Parliament) is
fairly obvious, and despite his protestations to the contrary, *Magnus
Merriman* has usually been interpreted as a semi-autobiographical
description of Linklater's own experiences of Scottish Nationalism
in the early 1930s; indeed some of the novel's characters are thinly
veiled portraits of contemporary friends and acquaintances.[34]
Moreover many of Merriman's attitudes towards modern poetry

and modernism in general echo Linklater's own, and Merriman's
eventual sense of isolation in Orkney may well have been a *'cri de
coeur'* of the author himself, for as Watson has stated: 'the impasse
of *Magnus Merriman's* fate may be revealingly honest about
Linklater's position in Scotland'.[35]

A major theme of the novel is the constant debunking of
Merriman's romantic notions of love, politics and art. As Bold has
pointed out, *Magnus Merriman* 'has the Christian name of a saint
and the surname of a sinner (as the narrow disciples of Knox made
merriment synonymous with sin)'. All Merriman's ideals and
ambitions are doomed to fail as 'fate lay before him treacherous as
a banana-skin'.[36] Nonetheless, Merriman's disillusionment, despite
its sadness, often invites laughter as he has such an over-romanti-
cised view of his lofty aims and ideals. Standing as a Nationalist in
an election at Kinluce on the east coast, Merriman finds inspiration
walking along the beach: 'Suddenly Magnus felt his heart fill with
passionate love for the very soil of Scotland, for the sea that broke
on its coasts, and the mountain airs that filled its sky with music'
(MM, 162), and with tears in his eyes he decides to appeal to the
electors' pure sense of patriotism. Only 'twenty or thirty oafish rus-
tics' attend his next meeting, however, and 'the lofty hortations that
were in Magnus's mind crumbled like dreams in the grey light of a
November morning' (MM, 164, 165).

Similarly, Merriman becomes overenthusiastically involved in
Orkney on his return there. 'He cleaned the stables and smelt
strongly of dung, he spoke with an Orkney accent, he discussed the
rotation of crops...' (MM, 210), but with the coming of bad weather,
his dreams of being an Orkney farmer wane dramatically as 'the
skies wept down his neck while he sat in a slow-moving cart or
scythed a load of sodden grass, and he took no pleasure in tramp-
ing through the farmyard mire' (MM, 221). Merriman's proposed
poem, 'The Returning Sun' was to 'picture a Scotland glorious in
the revisiting of its ancient pride' (MM, 80), but he gradually realises that 'his new Scotland was borrowing the unsubstantial foundations of Utopia' (MM, 221). Offered a post as literary critic of an
English newspaper, Merriman dreams of gaining a 'magnificent
reputation' (MM, 225) and realises that, after all, London is 'the
source of true delight' (MM, 230), only to become a second-rate

journalistic hack expected to write to the varying whims and dictates of the paper's editor and owner (MM, 251-53). Finally, on
returning to Orkney to marry Rose, Merriman expects his bride to
be docilely dependent on him, but quickly realises that behind her
youth and public shyness Rose is a very determined if not shrewish
young woman who soon has him well under her thumb. Before
long, Merriman's only show of independence consists of a defiant
sally down to the village to become blind drunk.

A very interesting and productive method of evaluating *Magnus
Merriman* is to compare and contrast it with Linklater's earlier semi-
autobiographical novel, *White-maa's Saga*, for the fictional characters of Flett and Merriman have much in common. Both of them
have as a home a farm in Orkney which is owned and run by a sister (though Flett's sister is single, whereas Merriman's is married);
both are very conscious of their Norse ancestry and have various
editions of the Old Norse sagas on their bookshelves (WMS, 74;
MM, 291). Orkney also tends to be a haven for both of them from
the trials and tribulations of the world and they use their sisters'
homes as a place to hide and lick their wounds, Flett after failing his
medical exams, Merriman after losing his election campaign, and
both of them after disillusioning love affairs. Moreover they both
have a different identity in Orkney, as they have local nicknames
which are never used elsewhere: Flett is White-maa (a sea-gull) and
Merriman is Mansie (a diminutive form of Magnus). Both men
have a deep distrust of the Celtic spirit, and both are rather chauvinistic in their attitudes towards women.

Despite their similarities, however, the two men are very different in temperament and achievement. *White-maa's Saga*, despite its
sometimes rather gauche style and melodramatic plot, is full of a
certain raw energy and the novel ends on a note of hope and ful-
fillment. In *Magnus Merriman*, however, the hero becomes frustrated and disillusioned at every turn of his career, and has little control over his own fate as he is the constant victim of untoward
events and a vacillating and easily manipulable character.

The change in tone between *White-maa's Saga* and *Magnus
Merriman* is quite notable and reveals a Linklater more distinctly
worldly-wise if not cynical. Hart's description of Merriman as
'White-maa grown older'[37] is thus not really accurate, for it is

Linklater who has grown older, not White-maa. But the truly interesting aspect of the change of tone in the two novels, especially as
concerns this book, is Linklater's strikingly different use of Old
Norse motifs in *Magnus Merriman*. In keeping with the ironic tone
of the novel, Merriman appears, at times, not so much a similar
character to Flett as a parody of him. Magnus claims his family
have been lairds in Orkney since the twelfth century and that he is
descended from St. Magnus (MM, 20-21). This claim is totally spu-
rious, however, not least because St. Magnus was a celibate and had
no descendants. In *White-maa's Saga* Flett, outside his formal boxing
matches, becomes involved in fights in self-defence or over such
serious subjects as politics or an attempted swindle at the County
Fair. Merriman, on the other hand, gets involved in a drinking
spree with the lecturer in Anglo-Saxon at Inverdoon in which:

> ... they quarrelled violently over the rival merits of Beowulf and
> The Saga of Burnt Njal. Continuing their argument in the street,
> they presently assaulted each other and were both arrested.
> (MM, 6)

Furthermore, Merriman twice becomes involved in brawls with his
best friend Meiklejohn over such an esoteric and, in the circumstances, rather frivolous subject as the relative merits of
Shakespeare and Racine (MM, 41-49; 125-32).

Unlike Flett, Merriman has no Nordic sea-going tradition in his
family, either. His father was a schoolteacher and his great-grandmother was a 'well-known witch' (MM, 88). Even Merriman's interest in fishing, in direct contrast to Flett's, is on inland lochs and not
the open sea. Merriman, in fact, is very much land-orientated, and
in contrast to Flett's plans to travel the world, his romantic dreams
are rather more mundanely centred on three hundred acres of good
land and fathering a large family on Rose (MM, 212).

Merriman's 'supernatural' experience in the novel, his attempt
to impress his American girlfriend with the story of his great-
grandmother being a witch is quickly deflated by Frieda's truly
macabre and horrific story of a disturbing case of witchcraft in the
United States (MM, 88-89, 92-93). As with Flett, Merriman also has
his future told at the County Fair, but in Merriman's case the

prophecy of Madame Vanda is uninspiringly mundane though highly accurate, for it is precisely after the dance the same evening that Merriman is seduced by Rose and she becomes pregnant, thus sealing his unexciting fate.

Aspects of Linklater's interpretation of the Viking ethos hinted at in *White-maa's Saga* and implied in *The Men of Ness* are also demythologised or treated ironically in *Magnus Merriman*. Lofty concepts of reputation and honour are mocked by exaggerated anecdotes causing drunken brawls in public houses:

> Here, with foul shirts and fouler breath, were Mars's heroes. Kings had fallen and nations perished, armies had withered and cities been ruined for this and this alone: that poor men in stinking pubs might have great wealth of memory. (MM, 40-41)

Merriman's early admiration of those who lived, Norse fashion, by their own strength (MM, 135) and his faith in 'the admirable spirit of Norse fatalism, that was active, not passive, and full of energy and ego even in the very face of doom', finally becomes, in the light of his failures, a far more uninspiring affirmation that: 'Nothing happens to a man except that which is intrinsically like him' (MM, 250). Most significant of all, perhaps, is his realisation that his idealistic vision of a Scotland returning to 'the odal laws of the Norsemen' was little more than an image of his odallers 'drinking, as had their Orkney forbears, the starkest ale in Albion' and that 'he could not stress too much this favouring glimpse, for the brewing of much stark ale is an economic flaw in the structure even of Utopias' (MM, 221).

It is thus fair to say that many of the Norse motifs and ideals presented so positively in *White-maa's Saga* and *The Men of Ness* are highly satirised if not ridiculed in *Magnus Merriman*. It is interesting to note that much had happened in Linklater's own life in the five years between the publication of *White-maa's Saga* and *Magnus Merriman*; his nationalist ideals had been destroyed by factional bickering, he had fought and lost a Parliamentary election, he had failed to repeat his best-selling success of *Juan in America*, and his personal freedoms and responsibilities had been somewhat curtailed by marriage and fatherhood. All of these points perhaps help

explain the more cynical and pessimistic tone underneath the comical surface of *Magnus Merriman*. But it is Linklater's sense of failure
as regards his *preceding* novel, *The Men of Ness*, that perhaps weighs
most here, for its lack of critical success in Britain had implied a
rejection or lack of interest in two of Linklater's most cherished
beliefs: the importance of the Old Norse heritage in Scotland and
his sense of being a modern-day 'makar'. To a certain extent, it
could be argued that Linklater never fully overcame his disappointment in 1932,[38] and the satirical treatment of Old Norse motifs
in *Magnus Merriman* can be seen as a reflection of Linklater's self-
scorning response to his conception and experience of the critical
failure of *The Men of Ness*.

Historian and Novelist 1955-68

The second, post-war period of Linklater's Norse-inspired works
can be divided into two categories: his historical books dealing
with the Viking past, and a novel, *The Dark of Summer* (1956), set
mostly in contemporary Shetland. Before discussing this final
Norse-inspired fictional work, a brief look at his history books is
necessary in order to summarise some of Linklater's main beliefs
concerning Old Norse history and literature.

   Although Linklater cannot be ranked as an historian in the
fullest academic definition of the word, he wrote many books pop-
ularising British political and military history. At least one of these,
The Prince in the Heather (1965), on Bonnie Prince Charlie, has been
reprinted several times.[39] It can come as no surprise, therefore, that
Linklater was bound, sooner or later, to turn his attention to his lifelong interest in Old Norse history and culture. The result can be
found in three interesting and readable books: *The Ultimate Viking*
(1955), his deeply personal review of Orkney and Old Norse history and literature; *Orkney and Shetland* (1965), a popular historical
and geographical survey of the Northern Isles with special and constant reference to their Norse past; and *The Conquest of England*
(1966), his sweeping survey of Viking history in northern and western Europe, especially the British Isles, from the eighth to the
eleventh century. These three books contain the fruits of a lifetime's
study of Linklater's favourite subject, in particular his three basic
assumptions as regards Old Norse history and culture. These were,

that the Norse ethos was primarily aesthetically motivated; that the Norse propulsion was vital to the civilisation of Western Europe; and that the Battle of Hastings in 1066 marked the ultimate Norse conquest of England.

The Aesthetic Impulse and the Norse Ethos

Linklater's theory on the aesthetic impulse underlying much of Old Norse attitudes to action and heroism is that which had helped inspire *The Men of Ness*. Indeed it may have been Linklater's sense of the failure of this novel which drove him to reiterate his beliefs nearly twenty-five years later, only this time in non-fictional form. The theme is boldly stated once more at the beginning of *The Ultimate Viking*: the Norsemen were so 'greedy of fame' and desparate to 'create a legend' that they were 'quite contemptuous of economic advantage and the safety of their skins':

> But they saw clearly a difference between right and wrong, and the difference was aesthetic. If what they did became a story that would please the ear, then it was right and beautiful. (UV, 8)

He supports this theory with a wealth of examples from Old Norse history and literature, especially *Orkneyinga Saga*, *Njal's Saga*, *Laxdaela Saga*, *Egil's Saga*, and *Grettir's Saga*. Typical instances of Linklater's conception of true Norse conduct are often found in the very high-points of the stories: Gunnar of Hlidarend's refusing to go into exile, even though he knows it will mean certain death (UV, 187-89); Njal and his wife remaining in their burning home rather than face the shame of being unable to avenge the deaths of their sons (UV, 199-201); Kjartan throwing down his sword rather than strike his blood-brother, knowing full well that the latter will slay him regardless (UV, 224-26). These, and many other incidents are given by Linklater as examples of the Norseman's ability not only to see and understand his fate, but also to embrace it.

Fascinating and attractive as Linklater's theory is, it does have three distinct drawbacks. Firstly, the presentation of some of his arguments are biased and unconvincing; secondly, some of the evidence he presents in fact disproves his theory; and thirdly, there is a vital question as to the veracity and reliablity of the saga evidence itself. An example of one of Linklater's biased and unconvincing arguments concerns the way in which he presents Sweyn Asleifsson's ostentatious defiance of Earl Rognvald at Lambaborg Castle, Caithness, in defence of his friend Margad (UV, 105-08). The garrison was eventually starved into submission, but not before Sweyn and Margad had made a daring escape down the cliffs. Earl Rognvald magnanimously spares Sweyn's men. The question here is whether Sweyn did not in fact leave his men in the lurch? Would his daring escape have seemed so honourable had the Earl massacred his men in retaliation? Linklater either fails to see this point of view – or resolutely refuses to comment on it if he does.

An example of the second drawback to Linklater's theory, his use of evidence which in fact refutes his own argument, again concerns Sweyn Asleifsson. In *The Ultimate Viking* Linklater describes the great Christmas feast at Earl Paul's in Orkney, during which one of the guests, Sweyn Breastrope, becomes jealous of Sweyn Asleifsson and mutters threats against him. Forewarned and armed by Eyvind Melbrigdason, Sweyn Asleifsson strikes down his namesake as he comes out of the Earl's hall. Linklater descibes this act as 'the expression of a studied intention':

> The blow was as deliberate – as expressive of a formulated purpose – as Aeschylus' choice, for a dramatic theme, of the misfortunes of the House of Atreus; as deliberate as the impersonality of Piero della Francesca's painting; as deliberate as Brahms's selection of G minor for the key of his first pianoforte quartet. (UV, 91)

The highly esoteric allusions cannot hide the fact that this claim is untenable. A detailed study of the incident, as it is described in *Orkneyinga Saga* (Ch.66, pp.112-15), clearly reveals that Eyvind Melbrigdason stage-manages the whole affair. Throughout the entire incident Sweyn Asleifsson appears to be little more than a passive and drunken agent who does exactly as he is told – and yet Linklater would have us believe that he is a completely free agent with a 'formulated purpose' who makes his own decisions and defiantly carries them out!

The third and final drawback to Linklater's theory lies in the very nature of the evidence itself, for there has been a long and continuing debate as to the veracity and reliability of Old Norse sagas as impartial records of the historical past. Linklater's approach to the sagas is that 'if they are impressionistically true, the impelling motives of their principal characters cannot have been twisted or mis-shapen' (UV, 171). This has been a valid and acceptable view in the past, but Old Norse scholars have recently become much more aware of the literary features of the sagas and their historical veracity has been increasingly questioned. Famous last words, prophetic speeches, and extemporary aphorisms have been uttered and recorded for posterity, but the high frequency of such dramatic, ironic, and epigrammatic comments in the sagas clearly suggests a literary rather than an oral origin.[40] The characters and events of such literary creations cannot, therefore, be regarded as historically accurate recordings of the life, times, or *aesthetic values* of real people, especially when they are written down at a distance in time of up to two to three hundred years, or may indeed be entirely fictitious.

More recent research has also shown that Linklater's views of Viking conduct are anachronistic in a saga context, for the saga-authors were concerned to stress the positive and peaceful aspects of settling disputes, along with the more socially acceptable forms of reasonable compromise. Apart from one or two exceptions (e.g *Egil's Saga*), the violent and unruly Viking who causes bloodshed and discord whilst seeking self-aggrandisement is implicitly deplored and criticised. As Paul Schach has expressed it:

> The *Íslendingasögur* were once believed to be the heirs and prose continuators of the heroic poetry of the North. Like so many of our former beliefs, this one has to be abandoned on the basis of recent research. In saga literature, the berserker and the viking are nearly always villains....[41]

Yet it was precisely this image of the bold, virile and aggressive Viking which Linklater believed the sagas eulogised and upon which he based his ideas of the Norse temperament. A warning against this kind of over-idealisation of the Vikings comes from E.J. Cowan, who may well have had Linklater in mind when describing Sweyn Asleifsson as 'a man persistently romanticised by commentators as one who epitomises the Viking way of life. Sweyn is an anachronism, his values decadent, in a twelfth century context'. More recent research has also revealed that the author of the *Orkneyinga Saga* is in fact highly critical of Sweyn and frequently describes him as an 'unfair, overbearing man'.[42] The aesthetic impulse which Linklater sees behind the Norse ethos thus seems little more than a literary artefact.

'The Norse Propulsion'

Both in *The Ultimate Viking* and *The Conquest of England*, Linklater is keen to emphasise the importance of Britain's Old Norse heritage in order to counterbalance the deep-rooted assumption that all the sources of civilisation came from the Mediterranean: Palestine, Rome, and Greece.

> But all the virtues in the world, and the moral, aesthetic, or administrative products of virtue, are worthless, because inoperative, without a physical ability, a strength of mind and body, to give them action and by example proclaim their value. And to all north-western Europe a prodigious reinforcement of that necessary strength – sometimes an addition to failing strength, sometimes the injection into apathy of a new impulse – came from the vigour of the Norse propulsion.[43]

The only unfortunate aspect of this assertion, however, is the slight but discernible suggestion that all morality, aesthetics, and virtue could degenerate into effeteness and decadence unless tempered with some vigorous display of virility. This emphasis on the idea that 'physical exhilaration must be accepted as a factor in Norse history' (UV, 4-5) leads Linklater to make some rather dubious justifications for Viking raids on churches and monasteries, and even to vindicate torture and killing by the Norwegian King Olaf Tryggvason in the latter's efforts to convert Norway to Christianity.[44] Any attempt to find mitigating circumstances for the use of torture is disturbing, and Linklater's sense of values must be called into question here. His apparent readiness to favour vigorous physical action, even violence, in preference to more passive or peaceful methods is best exemplified in his attitude to the patron saint of Orkney, Earl Magnus Erlendsson.

In both *The Ultimate Viking* and *Orkney and Shetland*, Linklater makes disparaging remarks about St. Magnus, being extremely sceptical of both his celibacy and his sanctity. Even Magnus's celebrated refusal to fight in the sea-battle in the Menai Straight is seen as 'so contrived, so theatrical a protest'[45] (cf. George Mackay Brown's attitude towards the saint in the following chapter). Linklater is clearly more impressed with the Norse world's two other saints: Earl Rognvald and King Olaf the Stout. The former, Magnus's nephew, was 'a poet, clean-limbed, well made, with light chestnut hair; he played the harp, he ran on skis, he could shoe a horse and read runes and shoot straight' (UV, 81). Linklater lovingly retells his lifestory in *The Ultimate Viking*, especially relishing the Earl's crusade to Jerusalem on which, en route, he had a love-affair with a young princess at Narbonne, and successfully attacked shipping in the Mediterranean. He says little of King Olaf, but although the latter was a rapacious and violent Viking who later became a convert to Christianity, Linklater believes that, 'it would be uncharitable to dispute his faith' (UV, 54). This is in marked contrast to his comments on St. Magnus. The reader is left with the uncomfortable feeling that Linklater's view of the three saints is not based on a serious investigation of their faith, but the simple fact that Earl Rognvald and King Olaf were lusty Vikings, whilst Earl Magnus was a celibate pacifist.

A further questionable aspect of Linklater's belief in the Norse propulsion is his tendency to see it in racial terms. Thus the Norse vitality and spirit 'irradiated with its hardihood and imagination the less urgent clay, the rich but quieter earth, of their Saxon and Celtic neighbours' (UV, 10). Linklater thus presents Anglo-Saxon England as decadent and lacking direction and makes disparaging remarks on early Gaelic culture. Such anti-Celtic prejudice is also much in evidence elsewhere in Linklater's historical writings[46] and has already been noted in connection with his first novel *Whitemaa's Saga*. Given the temper of the times and the ongoing Norse/Celtic debate in Scotland, Linklater's anti-Celtic prejudices in 1929 may be understandable if regrettable, but that he should continue to interpret history with such outmoded and discredited racial theories in the 1950s and 60s is rather deplorable and does little to enhance the validity of his hypothesis.

The Norse Conquest of Britain

Linklater's most interesting theory on Norse history concerns the Viking invasions of Britain. In *The Ultimate Viking* he makes the startling claim that the Battle of Clontarf in 1014 was not, as traditionally accepted, Irish resistance to Norse domination, or even a contest between Christianity and paganism. It was no less than a secret conspiracy by King Sweyn Forkbeard, the Danish King of England, for the total Norse domination of the British Isles. Linklater puts forward a lot of intriguing evidence for his theory, but it is flawed by two main points. Firstly, King Sweyn was dead before a sword was even drawn (UV, 51), and secondly, it would seem quite remarkable, if not totally beyond the bounds of credibility, that such a grandiose plan should have escaped the notice of the annalists and historians of the time.

Linklater later goes on to extend his theory and claim that what the Norsemen had failed to do at the Battle of Clontarf in 1014 they finally achieved at the Battle of Hastings in 1066. Indeed the whole of his book *The Conquest of England* is devoted to the thesis that the Norman Conquest was the final and successful Norse attempt to subjugate England. The fact that William the Conqueror was descended from Ganga-Rolf, a son of Earl Rognvald of More, has never been disputed, and this view of the Norman Conquest has been put forward many times before, especially in the last century. Nonetheless, this hypothesis does not bear close scholarly scrutiny. David C. Douglas, a recognised authority on Norman history, has quite convincingly and irrefutably disproved it in his *The Norman Achievement* (1969) in which he points out that although the Vikings certainly established a dynasty in tenth-century Normandy, they were only a tiny minority of the native population and the new ruling class from Scandinavia was rapidly absorbed into the surrounding Latin and Christian culture:

> When full allowance is made for the intensely individual character of the Normans in the eleventh century, it remains true that the conquests which they made between 1050 and 1100 were made by men who were French in their language, in the rudiments of their culture and in most of their political ideas.[47]

Despite this fundamental weakness in Linklater's theory, it remains a provocative and alternative view of the Norman Conquest, and one which still has its supporters to this day.[48] Many of Linklater's ideas about the Vikings, as recorded in his history books, are thus highly personal and subjective. Nonetheless, they reveal his passionate interest in the Norse heritage in Britain, and provide stimulating and challenging opinions for both the lay and the academic reader. Perhaps most important of all, his background research for *The Ultimate Viking* provided him with the inspiration for his last important piece of Norse-inspired fiction, *The Dark of Summer*.

The Dark of Summer

Set in the 1940s and 50s, mostly in Shetland and the Faroes, *The Dark of Summer* is not one of Linklater's better known novels, though it has perhaps been underrated. The novel has two major plots, the tracking down of a would-be collaborator in wartime Shetland, and the solving of a 200-year old murder and inheritance mystery. Woven between these narrative threads are sub-plots dealing with the themes of guilt, fear and atonement.

In the beginning of the novel, Tony Chisholm, an officer in the army, discovers the truth of the death, in action, of his brother: he had been shot whilst fleeing from the front line. Whilst recovering from the shock of this, Chisholm is sent to the Faroes, ostensibly as a Welfare Officer, but in reality to investigate rumours that a Nazi agent from Norway has landed there. Chisholm discovers that such an agent, Jon Jonsson, had indeed landed and been sheltered by two of Chisholm's Faroese friends, Bömlo and Tórur, but had accidentally died at their hands when he tried to bribe them. Chisholm learns from them that Jonsson intended to meet a friend of Vidkun Quisling (Norway's Nazi wartime leader) in Shetland; Silver, a Royal Navy captain helping Chisholm, recalls seeing Quisling in Oslo before the war with a certain Magnus Wishart from Shetland, and surmises that the latter is the probable Nazi contact. They sail to Shetland where Chisholm visits the Wisharts and befriends the two children Olaf and Gudrun, the latter giving him a book, *The Wishart Inheritance*, dealing with an unsolved murder and the litigation concerning the ownership of Weddergarth, Wishart's estate. Wishart subjects Chisholm to a semi-fascistic lecture on the necessi-

ty of renewing Norse blood in Britain, but on being confronted with
the evidence (i.e. Jonsson's body) angrily denies any connection
with Norwegian Nazis. As soon as Chisholm and Silver depart,
however, Wishart commits suicide.

The rest of the novel relates Chisholm's attempts, throughout the
rest of the Second World War, and later the Korean War, to come to
terms with his feelings of guilt over his brother's cowardice and
Wishart's suicide. He meets up with Olaf Wishart again in the
Korean War and the latter, now a young soldier, dies in Chisholm's
arms claiming he has atoned for his father's crime. Chisholm eventually returns to Shetland and marries Gudrun. Whilst making a
new road from Weddergarth to the beach the body of Dandy
Pitcairn, who had disappeared in 1747, is discovered. The final
proof that he had indeed been murdered establishes beyond all
doubt that the Wisharts had a moral as well as legal title to the
estate.

One of the more obvious uses of Norse background in the novel
is the idea of Nordic supremacy used by Jonsson and Wishart.
Before giving away his ulterior motives, Jonsson had impressed
Bömlo and Tórur with his theory of 'the great destiny of the
Atlantic islands and the sea-going races of Norse descent' which
would come into their own again once Germany and Russia had
destroyed each other.[49] Jonsson stressed that this was Quisling's
own idea and had nothing to do with Hitler. In his harangue to
Chisholm, Mungo Wishart extended the Norse blood links to
include England.

> What he said, in effect, was that all the achievements of England
> were due to men of Norman blood; to men who had some inheri-
> tance of flesh and spirit from the Norman conquest, or earlier set-
> tlements from the north. But now, he said, all England, and
> Scotland too, had lost that potency, that will to explore and con-
> quer and create in their own image. And the reason? The last
> dregs of Norse blood had run out, and there was no hope for
> Britain unless its heart could be replenished.
>
> Breaking a long silence, I said, 'I can't see where you're going to
> refill it.'
>
> 'There are sources,' he said darkly. 'Sources I know.' (DS, 149-50)

The intriguing point here is that Wishart's theory is an extension of Linklater's own belief in the efficacy of Norse blood in the Norman Conquest already referred to. Linklater was a virulent anti-Nazi,[50] so why did he give Wishart views which he himself half believed in? The answer, in fact, is that Linklater needed a neat solution to a delicate problem. It is essential to the novel that Mungo Wishart be viewed with some sympathy. The Nordic myth propounded in *The Dark of Summer* can be seen as a superficially attractive idea (Bömlo and Tórur are inspired by it) which, although classifiable as fascist nonetheless avoids the worst excesses of German Nazism and anti-semitism. Furthermore it is, from a military point of view, patently absurd, and presented as a peculiarly Scandinavian form of nazism, the brainchild of Quisling and not Hitler. All these points make it more acceptable that an eccentric Shetland landowner should idly flirt with collaboration during the last war. The reader's view of Wishart is thus of a highly unstable and misguided man who is the victim of folly rather than evil.

What could be regarded as further Old Norse influence in the novel is its examination of the concepts of heroism and atonement. These subjects are not explicitly related to an Old Norse ethos, but the prevailing Norse ambience of the novel (the setting in Shetland and the Faroes, the use of ideas of Nordic supremacy, and the names of Wishart's children) suggest an implicit connection. Chisholm is almost obsessed with trying to define the nature of cowardice, especially since he is confronted by paradoxical examples. His brother is shot by an officer for panicking, yet when he himself freezes with fear when attacked by tanks, the enemy panics, first enabling Chisholm to regain his nerve and ultimately be awarded a medal for the action (DS, 81). Conversely, Chisholm is curious to discover the source of bravery when a complete stranger risks his life to save his, and is then killed attempting to save yet another. 'Why, for the sake of two strangers, had he risked his life, and lost it? Pity, I suppose, but why should pity move a man so strongly?' (DS, 182). Chisholm eventually discovers an answer when he himself acts bravely and spontaneously in a vain effort to save the lives of men trapped in burning lorries:

> I had submitted to the impulse of compassion, in circumstances
> that menaced me with death for doing so, and although I had

failed to achieve anything ... I recognized, with enormous gratitude, the nature of my impulses; and for the first time in my life –
I think this is true – I felt I was a whole man. (DS, 201)

Both bravery and cowardice are thus natural human responses and
can occur in very similar circumstances; they are spontaneous and
unpredictable acts totally divorced from preconceived intentions or
notions. Moreover it is clear that Chisholm sees his own act of bravery as somehow expiating his brother's cowardice. This is not
atonement in the Old Norse sense (which would involve either
physical revenge or fiscal payment), but it may perhaps approach
Linklater's own conception of aesthetically motivated action. Such
a view is strengthened when Chisholm, in the Korean War, holds
the dying Olaf Wishart in his arms:

> Olaf opened his eyes, and looked at me with intense gravity, but
> without – as I thought – anxiety. I bent low above him to hear what
> he was saying, and slowly and very faintly he said, 'Do you think
> - this - will make up - for him?' I had no idea what he meant, but
> he wanted acquiescence, and I cried, 'Yes, yes. Of course it will.'
> (DS, 234)

Chisholm later realises, as does the reader, exactly what Olaf means
– he had given his life in atonement for his father's treachery in the
previous war. It is quite clear, too, that this is exactly what Linklater
wants us to infer. Within the context of the Korean War, Olaf's death
is insignificant, but to those who understand his motivation
(Chisholm, Gudrun and the reader) it achieves great meaning and
dignity. Olaf had completed a pattern. Chisholm, still haunted by a
sense of guilt over Wishart's suicide (DS, 272), also eventually
makes atonement, and a pattern, by marrying Gudrun and settling
at Weddergarth. These plot elements (especially the discovery of
Dandy Pitcairn's body) can of course be seen as a very neat tying
up of narrative loose ends, but the ending of the novel is still convincing, for, contrived or not, it has a satisfying rightness about it.

As mentioned earlier, *The Dark of Summer* has been perhaps
unfairly neglected. Parnell, for example, is full of praise for
Linklater's handling of the complicated plot, but otherwise mostly
concerns himself with the less important implications of the inher-

itance problem.[51] It is, in fact, perhaps one of Linklater's most successful post-war novels in terms of the merging of form and content, and the real strength of the novel lies in its serious, interesting
and sensitive study of the arbitrary nature of bravery and cowardice. Furthermore, his suggestion that a sense of selfless atonement may endow otherwise meaningless loss of life with some dignity and purpose, is the nearest Linklater comes to a successful
implementation, in a twentieth-century context, of his theory of the
aesthetic motivation of action inherent in the Norse ethos.

Old Norse history and literature have thus had an important
influence on Linklater's work throughout his life. Norse themes
and motifs give pattern, meaning and contrasts to his two semi-
autobiographical novels *White-maa's Saga* and *Magnus Merriman*,
and the Viking history of Orkney was the inspiration both for *The
Men of Ness*, a novel which was clearly important to him, and for
the pageant for St. Magnus' Cathedral. In the post-war years his
love of the sagas and Norse history gave him the solid background
for his two history books and a guide to the Northern Isles. It also
provided him with renewed inspiration to explore once again his
interpretation of the Norse ethos in a contemporary context in *The
Dark of Summer*.

Most notable of all, perhaps, is the possibility that Linklater's
love of Viking history and literature influenced his own personal
beliefs and behaviour. Like his characters Peter Flett and Magnus
Merriman – and the 'Ultimate Viking' Sweyn Asleifsson – Linklater
spent long forays around the world before returning to his safe
domestic haven in Orkney. In his case, of course, his 'plunder' was
material for his novels, histories and journalism. His admiration for
Viking daring and fighting skills reflected the fact that, despite his
abhorrence of the pointlessness and destructiveness of war, he
always remained fascinated by military combat and army life.[52]
His interest in what he believed to be the aesthetic motivation
behind the Norse ethos paralleled his deep concern for the ethics of
conduct in modern warfare, most notably recorded in *Private
Angelo* and *The Dark of Summer*. Indeed, Linklater was so steeped in
Old Norse lore and literature in both his personal and literary life,
that it would be perhaps appropriate to give him the epitaph of the
'Ultimate Viking' of modern Scottish literature.

NOTES

1 Eric Linklater, *Fanfare for a Tin Hat* (London, 1970), pp.27-30.
2 Michael Parnell, *Eric Linklater: A Critical Biography* (London, 1984), p.6.
3 *Fanfare for a Tin Hat*, p.132.
4 Eric Linklater, *The Ultimate Viking* (London, 1955), p.295. All further references in the text are to this edition, abbreviated UV.
5 *Fanfare for a Tin Hat*, p.14.
6 Eric Linklater, *The Man on My Back* (London, 1941), p.328.
7 'Spilt Wine', in *Alma Mater*, 21.10.21, pp.9-10.
8 For details, see Marjorie Linklater, 'Looking Back to the Octocentenary Pageant [1937]', in *St. Magnus Cathedral: 850 Years - A Celebration*, ed. Alastair and Anne Cormack (Kirkwall, 1987), pp.61-74. The script to the pageant is in the Orkney Archives, D1/98.
9 *The Man on My Back*, pp.225, 227.
10 Quoted in Parnell, p.126.
11 Parnell, p.127. Unfortunately no trace of these papers or any such radio broadcast can be found in the NLS, the Orkney Library, the BBC Archives, or the private papers of Mrs Marjorie Linklater.
12 *Fanfare for a Tin Hat*, p.132.
13 Eric Linklater, *The Men of Ness* (1932), 2nd edn., with Introduction by Marjorie Linklater (Kirkwall, 1983), p.223. All further references to the novel are to this edition, abbreviated MN.
14 *Fanfare for a Tin Hat*, p.132.
15 Marjorie Linklater, Introduction to *The Men of Ness*, n.p.
16 *Njal's Saga*, trans. Magnus Magnusson and Hermann Pálsson (Harmondsworth, 1960). All further references to the saga are to this edition.
17 See *The Saga of the Jómsvíkings*, trans. Lee M. Hollander (Austin, 1955), Ch.23, pp.107-14.
18 *The Saga of Grettir the Strong*, trans. G.A. Hight and ed. Peter Foote, 2nd edn. (London, 1972). All further references to *Grettir's Saga* are to this edition.
19 *Egil's Saga*, trans. Hermann Pálsson and Paul Edwards (Harmondsworth, 1976). All further references to the saga are to this edition. Linklater overlooks the point that Skallagrim is in fact a nickname and not a proper name (lit. 'Bald Grim'), and thus incongruously gives his character a shock of black hair. Rider Haggard makes a similar error in *Eric Brighteyes* (1891).
20 *Laxdaela Saga*, trans. Magnus Magnusson and Hermann Pálsson (Harmondsworth, 1969). All further references to the saga are to this edition.
21 *The Man on My Back*, p.228. The Icelandic reviewer is probably Stefán Stefánsson; see *Eimreiðin* 39:4 (1933), 455-56.
22 *Fanfare for a Tin Hat*, p.133.
23 Storm Jameson, review in *Now and Then* (Winter, 1932), 34.
24 Parnell, p.130; Marjorie Linklater, Introduction to *The Men of Ness*;

Bengtsson's *The Long Ships* was a world-wide bestseller and has been fre- quently reprinted in English translation.

25   Watson, p.377; Wittig, p.326; Hart, *The Scottish Novel*, p.251; Parnell, pp.134-35.

26   *Fanfare for a Tin Hat*, pp.133-35

27   *The Man on My Back*, p.244.

28   Watson, p.377; Murray, 'Novelists of the Renaissance', p.111; Marjorie Linklater, Introduction to *The Men of Ness*; Hart, *The Scottish Novel*, p.252.

29   In *God Likes Them Plain* (London, 1935), pp.61-76. All further references to 'Wineland' are to this edition.

30   See, for example, the murderous feud between Bergthora and Hallgerda in *Njal's Saga* Chs.35-98, pp.97-123.

31   Parnell, p.180.

32   *White-maa's Saga* (1929), 2nd edn. (Edinburgh, 1983). All further references are to this edition, abbreviated WMS.

33   Parnell, p.102.

34   E.g. 'Francis Meiklejohn' is based on Moray McLaren and 'Hugh Skene' on Hugh MacDiarmid.

35   Watson, p.377.

36   Bold, *Modern Scottish Literature*, p.186; Eric Linklater, *Magnus Merriman* (1934), Canongate Classics 35 (Edinburgh, 1990), p.22. All further refer- ences in the text are to this edition, abbreviated MM.

37   *The Scottish Novel*, p.252.

38   His bitterness is still evident in *Fanfare for a Tin Hat* (pp.133-35) written nearly forty years later.

39   For a full list of Linklater's historical works, see Parnell, pp.363-64.

40   For further comment on this, see Paul Schach, *Icelandic Sagas*, Twayne's World Authors Series 717 (Boston, 1984), p.130; Jónas Kristjánsson, *Eddas and Sagas*, trans. Peter Foote (Reykjavik, 1988), pp.166, 204-06.

41   Schach, p.173.

42   E.J. Cowan, 'What is *Orkneyinga Saga* about?', *Northern Studies* 2 (1973), 20; Peter Foote, 'Observations on *Orkneyinga Saga*', in *St Magnus Cathedral and Orkney's Twelfth Century Renaissance*, ed. Barbara E. Crawford (Aberdeen, 1988), pp.196-97.

43   *The Conquest of England* (London, 1966), p.15.

44   *Conquest of England*, p.14; *Ultimate Viking*, p.266.

45   *Orkney and Shetland* (London, 1965), pp.48-49; *Ultimate Viking*, p.74.

46   See for example *The Conquest of England*, pp.4-6, 84 and *The Survival of Scotland* (London, 1968), pp.16, 25, 28, 31, 32, 257, 327.

47   David C. Douglas, *The Norman Achievement*, 2nd edn. (London, 1972), p.29.

48   E.g. Magnús Fjalldal, 'Norrænir menn í vesturvíking - hin hlíðin', ['Norse Raids in the West – the Other Story'] in *Skírnir* 161 (1987), 106-17.

49   *The Dark of Summer* (1956; London, 1957), p.85. All references are to this edi- tion, abbreviated DS.

50   See for example Parnell, pp.162-63.

51   Parnell, pp.301-02.
52   This is particularly notable in his histories of campaigns and regiments. His autobiographical volumes, *Fanfare for a Tin Hat*, *The Man on my Back*, and *A Year of Space* (London, 1953), also contain much comment on soldiering in both World Wars. *The Art of Adventure* (London, 1947) has articles on war heroes.

12. GEORGE MACKAY BROWN

George Mackay Brown (1921-96) is indisputably Orkney's best known and most successful post-war writer. His books of poetry, plays, novels and collections of short stories dealing predominantly with the ordinary farmers and fishermen of Orkney from ancient times until the present day have captivated a growing number of readers with their simplicity and sincerity. His artistic versatility is evident in the variety of literary forms he has been willing to use, though whether writing poems, plays or stories he has always had a distinctive style, employing a deceptively simple but exact diction with mythic and symbolic overtones. His work has a very special ambience, a distinct blend of folklore and religious mysticism. Moreover his insistence on stressing the values of the elemental forces of life, as opposed to those of modern technology, has struck a resonant chord in the late twentieth century with its increasing social and ecological problems. His readership and reputation now extend well beyond the Orkney Isles to Europe and the wider world.

Old Norse Style

One of the most notable features of Mackay Brown's increasingly popular poetry and fiction is the influence of Old Norse literature on his work, a direct result of his love and admiration for the sagas and skaldic poetry of medieval Scandinavia. This should come as no great surprise, bearing in mind Orkney's immense Norse heritage, and its influence is immediately apparent in Mackay Brown's spare and sometimes laconic prose style, so reminiscent of the Icelandic sagas, and also in the sheer number of his poems and stories based on Viking history and literature. Virtually every novel and collection of short stories or poems by Mackay Brown contains subject matter from the Viking Age.[1]

Most notable in his poetry, perhaps, is his experimentation with so-called 'rune' poems and modern versions of 'kennings' or skaldic metaphors; these were a vital feature of Old Norse skaldic poetry, a form of imagery whereby two unrelated words are juxtaposed to create a more poetic name for the more common and elemental facts of Viking life and culture. In his poem 'The Sea: Four Elegies',[2] for example, Mackay Brown actually lists many kennings for the sea: 'Swan's Path', 'Whale's Acre', etc. Such kennings, including those Mackay Brown creates himself, are in fact endemic in his poetry, and particularly in poems dealing with Viking subject matter. Some of the most frequent are: 'salt furrow' (boat ploughing through the sea), 'hawkfall' (death), 'earth-gold' and 'cargoes of summer' (harvest), and 'blue hills' (whales). Yet such kennings are not restricted to his Viking poems alone, for he uses them in other poems and even in his prose works, as in the title of a collection of short stories: *Hawkfall* (1974). The effect of these kennings is perhaps first and foremost to capture the very sound and spirit of skaldic poetry in his Viking poems, but they are just as effective in his more contemporary works in their powerful compression of meaning and imagery, for example 'red coat' or 'red shirt', meaning execution by fire.

Runes were the letters of the earliest alphabet of the Germanic races and were often regarded as secret and magical. Old Norse runic inscriptions were thus usually terse and cryptic and often open to more than one interpretation. Mackay Brown seems to have been fascinated by this form of expression and even wrote a short story on the possible origins and meaning of the intriguing runic inscriptions to be found in the Maeshowe burial chamber in Orkney.[3] Moreover he adapted this terse, cryptic style in some of his own poetry for artistic and symbolic effect. The resulting 'Rune Poems' are often striking and varying. They can present perfect imagistic cameos:

> The sun-dipped isle was suddenly a sheep
> Lost and stupid, a dense wet tremulous fleece.

They can present humorous capsules of life:

> A man-of-war enchanted
> Three boys away.
> Pinleg, Windbag, Lord Rum returned.

They can be disturbingly brutal and enigmatic:

> Here lies Sigurd the fisherman
> Dead of hooves.[4]

Perhaps the best example of the power, concision and compression of these poems can be seen in Mackay Brown's vivid presentation of the danger and hardships of the fisherman's life-cycle in the following deceptively simple lines:

> Cod, give needles and oil.
> Winter hands
> Must sew shrouds by lamplight.[5]

Much of Mackay Brown's poetry is full of rhythmic alliteration very reminiscent of Old Norse poetry, whereby specific consonants in one line are to be repeated in the next. However, it is best perhaps not to place too much emphasis on possible Norse influence here, as alliteration is a very common form of poetic technique in many languages, and was much used by both Dylan Thomas and Gerard Manley Hopkins, two poets who have had a strong influence on Mackay Brown's work.[6] There can be little doubt, however, that his use of alliteration in his Viking poems was a very deliberate effort to capture the appropriate rhythms and cadences of ancient Scandinavian literature, though it was not always the method he used in creating modern forms of skaldic verse as a study of his versions of Earl Rognvald's strophes from *Orkneyinga Saga* will reveal.

A more definite and pervasive influence of Old Norse literature on Mackay Brown's style can be traced to his avid reading of the sagas, in particular *Orkneyinga Saga* and *Njal's Saga*, the latter, he declared, being 'amongst my greatest treasures'.[7] Mackay Brown was very explicit in his admiration for the sagas and the way their authors present their material:

> I admire the 'pure' art of the sagamen; everything extraneous, such as detailed descriptions of people and places and comments by the author on what is happening, is ruthlessly excluded.[8]

Elsewhere he states that the Icelandic sagas 'confirmed that a well-told story is conceived in simplicity and grows surrounded by silences'.[9] It is precisely this unemotional, impersonal concision of language that Mackay Brown successfully tried to emulate in his prose and poetry. The grim laconic style of the sagas is vividly recreated in such poems as 'A Battle in Ulster' (*Winterfold*, p.28) and 'Five Voyages of Arnor' (*Selected Poems*, pp.67-68) as well as such stories as 'The Story of Jorkel Hayforks' (*Calendar*, pp.118-26) and 'Tartan'.[10] This style was not exclusively reserved for Viking material, however, and he sometimes imitated the saga style to achieve ironic effects in stories dealing with contemporary themes and situations. In the novel *Greenvoe*, for example, the laird's granddaughter is anxious for a sexual encounter with a local 'peasant' after reading D.H. Lawrence's *Women in Love*. She thus persuades the rough ferryman Ivan Westray to take her with him on his boat-trip to a lighthouse. On the way back, however, Westray cynically rapes her, and the aftermath is described in the mockingly grim tones of a Norse saga:

> Ivan Westray put the kettle on the gas-ring and cut slices of bread and stabbed a tin of corned beef with an opener.
> Inga watched in silence.
> The granddaughter of the chief man in Hellya asked a certain boatman to take her to the sea tower. There was much fog on the way back. The boatman whose name was Ivan forced Inga to lie with him in the cabin of the boat called *Skua*. Inga said he had done her a great wrong that day and that he would suffer for it. Ivan laughed. He said they would see about that.[11]

As Murray and Tait have pointed out, the effectiveness of this Norse diction is due to the whole chapter being related in two other narrative voices apart from the traditional saga-voice: a prosaic twentieth-century one and a late medieval one (Shakespeare and Donne) which expresses a very different view of love than that shown by Westray. 'The main impact of the scene', Murray and Tait argue, 'is in the juxtaposition of these three voices'.[12]

Rowena Murray has analysed the influence of Old Norse on Mackay Brown's diction in some detail, particularly stressing its effectiveness when contrasted with a different period of time. This is very notable, for example, in the execution scene of *Magnus*,

> ... where the spare, laconic utterances of the saga style are appropriate to the tone of blank acceptance in the voice of the concentration camp cook, chosen to perform the execution, and suggests both the numbness brought on by repeated horror and the resignation of the victims: Magnus and Bonhoeffer.[13]

Murray in fact claims that there is a distinct progression in Mackay Brown's assimilation of the saga-style from *An Orkney Tapestry* (1969), a marvellously lyrical portrayal of Orkney and its people, past and present, through his novels *Greenvoe* (1972) and *Magnus* (1973) to *Time in a Red Coat* (1984):

> In *Time in a Red Coat*, finally, the saga style is gone; or rather the voice of the saga-man is gone. In its place we have a compression that mimics the workings of the mind itself, with its complex movement and unknown, or perhaps simply unspoken, motives. All of Brown's characters are now presented in a kind of indirect, often impersonal, speech; their interior worlds are all rendered with that lack of explanation of motive, that economy, that compression which Brown learned from the sagas.[14]

The final two sentences of this quotation are indeed an accurate comment on Mackay Brown's style, but to see its full emergence as incomplete until 1984 is to underestimate his innate literary skills. It seems to the present writer that Mackay Brown's laconic and impersonal style had already attained its precision and effectiveness in his earliest short stories, his authorial detachment often enabling the reader to have complete empathy with his characters. Thus Mackay Brown, a devout Catholic, could nonetheless create a harrowing and intensely moving picture of atheism and alcoholic despair in 'Celia' (*A Time to Keep*, pp.1-37), one of his 'major achievements'.[15]

In spite of all that has been said, however, there should be some caution in associating all of Mackay Brown's style with Old Norse influence, for as J. Graeme Roberts has pointed out, 'the narrative economy that Brown admires in Norse sagas and oral tales is, of course, a widely recognised feature of folk literature'. Roberts then illustrates in detail Mackay Brown's use of repetition, patterning (especially triadic groupings) and framing devices:

> It is for this reason that narrative economy, whether of subject matter or style, is probably a less significant example of the effect of tradition on Brown's approach to the short story than another characteristic of his earlier work, his use of very marked verbal and structural patterns, something that seems to derive from orally composed and transmitted narratives like the ballad.[16]

Indeed, perhaps it is this blending of the laconic and aphoristic diction of his Norse inheritance with traditional folklore structures which provides Mackay Brown with his distinctive and effective style.

Old Norse History in Prose and Poetry

The major and most obvious Old Norse influence on Mackay Brown, however, is that of subject matter. In many of his poems, short stories and two novels, he sought his plots and themes from the *Orkneyinga Saga*, the Icelandic family sagas, and Viking history in general. But, as with his style, Mackay Brown's presentation of the Vikings is a very distinct and personal one. Unlike many nineteenth- and twentieth-century writers, and fellow Orcadian Eric Linklater in particular, Mackay Brown was least impressed by, or interested in, ideas of Nordic supremacy or Viking military prowess, for as he stated very succinctly, racial myths and an uncritical adoration of physical power had produced in Germany 'the greatest nightmare in history':

> If the Viking myth is true, it is true with so many reservations and qualifications as to be almost meaningless. No harm is done, except that the corridors of history get filled with unreal figures and hollow voices, and so we ourselves become part of a phantasmagoria. In this book an attempt is made to see the Vikings plain.[17]

And see them plain we do, not only in *An Orkney Tapestry*, but throughout many of his poems and short stories. Mackay Brown made no attempt to glorify the Norse invasion of Orkney or their propensity for violence. In the story 'The Day the Vikings Came',[18] for example, the young Orcadian Skom sees his whole village destroyed by marauding Vikings and his sweetheart dragged into a longship. A Norseman stands next to Skom, laughing contemptuously. Skom kills the Norseman and rushes down to the beach to share the fate of his people. In 'The Day of the Ox' an Orcadian seer has a premonition of disaster and the story ends with the arrival of a longship and 'axe-glitterings'.[19] The poem 'The Stone Cross' relates very austerely the unbelievably callous massacre of monks by Viking raiders (*Winterfold*, pp.51-52). More recently, however, Mackay Brown also stressed some of the peaceful ways in which the Celts and Vikings met and mingled: either through trade and art, as in the story 'The Stone Rose', or through Christian worship, as in 'The Nativity Bell and the Falconer'.[20]

Mackay Brown's critical presentation of the Vikings' use of aggression was indeed highly influenced by his Christian point of view. Converted to Roman Catholicism in 1961, he consistently deprecated the wanton use of violence, both in Viking and modern times, regarding it as inhuman and essentially contradictory to the basic message of Christianity. This attitude is clearly formulated in the section called 'Warrior' in *An Orkney Tapestry*, for here he relates some of the life and adventures of Earl Sigurd of Orkney, culminating in his death at Clontarf in 1014. Mackay Brown first duly presents the heroic values which dominated the Norse world:

> Of only a few abstract qualities could a man be sure – of courage, for example, and of loyalty, and of generosity. These were the jewels that a man could save out of the flux. If you were lucky, perhaps some sagaman would set your actions in the horn and silver of his prose; that was the only kind of immortality a man could hope for. (OT, 56)

It was thus only natural that Earl Sigurd should fight at Clontarf as he 'wanted nothing but the centre of the battle and a place in the story', and Mackay Brown pays tribute to his 'courage, loyalty, generosity' (OT, 60). Nonetheless, Mackay Brown makes it clear that, in his opinion, the Norsemen were doomed to adhere to these values simply because they were ignorant of any others: 'Christ's charity meant nothing as yet to Earl Sigurd' (OT, 57). The battle of Clontarf was thus not a part of a great Norse conspiracy to conquer the British Isles, as Linklater believed, but, a more traditional view, a battle 'between Christ and Odin for the soul of Ireland' (OT, 62). Mackay Brown ends the chapter by quoting Gray's 'The Fatal Sisters', claiming it as a savage mockery of so-called heroes who were, in fact, no more than 'servants of Valkyries' who embroiled nations in carnage and war. In terms of bloodshed Earl Sigurd was thus simply a 'small-time huckster' (OT, 66-68).

This very critical view of the Vikings' willingness to achieve fame with the sword is also reflected in Mackay Brown's ironic treatment of Norsemen in his poems and stories. In the poem 'Bjorn the Shetlander Sails to Largs 1263' (*Winterfold*, p.26), for example, a fifteen year old boy eagerly awaits going on his first Viking voyage, the knowledgeable reader already aware that King Hakon's expedition ends in failure and defeat. In 'A Battle in Ulster', Rolf tries to receive a nasty wound in order to impress the girl he is courting. But at the end of fighting he reports: 'All I have got / Is a broken tooth, an eye blue as an oyster, / And my pinkie scratched. / From now on, Gudrun, / I will court less particular girls.' (*Winterfold*, p.28). In the poem 'Voyager' an old Viking languishes in Ireland, forced to speak Gaelic and sorely missing his home in Trondheim;[21] the poem 'Orkneyman at Clontarf' relates how Finn had boasted of being a soldier of Earl Sigurd's, but now crawls from ditch to ditch, dying from an arrow wound in his chest (*Voyages*, pp.40-42).

A more humorous irony can be found in 'The Story of Jorkel Hayforks' in which, after many misadventures, Jorkel reaches Orkney and kills the seducer of his sister in Norway. Jorkel is badly injured by hayforks in the subsequent brawl and is forced to spend the rest of his life in Orkney, ultimately, an old man, paying for a mass for the man he slew. 'Sylvanus, A Monk of Eynhallow' (*Masked Fisherman*, pp.127-43) relates how two Vikings, Sven [sic] and Ragnar, finally make it back to Orkney after a disastrous Viking expedition. Ragnar dies of his wounds, and the chastened Sven becomes a monk. Perhaps Mackay Brown's best 'anti-saga' in prose, however, is the story 'Tartan' in which four Vikings raid a Scottish clachan and are almost farcically outwitted by the villagers. The men finally make away with two sheep and a roll of tartan, but the most arrogant and boastful Viking, Kol, has his throat cut whilst in a drunken stupor.[22]

The main element in all these stories and poems, again ultimately influenced by Mackay Brown's Christian values, is that their heroes or personas are not generally the earls, kings, and chieftains of the sagas, but the ordinary 'man-in-the-longship', the cannon-fodder, so to speak, of Viking history. As Mackay Brown himself commented on *Orkneyinga Saga*, 'the common people ... make rare appearances'.[23] This is the other side of the Norse heroic coin, for what the saga-writers recorded as bringing fame and glory to kings and earls could also bring an agonising death, fearful disfigurement or years of slavery and humiliation to other Norsemen. Mackay Brown thus sets the record straight and reveals that many Vikings were as much victims as heroes, ordinary Orcadians or Norwegians who shared and suffered the vicissitudes of medieval life with the rest of mankind.

Historical Contrasts

One very notable feature of Mackay Brown's use of Old Norse (and indeed other) historical material, is the schematic contrasts between past and present within a single poem or story, or sequence of poems and stories. A good example of this is the short story 'The Three Islands' (*Calendar*, pp.52-60) in which three present-day fishermen are collecting lobster-creels off three Orkney isles: Eynhallow, Geirsay, and Egilsay; at each place they comment on their catch and how dull and miserable the islands look. Between each stop to haul in the lobster-creels, however, Mackay Brown inserts a short glimpse of life on these isles in the Viking Age: the monks writing their beautiful holy books on Eynhallow, the thriving community of the great Viking Sweyn Asleifson [sic] on Geirsay, and the tragic murder of St. Magnus on Egilsay. The story thus effectively comments on the poverty and ignorance of the fishermen in contrast to the apparent wealth and glory of Orkney's Norse Age.

His poem sequence 'The Masque of Princes' (*Selected Poems*, pp.77-88) presents the cruelty, vanity, and indifference of royal leaders (beginning with the Old Norse 'Sea Jarl') through the ages and ends with a prose-poem on the poverty-stricken circumstances surrounding the birth of the one true king at Jerusalem. An interesting and effective use of this technique can be found in the short story 'The Eye of the Hurricane' (*Time to Keep*, pp.155-82) in which a young author has come to Orkney to write a novel on Earl Rognvald Kolsson's pilgrimage to the Holy Land in 1151-53. A vital part of the novel was to deal with the earl's love affair with Princess Ermengarde in Narbonne. As the young novelist comments:

> In this Chapter Five I had somehow to communicate to the twentieth-century common reader, accustomed to the last hectic boring obscenities of romantic love, its sacred ceremonial root. (*Time to Keep*, p.168)

The author's concentration becomes increasingly disturbed by the drinking bouts of his landlord, Captain Stevens, who lives upstairs, and erotic fantasies concerning his landlord's cleaning woman, Miriam. The writer gradually realises that Captain Stevens has been driven to drink through intense suffering: after only a year of marriage his passionately loved wife had died in childbirth. Stevens eventually dies after a particularly harrowing session with rum. The author's novel continues to progress – except for the section on Earl Rognvald and Ermengarde. Compared to his own contemporary, sterile fantasies about Miriam and the agonising passion of Captain Stevens, he realises he is probably incapable of recreating a true and moving historical account of the aging earl's love for the young princess:

> Chapter Five remains unfinished. I shall return to it later, when a great deal that is confused and uncertain now clarifies in my mind. Love is too deep a subject for prose – only music and poetry can build bridges between the rage of the seed in the furrow, the coupling of beasts, the passion of man and woman, the saint's prayer. (*Time to Keep*, p.180)

In 'Hawkfall' we follow the fortunes of a family with a distinct facial feature, a flattened nose, through a series of episodes in Orcadian history.[24] In the Stone Age the main character is simply a fisherman; in Norse times he is called William Otter or Flatnose and is given land by Earl Thorfinn; in 1593 a flat-nosed farmer called Adam Thorfinnson [sic] is tortured to make him sign away his land to Earl Patrick Stuart in exchange for the barren soil of Lang Klett; in the nineteenth century, Tom Langclett, nicknamed Tammag Flatnose, is obliged to let his bride spend the wedding night with the laird (*droit de seigneur*); finally, in the twentieth century, Humphrey Langclett, a widower and shopkeeper in Hamnavoe, is faced with the fact that his family will probably die out, for his daughter seems an eternal spinster and her spiteful machinations may well prevent him from remarrying. This ending is made even more sad and depressing precisely because the reader has been made fully aware of the struggles of the Otter-Thorfinnson-Langclett family throughout the ages, only to be defeated by petty selfishness and a vindictive sense of propriety.

A final example of this contrastive technique is in the novel *Greenvoe*, which tells the story of the last few days of the small Orkney island of Hellya before it is due to be taken over by the 'Black Star' nuclear defence project. Every evening the unemployed fisherman Skarf reads aloud his own history of the island in the small hotel bar. A whole section of this history concerns the Norse settlement of Hellya, and in particular one Thorvald Harvest-Happy who died craving meat during Lent whilst a whale lay stranded on the beach because the Church could not decide if whale flesh was meat or fish! Most of Skarf's listeners are, sadly, totally ignorant of their island's history. '"I had no idea all them things happened here in Hellya"', the landlord of the hotel tells Skarf. But this does not prevent him from allowing his hotel to be torn down for 'extravagant compensation'.[25] George Mackay Brown thus uses Skarf's retelling of Hellya's rich and eventful past, just before the whole island is to be evacuated, to underline the tragedy and poignancy of the wanton destruction of a centuries-old community.

A further aspect of Mackay Brown's use of historical material can be found in his use of Old Norse sagas or mythology in recent or contemporary fiction. Examples of this can be found in two works of fiction, *Time in a Red Coat* (1984) and *The Golden Bird* (1987). The former tells the story of a young princess in ancient China who

travels through time and space to reach Orkney in the late nineteenth or early twentieth century.[26] She sets out on her journey
arrayed in a white dress, but by the time she reaches Orkney it has
become torn and coloured red, for she has brought help and suc-
cour to victims of war throughout the ages en route. The novel is
indeed a strong plea for peace in modern times and a protest
against the use of war as a political means, especially against
unarmed and innocent civilians.

There is Old Norse influence in this work, for the apparently
ageless girl's presence at or near the major battlefields of Europe
recalls the Valkyrie legend, though the girl's role is to protect and
preserve life as well as she can, and not to gather the slain for
Valhalla. In one major scene she visits a surrealistic Museum of War
(where future conflicts are also recorded), the owner of which has
lost one of his eyes and his right hand in battle.[27] The knowledgeable reader cannot but note the Old Norse symbolism here, for significantly enough Odin, the God of War, has only one eye, and his
son Tyr, the God of Victory, loses his right hand to the wolf Fenrir.
The title story of the book of the same name, 'The Golden Bird',[28]
relates, among other things, the destruction of a great friendship
between two men by a bitter and vindictive feud between their
wives Mary Jean and Tomina. The inspiration for this plot clearly
comes from *Njal's Saga*,[29] for although the women do not goad others to murder, as in the saga, their spite and acts of vandalism are
very reminiscent of the vicious (and in the saga, unsuccessful)
attempts of Hallgerda and Bergthora to destroy the close friendship
of Njal and Gunnar.[30]

This use of Old Norse and other historical material can thus provide an effective literary technique, but it is not without its weaknesses. Mackay Brown's dislike and distrust of the modern world and
technological progress (especially all applications of nuclear power) is
very specifically related in *An Orkney Tapestry* (pp.20-23), and is evident throughout all his work. Some critics, however, have pointed out
that Mackay Brown's responding glorification of former times is both
simplistic and limited. As Robin Fulton has commented:

> He [Mackay Brown] is liable to make references back in time in
> order to gain a stance from which he can militate against the kind

of society most of us in North Europe and North America now
live.... Over against the alleged false gods of the new age he sets
qualities derived from religious tradition both pagan and
Christian, but again such reference is utilised to show that all the
rest of us are out of step.[31]

Thus, in another context, Fulton argues that Mackay Brown's 'pseu-
do-historical reconstructions are least credible when they are
manipulated to show that the new life is shabbier than the old
one'.[32] In the case of 'The Three Islands' mentioned above, however, this is surely missing the point. Mackay Brown is not here implying that the present is shabbier than the past, but that the past can
enrich the present. The sheer ignorance of the fishermen of their
own history and heritage deprives them of a whole spectrum of
emotions and values. A knowledge of the three islands' histories
would have given them another way of seeing them, helped enliv-
en a dreary fishing-trip, and provided them with a more satisfying
emotional and intellectual experience to compensate for their poor
catch.[33]

Old Norse History and Didacticism

There is an element of truth in Fulton's criticism, however, for
Mackay Brown did occasionally use historical comparisons for
overtly didactic purposes. Two good examples of this can be found
in the poetry of *Fishermen with Ploughs* and the prose stories of
Andrina. *Fishermen with Ploughs* is a long sequence of poems
describing the history of Rackwick in Orkney, from its original
Norse settlement to its depopulation and eventual resettlement
after a projected nuclear holocaust in the not too distant future.
Mackay Brown's pessimistic view of modern technology and the
fate of mankind is only too evident in these poems. They present a
clear statement on his belief in the importance of man's relationship
with nature, especially reflected in his frequent use of the 'ploughing – sowing – harvesting – bread and ale' imagery.

The Old Norse material in this work comprises thirteen poems in
two sections, 'Dragon and Dove' and 'Our Lady', or about a quarter of the whole, but as Mackay Brown is here using Viking history
to illustrate his own preconceived ideas of human destiny, the

poems are nowhere near as powerful as some of those mentioned earlier. Individual lines are stylistically impressive, but, apart perhaps from the poem 'Helmsman' (pp.20-21), the overall effect is disappointing, as the Norse folk presented here are not vivid recreations of historical people, but verbal metaphors in highly stylised pieces; they represent a good example of what Fulton sees as the dangers of Mackay Brown's ritualised symbolism: 'The elemental images of birth, marriage, death, of wave and field, fish and corn, fiddle and ale, tend to be moved round like counters in all too predictable patterns'.[34]

An example in prose of Mackay Brown's didactic use of historical comparisons is his sequence of short stories 'Poets' in *Andrina* (pp.44-70). It is comprised of four tales: 'The Satirist', on a poet from ancient China; 'The Skald in the Cave', on a Norse poet; 'Lord of Silence', on an eighteenth-century Scottish bard; and 'Gold Dust', on a modern poet in Scotland. The first story stresses the social and political importance of poetry, the second the necessity for natural inspiration, the third the value of poetic silence. The fourth, however, presents a modern poet, Frank Kern, a man living on social security and his mother, proudly and ostentatiously showing off a poem, 'an inch of cyclostyled type' (p.69), which he has just had published in a new, obscure, and very cheaply produced quarterly. Mackay Brown thus rather melodramatically presents the role and value of poetry in the twentieth century as having dwindled into irrelevance and pretentiousness.

The Old Norse section, 'The Skald in the Cave' has the earl's poet, Arvid, dying and planning to pass on symbolically his ivory harp to one of his five sons. Three of them have received some poetic training: Thord, the lawyer and trader, Ottar, the Viking, and Rolf, the lascivious tax-collector. Arvid rejects all these, and also Solmund, who is a monk. Instead he chooses as his successor Jon, for unlike his brothers, who have excelled in warfare, trade, sex and religion, Jon has remained a simple fisherman and crofter; as he says in his own words: '"I learned only to put a stitch in a net. I can bind sheaves in a harvest"' (p.56). The story is very patterned and symbolic, but its general point, that worldly knowledge is not always necessary for poetic inspiration, is clearly and plainly stated. Standing on its own, 'The Skald in the Cave' would be a neat if not particularly profound story, but its individual point is virtually lost within the sequence 'Poets', for it is so obviously being used for didactic purposes; skaldic poetry has simply become an historical stick with which to beat modern verse.

A final and very good example of Mackay Brown's didactic use of Old Norse material (though not in the context of historical contrast) is the short story 'The Fires of Christmas' (*Hawkfall*, pp.59-65). In this story, Mackay Brown retells two incidents from *Orkneyinga Saga*, Earl Thorfinn's burning of Rognvald Brusison in 1046, and the killing of Sweyn Breastrope [sic] by Sweyn Asleifson [sic] in 1135.[35] At the end of these two accounts Mackay Brown adds a paragraph in which he simply states that, although there had been eighty-nine years between the events:

> ... in the meantime the blood of Saint Magnus had been shed. The second drama is not so dark and hopeless as the first. Fate had given way, to some extent at least, to grace. (*Hawkfall*, p.65)

Even a convinced Christian with a good historical knowledge of these events must find Mackay Brown's argument hard to follow. The first killing is both a self-defensive act of revenge (Rognvald had previously attempted to burn Earl Thorfinn to death in his hall) and an unfortunate necessity to ensure that Rognvald would never again treacherously disturb the peace and prosperity of Orkney. Moreover the firing at Paplay was scrupulously conducted according to the conventions of the time: women, children, and unarmed men were allowed out of the burning building. The murder of Sweyn Breastrope, Earl Paul's retainer, on the other hand, was carried out by a guest of Earl Paul's in his own homestead, and was the result of a stupid and drunken jealousy. One cannot deny, of course, that both killings were brutal and unpleasant, but the Thorfinn/Rognvald confrontation had some weighty reasons behind it, whereas the incident involving the two Sweyns seems petty and despicable. Indeed, as I have pointed out in the previous chapter on Linklater, the murder was apparently connived at by Eyvind Melbrigdason. So it seems hard to see how Mackay Brown perceives any distinct advance in human moral progress, and the whole point of the story must be brought into question. It is an understandable failure as Mackay Brown is clearly trying to twist historical facts to fit in with his sometimes dogmatic Christian beliefs.

This overt didacticism is, fortunately, not common. Even Robin Fulton concedes that although Mackay Brown's sometimes simplistic attitude towards Progress cannot be ignored, 'it is worth stressing that it is most evident when his work is at its weakest'.[36] As I hope the evidence above will show, however, Mackay Brown's overall application of Old Norse literature and history, whether for imaginative historical recreations, historical contrasts, or stylistic purposes, is usually interesting, enlightening and effective. Beyond Mackay Brown's general love and knowledge of Old Norse culture, however, two incidents from Orkney's Norse history seemed to have captured his imagination above all others: the martyrdom of St. Magnus in 1117 and the pilgrimage of Earl Rognvald Kolsson c.1151-53; these two subjects therefore demand more detailed study and evaluation.

Earl Rognvald Kolsson and Skaldic Poetry

It is not surprising that Mackay Brown should have been drawn to the history of Earl Rognvald (1136-58) as he is beyond doubt one of the most attractive characters in *Orkneyinga Saga*.[37] A brave and resourceful man, patient and magnanimous to his enemies, his greatest achievement was the founding of St. Magnus Cathedral in 1137, still the magnificent centrepiece of Orkney. Mackay Brown reveals his admiration for Rognvald in his eulogistic 'Crusader' section of *An Orkney Tapestry* (pp.102-23) in which he lovingly retells the saga story of Rognvald, dwelling especially on his pilgrimage to Jerusalem, including the romantic interlude with Princess Ermengarde in Narbonne, the defeat of a tyrant in Galicia, and the sinking of a dromond in the Mediterranean. Mackay Brown ends his account with an entirely fictitious description of Rognvald and his men participating in the Stations of the Cross in the Church of the Holy Sepulchre in Jerusalem.

Besides being a crusader, the builder of St. Magnus Cathedral, and canonised saint (1192), Rognvald Kolsson was bound to have excited the sympathy and imagination of Mackay Brown for two additional reasons. Firstly, Rognvald was very much a man of the people. He happily accepts the humble hospitality of local farmers when shipwrecked in Shetland, and on another occasion he rows out to sea, incognito, with an old man desperately in need of a fishing partner.[38] The whole incident, including a Shetland woman jeering at the disguised earl when he falls in the mud, and the earl's humorous poem on the occasion, has been retold by Mackay Brown in his story 'The Masked Fisherman' in the collection of the same title (pp.127-35). And secondly, Rognvald was a highly accomplished poet who attracted other skalds to his Orkney court. This is an important point, for apart from the general influence of Old Norse skaldic poetry on Mackay Brown's own work, discussed above, it was only when writing about Earl Rognvald that he made a serious attempt to present modern versions of skaldic verses. These verses are not translations as Mackay Brown knew no Old Norse, but modern versions of A.B. Taylor's translations.[39] As Mackay Brown himself explained:

> I have had to wrench skaldic verse into a shape acceptable to modern readers. Any attempt to reproduce something like the original is impossibly difficult.... I expect no delight at all for my very free paraphrase; only that perhaps it is more in accord with modern taste. (OT, 2-3)

Skaldic verse is indeed notoriously difficult to understand, let alone translate.[40] Nonetheless, translating such poetry is only *impossibly* difficult for those who have no knowledge of Old Norse, for a very good attempt has been made to approximate both the style (alliterative patterning) and the meaning of *Orkneyinga Saga's* skaldic verses in Pálsson's and Edwards' most recent translation. Mackay Brown's versions of Earl Rognvald's and his skalds' strophes must be judged on their own terms, therefore: as modern responses to Taylor's translations. A comparison between the two writers' renderings is revealing.

In general terms Taylor's translations are accurate versions of the meanings of the verses,[41] but although they give some hint of the original style, they are not very striking as poetry. Mackay Brown's poems, paying less attention to the Norse fondness for alliteration, are much more concise, compressed and effective. Compare for

example the two versions of a strophe by one of Rognvald's skalds
(Armod) on a sexually frustrated seaman on watch:

Taylor (p.298):	*Orkney Tapestry* (p.117):
We watch o'er the sea-steed	Night. Sheets of salt.
When o'er the stout gunwale	Armod on watch.
The billow breaks wildly.	A heave and wash of lights
Thus duty is done.	from the island.
While the lazy land-lubber	The lads of Crete
Sleeps by some maiden	Toss in hot tumbled linen.
Soft-skinned and kind,	This poet on watch
Over my shoulder	Cold, burning, unkissed.
I gaze towards Crete.	

Mackay Brown's jagged, paratactic syntax is much more successful
than Taylor's clausal subordination in drawing out the mood of taut
awareness and sexual frustration of the man on watch. Similarly,
Mackay Brown's version of Armod's strophe on the stormy coast of
Northumberland (OT, 104; Taylor, p.285) captures much more succinctly the sarcasm of the sailor towards those safe on dry land.
Mackay Brown's artistry is most strikingly apparent, however, in
his invariably effective use of imagery. Feeling unable to mimic all
the linguistic patterns of skaldic poetry in modern verse forms, he
cleverly seized on implied images in the strophes and used them as
structural matrixes, often contrapuntally. Thus in a strophe in *An
Orkney Tapestry* (pp.104-5) the images of drinking and horse-riding
in the first half are turned into metaphors in the second half
through 'hogsheads of salt' as the earl 'spurs the ship'. Similarly the
red wine and silver-white hair of Ermengarde are contrasted with
the redness of blood and the 'sharp whiteness' of swords (OT, 109;
Taylor, p.290); in another strophe Sigmund thinks of his lover's
spinning wheel in Orkney whilst he himself is involved in the 'red
wheel of war' (OT, 110; Taylor, p.291).

   Other notable comparisons can be made between Mackay Brown's
own different versions of Rognvald's strophes, for although two of
them were repeated with very minor and insignificant changes in
Winterfold, two others were rewritten with very different nuances.
Compare, for example, the two versions below (Taylor, p.286):

An Orkney Tapestry (p.106):   *Winterfold* (p.23):

Golden one,   Your hair, lady
Tall one,   Is long, a bright waterfall.
Moving in perfume and onyx,   You move through the warriors
Witty one,   Rich and tall as starlight.
You with the shoulders   What can I give
Lapped in long silken hair   For the cup and kisses brought
Listen: because of me   to my mouth ?
The eagle has a red claw.   Nothing.
                                     This red hand, a death-dealer.

Here we can see a distinct shift in emphasis; in the earlier version
the 'red claw' of Rognvald is clearly meant to impress the princess,
whereas in the later version the earl has become more demure and
unsure of himself. There are further differences in the following
strophes, also translations of compositions by Rognvald (Taylor,
p.287):

An Orkney Tapestry, (p.111):   *Winterfold*, (p.23):

The small mouth of Ermengarde   The summer mouth of Ermengarde
Commands two things -   Commands two things -
A sea strewn with wreckage   A sea of saga-stuff, wreckage, gold,
As far as Jordan,   As far as Jordan,
And later, in autumn   And later, at leaf-fall,
With other migrant wings   On patched homing wings
A returned prow.   A sun-dark hero.

In the earlier version the 'small mouth of Ermengarde' has implicit
sexual undertones reinforced by 'a returned prow'. In the later version, however, the 'summer mouth of Ermengarde' removes all sen-
suality from the verse and the earl will return as a conventional
'sun-dark hero' rather than a lover. Mackay Brown clearly wished
to present a gentler, more chivalrous crusader in *Winterfold* than the
more aggressive earl in *An Orkney Tapestry*, probably reflecting
Mackay Brown's increasing interest in the religious rather than military aspects of Rognvald's saintliness. Indeed, Mackay Brown's
concern with presenting Rognvald and his men as true Christians

often seems to result in his creating meanings and nuances completely at variance with the original Old Norse versions. In one
instance, for example, the monks of Westray are ironically
described by Rognvald (in translation) as 'sixteen young women ...
bevies of maidens with heads bald and bare' (Taylor, p.252),[42] but
Mackay Brown presents them as 'sixteen walkers' with heads 'bare
as stone', and only in the last line does he add: 'Demure and harm-
less as girls' (*Winterfold*, p.21). Rognvald's implied sarcasm and
amusing metaphor is completely removed by Mackay Brown, who
replaces it with a very tame simile; again perhaps his own religious
sensitivity prevents him from retelling Rognvald's irreverent jest.
Indeed, Mackay Brown's determination to emphasise Rognvald's
Christianity produces even greater divergences from the texts and
he changes completely the last few lines of the earl's strophe on the
latter's departure from the Holy Land for Constantinople and the
Byzantine court:

Taylor (p.301):	*An Orkney Tapestry* (p.122):
Let us take the bounty	We will be the Emperor's
Of the mighty Monarch	husbandmen,
Push on to clash of sword,	Winnowing chaff from the holy
Redden the wolf's jaws,	grain
And honour the King.	May we be worthy at last
	For the glory of Christ the King
	To break bread in the white
	churches.

Seeking plunder and fame in the service of the Byzantine Emperor
is thus turned into a statement of religious fervour, with the worldly 'King' of the original becoming 'Christ the King' in Mackay
Brown's version. He changes the strophe even further in *Winterfold*
(p.24), now introducing a laudatory chant from the Mass:

Sin darkens the grain-hold.
We have branded their coasts with rage and lust,
The old dragon-breath.
No end of sorrow, soultroth, seeking, still.
Kyrie, Christe, Kyrie eleison

> The Golden Harvester
> Comes out to grace, with robe and ring,
>   the swineherd.

There is at least some mention of violence here, but in tones of guilt
and regret which are simply not present in Earl Rognvald's original
strophe. Mackay Brown has completely transformed Rognvald's
verse from a traditional expression of Norse expectations of battle
and honour into what amounts to a confessional homily.[43] Mackay
Brown's apparent need to mute the earl's more violent history and
foreground his Christian sensibility is in stark contrast to
Linklater's approach to medieval Scandinavian holy men; indeed in
his own though very different way, Mackay Brown was as biased as
his fellow Orcadian in his presentation of saints, a point which will
become even clearer with a study of Mackay Brown's lifelong
admiration for St. Magnus the Martyr.

St. Magnus, Earl of Orkney

The story of the earl and saint, Magnus Erlendsson, is perhaps the
most famous episode in Orkney's history (*Orkneyinga Saga* Chs.39-
52). Renowned for his religious sensibility and celibate marriage,
Magnus ruled Orkney jointly with his cousin Earl Hakon Paulsson
in peace and co-operation in the early part of the twelfth century.
Rival supporters of the two earls gradually stirred up animosity
between the cousins, however, and faced with outright civil war the
two factions met fully armed at the Orkney Thing where open conflict was only averted by a peace treaty to be ratified on the isle of
Egilsay on Easter Sunday 1116 or 1117. Magnus duly arrived at
Egilsay with two warships, as agreed, but Hakon arrived with
eight, a clear indication of his treacherous intentions. Faced with
the inevitable, Magnus at first tried to come to terms with Hakon
and made three offers: firstly, that he, Magnus, would go on a pilgrimage to Jerusalem and then remain in permanent exile from
Orkney; secondly, he would retire to a monastery and take no further part in political life; and thirdly, he would submit to mutilation
and permanent imprisonment. Hakon refused the first two offers,
but was willing to accept the third. His men, however, would hear
of no compromise and insisted on the death of one of the two earls.

'"Better kill him then," said Hakon. "I don't want an early death; I much prefer ruling over people and places."'[44] None of Hakon's men would actually do the deed and he was forced to order his cook, Lifolf, to carry out the execution. Magnus knelt in prayer before being killed by a single blow of an axe to the head. Shortly after Magnus had been interred at Birsay, miracles began to happen at his tomb and he was canonised as a martyr c.1137, or twenty years after his death.[45]

The story of Magnus was a constant inspiration for Mackay Brown and implicit and explicit references to the life and death of St. Magnus can be found throughout his poems, plays and stories. In one five-year period, however, Mackay Brown produced three important renderings of the St. Magnus story: the 'Martyr' section of *An Orkney Tapestry* (1969), the play *The Loom of Light* (staged 1972)[46] and the novel *Magnus* (1973). The notable feature of these works is that Mackay Brown gradually expands and changes his material over the period, and a detailed study of this development reveals several interesting facets of the author's vision of the saint and his martyrdom.

In 'Martyr', Mackay Brown presents a relatively straightforward retelling of the saga with additional comments and certain literary embellishments including a fictional one-act drama concerning two Orkney tinkers, Jock and blind Mary, the latter regaining her sight as a result of Jock's prayers at Magnus's tomb. Although admitting that Magnus's monkish biographers were biased in their presentation of the saint's life, Mackay Brown nonetheless argues that: 'The events that gather about him are so extraordinary, and were witnessed by so many people, and were enacted in such a hard light, that there is no faking of the record' (OT, 72). He also adds his own personal slant to the story by presenting Hakon as a religious as well as a political rival, for 'fame in history was probably the only kind of immortality this young Norseman believed in: a resurrection of the word' (OT, 71). Hakon is thus clearly associated with the Old Norse pagan values which Mackay Brown had already condemned in the earlier 'Warrior' section on Earl Sigurd. Hakon's repentance over the slaying of Magnus and his pilgrimage to the Holy Land can consequently be seen as the ultimate victory of Magnus's Christian faith.

Near the end of 'Martyr', Mackay Brown writes: 'The story of
Magnus and Hakon unfolds like a drama. Some day a play will be
written about it; I have not the ability myself' (OT, 87). He evident-
ly changed his mind soon after, however, for in 1972 his play *The
Loom of Light* was produced in Kirkwall. Scene 1 opens with two
Orkney peasants, Mans and Hild, struggling to plough their field
whilst across the water on Birsay Earl Paul is marrying Thora, the
future mother of Magnus. Scene 2, set ten years later, presents
Magnus and Hakon as schoolboys on Birsay; Hakon is already
aggressive and wilful, whereas Magnus is significantly concerned
over a wounded seal on the beach. Scene 3 presents one of the most
famous incidents in Magnus's career: his refusal to fight alongside
his king against the Welsh in the Menai Strait. Whilst the sea-battle
rages Magnus steadfastly reads aloud from his psalter, ignoring the
king's disapproval and Hakon's taunts of cowardice. At the end of
hostilities, Magnus binds the wounds of Mans, who is now one of
the longship's oarsmen. In Scene 4, seventeen years later, we return
to Mans and Hild who are desperately trying to save their land
from the depradations of both Hakon's and Magnus's men; the
whole of Orkney is aflame in civil war. In Scene 5 the leading men
of both factions approach the bishop on Birsay in an attempt to
involve him in negotiations for peace. The bishop declines the invitation, ominously commenting: 'What is desperately needed in
Orkney this Easter is something more in the nature of a sacrifice:
the true immaculate death of the dove' (*Plays*, p.32). Scene 6 presents the confrontation on Egilsay. Here Mackay Brown makes an
important change from the saga, for it is now Hakon who makes
the proposals (here reduced from three to two) to his men; Magnus
is not even present and only appears after the decision to kill him
has been taken. The significance of this change will be discussed
below in connection with the novel *Magnus*. Mackay Brown's stage
directions for the actual killing ('The witnesses gather round, hiding Magnus and Lifolf'; *Plays*, p.42) are interesting in that they seem
almost certainly copied from Linklater's and Clouston's pageant of
1937.[47] The final scene of the play is an expanded version of the
one-act drama from 'Martyr', the tinkers Jock and Mary begging
from Mans and Hild before continuing on their journey to St.
Magnus's tomb and the miracle.

Mackay Brown's dramatisation of the saga events seems primarily aimed at underlining the ritual necessity of sacrifice and that Magnus was specifically *chosen* for the Christ-like role. Nonetheless Mackay Brown appears to have been unconvinced that he had done full justice to this vision, for as he explained in the preface to his plays: 'Some writers are never content to leave well alone. On to the stark framework of the play I rigged the novel *Magnus*' (*Plays*, p.ix). This novel is indeed the culmination of Mackay Brown's study and interpretation of the Orkney saint's life. Its first three chapters are greatly expanded prose versions of the first three scenes of the play with Mackay Brown naturally 'making as full use as possible of the more varied techniques at the novelist's disposal' (*Plays*, p.x). Effective additions in the novel include details of the wedding and nuptial night of Magnus's parents which underline the ploughing and sowing symbolism. This was already hinted at through the parallel of Mans's and Hild's working in the fields.

The fourth chapter, 'The Temptations', is a completely new and ambitious addition to the story, for here Mackay Brown introduces the Keeper of the Loom or Magnus's guardian angel who appears to him and informs him of the weaving of a seamless garment in preparation for his being bidden to a marriage feast. He is also warned to beware the Tempter, and indeed for the remainder of the chapter we see Magnus resisting the varying temptations of lust, power, war and resignation from life. This section of the novel, with its pervasive biblical and religious motifs, is often the most difficult for readers to understand.

The fifth chapter, 'Scarecrow', contains the same material as Scene 4 of the play, but this time with more harrowing scenes of pillaging and murder as the earls' factions ride roughshod over the rights of the Orcadians in their military struggle for power. The sixth chapter, 'Prelude to the Invocation of the Dove', is centred on the leading men's appeal to the bishop (cf. Scene 5 of the play), but has an additional section in which the bishop composes a homily, 'Concerning the Two Coats, of Caesar and of God, that cover Adam's Shame', which once more reiterates the garment symbolism prevalent throughout Mackay Brown's renderings of the Magnus story. As in the play, the chapter ends with the bishop's premonition of the necessity of a blood sacrifice.

The seventh chapter, 'The Killing', takes place on Egilsay, only the proposals concerning Magnus's fate (again reduced to two) are now mooted by Magnus's leading men, Finn Thorkelson and Hold Ragnarson.[48] Hakon's men rudely reject them and Magnus is condemned to death, once more in his absence. The chapter also contains a long digression on the nature and meaning of sacrifice and the Catholic mass, and the startling introduction of Brechtian *Verfremdungseffekte*. Mackay Brown not only has twentieth-century journalists reporting on the events on Egilsay, he also translocates the execution scene to a Nazi concentration camp; the victim is now not Magnus, but Dietrich Bonhoeffer, a Lutheran priest who had been a steadfast opponent of Hitler's regime and who was hanged on 8 April 1945. The executioner, still called Lifolf, is now the camp butcher, and Hakon is the Commandant, his leading men SS officers of varying rank. Mackay Brown uses this technique, Bold claims, to imply that 'the martyrdom is as relevant today as it was in the twelfth century'.[49] It is certainly a startling innovation in what had purported to be an historical novel set in medieval Orkney, and one which has been both admired and criticised, as we shall see.

The final chapter, 'Harvest', once again returns to the twelfth century and the pattern established in *An Orkney Tapestry* and *The Loom of Light*: the tinkers Jock and Mary on their way to Birsay and begging from Mans and Hild, now enjoying the peace and prosperity of Hakon's reign, the 'harvest' made possible by the spilling of Magnus's blood.

Magnus is an ambitious and daring novel, and critical evaluations of it have varied. Elizabeth Huberman asserts that it is 'a novel which transforms a suspect genre and an unfashionable subject into a true and timeless work of the imagination' whilst Bold views it more harshly as 'a theological discourse with fictional asides'. A reviewer for the *Times Literary Supplement* sees both positive and negative aspects of the novel, summing up *Magnus* as 'a collection of magnificent pieces which do not quite fit together to achieve the desired unity'.[50] There are quite clearly both strengths and weakness in the novel. For religious readers it must provide a poignant and dramatic affirmation of faith in Christ's death and resurrection. Stylistically, too, some of its scenes, especially those concerning the peasants Mans and Hild and the tinkers Jock and Mary contain some of Mackay Brown's finest writing and reveal his deep compassion for ordinary folk struggling against the vicissitudes of life. The callous scenes in the civil war section provide a very effective condemnation of the pointlessness and barbarity of violence. The use of *Verfremdungseffekte* may disturb the unity of the novel for some readers, but on the whole they are imaginative and daring, and at the very least display a certain stylistic virtuosity.

Two of the main flaws in the novel, as Bold has pointed out, are the rather nebulous characterisation of the eponymous hero and the long sections of liturgical imagery and theological moralising which may well prove somewhat irksome, if not incomprehensible, to non-Roman Catholic readers. Bold particularly criticises Mackay Brown for tacitly assuming 'that the martyrdom was ordained by God' and for 'dogmatically accepting' the sanctity of Magnus. By making Magnus 'a particular chosen seed, a summoned one' (*Magnus*, p.26) and by giving him a guardian angel who foretells his fate, Mackay Brown 'deprives Magnus of a free will' and removes all dramatic tension from the novel. Bold is also unimpressed with Mackay Brown's introduction of the Dietrich Bonhoeffer parallel, pointing out that the passive martyrdom of Magnus bears no comparison with the active anti-Nazi resistance of the Lutheran pastor.[51]

One other feature of *Magnus*, however, apparently overlooked or ignored by the critics, needs further consideration. This concerns Mackay Brown's unobtrusive manipulation of Old Norse history mentioned earlier. Most critics, and presumably most readers, tacitly assume that apart from the obvious fictional embellishments, the story of Magnus is that of the saga. A careful study of *Orkneyinga Saga* and Mackay Brown's other major source, John Mooney's *St. Magnus: Earl of Orkney* (1935), reveals that this is not the case, however. In three specific incidents Mackay Brown has changed the facts to suit his own purposes. The first is in Magnus's relations with his namesake King Magnus Barelegs of Norway both before and during the sea-battle in the Menai Strait. In both *The Loom of Light* (*Plays*, p.20) and *Magnus* (pp.62-63) Mackay Brown has King Magnus confirm the fathers of Magnus and Hakon as joint earls of Orkney. This is a total contradiction of the saga, in which

King Magnus actually *deposes* Earls Paul and Erlend (sending them into exile in Norway where they die) and proclaims his own son as overlord of the Northern Isles.[52] Mackay Brown does in fact give the saga version in *An Orkney Tapestry* (p.70), but why does he depart from the saga in the play and the novel?

The answer would seem to be that, contrary to Huberman's claims, he wishes to remove all ambiguity from Magnus's actions; in Bold's words, Mackay Brown must 'scan the saga account of Magnus's life and isolate the quality of saintliness'.[53] Thus Magnus's refusal to fight King Magnus's Welsh enemies, for example, must be seen as a specific act of Christian non-belligerence and not as a political protest against the king's disinheriting his father (and ultimately himself) of the Orkney earldom. Furthermore, the supposition that Magnus's intentions were in actuality more worldly than religious gains further credence when possible political links between Magnus and the Welsh are taken into account.[54] Moreover Mackay Brown's claims for the uniqueness of Magnus's action (OT, 74) are also inaccurate; although unusual, a refusal to fight was not without precedent in the Norse world. King Brian Boru refused to bear arms at the Battle of Clontarf on Good Friday in 1014, and in *Laxdaela Saga* Kjartan Olafsson threw down his sword and accepted death at the hands of his cousin Bolli rather than kill the latter himself.[55]

A second important instance of Mackay Brown's deviation from the saga concerns the civil war between the earls Magnus and Hakon. In *An Orkney Tapestry* Mackay Brown stresses that Orkney 'had been torn and bloodied with centuries of civil strife' and that all the earls 'had given most of their wealth and energy to war' (p.77). In *The Loom of Light* and *Magnus* Mackay Brown therefore presents the reader with vivid portrayals of the rapine and looting of Magnus's and Hakon's men. Most critics seem to take these scenes at face value,[56] but they are completely at variance with the facts. The latter part of Earl Thorfinn's reign was blessed with peace and splendour and Earls Paul and Erlend had ruled jointly and harmoniously for decades, only finally becoming alienated by the rivalry of their sons. Even then, however, the Orkney magnates always brought about reconciliations through turbulent but non-violent negotiations. There may have been the occasional brawl between rival supporters of Hakon and Magnus, but there was never open war between them. Indeed the last major conflict between two Orkney earls, Thorfinn and Rognvald Brusison, had been in 1046. In other words Orkney had enjoyed relative peace and security for almost three generations before the Hakon-Magnus confrontation ended in murder in c.1117.[57] Mackay Brown's aim in creating a fictitious war between Hakon and Magnus seems clear, for it gives far greater meaning to Magnus's death if it ended a vicious civil war rather than simply averted one. Within the terms of artistic license this is perhaps perfectly justifiable in that civil war *would* almost certainly have broken out had the earls both continued to live in dispute. Nonetheless it underlines Mackay Brown's assiduous, if not anxious, concern to magnify the relevance of Magnus's martyrdom, even if it meant modifying the saga.

The final incident revolves around the proposals mooted on Egilsay in an attempt to avoid bloodshed. In *An Orkney Tapestry* (p.81) Mackay Brown faithfully presents the saga version of the incident, with Magnus making the three offers to Hakon. In the play and novel, however, as previously mentioned, these proposals are reduced in number and put forward either by Hakon or Magnus's men, in each case with Magnus absent. Why does Mackay Brown make this important change from the saga? Again, the answer seems to be that he is trying to make Magnus as non-worldly as possible. In the saga, Magnus's attempts to come to terms with Hakon and save his own life are perfectly natural and reveal a normal and fallible human being. By removing Magnus from the negotiations altogether, Mackay Brown also removes this worldly blemish from his martyrdom and underlines the preordained nature of his fate. This interpretation supports Bold's assertion that 'Magnus is conspicuous by his corporeal absence' and helps explain the rather nebulous characterisation of Magnus.[58]

All these divergences from the saga show, as with his treatment of Earl Rognvald, that Mackay Brown is determined to play down the fallible and human aspects of Magnus and to emphasise his saintliness. The modification of historical fact for purposes of narrative fiction is not unknown, of course, indeed in the Scottish tradition itself Sir Walter Scott set a notable precedent,[59] and Mackay Brown was justified in presenting his vision of St. Magnus in whatever form he felt most effective. Nonetheless, when such literary refractions and rearrangements are noted by readers with a knowledge of Orcadian history, the result may be a greater wariness and scepticism towards Mackay Brown's intentions, especially if these seem overtly didactic. In this sense, Mackay Brown's manipulation of the saga may have defeated his own ends.

As all the above comments suggest, understanding and evaluating *Magnus* is a complex process involving shifting historical, religious and artistic viewpoints. Indeed this complexity is at the heart of the work's achievement. This is particularly notable in that a reader with no particular knowledge of Roman Catholicism or the history of Orkney can nonetheless engage deeply with the novel. Despite Bold's criticism, the identification of Magnus's fate with that of Bonhoeffer's, for example, can give a poignant reading as a moving and explicit statement of '*la condition humaine*' in which justice does not always triumph and truly good men of all ages and races are often mercilessly destroyed in the unscrupulous pursuit of political power and ideological hegemony. As Huberman has summarised: 'The choices presented in archaic terms to the twelfth-century Magnus are suddenly the choices presented to us in the conflicts of conscience of this century'.[60]

After *Magnus*, Mackay Brown never again dealt with the story of the Orkney earl in such detail, though he did write what were, in effect, epilogues. The short story 'The Feast at Paplay' (*Andrina*, pp.105-24) presents a grim retelling of the saga incident in which Earl Hakon, after the killing of Magnus, visits Thora, Magnus's mother, who has prepared a feast to celebrate what everyone had thought would be a peace treaty. The feast thus becomes a wake, and, true to the saga, the story ends with the overwrought Hakon bursting into tears and granting Thora permission to bury her son in consecrated ground. More recently Mackay Brown collaborated with artists of various kinds in producing beautifully illustrated editions (with musical scores, drawings, and photographs) of his poetry and prose works celebrating the canonisation of St. Magnus and Earl Rognvald's founding of the cathedral in 1137.[61] In terms of the themes of Christian saintliness and non-violence, however, Mackay Brown made his most direct and succinct statement in his final Viking novel *Vinland*.

Vinland: **Ranald Sigmundson, Secular Saint**

Mackay Brown's *Vinland* relates the life and times of the Orcadian Norseman Ranald Sigmundson. As a boy of twelve he deserts his bullying father on a trading expedition in Iceland and stows away on the ship of Leif Ericson [sic], thus becoming one of Vikings who first land in America, or Vinland as it was known in the Norse world. After the failure of attempts to come to peaceful terms with the natives and make a settlement there, he returns to Greenland with Leif where he wins a famous horse race. On visiting Norway he is entertained by King Olaf, anxious for news of the new continent, and on returning to Orkney he outwits Earl Sigurd's treasurer in the payment for the cargo his ship is carrying. He then successfully reclaims his inherited land at Breckness and becomes a prosperous and influential farmer, a member of the Orkney Thing, and privy to the Earl's family and political machinations. Thus in 1014 he accompanies the Earl to Ireland and takes part in the famous battle at Clontarf, and some five years later is present at the feast where Earl Einar is murdered. He lives to see the struggle for power between Earls Thorfinn and Rognvald, which ends with the latter's death at the Burning of Paplay, and he finally dies as the victorious Thorfinn is about to set off for Rome with the Scottish king, Macbeth, around about the year 1050.

As this brief summary of *Vinland* illustrates, Ranald Sigmundson's life encompasses some of the most stirring events in the Norse world in the first half of the eleventh century. Indeed, his journey to Vinland, meeting with King Olaf, participation at Clontarf, and his relations and dealings with some of the most famous Norsemen of his time, all at first indicate that Ranald will have an illustrious career as a typical Viking who will 'play his part in the story'. A reader familiar with Mackay Brown's work may well find this an unlikely departure from the usual ambience of his Viking fiction, and these suspicions are confirmed half way through the novel when there comes a dramatic change in Ranald's role and attitude. He is so appalled by the treachery and bloodshed at Clontarf that he is reluctant to talk about his experiences there and his distaste for the crudity and barbarity of Orcadian intrigues reaches a climax with the murder of Earl Einar by Thorkel, Thorfinn's loyal supporter. Einar's murder is justifiable in that

Einar himself had planned to ambush and kill Thorkel, but nonetheless Ranald rejects his former friendship with Thorkel and quite literally resigns from public life, never again attending the Thing or the earls' conferences but resolutely minding his own business. He later explains to his grandchildren how

> ... a deep disgust had entered into his heart at human folly and cruelty, his own included; and how he had seen that power drives men mad, and how Earl Einar of the Twisted Mouth had fallen into his own web-of-treachery at Skaill in Sandwick; and how he had decided to wash his hands of politics and violence and attend only to the farm of Breckness. (V, 226)[62]

For the rest of his life Ranald tends to shun the company of the wealthy and powerful and seeks instead the company of lowly fishermen, boat-builders and peasants. He provides loans on generous terms for other farmers in difficulty and gives away food and clothing to beggars. The death of his favourite child, Margaret, makes him even more reclusive and he hands over the running of Breckness to his son Sumarlid and eventually takes up abode in a delapidated hovel on a nearby hill. He becomes increasingly devout, especially after talks with the monk Fergus and the abbot Peter, and plans to set sail again for Vinland in a boat being built for him by his friend Lodd, long-since dead. However, he dies, significantly enough on an Easter Monday, before he can make this impossible dream come true. In Mackay Brown's view, Ranald Sigmundson has thus redeemed himself to become a true Norse hero: a once typical Viking who in the pride of life rejects the vanities of this world to live a simple, honest Christian life by trying to be at peace with all men, the world of nature and his God. But how successful is this new approach now that Mackay Brown has used a fictional secular saint instead of an historically canonised one?

Vinland: Historical Background and Narrative Structure

As might be expected, Mackay Brown bases most of the events of his novel on *Orkneyinga Saga* and the *Vinland Sagas* and for the most part he remains faithful to them. Like Grassic Gibbon and Linklater before him, he conflates the various versions of the discovery of

Vinland into one simplified story: though the historical Leif never saw any natives, Mackay Brown has him trade and later fight with them, and the famous grapes are given to the Norsemen by the Indians themselves. This imaginative conflation of the sources is perfectly acceptable within the artistic structure of the novel, for, as we shall see, the exact details of the Norse discovery of Vinland are subordinate to its symbolic significance for the character of Ranald. Nonetheless, there are some historical errors: Reykjavik was certainly not a port c.1000, and the 'burning mountain', presumably a reference to Hekla, is not visible from there (V, 4); nor would the Indians have scalped the Norsemen they killed in Vinland (V, 20) as this practice was only introduced to them by the British and French more than five centuries later; and when Ranald reaches Bergen there are references to a castle, dungeons and 'an arched heraldic gate' (V, 38, 44) at a time when large stone buildings and heraldry were unknown in Norway.

These minor slips are, of course, unimportant in terms of the novel as a whole, but a more serious anachronism is evident in Leif Ericson's comments when he claims that, in comparison with the native Americans, the Norsemen are 'wasteful gluttons' who are irresponsible in their utilisation of wildlife and natural resources; he later relates a dream in which he predicts that the Indians' harmonious relations with the animal and natural world will be destroyed by the 'cunning and greed' of the white man (V, 24, 32). Such ecological concern is glaringly incongruous in an eleventh-century context, and Leif comes across, bizarrely, as more of a modern-day Greenpeace spokesman (complete with anti-whaling comments) than a Viking leader. This overtly didactic interpolation of Old Norse sources could, as in *Magnus*, disconcert the reader and make him unduly wary of Mackay Brown's intentions.

A further literary problem in *Vinland* concerns its narrative structure. The story is related entirely from Ranald's point of view, but, as the plot synopsis above reveals, about half way through the novel Ranald completely retires from public life. In order to justify this, however, and make this gesture seem valid, the reader must still be able to witness the treacherous and bloody events of Thorfinn's struggle to become the sole earl in Orkney. But how is this to be done if Ranald no longer takes part in Orcadian politics?

Mackay Brown's solution is to have all the news brought to Ranald (and thus the reader) by those who saw or heard of the relevant incidents, for example: 'these matters Ranald of Breckness learned from the men who came to visit him ...' (V, 138) and 'news of the earls' quarrels and manoeuvrings was brought to him from time to time ...' (V, 162). His informants are merchants, skippers and other farmers, and later on his son Ranald and son-in-law Ramir (for example: V, 165, 179, 193, 217, 225, 198, 204).

There are two main drawbacks with this device; firstly, the 'news came to Ranald' formula occurs more than a dozen times and thus becomes a very repetitive, if not distancing form of narrative, and secondly, as these reports only refer to the actions of the earls, there is a danger that the reader will begin to experience the novel as a simple retelling of the *Orkneyinga Saga* and not an independent work of fiction. To be fair to Mackay Brown, though, it is hard to see how else he could have surmounted this narrative problem; the reader *must* see the bloody events as they enfold while Ranald *must* remain on his farm in silent, peaceful protest, for any poignant contrast to be made. Moreover Mackay Brown does at least avoid another possible weakness concerning an inactive main protagonist: although Ranald takes no part in the politics of Orkney he is always shown doing small acts of piety, kindness and friendship in between the bloody scenes of intrigue. He thus never becomes as nebulous a character as some readers find the eponymous hero of *Magnus*. On the other hand, Ranald's insistence, near the end of his life, that his friend Lodd is building him a boat for his projected journey to Vinland, could lead to an ambiguous response from the reader, for Lodd has already been dead for several years. Does this mean to infer that Ranald's spiritual vision now transcends corporeal restrictions, or is he simply losing his memory? The last possibility is a little disconcerting, for it could be interpreted as evidence, not of saintliness, but of senility, consequently undermining what Mackay Brown clearly intends to be the importance and validity of Ranald's plans for one final expedition to the west.

The above criticisms of Mackay Brown's anachronisms and imprecise narrative technique may sem to imply that the novel is not a convincing work of art, but, as with *Magnus*, in spite of its flaws, *Vinland* remains a gripping, thought-provoking, and ultimately moving piece of fiction. This is a result of Mackay Brown's skillful weaving together of two major themes: a telling and per- suasive contrast of the Norse concept of fate and the Christian view of free will, and the powerful and unifying symbol of Vinland itself.

Ranald Sigmundson and Fate

As has seen previously noted, Mackay Brown had criticised the Norse concept of fate as early as 1969 in his *Orkney Tapestry*. In *Vinland*, however, this subject provides the central debate of the novel. Throughout his life, Ranald is troubled by the 'riddle of fate and freedom' (V, 227) and he neatly summarises how a belief in the Norse view of fate can give a man an apparent sense of free will:

> 'Believing this – it is in the very marrow of our bones, it is carved deep in our hearts – bestows a kind of wild freedom. Let us wring what we can out of the tight fist of fate. Then we can go down with a certain carelessness, even with laughter, into the invisible dust....' (V, 185)

But events in Ranald's life gradually undermine this belief. Earl Sigurd, for example, would '"rather fish in the burn for trout or shoot grouse on Greenay hill"' (V, 85), but fear of society's con- tempt, and his mother's sarcastic tongue, drive him to go a-Viking in Ireland. True to the fate his mother had prophesied, he dies in battle at Clontarf and 'earns his place in the story'. Essentially, how- ever, the impression is gained that Sigurd is in reality a hen-pecked man and a slave to conformity. He had little real choice in going to Clontarf, and his death, in practical terms, achieves absolutely nothing. The careers of Earls Einar and Rognvald Brusison can also be seen in this light. They certainly achieve fame but in reality their deaths are rather ignominious: Sigurd dies wrapped in his own banner because no one else will carry it; Einar's Viking raids always fail and his head is split with an axe while drunk; and the hand- some and dashing Rognvald is butchered in a boathouse, betrayed by his own dog. Even the brave and resolute Thorfinn, with his many admirable qualities, can be guilty of appalling acts of cold- blooded murder to achieve his ends (V, 210). In other words, Mackay Brown seems to impy, a belief in fate provides no reassurance in the vicissitudes of life: it actually encourages ruthless ambition and anarchic violence. As Ranald's mother Thora comments:

> 'There is still too much talk of fate and the old gods here in the north. It has made men hard and bitter and cruel.... I hope I will hear no more talk of the inexorable workings of fate, for only cruelty and rage and ugliness come out of such a belief.' (V, 112-13)

Indeed there are hints throughout the novel that fate is not as inexorable as medieval Norsemen believed. Earl Sigurd's mother, Eithne, had woven a magic Raven banner which would guarantee victory though its bearer would die. Sigurd duly dies literally wearing the banner – but on the losing side, a point on which the author of *Orkneyinga Saga* remains curiously silent. Moreover Eithne's prophecies concerning Ranald turn out to be inaccurate. She admittedly predicts years of prosperity and happiness (and even his wife, Ragna), but then she also states:

> 'The worst thing that can happen to a man ... is to grow old in stupidity and complacency. The silver hairs come into his beard. He gets aches in his joints, his breath comes short, his children pay no attention to his advice and go here and there about their own affairs.... He thinks people are mocking him behind his back – and so they are, most like, and little wonder.... That, Ranald Sigmundsson, is the kind of death that men seem to want nowadays. But it won't happen to you, I'm glad to say.' (V, 87-88)

Ironically, of course, this is more or less exactly how Ranald *does* die (he is referred to as an 'old dottled farmer', for example, V, 183), but the important point is that this is because Ranald *chooses* to die this way: Ranald takes his fate into his own hands and makes what he wants of his life, in this case a dedication to pacifism and a contemplation of the real meaning of existence. He successfully refuses to conform to the dictates of the prevailing ethos of his time. Ranald gains neither gold nor glory, but his death, though non-violent, is really much more dignified than those of the earls mentioned previously. The values Ranald lives for are summarised in a long lyrical speech made by the abbot Peter:

'... always, at night, a good man may lie down at peace with him-self and sleep.

'Yet, even so, he may think, searching his conscience before sleep, 'I have wrought no evil on earth today as far as I know, and I have helped my neighbour in this small matter and that, but does it matter in the end? This sleep that will soon fall on me at mid-night is a foreshadowing of death, the last endless sleep. Then it will be as if a poor crofter or fisherman like me had never lived. I might indeed have lived more comfortable nowadays with my wife and children if I had gone viking in the days of my strength, and gotten fame and gold ...' But the good man knows indeed that, though he is poor, it is a better treasure to lie down at night with an unburdened heart....

'The piece of the light that we tend and trim in our hearts will outlast the darkness and the dust of death....

'And so, dear children of the light, go out in peace to your fields and your fishing-boats.' (V, 189-90)

This simple, but beautifully expressed view of the positive and uplifting values of Christian pacifism seems a more positive achievement than the death and destruction which follow in the wake of the earls' greed for fame and is in stark contrast to the aggressive ways of contemporary Norsemen. This vision of humil-ity and non-aggression is succinctly and effectively symbolised by the emotional impact of the most memorable event of Ranald's life: his participation in the discovery of Vinland.

Vinland: Journey's End

It can come as a surprise after a first reading of *Vinland* to realise that only 11 of its 232 pages are actually concerned with the first Norse attempt to establish a settlement in America. But shortlived though it be, this adventure is to have an enduring influence on the twelve-year old Ranald's imagination, and Vinland eventually becomes a convincing and unifying symbol for all his beliefs and aspirations. Two things in particular make a great impression on him: the vision of harmony between man and nature, as portrayed in the lifestyle of the Indians (the 'web of creation', so often referred to in Mackay Brown's works), and a sense of the lost opportunity of creating a lasting and friendly relationship with the natives of the

new continent. The 'skraelingar', as the Norsemen call them, greet
Leif Ericson and his men peacefully and courteously and attempt to
communicate and trade with them. Ranald himself strikes up a sort
of friendship with a young boy of his own age, the two of them
happily splashing each other with water down on the beach.
Unfortunately, however, the Norsemen give the Indians alcohol,
which they have never drunk before, and one of them, making a
boisterous gesture is misunderstood by a quick-tempered
Norseman who instantly kills him. A fight ensues and from then on
relations between the two groups are marked by suspicion, fear and
violence; Ranald himself is struck by a stone thrown by the Indian
boy. Constantly besieged and outnumbered, the Greenlanders
eventually give up their attempt at settlement and return home.

For the rest of his life Ranald always remembers his transient
friendship with the Indian boy. What haunts him most, especially
when his life takes a dramatic turn after the murder of Earl Einar, is
this missed opportunity: the *promise*, the *possibility*, of two races,
previously unknown to each other, meeting, communicating and
living together in mutual respect and understanding in an integrat-
ed community; a possibility which, by analogy, also extends to all
peoples at all times. Thus, in his old age, yearning for a world of
peace and reconciliation instead of violence and confrontation,
Ranald talks of building a boat and sailing to Vinland to try and
renew his friendship with the Indian. He knows, of course, that in
reality this is impossible, but the projected return to Vinland is an
inspiring dream to uplift his last frail years; it neatly represents all
that he has learnt and valued in his life.

The symbolic meaning of Vinland is cleverly reinforced by the
parallel Celtic legend of a magic land far to the west. Ranald is
especially impressed by the monk Fergus's tale of Saint Brandon
who found an 'unutterably delightful' earthly paradise in the
Atlantic, where everyone is young, but is nonetheless informed by
one of the inhabitants that 'heaven was further west still ...' (V,
180). This is part of the same Celtic tradition which embraces the
fantastic sea-journey of Mael Duin and the Gaelic Otherworld of
Tir-nan-Og, the Land of Everlasting Youth, all far to the west.[63] As
the title of the last chapter 'Tir-nan-Og' suggests, Mackay Brown
has synthesised pagan and Christian myths and Norse and Celtic

sagas and legends to provide a perfect symbol for Ranald's aspirations and the duality of man's nature: the search for a new, peaceful and *real* world where men may live together in harmony (Vinland), and a visionary *ideal* world of complete perfection and immortality (Tir-nan-Og/Heaven).

What ultimately makes the duality of this symbol convincing and effective is the character of Ranald himself. It is notoriously difficult for an author to create a truly 'good' character without making him seem unbelievable or priggish, but in Ranald Sigmundson Mackay Brown has presented a convincing portrayal of a man who tries to be benevolent and sincere while remaining strikingly human and credible. Throughout all the turbulent events of his lifetime, the young Viking and aging recluse remains constant in his basic integrity. He may die a disreputable 'straw death' in contemporary Norse terms, but in the eyes of a modern reader he can be seen as an ordinary and fallible human being who, against the many odds of his time and society, managed to live a life of basic honesty and decency which is inspiring in its humility and dignity. As Ranald once says to his son Somarlid:

> 'Who knows how many saints there are among those poor humble men? Not only in the little churches either, but in the crofts and fishing-bothies there are men and women of great goodness, though their lives are often hard.' (V, 195)

As the whole of *Vinland* implies, Ranald Sigmundson is indeed one of these saints and his character one of Mackay Brown's most appealing representatives of his Christian faith.

Orkney Skald

As all the above evidence reveals, Old Norse history and literature had a profound influence on George Mackay Brown, and in terms of style, subject matter and ambience they are pervasive throughout all his work. Moreover they were not intellectual elements occasionally grafted on to his poems and stories (cf. Lindsay, MacDiarmid, and, to some extent, Mitchison and Buchan), they were totally and unselfconsciously part of Mackay Brown's total experience.

The use of saga and skaldic diction and plots and motifs from *Orkneyinga Saga* and other Old Norse works have been detailed above and need no further comment. Two important aspects of Mackay Brown's Norse-inspired poetry and fiction are perhaps worth reiterating, however. Firstly, Mackay Brown's deep Christian values considerably affected the way he saw the Vikings. On the negative side this has meant rather biased presentations of the Orkney saints, Magnus and Rognvald, but on the positive side, this has meant a much more rounded picture of eleventh- and twelfth-century Norsemen as Christians as well as pagans, as peacemakers as well as warmongers. Secondly, and related to the first aspect, Mackay Brown's love and appreciation of the everyday life of ordinary folk has resulted in the literary creation of totally believable Norsemen. The stereotype axe-wielding, all-conquering Viking, winning fame and fortune is not eulogised in Mackay Brown's poetry or fiction, for alongside the usual Norse earls and kings we are presented with Vikings who are peasants, fishermen, tax-collectors, tinkers, longship rowers, wounded soldiers, deserters, and even monks. Mackay Brown did not see the Vikings as creators of a particular ethos (cf. Linklater and Gunn), or as archetypal heroes (cf. Buchan and Linklater), or as bearers of an influential mythology (cf. Lindsay), but simply, and essentially, as ordinary, fallible, medieval Orcadians. In this respect it is probably fair to say that Mackay Brown's attempts to 'see the Vikings plain' (OT, 20) must be considered as having provided modern Scottish literature with its most convincing and effective realisation and interpretation of Scotland's Old Norse heritage.

NOTES

1   The only major exception would appear to be the collection of short stories *The Sun's Net* (London, 1976).
2   *Winterfold* (London, 1976), p.30.
3   'Stone Poems', in *A Calendar of Love* (1967; London, 1987), pp.115-17.
4   From 'Weather Bestiary' and 'Runes from a Holy Island', *Selected Poems* (London, 1977), pp.44, 89; 'Grave Stone', *Fishermen with Ploughs: A Poem Cycle* (London, 1979), p.30.
5   'Runes from a Holy Island', *Selected Poems*, p.90.

6   Alan Bold, *George Mackay Brown* (Edinburgh, 1978), p.16.
7   *Letters from Hamnavoe* (Edinburgh, 1975), p.86
8   Introduction to *Witch and Other Stories* (London,1977), p.x.
9   'Writer's Shop', in *Chapman* 16 (Summer, 1976), 22.
10   *A Time to Keep and Other Stories* (1969; London, 1976), pp.135-40.
11   *Greenvoe* (1972), Penguin edn. (Harmondsworth, 1976), p.207.
12   Murray and Tait, *Ten Modern Scottish Novels*, p.166.
13   Rowena Murray, 'The Influence of Norse Literature on the Twentieth-Century Writer George Mackay Brown', in *Scottish Language and Literature, Medieval and Renaissance*, Scottish Studies Vol.4, ed. Dietrich Strauss and Horst W. Drescher (Frankfurt am Main, 1986), p.553.
14   Rowena Murray, p.548.
15   Bold, *Mackay Brown*, p.57.
16   J. Graeme Roberts, 'Tradition and Pattern in the Short Stories of George Mackay Brown', in *Literature of the North*, ed. David Hewitt and Michael Spiller (Aberdeen, 1985), pp.179, 180.
17   *An Orkney Tapestry* (1969; London, 1978), p.20. All references are to this edition, abbreviated OT
18   *New Shetlander* 24 (1950), 2-3.
19   *Andrina and Other Stories* (London, 1983), p.129.
20   *The Masked Fisherman and Other Stories* (London, 1989), pp.111-26; 145-51.
21   *Voyages* (London, 1983), pp.27-28.
22   *A Time to Keep*, pp.135-40.
23   *Masked Fisherman*, p.ix.
24   In *Hawkfall* (1974; London, 1983), pp.9-58. Ketil Flatnose was a renowned ninth-century settler in the Hebrides and the father of Aud the Deep-Minded; see Crawford, *Scandinavian Scotland*, pp.47-48.
25   *Greenvoe*, pp.27, 217.
26   The plot, consisting of a heroine with magic powers moving through space and time, is reminiscent of Naomi Mitchison's *Travel Light*; see Chapter 9.
27   *Time in a Red Coat* (London, 1984), p.187.
28   In *The Golden Bird: Two Orkney Stories* (London, 1987), pp.3-129.
29   Confirmed in a letter from Mackay Brown, 30.12.87.
30   See *Njal's Saga*, Chs. 35-48, pp.97-123.
31   Robin Fulton, *Contemporary Scottish Poetry: Individuals and Contexts* (Loanhead, 1974), p.113.
32   Robin Fulton, 'Argus: a Scottish Survey', *New Edinburgh Review* 4 (1969), 6.
33   For a fuller discussion of this aspect of 'The Three Islands', see Berthold Schoene, *The Making of Orcadia: Narrative Identity in the Prose Work of George Mackay Brown*, Anglo-American Studies 6 (Frankfurt am Main, 1995), pp.84-88.
34   Fulton, *Contemporary Scottish Poetry*, p.112.
35   *Orkneyinga Saga*, Chs.29 and 66, pp.67-68, 112-15.
36   Fulton, *Contemporary Scottish Poetry*, p.113.
37   See Chs.64-104, pp.109-190.
38   *Orkneyinga Saga*, Ch.85, pp.139-43.

39 Mackay Brown intended studying Old Norse under Hermann Pálsson at
    the University of Edinburgh, but the proposed text book proved too expen-
    sive! Conversation with Mackay Brown, August 1988. *The Orkneyinga Saga*,
    trans. A.B. Taylor (Edinburgh, 1938).

40 To appreciate the problems involved one need only read a study of
    Rognvald's poetry (with English paraphrases) in which all the strophes are
    analysed in detail, revealing all the complex intricacies and opacity of Old
    Norse kennings: Paul Bibire, 'The Poetry of Earl Rognvaldr's Court', in *St
    Magnus Cathedral*, ed. Barbara E. Crawford (Aberdeen, 1988), pp.208-40.

41 With one notable exception. Taylor inexplicably translates ON 'siau'
    (seven) as 'three', an error Mackay Brown carries over into his own version;
    see *Orkneyinga saga*, ed. Sigurður Nordal (Copenhagen, 1913), p.244; Taylor,
    p.293; *Orkney Tapestry*, pp.104-5; see also Bibire, p.235.

42 For another version, see Bibire, p.22.

43 For a less critical view of Mackay Brown's versions of these strophes, see
    David Annwn, *Inhabited Voices* (Frome, 1984), pp.203-4.

44 *Orkneyinga Saga*, Ch.49, p.87.

45 The most detailed biography of St. Magnus is John Mooney's *St. Magnus,
    Earl of Orkney* (Kirkwall, 1935).

46 George Mackay Brown, *Three Plays* (London, 1984), pp.1-55. All further ref-
    erences to the play are to this edition, abbreviated *Plays*.

47 See Eric Linklater and J. Storer Clouston, 'Octocentenary Celebration of St
    Magnus Cathedral - 1937', Scene 3, p.7; Orkney Archives, D1/98.

48 *Magnus* (1973), Richard Drew edn. (Glasgow, 1987), pp.147-62.

49 Bold, *Mackay Brown*, p.106.

50 Elizabeth Huberman, 'George Mackay Brown's *Magnus*', *Studies in Scottish
    Literature* 16 (1981), 133; Bold, *Mackay Brown*, p.101; *Times Literary
    Supplement* (Sept. 1973), p.1101.

51 Bold, *Mackay Brown*, pp.100, 101, 104, 108.

52 *Orkneyinga Saga*, Ch.39, p.78. See also Mooney, *St. Magnus*, p.83, and
    William P.L. Thomson, *History of Orkney* (Edinburgh, 1987), p.55.

53 Huberman, pp.122-27; Bold, *Mackay Brown*, p.101.

54 Thomson (pp.56-57) is very persuasive on this point.

55 *Njal's Saga*, Ch.157, p.347; *Laxdaela Saga*, Ch.49, p.175.

56 For example Huberman, pp.127-28; Bold, *Mackay Brown*, p.105; Schoene,
    p.222.

57 Thomson, pp.45-46, 54-55.

58 Bold, *Mackay Brown*, p.109.

59 Scott, however, usually added copious notes to his works outlining what
    the real historical facts were and why he had changed them.

60 Huberman, p.132

61 George Mackay Brown, Gunnie Moberg and Simon Fraser, *The Loom of Light*
    (Nairn, 1986) and *A Celebration for Magnus* (Nairn, 1987).

62 *Vinland* (London, 1992). All further references are to this edition, abbreviat-
    ed V.

63 Details of this background Celtic mythology are outside the scope of this
    work, but those interested may care to consult *The Voyage of Bran*, trans.
    Kuno Meyer (London, 1895) and Alfred, Lord Tennyson, *The Voyage of
    Maeldune* (London, 1892). On Tir-nan-Og, see F. Marian McNeill, *The Silver
    Bough, Vol.I Scottish Folk-lore and Folk-Belief* (1957), Canongate Classics 24
    (Edinburgh, 1989), pp.104-7; on the historical background to Brendan's
    explorations, see Gwyn Jones, *The Norse Atlantic Saga*, pp.33-34.

BIBLIOGRAPHY

I: OLD NORSE PRIMARY SOURCES (IN TRANSLATION)

Where the authorship is unknown or uncertain, the sagas are listed in alphabetical order.

Egil's Saga, trans. Hermann Pálsson and Paul Edwards (Harmondsworth, 1976)
   See also *Story of Egil Skallagrimsson, The*
Eirik's Saga, see *Vinland Sagas, The*
Eyrbyggja Saga, trans. Hermann Pálsson and Paul Edwards (1972), Penguin edn.
   (Harmondsworth, 1989)
   See also *Story of the Ere-Dwellers, The*
Gisli's Saga, see *Saga of Gisli, The*
Greenlanders' Saga, The, see *Vinland Sagas, The*
Grettis Saga: the Story of Grettir the Strong, trans. William Morris and Eiríkr [sic]
   Magnússon (London, 1869)
   See also *Saga of Grettir the Strong, The*
Gunnlaug's Saga, see *Saga of Gunnlaug Snake-Tongue, The*
Hávamál, see *Poetic Edda, The*
Heiðarvíga Saga, see *Story of the Heath-Slayings, The*
Heimskringla, see Sturluson, Snorri
Hrafnkel's Saga and Other Stories, trans. Hermann Pálsson (Harmondsworth, 1971)
Jómsvíkinga Saga, see *Saga of the Jómsvíkings, The*
King Harald's Saga, trans. Magnus Magnusson and Hermann Pálsson
   (Harmondsworth, 1966)
Landnámabók, see Thorgilsson, Ari
Laxdaela Saga, trans. Muriel C. Press (London, 1899)
Laxdaela Saga, trans. Magnus Magnusson and Hermann Pálsson
   (Harmondsworth, 1969)
Njal's Saga, trans. Magnus Magnusson and Hermann Pálsson (Harmondsworth,
   1960)
   See also *Story of Burnt Njal, The*
Orkneyinga Saga, trans. Jón Hjaltalín and Gilbert Goudie (Edinburgh, 1873)
Orkneyinga Saga, The, trans. A.B. Taylor (Edinburgh, 1938)
Orkneyinga Saga: The History of the Earls of Orkney, trans. Hermann Pálsson and
   Paul Edwards (Harmondsworth, 1981)
Poetic Edda, The [including *Hávamál* and *Völuspá*], trans. Lee M. Hollander, 2nd.
   rev. edn. (Austin, 1986)
Saga of the Faroe Islanders, The, trans. Muriel C. Press (London, 1934)
Saga of Gisli, The, trans. George Johnston (1963), rev. edn. (London, 1987)
Saga of Grettir the Strong, The, trans. G.A. Hight, ed. Peter Foote, 2nd. edn.
   (London 1972)

Saga of Gunnlaug Snake-Tongue, The, trans. Alan Boucher (Reykjavik, 1983)

Saga of Hrolf Kraki, The, trans. Stella M. Mills (Oxford, 1933)

Saga of the Jómsvíkings, The, trans. Lee M. Hollander (Austin, 1955)

Saga of the Volsungs, The: The Norse Epic of Sigurd the Dragon Slayer, trans. Jesse L. Byock (Berkeley & Oxford, 1990)
    See also *Völsunga Saga*

Story of Burnt Njal, The, trans. with Introduction by George Webbe Dasent (Edinburgh, 1861)

Story of the Ere-Dwellers, The [Eyrbyggja Saga], trans. William Morris and Eiríkr Magnússon, The Saga Library Vol.II (London, 1892)

Story of Egil Skallagrimsson, The, trans. William Charles Green (London, 1893)

Story of the Heath-Slayings, The [Heiðarvíga Saga], trans. William Morris and Eiríkr Magnússon, The Saga Library Vol.II (London, 1892)

Sturluson, Snorri, *Edda [The Prose Edda]*, trans. Anthony Faulkes (London, 1987)

——, *Heimskringla; or the Chronicle of the Kings of Norway*, trans. with 'Preliminary Dissertation' by Samuel Laing (London, 1844)

——, *Heimskringla: the History of the Kings of Norway*, trans. Lee M. Hollander (Austin, 1984)

——, *The Prose or Younger Edda*, trans. G.W. Dasent (London, 1842)

Thorgilsson, Ari, *The Book of Settlements [Landnámabók]*, trans. Hermann Pálsson and Paul Edwards (Winnipeg, 1972)

Viga Glum's Saga, trans. Edmund W. Head (London, 1866)

Viga Glums Saga, trans. John McKinnell (Edinburgh, 1987)

Vigfusson, Gudbrandur, and Frederick York Powell, *Corpus Poeticum Boreale*, 2 vols (Oxford, 1883)

——, *Origines Islandicae*, 2 vols (Oxford, 1905)

Vinland Sagas, The: The Norse Discovery of America (comprising *The Greenlanders' Saga* and *Eirik's Saga*), trans. Magnus Magnusson and Hermann Pálsson (Harmondsworth, 1965)

Völsunga Saga, trans. Eiríkr Magnússon and William Morris (London, 1870)

Völuspá, see *Poetic Edda, The*

II: SCOTTISH PRIMARY SOURCES

Anderson, Basil Ramsay, *Broken Lights: Poems and Reminiscences*, ed. Jessie M.E. Saxby (Edinburgh, 1888)

Balfour, David, *Ancient Orkney Melodies* (1885), rpt. with Foreword by Howie Firth (Kirkwall, 1985)

'Ballad of Hildina, The', trans. W.G. Collingwood, *Orkney and Shetland Miscellany* 1 (1907-08), 211-16

Ballantyne, R.M., *Erling the Bold* (London, 1869)

——, *The Norsemen in the West or America Before Columbus* (London, 1872)

Banks, William Mitchell, *A Narrative of the Voyage of the Argonauts in 1880* (Edinburgh, 1881)

Barry, George, *The History of the Orkney Isles* (Edinburgh, 1805)

Bird, Vivian, 'Back Again from the Dark', *New Shetlander* 43 (1956), 17-19

Blair, Hugh, *A Critical Dissertation on the Poems of Ossian, Son of Fingal* (London, 1763)

Bourke, Rev. U.J., *The Aryan Origin of the Gaelic Race and Language* (London, 1875)

Bremner, Robert Locke, *The Norsemen in Alban* (Glasgow, 1923)

Brown, George Mackay, *Andrina and Other Stories* (London, 1983)

——, *Beside the Ocean of Time* (London, 1994)

——, *A Calendar of Love* (1967; London, 1987)

——, 'The Day the Vikings Came', *New Shetlander* 24 (1950), 2-3

——, 'Edwin Muir at Newbattle', *Akros* 16 No.47 (1981), 6-13

——, *Fishermen with Ploughs: A Poem Cycle* (London, 1979)

——, *The Golden Bird: Two Orkney Stories* (London, 1987)

——, *Greenvoe* (1972), Penguin edn. (Harmondsworth, 1976)

——, *Hawkfall* (1974; London, 1983)

——, *Letters from Hamnavoe* (Edinburgh, 1975)

——, *Magnus* (1973), Richard Drew edn. (Glasgow, 1987)

——, *The Masked Fisherman and Other Stories* (London, 1989)

——, *An Orkney Tapestry* (1969; London, 1978)

——, 'Prayer to Magnus', *New Shetlander* 6 (1947), 3

——, *The Sea King's Daughter* and *Eureka* (Nairn, 1991)

——, *Selected Poems* (London, 1977)

——, *Selected Poems 1954-1983* (London, 1990)

——, *The Storm and Other Poems* (Kirkwall, 1954)

——, *The Sun's Net* (London, 1976)

——, *Three Plays: The Loom of Light; The Well; The Voyage of St Brandon* (London, 1984)

——, *Time in a Red Coat* (London, 1984)

——, *A Time to Keep and Other Stories* (1969; London, 1976)

——, *Voyages* (London, 1983)

——, *Winterfold* (London, 1976)

——, *Vinland* (London, 1992)

——, *Witch and Other Stories* (London, 1977)

——, *The Wreck of the Archangel: Poems* (London, 1989)

——, 'Writer's Shop', *Chapman* 16 (Summer, 1976), 21-24

——, and Gunnie Moberg and Simon Fraser, *The Loom of Light* (Nairn, 1986)

——, and Gunnie Moberg, Simon Fraser, *et al.*, *A Celebration for Magnus* (Nairn, 1987)

Bruce, Michael, *Poems on Several Occasions* (Edinburgh, 1770)

Buchan, John, *The Adventures of Dickson McCunn*, Penguin Omnibus edn. [*Huntingtower* (1922), *Castle Gay* (1930), *The House of the Four Winds* (1937)] (Harmondsworth 1994)

——, *The Courts of the Morning* (London, 1929)

——, *Greenmantle* (1916), OUP World's Classics edn. (Oxford, 1993)

——, *The Half-Hearted* (1900; London, 1922)

——, 'The Heroic Age of Ireland', in *Some Eighteenth Century Byways* (London, 1908), pp.301-307

——, 'The Highland Clearances', *The Spectator* Vol.112 (6 June 1914), 955-57

——, 'The Iceland Colony', in *Canadian Occasions* (London, 1940), pp.28-30

——, *The Island of Sheep* (1936), Penguin edn. (Harmondsworth, 1975)

——, *John Macnab* (1925), OUP World's Classics edn. (Oxford, 1994)

——, *The Long Traverse* (London, 1941)

——, *A Lost Lady of Old Years* (London, 1899)

——, *Memory Hold-the-Door* (London, 1940)

——, *Midwinter* (1923), B&W edn. (Edinburgh, 1993)

——, *The Path of the King* (London, 1921)

——, *A Prince of the Captivity* (1933), Hamlyn edn. (London, 1981)

——, *The Runagates Club* (1928; London, 1954)

——, *Sick Heart River* (1941), Penguin edn. (Harmondsworth, 1985)

——, 'Some Scottish Characteristics', in *The Scottish Tongue* (London, 1924), pp.49-88

——, *Mr Standfast* (1919), OUP World's Classics edn. (Oxford, 1993)

——, *The Thirty-Nine Steps* (1915), OUP World's Classics edn. (Oxford, 1993)

——, *The Three Hostages* (1924), OUP World's Classics edn. (Oxford, 1995)

——, *The Watcher by the Threshold* (1902; London, 1951)

——, *Witch Wood* (1927), OUP World's Classics edn. (Oxford, 1993)

Buchanan, Robert Williams, 'Balder the Beautiful', *Contemporary Review* 29 (1876-77) 691-710; 800-827; 1004-1026.

——, *Ballad Stories of the Affections from the Scandinavian* (London, 1866)

Burgess, J.J. Haldane, File of reviews, Shetland Archives D2/73

——, Newspaper cuttings and papers, Shetland Archives D6/292/4

——, *Rasmie's Buddie: Poems in Shetlandic* (Lerwick, 1891)

——, *Young Rasmie's Kit: A Book of Verse* (Lerwick, 1928)

——, *The Viking Path* (Edinburgh & London, 1894)

Campbell, Dr. John, and William Oldys, *A Polite Correspondence: Or Rational Amusement* (London, 1741)

Campbell, John Francis, (ed. and trans.) *Popular Tales of the West Highlands Orally Collected*, 4 vols (Edinburgh, 1860-62)

Carlyle, Thomas, *The Early Kings of Norway* (London, 1875)

——, *Sartor Resartus* and *On Heroes and Hero-Worship* (1838, 1840), Everyman's Library 278 (London, 1967)

Carmichael, Alexander, *Carmina Gadelica*, 5 vols, 2nd. edn. (London, 1928)

Chambers, Robert, *Tracings of Iceland and the Faröe Islands* (Edinburgh & London, 1856)

Clark, W. Fordyce, *The Story of Shetland* (Edinburgh, 1906)

Clouston, J. Storer, *Vandrad the Viking: or the Feud and the Spell* (Edinburgh & London, 1898)

Costie, C.M., *Benjie's Bodle* (Kirkwall, 1956)

——, *The Collected Orkney Dialect Tales of C.M. Costie* (Kirkwall, 1976)

Craigie, Sir W.A., 'Gaelic Historical Songs', *Scottish Review* 18 (1891), 301-41

——, *The Icelandic Sagas* (Cambridge, 1913)

——, *The Religion of Ancient Scandinavia* (London, 1906)

——, *Scandinavian Folk-lore* (London & Paisley, 1896)

——, and John Buchan, *The Scottish Tongue* (London, 1924)

Dennison, W. Traill, *The Orcadian Sketch-Book* (Kirkwall, 1880)

Dunnett, Dorothy, *King Hereafter* (London, 1982)

Elphinstone, Margaret, *Islanders* (Edinburgh, 1995)

Erskine, R., 'Celt, Slav, Hun, and Teuton', *Scottish Review* 37 No.75 (1914), 315-25

——, 'The Two Cultures', *Scottish Review* 37 No.74 (1914), 283-306

Frazer, J.G., *Balder the Beautiful*, 2 vols, Part VII of *The Golden Bough: A Study in Magic and Religion*, 3rd edn. (London, 1913)

Galt, John, *The Collected Poems of John Galt 1779-1839*, ed. Hamilton Baird Timothy, 2 vols (London & Ontario, 1969)

——, *The Literary Life and Miscellanies of John Galt*, 3 vols (Edinburgh, 1834)

Gibbon, Lewis Grassic, *A Scots Hairst: Essays and Short Stories*, ed. Ian S. Munro (1967), 3rd. edn. (London, 1983)

——, *A Scots Quair* (1946), Canongate Classics 59 (Edinburgh, 1995)

——, *Sunset Song* (1932), Canongate Classics 12 (Edinburgh, 1988)

——, and Hugh MacDiarmid, *Scottish Scene: or The Intelligent Man's Guide to Albyn* (London, 1934)

See also Mitchell, J. Leslie

Graham, John J., *Shadowed Valley* (Lerwick, 1987)

——, and T.A. Robertson, *Nordern Lichts: An Anthology of Shetland Verse and Prose* (Lerwick, 1964)

Graham, R.B. Cunninghame, 'Snækoll's Saga', in *The Ipané* (London, 1901), pp.204-25

Gray, Joseph, *Lowrie* (Lerwick, 1933)

Grieve, C.M., 'Mannigfaltig', *New Age* 35 (14 August 1924), 185-86

See also MacDiarmid, Hugh

Gunn, Neil M., *The Atom of Delight* (1956), Polygon edn. (Edinburgh, 1986)

——, *Butcher's Broom* (1934), Souvenir Press edn. (London, 1977)

——, 'Caithness and Sutherland', in *Scottish Country*, ed. G. Scott-Moncrieff (London, 1935), pp.59-76

——, 'The Gael Will Come Again', *Scots Magazine* 14 (Feb. 1931), 324-27 [using the pseudonym 'Dane McNeil']

——, *The Green Isle of the Great Deep* (1944), Souvenir Press edn. (London, 1975)

——, *The Grey Coast* (1926), Souvenir Press edn. (London, 1983)

——, *Hidden Doors* (Edinburgh, 1929)

——, *Highland River* (1937), Canongate Classics 37 (Edinburgh, 1991)

——, *Landscape and Light: Essays by Neil M. Gunn*, ed. Alistair McCleery (Aberdeen, 1987)

——, *The Lost Chart* (London, 1949)

——, *The Lost Glen* (1932), Richard Drew edn. (Glasgow, 1985)

——, *The Man Who Came Back: Short Stories and Essays*, ed. Margery McCulloch (Edinburgh, 1991)

——, *Morning Tide* (1931), Souvenir Press edn. (London, 1982)

——, Notebooks, papers and letters. NLS Dep.209 Boxes 1, 10, 17

——, *Off in a Boat* (London, 1938)

——, *The Silver Darlings* (1941; London, 1978)

——, *Sun Circle* (1933), Souvenir Press edn. (London, 1983)

——, *The Well at the World's End* (1951), Souvenir Press edn. (London, 1985)

Hayton, Sian, *Cells of Knowledge* (Edinburgh, 1989)

——, *Hidden Daughters* (Edinburgh, 1992)

——, *The Last Flight* (Edinburgh, 1995)

Henderson, Ebenezer, *Iceland: or the Journal of a Residence in that Island during the Years 1814 and 1815* (Edinburgh, 1818)

Henderson, George, *The Norse Influence on Celtic Scotland* (Glasgow, 1910)

Hogg, James, *Memoirs of the Author's Life and Familiar Anecdotes of Sir Walter Scott*, ed. Douglas S. Mack (Edinburgh & London, 1972)

——, *Queen Hynde* (Edinburgh, 1825)

——, *The Three Perils of Man: War, Women and Witchcraft* (1822), ed. Douglas Gifford, Scottish Classics Series 9 (Edinburgh, 1989)

Home, Henry (Lord Kames), *Sketches of the History of Man* (1774), 4 vols (Glasgow, 1802), I, 78-94

Home, John, *Alfred: A Tragedy* (London, 1788); rpt. in *The Plays of John Home*, ed. James S. Malek (London & New York, 1980)

Hunter, John J., *Taen wi da Trow* (Lerwick, 1952)

Jamieson, John, *An Etymological Dictionary of the Scottish Language* (Edinburgh, 1808)

Jamieson, Robert, *Popular Ballads and Songs*, 2 vols (Edinburgh, 1806)

——, and H. Weber, *Illustrations of Northern Antiquities* (Edinburgh, 1814)

Jamieson, Robert Alan, *Shoormal* (Edinburgh, 1986)

——, *Soor Hearts* (Edinburgh, 1984)

——, *Thin Wealth* (Edinburgh, 1986)

Johnstone, James, *Anecdotes of Olave the Black, King of Man* (Copenhagen, 1780)

——, *Antiquitates Celto-Scandicae* (Copenhagen, 1786)

——, *The Norwegian Account of King Haco's Expedition Against Scotland A.D. 1263* (Copenhagen, 1782)

Ker, W.P., *The Dark Ages* (London, 1904)

——, *Epic and Romance* (1897; London, 1926)

Laing, Samuel, 'Preliminary Dissertation'; an introduction to his translation of Snorri Sturluson's *Heimskringla* (London, 1844)

Lang, Andrew, (ed.) *The Book of Dreams and Ghosts*, 2nd. edn. (London, 1899)

——, 'The Celtic Renascence', *Blackwood's Magazine* 161 (1897), 181-91

——, *Homer and the Epic* (London, 1893)

——, *Homer and his Age* (London, 1906)

——, 'The Sagas', in *Essays in Little* (London, 1891), pp.141-52

——, (ed.) *The Red Fairy Book* (London, 1890)

Laurenson, Arthur, *Arthur Laurenson: His Letters and Literary Remains*, ed. Catherine Spence (London, 1901)

Leighton, Robert, *Olaf the Glorious: A Historical Story of the Viking Age* (London, 1894)

——, *The Thirsty Sword: A Story of the Norse Invasion of Scotland (1262-63)* (London, 1892)

Leyden, John, 'Danish Ode', *Edinburgh Magazine* 5 (April 1795), 301-302

——, 'The Descent of Odin', *Edinburgh Magazine* 6 (Sept. 1795), 222

——, 'The Incantation of Hervor', *Edinburgh Magazine* 6 (Nov. 1795), 382-83

Lindsay, David, *The Adventures of M. de Mailly* (London, 1926)

——, *Devil's Tor* (London, 1932)

——, *The Haunted Woman* (1922), Canongate Classics 9 (Edinburgh, 1987)

——, 'Sketch Notes for a New System of Philosophy', TS, NLS, Acc. No.5616

——, *The Sphinx* (London, 1923)

——, *The Violet Apple* and *The Witch*, ed. J.B. Pick (Chicago, 1976)

——, *A Voyage to Arcturus* (1920), Canongate Classics 47 (Edinburgh, 1992)

Linklater, Eric, *The Art of Adventure* (London, 1947)

——, *The Conquest of England* (London, 1966)

——, *The Dark of Summer* (1956; London, 1957)

——, *Fanfare for a Tin Hat* (London, 1970)

——, *God Likes Them Plain* (London, 1935)

——, *Juan in America* (London, 1931)

——, *Magnus Merriman* (1934), Canongate Classics 35 (Edinburgh, 1990)

——, *The Man on my Back* (London, 1941)

——, *The Men of Ness* (1932), 2nd. edn with Introduction by Marjorie Linklater (Kirkwall, 1983)

——, 'Orkney', in *Scottish Country*, ed. George Scott-Moncrieff (London, 1935), pp.77-97

——, *Orkney and Shetland* (London, 1965)

——, *The Prince in the Heather* (London, 1965)

——, *Private Angelo* (1946), Canongate Classics 44 (Edinburgh, 1992)

——, 'Spilt Wine', in *Alma Mater*, 26.10.21, pp.9-10

——, *The Survival of Scotland* (London, 1968)

——, *The Ultimate Viking* (London, 1955)

——, *White-maa's Saga* (1929; Edinburgh, 1983)

——, *A Year of Space* (London, 1953)

——, and J. Storer Clouston, 'Octocentenary Celebration of St Magnus Cathedral - 1937', TS in Orkney Archives, D1/98

Livingstone, William, *Duain agus Orain* (Glasgow, 1882)

Lockhart, John G., *Memoirs of the Life of Sir Walter Scott*, 7 vols (Edinburgh & London, 1837-38) Vol.I

Logan, James, *The Clans of the Scottish Highlands*, 2 vols (London, 1845-7)

——, *The Scottish Gaël; or Celtic Manners as Preserved Among the Highlanders*, 2 vols (London, 1831)

Longmuir, John, 'Memoir of Dr. Jamieson', in *Jamieson's Dictionary of the Scottish Language*, rev. and ed. John Longmuir (Paisley, 1912), pp.ix-xviii

Low, George, *A Tour through the Islands of Orkney and Schetland* [sic] (1879), rpt. (Inverness, 1978)

Mac Colla, Fionn, *At the Sign of the Clenched Fist* (Edinburgh, 1967)

——, *Too Long in this Condition* (Thurso, 1975)

MacDiarmid, Hugh, *At the Sign of the Thistle: A Collection of Essays* (London, 1934)

——, *The Complete Poems of Hugh MacDiarmid*, ed. Michael Grieve and W.R. Aitken, 2nd. rev. edn., 2 vols (Harmondsworth, 1985)

——, (ed.) *Contemporary Scottish Studies* (1926), 2nd. rev. edn. (Edinburgh, 1976)

——, *A Drunk Man Looks at the Thistle* (1926), ed. Kenneth Buthlay (Edinburgh, 1987)

——, *The Islands of Scotland* (London, 1939)

——, *The Letters of Hugh MacDiarmid*, ed. Alan Bold (London, 1984)

——, *Lucky Poet* (London, 1943)

——, *Selected Essays of Hugh MacDiarmid*, ed. Duncan Glen (London, 1969)

——, *The Uncanny Scot: A Selection of Prose*, ed. Kenneth Buthlay (London, 1968)

——, and Lewis Grassic Gibbon, *Scottish Scene: or The Intelligent Man's Guide to Albyn* (London, 1934)

    See also Grieve, C.M.

Mackay, Colin, *The Song of the Forest* (Edinburgh, 1986)

Mackenzie, Sir G.S., *Travels in the Island of Iceland During the Summer of the Year 1810* (Edinburgh, 1811)

Mackenzie, Henry, *The Works of Henry Mackenzie, Esq.*, Vol.VIII (Edinburgh, 1808)

Macleod, Fiona, *Barbaric Tales* (London, 1903)

——, *Pharais and The Mountain Lovers*, in *The Works of Fiona Macleod*, Uniform edn. Vol.I (London, 1910)

    See also Sharp, William

Macpherson, James, *Poems of Ossian* (1805), rpt. with Introduction by John MacQueen, 2 vols (Edinburgh, 1971)

——, *The Poetical Works of James Macpherson* (Edinburgh, 1802)

Marwick, Ernest, (ed.) *An Anthology of Orkney Verse* (Kirkwall, 1949)

Marwick, Hugh, *Orkney* (London, 1951)

——, *The Orkney Norn* (Oxford, 1929)

Mitchell, J. Leslie, *The Lost Trumpet* (London, 1932)

——, *The Thirteenth Disciple* (1931), Scottish Fiction Reprint Library (Edinburgh, 1981)

——, and Lewis Grassic Gibbon, *Nine Against the Unknown: A Record of Geographical Exploration* (London, 1934)

    See also Gibbon, Lewis Grassic.

Mitchison, Naomi, *All Change Here: Girlhood and Marriage* (London, 1975)

——, *An End and a Beginning and Other Plays* (London, 1937)

——, *Barbarian Stories* (London, 1929)

——, *Beyond This Limit: Selected Shorter Fiction of Naomi Mitchison*, ed. Isobel Murray (Edinburgh, 1986)

——, *The Big House* (London, 1950)

——, *The Blood of the Martyrs* (London, 1939)

——, *The Bull Calves* (London, 1947)

——, *The Conquered* (London, 1923)

——, *The Corn King and the Spring Queen* (London, 1931)

——, *The Delicate Fire: Short Stories and Poems* (London, 1933)

——, *Five Men and A Swan* (London, 1957)

——, *The Fourth Pig: Stories and Verses* (London, 1936)

——, *Graeme and the Dragon* (London, 1954)

——, *The Hostages and Other Stories for Boys and Girls* (London, 1930)

——, *Karensgaard: The Story of a Danish Farm* (London, 1961)

——, *The Land the Ravens Found* (London, 1955)

——, 'Leaving Denmark', *Chapman* 50-51 (Spring 1987), 25

——, *Mucking Around: Five Continents over Fifty Years* (London, 1981)

——, *Naomi Mitchison*, Saltire Self-Portraits 2 (Edinburgh, 1986)

——, *The Oath-Takers* (Nairn, 1991)

——, *Sea-Green Ribbons* (Nairn, 1991)

——, *Small Talk: Memories of an Edwardian Childhood* (London, 1973)

——, *Solution Three* (London, 1975)

——, *The Swan's Road* (London, 1954)

——, *Travel Light* (1952), Virago Modern Classics (London, 1985)

——, *What Do You Think Yourself?* (Edinburgh, 1982)

——, *When the Bough Breaks and Other Stories* (London, 1924)

——, *You May Well Ask: A Memoir 1920-1940*, 2nd. edn. (London, 1986)

Motherwell, William, *The Poetical Works of William Motherwell*, ed. William Kennedy, 3rd. edn. (Glasgow, 1849)

Muir, Edwin, *An Autobiography* (1954), 2nd edn. (London, 1987)

——, *The Complete Poems of Edwin Muir*, ed. P.H. Butter (Aberdeen, 1991)

——, Notebook in NLS, MS.19663

——, 'Returning to Orkney', TS, in NLS, MS.19662, pp.45-61

——, *Scott and Scotland* (1936; Edinburgh, 1982)

——, *Scottish Journey* (1935; London, 1985)

——, *Selected Letters of Edwin Muir*, ed. P.H. Butter (London, 1974)

Muir, Willa, *Belonging: A Memoir* (London, 1968)

Nicolson, Laurence J., *Songs of Thule* (Paisley, 1894)

Oswald, Elizabeth Jane, *By Fell and Fjord: or Scenes and Studies in Iceland* (Edinburgh, 1882)

Pinkerton, John, *An Enquiry into the History of Scotland Preceeding the Reign of Malcolm III or the Year 1056* (1789), 2nd. edn., 2 vols (Edinburgh, 1814)

——, 'An Essay on the Origins of Scotish [sic] Poetry', in *Ancient Scotish* [sic] *Poems*, 2 vols (London, 1786), I, xxi-lxxiv

Power, William, *Scotland and the Scots* (Edinburgh & London, 1934)

Rendall, Robert, *Orkney Variants and Other Poems* (Kirkwall, 1951)

Renwick, Jack, 'The Shadowed Wave', *Scotia Review* 20 (1978), 52-56

Richardson, William, *The Maid of Lochlin, a Lyrical Drama. With Legendary Odes and Other Poems* (London, 1801)

Robertson, Duncan J., *Wraith and Wrack* (London, 1918)

Robertson, E. William, *Scotland under her Early Kings: a History of the Kingdom to the Close of the Thirteenth Century*, 2 vols (Edinburgh, 1862)

Robertson, T.A., *The Collected Poems of Vagaland*, ed. M. Robertson, 2nd edn. (Lerwick, 1980)

Roger, James Cruickshank, *Celticism a Myth* (London, 1884)

Rolleston, T.W., *Myths and Legends of the Celtic Race* (1911), Constable Reprint (London, 1985)

Saxby, Jessie M.E., *Daala-Mist: or Stories of Shetland* (Edinburgh, 1876)

——, *Shetland Traditional Lore* (Edinburgh, 1932)

Scott, Sir Walter, 'An Abstract of the Eyrbiggia-Saga' [sic], in *Illustrations of Northern Antiquities*, ed. Robert Jamieson and H. Weber (Edinburgh, 1814), pp.477-513

——, *The Antiquary* (1829), Waverley Novels, Centenary edn., Vol.III (Edinburgh, 1886)

——, *Count Robert of Paris* (1833), Waverley Novels, Centenary edn., Vol.XXIV (Edinburgh, 1887)

——, *Ivanhoe* (1819), Penguin Classics (Harmondsworth, 1986)

——, *The Pirate* (1822), Waverley Novels, Centenary edn., Vol. XIII (Edinburgh, 1886)

——, *The Poetical Works of Sir Walter Scott*, Albion edn. (London, 1894)

Scott-Moncrieff, George, (ed.) *Scottish Country* (London, 1935)

Sharp, William, 'Icelandic Literature', in *Library of the World's Best Literature, Ancient and Modern*, ed. Charles Dudley Warner, Vol. XX (New York, 1896-97), 7865-7895

See also Macleod, Fiona

Skene, W.F., *The Highlanders of Scotland: their Origins, History and Antiquities*, 2 vols (London, 1837)

Stevenson, Robert Louis, 'The Waif Woman', in *The Strange Case of Dr. Jekyll and Mr. Hyde, Fables and Other Stories and Fragments*, Tusitala edn. Vol.V (London, 1924), pp.159-79

Sutherland, Stella, *Aa My Selves: Poems 1940-1980* (Lerwick, 1980)

Symington, Andrew, *Pen and Pencil Sketches of Faröe and Iceland* (London, 1862)

Tait, William J., *A Day Between Weathers: Collected Poems 1938-1978* (Edinburgh, 1980)

Tennant, William, *The Comic Poems of William Tennant*, ed. Alexander Scott and Maurice Lindsay (Edinburgh, 1989)

——, *The Thane of Fife* (Edinburgh, 1822)

Tranter, Nigel, *Lord of the Isles* (London, 1983)

——, *Macbeth the King* (Sevenoaks, 1978)

Urquhart, Alexander, 'Celt and Norseman', *Scots Magazine* 14 (Jan. 1931), 246-51

'Vagaland', see Robertson, T.A.

Vedder, David, *Orcadian Sketches: Legendary and Lyrical Pieces* (Edinburgh, 1832)

——, *Poems, Lyrics, and Sketches*, ed. Rev. George Gilfillan (Kirkwall, 1878)

Wardlaw, Lady Elizabeth, *Hardyknute: a Fragment* (Edinburgh, 1719), pub. anon. Rpt. in *Longer Scottish Poems Vol.II: 1650-1830*, ed. Thomas Crawford, David Hewitt and Alexander Law (Edinburgh, 1987), pp.7-14

III: SECONDARY, ENGLISH, AND OTHER SOURCES

Albert, L., *Six Thousand Years of Gaelic Grandeur Unearthed* (London, 1936)

Aldrich, Ruth I., *John Galt*, Twayne's English Authors 231 (Boston, 1978)

Allan, John R., *North-East Lowlands of Scotland*, 2nd. edn. (London, 1974)

Allen, Ralph Berger, *Old Icelandic Sources in the English Novel* (Philadelphia, 1933)

Angus, Stewart, 'The Novels of Neil M. Gunn', *Scottish Periodical* 1:2 (1948), 94-103

Annwn, David, *Inhabited Voices: Myth and History in the Poetry of Geoffrey Hill, Seamus Heaney and George Mackay Brown* (Frome, 1984)

Arendt, Hannah, *The Origins of Totalitarianism* (London, 1958)

Arnold, Matthew, 'Balder Dead' (1858), in *The Poems of Matthew Arnold 1840-1867*, ed. Sir A.T. Quiller-Couch (London, 1937), pp.238-68

——, 'On the Study of Celtic Literature' (1862), in *The Complete Prose Works of Matthew Arnold*, ed. R.H. Super, Vol.III *Lectures and Essays in Criticism* (Ann Arbor, 1962), pp.291-395

Asbjörnsen, P.C. and Jörgen Moe, *Popular Tales from the Norse*, trans. Sir G.W. Dasent (Edinburgh, 1859)

Auden, W.H. and Louis MacNeice, *Letters from Iceland* (1937; London, 1965)

Baring-Gould, Sabine, *Iceland: Its Scenes and Sagas* (London, 1863)

——, *The Icelander's Sword, or the Story of Oraefadal* (London, 1894)

Barnes, Michael, 'Orkney and Shetland Norn', in *Language in the British Isles*, ed. Peter Trudgill (Cambridge, 1984), pp.352-66

Batho, Edith, *The Ettrick Shepherd* (1928; New York, 1969)

——, 'Scott as Mediaevalist', in *Sir Walter Scott Today*, ed. H.C. Grierson (London, 1932), pp.133-57

——, 'Sir Walter Scott and the Sagas: Some Notes', *Modern Language Review* 24 (1929), 409-15

Bedell, Jeanne F., 'Romance and Moral Certainty: The Espionage Fiction of John Buchan', *Midwest Quarterly* 22:3 (1981), 230-41

Bengtsson, Frans G., *The Long Ships: A Saga of the Viking Age*, trans. Michael Meyer (London & Glasgow, 1956)

Bennett, J.A.W., 'The Beginnings of Norse Studies in England', *Saga-Book* 12 (1937), 35-42

Benton, Jill, *Naomi Mitchison: A Century of Experiment in Life and Letters* (London, 1990)

Bibire, Paul, 'The Poetry of Earl Rognvaldr's Court', in *St Magnus Cathedral*, ed. Barbara E. Crawford (Aberdeen, 1988), pp.208-40

Biddiss, Michael D., *Father of Racist Ideology: The Social and Political Thought of Count Gobineau* (New York, 1970)

Blackwood, Frederick T. Hamilton, Marquis of Dufferin and Ava, *Letters from High Latitudes* (London, 1857)

Bold, Alan, *George Mackay Brown* (Edinburgh, 1978)

——, *Hugh MacDiarmid: The Terrible Crystal* (London, 1983)

——, *MacDiarmid: Christopher Murray Grieve. A Critical Biography* (London, 1988)

——, *Modern Scottish Literature* (London, 1983)

Borgstrøm, Carl Hj., 'On the Influence of Norse on Scottish Gaelic; Preaspiration of Stops and Pitch Patterns', *Norsk Tidsskrift for Sprogvidenskap* 11 (*Lochlann* 6) (1974), 91-103

Borrow, George, *The Works of George Borrow*, ed. Clement Shorter, 16 vols (London, 1923-24)

Bosworth, Joseph, *Scandinavian Literature, with Short Chronological Specimens of the Old Danish, Icelandic, Norwegian and Swedish* (London, 1839)

Branston, Brian, *Gods of the North*, 2nd. rev. edn. (London, 1980)

Brooke, Charlotte, (trans.) *Reliques of Irish Poetry* (Dublin, 1789)

Brøgger, A.W., *Ancient Emigrants: A History of the Norse Settlements of Scotland* (Oxford, 1929)

Brøndsted, Johannes, *The Vikings* (1960), trans. Kalle Skow (Harmondsworth, 1965)

Buchan, David, *The Ballad and the Folk* (London, 1972)

Burchardt, C.B., *Norwegian Life and Literature* (London, 1920)

Burton, Sir Richard F., *Ultima Thule: or a Summer in Iceland*, 2 vols (London & Edinburgh, 1875)

Buthlay, Kenneth, *Hugh MacDiarmid*, Scottish Writers Series 2 (Edinburgh, 1982)

Butter, P.H., *Edwin Muir: Man and Poet* (Edinburgh & London, 1966)

Caird, James B., 'Gaelic Elements in Neil Gunn', *Studies in Scottish Literature* 15 (1980), 88-94

Calderwood, A.A., 'Danish Libraries in Britain', *Denmark* (June 1948), 8-9; (July 1948), 13-14

Campbell, Ian, *Lewis Grassic Gibbon*, Scottish Writers Series 6 (Edinburgh, 1985)

Chaillu, Paul du, *Ivar the Viking* (London, 1893)

Chamberlain, Houston Stewart, *The Foundations of the Nineteenth Century*, trans. John Lees, 2 vols (London, 1911)

Chapman, Malcolm, *The Gaelic Vision in Scottish Culture* (London & Montreal, 1978)

Christiansen, Reidar Th., 'Scotsmen and Norsemen: Cultural Relations in the North Sea Area', *Scottish Studies* 1 (1957), 15-57

——, *The Vikings and the Viking Wars in Irish and Gaelic Tradition* (Oslo, 1931)

Clyne, Norval, *The Romantic Scottish Ballads and the Lady Wardlaw Heresy* (Aberdeen, 1859)

Cohen, Bronwen, 'Norse Imagery in Shetland: an historical study of intellectuals and their use of the past in the construction of Shetland's identity, with particular reference to the period 1800-1914', unpublished Ph.D thesis, University of Manchester, 1983

Coles, John, *Summer Travelling in Iceland* (London, 1882)

Collingwood, W.G., and Jón Stefánsson, *A Pilgrimage to the Saga-Steads of Iceland* (Ulverston, 1899)

Cowan, Edward J., *Icelandic Studies in Eighteenth and Nineteenth Century Scotland*, Studia Islandica 31 (1972), 107-51

——, 'The Sage and the Sagas: the Brothers Carlyle and *Early Kings*', *The Bibliotheck* 9 (1978-79), 161-183

——, 'What is *Orkneyinga Saga* about ?', *Northern Studies* 2 (1973) 19-22

Crawford, Barbara E., (ed.) *St Magnus Cathedral and Orkney's Twelfth Century Renaissance* (Aberdeen, 1988)

——, *Scandinavian Scotland* (Leicester, 1987)

——, 'Scotland's Foreign Relations: Scandinavia', in *Scottish Society in the Fifteenth Century*, ed. Jennifer M. Brown (London, 1977), pp. 85-100

Crawford, Iain, Review of Naomi Mitchison's *The Swan's Road*, *Saltire Review* 1:3 (Winter, 1954), 93

Crossley-Holland, Kevin, *The Norse Myths* (London, 1980)

Curtis, L.P., *Anglo-Saxons and Celts: A Study of Anti-Irish Prejudice in Victorian England* (Bridgeport, Mass., 1968)

Daniell, David, *The Interpreter's House: A Critical Assessment of John Buchan* (London, 1975)

D'Arcy, Julian M., and Kirsten Wolf, 'Sir Walter Scott and *Eyrbyggja Saga*', *Studies in Scottish Literature* 22 (1987), 30-43

Darwin, Charles, *The Descent of Man*, 2 vols (London, 1871)

——, *On the Origin of Species by Means of Natural Selection* (London, 1859)

Dasent, George Webbe, 'England and Norway in the Eleventh Century', *The North British Review* 42 (1865), 357-412

——, 'Harald Hardrada', *The North British Review* 40 (1864), 93-143

——, 'Harald Hardrada and Magnus the Good', *The North British Review* 39 (1863), 493-537

See also Section I for translations from Old Norse

Deane, Seamus, *A Short History of Irish Literature* (London, 1986)

Dickinson, W. Croft, 'Some Scandinavian Influences in Scottish Legal Procedure?', *Arv* 15 (1959), 155-59

Dickson, Beth, 'From Personal to Global: The Fiction of Naomi Mitchison', *Chapman* 50-51 (Spring, 1987), 34-40

Dixon, Keith, 'Lewis Grassic Gibbon, Scotland and Nationalism', in *Nationalism in Literature*, ed. Horst W. Drescher and Hermann Völkel, Scottish Studies Vol.8 (Frankfurt am Main, 1989), pp.201-12

Dobell, Sydney T., *Balder* (London, 1854)

Donaldson, Gordon, *A Northern Commonwealth: Scotland and Norway* (Edinburgh, 1990)

——, 'Problems of Sovereignty and Law in Orkney and Shetland', in *Stair Society Miscellany Two* (1984), pp.13-40

Dooley, Anne, 'Hugh MacDiarmid and the Gaelic Muse', in *The Celtic Consciousness*, ed. Robert O'Driscoll (Edinburgh & Portaloise, 1982), pp.459-66

Douglas, David C., *The Norman Achievement*, 2nd. edn. (London, 1972)

Downie, R. Angus, *Frazer and the Golden Bough* (London, 1970)

Drescher, Horst, (ed.) *Thomas Carlyle 1981*, Scottish Studies Vol.1 (Frankfurt am Main, 1983)

Duckett, Eleanor Shipley, *Alfred the Great* (London & Chicago, 1956)

Dufferin, Marquis of, see Blackwood, Frederick Temple

Duncan, Archibald A.M., *Scotland: The Making of the Kingdom*, Edinburgh History of Scotland, Vol.I (Edinburgh, 1975)

Eddison, E.R., *Styrbjorn the Strong* (London, 1926)

Emerson, Ralph Waldo, *English Traits* (1856), rpt. in *The Selected Writings of Ralph Waldo Emerson*, ed. Brooks Atkinson, 2nd. edn. (New York, 1950), pp.523-690

Evans, D. Wyn, 'A Note on the Content of the Thorkelin Collection in the National Library of Scotland', *The Bibliotheck* 4 (1963), 79-80

Evans, Evan, (trans.) *Some Specimens of the Poetry of the Antient Welsh Bards* (London, 1764)

Fairchild, F.N., *The Noble Savage: A Study in Romantic Naturalism* (New York, 1928)

Fallis, Richard, *The Irish Renaissance: An Introduction to Anglo-Irish Literature* (Dublin, 1978)

Falnes, Oscar J., *National Romanticism in Norway* (London & New York, 1933)

Farley, Frank Edgar, *Scandinavian Influences in the English Romantic Movement* (Boston, 1903)

Faverty, Frederic E., *Matthew Arnold the Ethnologist* (Evanston, 1951)

Fenton, Alexander, and Hermann Pálsson, (eds.) *The Northern and Western Isles in the Viking World* (Edinburgh, 1984)

Fisher, M.G., (ed.) *Session Cases 1963* (Edinburgh, 1963)

Fjalldal, Magnús, 'Norrænir menn í vesturvíking - hin hlíðin' ['Norse Raiders in the West - the Other Story'], *Skírnir* 161 (1987), 106-17

Flom, George T., *Scandinavian Influence on Southern Lowland Scotch* (New York, 1900)

Foote, Peter, 'Observations on *Orkneyinga Saga*', in *St Magnus Cathedral*, ed. Barbara E. Crawford (Aberdeen, 1988), pp.192-207

——, and D.M. Wilson, *The Viking Achievement* (London, 1971)

Fulk, R.D., 'The Moral System of *Hrafnkels Saga Freysgoða*', *Saga-Book* 22 (1986-89), 1-32

Fulton, Robin, 'Argus: a Scottish Survey', *New Edinburgh Review* 4 (1969), 6-9

——, *Contemporary Scottish Poetry: Individuals and Contexts* (Loanhead, 1974)

Gathorne-Hardy, G.M., *The Norse Discoverers of America* (Oxford, 1921)

Geipel, John, *The Viking Legacy: The Scandinavian Influence on the English and Gaelic Languages* (Newton Abbot, 1971)

Gibson, O.D. Macrae, 'The Other Scottish Language—*Orkneyinga Saga*', in *Bryght Lanternis: Essays on the Language and Literature of Medieval and Renaissance Scotland*, ed. J. Derrick McClure and Michael G. Spiller (Aberdeen, 1989), pp.420-28

Gifford, Douglas, *James Hogg* (Edinburgh, 1976)

——, *Neil M. Gunn and Lewis Grassic Gibbon* (Edinburgh, 1983)

——, 'Neil Gunn and the Mythic Regeneration of Scotland: The Two Great Epic Cycles', in *Neil Gunn's Country: Essays in Celebration of Neil Gunn*, ed. Dairmid Gunn and Isobel Murray (Edinburgh, 1991), pp.75-111

——, and Alexander Scott, (eds.) *Neil M. Gunn: The Man and the Writer* (Edinburgh, 1973)

Gobineau, Count Joseph Arthur de, *Essai sur l'Inégalité des Races Humaines*, 4 vols (Paris, 1853-55)

Gosse, Edmund William, *King Erik: A Tragedy* (London, 1876)

——, *Studies in the Literature of Northern Europe* (London, 1879)

Gourlay, Robert B., 'Before the Vikings: The Pre-Norse Background in Caithness', in *The Viking Age in Caithness, Orkney and the North Atlantic*, ed. Colleen E. Batey, Judith Jesch and Christopher D. Morris (Edinburgh, 1993), pp.111-19

Graham, Laurence, and Brian Smith, (eds.) *MacDiarmid in Shetland* (Lerwick, 1992)

Gray, Thomas, *Gray's Poems, Letters and Essays*, ed. John Drinkworth, Everyman's Library 628 (London, 1966)

Green, Roger Lancelyn, *Andrew Lang: A Critical Biography* (Leicester, 1946)

Greenway, John L., *The Golden Horns: Mythic Imagination and the Nordic Past* (Athens, Georgia, 1977)

Grimble, Ian, *Scottish Clans and Tartans*, 2nd. edn. (London, 1977)

Grimond, Lord J., Introduction to Edwin Muir, *An Autobiography* (London, 1987)

Grønneberg, Roy, *Jakobsen and Shetland* (Lerwick, 1981)

Guest, Lady Charlotte, (trans.) *The Mabinogion*, 3 vols (London & Llandovery, 1838-49)

Gunn, Dairmid, 'My Uncle and I', in *Neil Gunn's Country: Essays in Celebration of Neil Gunn*, ed. Dairmid Gunn and Isobel Murray (Edinburgh, 1991), pp.3-17

Gunn, Mark Rugg, *History of the Clan Gunn* (Glasgow, n.d. [1969])

Haggard, H. Rider, *Eric Brighteyes* (1891; Hollywood, 1974)

Hart, Francis Russell, 'Beyond History and Tragedy: Neil Gunn's Early Fiction', in *Essays on Neil M. Gunn*, ed. David Morrison (Thurso, 1971), pp.52-67

——, *The Scottish Novel: From Smollett to Spark* (Cambridge, Mass., 1978)

——, and J.B. Pick, *Neil M. Gunn: A Highland Life* (London, 1981)

Harvie, Christopher, 'Second Thoughts of a Scotsman on the Make: Politics, Nationalism and Myth in John Buchan', in *Nationalism in Literature*, Scottish Studies Vol.8, ed. Horst Drescher and Hermann Völkel (Frankfurt am Main, 1989), pp.213-36.

Haugen, Einar, *Language Conflict and Language Planning: The Case of Modern Norwegian* (Cambridge, Mass., 1966)

Haws, Charles H., 'Carlyle's Concept of History in *Heroes and Hero-Worship*', in *Thomas Carlyle 1981*, ed. Horst Drescher, Scottish Studies Vol.1 (Frankfurt am Main, 1983), pp.153-63

Herbert, William, *Select Icelandic Poetry Translated from the Originals with Notes*, 2 parts (London, 1804-06)

Herbert, W.N., *To Circumjack MacDiarmid: The Poetry and Prose of Hugh MacDiarmid* (Oxford, 1992)

Herdman, John, 'The Previously Unpublished Novels of David Lindsay', *Scottish Literary Journal*, Supplement No.3 (1976), 14-25

Herford, C.H., 'Norse Myth in English Poetry', *Bulletin of the John Rylands Library* 5 (1919), 75-98

Hewitt, David, and Michael Spiller, (eds.) *Literature of the North* (Aberdeen, 1983)

Hewitt, Heather, Review of *A Distant Isle* by George Marshall in *Scottish Literary Journal*, Supplement No.28 (1988), 15-17

Higgins, D.S., *Rider Haggard: The Great Storyteller* (London, 1981)

Himmelfarb, Gertrude, *Victorian Minds* (London, 1968)

Holtsmark, Anne, 'Bjarne Kolbeinsson og hans forfatterskap', *Edda* 37:1 (1937), 1-17

——, 'Vefr Darraðar', *Maal og Minne* (1939), 74-96

Howitt, William and Mary, *The Literature and Romance of Northern Europe*, 2 vols (London, 1852)

Huberman, Elizabeth, 'George Mackay Brown's *Magnus*', *Studies in Scottish Literature* 16 (1981), 122-34

Hume, Kathryn, *Fantasy and Mimesis: Responses to Reality in Western Literature* (London & New York, 1984)

——, 'Visionary Allegory in David Lindsay's *A Voyage to Arcturus*', *Journal of English and Germanic Philology* 77 (1978), 72-91

Hustvedt, Sigurd Bernhard, *Ballad Criticism in Scandinavia and Great Britain during the Eighteenth Century* (New York, 1916)

Hægstad, Marius, *Hildinakvadet med utgreiding um det norske maal paa Shetland i eldre tid* (Christiania [Oslo], 1900)

Jakobsen, Jakob, *The Dialect and Place Names of Shetland* (Lerwick, 1897)

——, *An Etymological Dictionary of the Norn Language in Shetland*, trans. Anna Horsbøl, 2 vols (London & Copenhagen, 1928-32)

Jameson, Storm, Review of Eric Linklater's *The Men of Ness* in *Now and Then* (Winter 1932), 32-34

Johnson, Edgar, *Sir Walter Scott: The Great Unknown*, 2 vols (London, 1970)

Johnson, W.T., (ed.) *Thorkelin and Scotland*, Sgann Microfilms (Edinburgh, 1982)

Johnston, A.W., 'Orkney and Shetland Folk 880-1350', *Saga-Book* 9 (1920-25), 372-407

Jones, Gwyn, *A History of the Vikings*, 2nd. rev. edn. (Oxford, 1984)

——, *The Norse Atlantic Saga*, 2nd. rev. edn. (Oxford, 1986)

Kamenetsky, Christa, *Children's Literature in Hitler's Germany: The Cultural Policy of National Socialism* (Athens, Ohio, 1984)

Katz, Wendy R., *Rider Haggard and the Fiction of Empire* (Cambridge, 1987)

Kearney, Hugh, *The British Isles: A History of Four Nations* (Cambridge, 1989)

Keary, Annie and Eliza, *Heroes of Asgard and the Giants of Jötunheim* (London, 1857)

Kendon, Frank, Review of Neil Gunn's *Sun Circle* in *John O'London's Weekly*, 3 June 1933, p.309

Kendrick, T.D., *A History of the Vikings* (London, 1930)

Kidd, Colin, 'Teutonist Ethnology and Scottish Nationalist Inhibition 1780-1880', *The Scottish Historical Review* Vol.LXXIV 1: No.197 (1995), 45-68

Kingsley, Charles, *Hereward the Wake* (London, 1866)

——, *The Roman and the Teuton, Works of Charles Kingsley* Vol.X (London, 1879)

Kliger, Samuel, *The Goths in England: A Study in Seventeenth and Eighteenth Century Thought* (Cambridge, Mass., 1952)

Knox, Robert, *The Races of Men: a Fragment* (London, 1850-62)

Kristjánsson, Jónas, *Eddas and Sagas*, trans. Peter G. Foote (Reykjavik, 1988)

Kruse, Juanita, *John Buchan (1875-1940) and the Idea of Empire* (Lampeter, 1989)

Kusch, Robert W., 'Pattern and Paradox in *Heroes and Hero-Worship*', *Studies in Scottish Literature* 6 (1969), 146-55

Lieder, Paul Robert, 'Scott and Scandinavian Literature', *Smith College Studies in Modern Languages* I, No.2 (1920), 8-57

Lindsay, Maurice, *History of Scottish Literature* (London, 1977)

Linklater, Marjorie, Introduction to Eric Linklater's *The Men of Ness*, 2nd. edn. (Kirkwall, 1983)

——, 'Looking Back to the Octocentenary Pageant [1937]', in *St. Magnus Cathedral: 850 Years - A Celebration*, ed. Alastair and Anne Cormack (Kirkwall, 1987), pp.61-74

Litzenberg, Karl, *The Victorians and the Vikings*, University of Michigan Contributions in Modern Philology 3 (Ann Arbor, 1947)

——, 'William Morris and Scandinavian Literature: A Bibliographical Essay on Anglo-Norse Literary Relations', *Scandinavian Studies and Notes* 13 (1933-35), 93-105

Lock, C.G.W., *The Home of the Eddas* (London, 1879)

Longford, Elizabeth, Introduction to *Travel Light* by Naomi Mitchison, Virago Modern Classics (London, 1985)

Lownie, Andrew, *John Buchan: The Presbyterian Cavalier* (London, 1995)

Loyn, H.R., *The Vikings in Britain* (New York, 1977)

Lytton, Edward Bulwer, *Harold: The Last of the Saxon Kings* (1848), Everyman's Library 15 (London, 1970)

MacBain, Alexander, 'Macpherson's *Ossian*', *Celtic Magazine* 12 (1887), 193-201

Mac Cana, Proinsias, 'The Influence of the Vikings on Celtic Literature', in *Proceedings of the International Congress of Celtic Studies 1959*, ed. Brian Ó'Cúív (Dublin, 1962), pp.78-118

McCleery, Alistair, (ed.) Introduction to *Landscape and Light: Essays by Neil M. Gunn* (Aberdeen, 1987)

McClure, J. Derrick, '*Devil's Tor*: A Rehabilitation of David Lindsay's "Monster"', *Extrapolation* 21:4 (1980), 367-378

——, 'Language and Logic in *A Voyage to Arcturus*', *Scottish Literary Journal* 1:1 (1974), 29-38

McCulloch, Margery, 'Edwin Muir and Scotland', *Akros* 16 No.47 (1981), 67-81

——, *Edwin Muir: Poet, Critic and Novelist* (Edinburgh, 1993)

——, *The Novels of Neil M. Gunn: A Critical Study* (Edinburgh, 1987)

MacDonald, Rev. Allan, 'The Norsemen in Uist Folklore', *Saga-Book* 3 (1901-03), 413-33

MacDonald, Donald A., 'The Vikings in Gaelic Oral Tradition', in *The Northern and Western Isles in the Viking World*, ed. Alexander Fenton and Hermann Pálsson (Edinburgh, 1984), pp.265-79

Mackay, Rev. Neil, 'The Influence of the Norse Invasions on the Language and Literature of the Scottish Highlands', *Transactions of the Gaelic Society of Inverness* 20 (1894-96), 78-103

McKillop, A.D., 'A Critic of 1741 on Early Poetry', *Studies in Philology* 30 (1933), 504-21

McLaren, Moray, *The Scots* (Harmondsworth, 1951)

Maclean, Magnus, *The Literature of the Celts* (Glasgow & Dublin, 1902)

——, *The Literature of the Highlands* (Glasgow & London, 1903)

Maclean, Sorley, 'The Poetry of William Livingstone', *Transactions of the Gaelic Society of Inverness* 39-40 (1942-50), 1-19

MacNeice, Louis, see Auden, W.H.

McNeill, F. Marian, *The Silver Bough, Vol.I Scottish Folk-Lore and Folk-Belief* (1957), Canongate Classics 24 (Edinburgh, 1989)

McNeill, Peter, and Ranald Nicholson, *An Historical Atlas of Scotland c.400-c.1600* (St. Andrews, 1975)

McQuillan, Ruth A., 'MacDiarmid's Other Dictionary', *Lines Review* 66 (1978), 5-14

Magnusson, Sally, 'The Victorian and the Norseman', *Northern Studies* 12 (1978), 3-15

Malcolm, William K., *A Blasphemer and Reformer: A Study of James Leslie Mitchell (Lewis Grassic Gibbon)* (Aberdeen, 1984)

Manlove, Colin, *Scottish Fantasy Literature: A Critical Survey* (Edinburgh, 1994)

Marshall, George, *In A Distant Isle: The Orkney Background of Edwin Muir* (Edinburgh, 1987)

Mathias, Roland, *Anglo-Welsh Literature: An Illustrated History* (Bridgend, 1987)

Mawer, Allen, *The Vikings* (Cambridge, 1913)

Melchers, G., 'Narrowing and Extension of Meaning in the Scandinavian-based Vocabulary of Shetland Dialect', *Scottish Language* 5 (1986), 110-119

Meyer, Kuno, (trans.) *The Voyage of Bran* (London, 1895)

Mooney, John, *St. Magnus, Earl of Orkney* (Kirkwall, 1935)

Morris, William, *The Earthly Paradise*, 4 vols. (London, 1868-70)
    See also Section I for translations of sagas.

Morrison, David, (ed.) *Essays on Neil M. Gunn* (Thurso, 1971)

Munro, Ian S., *James Leslie Mitchell: Lewis Grassic Gibbon* (Edinburgh & London, 1966)

Murison, David, 'Norse Influence on Scots', *Lallans* 13 (1979), 31-34

——, 'Shetland Speech Today', *Fróðskaparrit* 13 (1964), 122-29

Murray, Isobel, 'Human Relations: An Outline of Some Major Themes in Naomi Mitchison's Adult Fiction', in *Studies in Scottish Fiction: Twentieth Century*, Scottish Studies Vol.10, ed. Joachim Schwend and Horst Drescher (Frankfurt am Main, 1990), pp.243-56

——, Introduction to Naomi Mitchison, *Beyond This Limit* (Edinburgh, 1986)

——, 'Novelists of the Renaissance', Ch.7 of *The History of Scottish Literature* Vol.4, ed. Cairns Craig (Aberdeen, 1987), pp.103-17

——, and Bob Tait, *Ten Modern Scottish Novels* (Aberdeen, 1984)

Murray, Rowena, 'The Influence of Norse Literature on the Twentieth-Century Writer George Mackay Brown', in *Scottish Language and Literature, Medieval and Renaissance*, Scottish Studies Vol.4, ed. Dietrich Strauss and Horst W. Drescher (Frankfurt am Main, 1986), pp.547-57

Nansen, Fridtjof, *In Northern Mists*, 2 vols (London, 1911)

Nicolaisen, W.F.H., *Scottish Place-Names: Their Study and Significance* (London, 1976)

Nordby, Conrad Hjalmar, *The Influence of Old Norse Literature upon English Literature* (New York, 1901)

Oftedal, Magne, 'Gaelic: Norse Influence', in *The Companion to Gaelic Scotland*, ed. Derick S. Thomson (Oxford, 1983), pp.98-99

Olrik, Axel, *Viking Civilisation*, rev. by Hans Ellekilde, trans. Jacob W. Hartmann (London, 1930)

——, and Hans Ellekilde, *Nordens Gudeverden*, 2 vols (Copenhagen, 1926-51)

Olsen, Magnus, 'Orknø-Norn og Norrøn Diktning paa Orknøene', *Maal og Minne* (1932), 139-53

Omberg, Margaret, *Scandinavian Themes in English Poetry 1760-1800*, Studia Anglistica Upsaliensia 29 (Uppsala, 1976)

Orkneyinga saga, ed. Sigurður Nordal (Copenhagen, 1913)

Parnell, Michael, *Eric Linklater: A Critical Biography* (London, 1984)

Percy, Thomas, *Five Pieces of Runic Poetry from the Icelandic Language* (London, 1763)

Perkins, Richard, 'Rowing Chants and the Origins of *Dróttkvæðr Háttr*', *Saga-Book* 21 (1984-85), 155-221

Pick, J.B., 'David Lindsay and the Sublime', *Cencrastus* 2 (Spring 1980), 15-17

——, *The Great Shadow House: Essays on the Metaphysical Tradition in Scottish Fiction* (Edinburgh, 1993)

——, Introduction to David Lindsay, *The Haunted Woman*, Canongate Classics 9 (Edinburgh, 1987)

——, and Colin Wilson and E.H. Visiak, *The Strange Genius of David Lindsay* (London, 1970)

Pike, Luke Owen, *The English and their Origin: a Prologue to Authentic English History* (London, 1866)

Poliakov, Léon, *The Aryan Myth: A History of Racist and Nationalist Ideas in Europe* (London, 1974)

Price, Richard, *The Fabulous Matter of Fact: The Poetics of Neil M Gunn* (Edinburgh, 1991)

Rabkin, Eric S., 'Conflation of Genres and Myths in David Lindsay's *A Voyage to Arcturus*', *The Journal of Narrative Technique* 6 (1977), 149-55

Rask, Rasmus C.N., *A Grammar of the Icelandic or Old Norse Tongue*, trans. G.W. Dasent (London, 1843)

Reid, Alexander, 'Neil Gunn's Mysticism', in *Neil M. Gunn: The Man and the Writer*, ed. Alexander Scott and Douglas Gifford (Edinburgh, 1973), pp.344-59

Rendboe, Laurits, 'How "worn-out" or "corrupted" was Shetland Norn in its final stage?', *North-Western European Language Evolution* 3 (1984), 53-88

——, *The Shetland Literary Tradition*, 2 vols (Odense, 1986)

Rescanières, Marie-Hélène, 'Scottish Saga: *Sun Circle* and *Butcher's Broom*', in *Neil M. Gunn: The Man and the Writer*, ed. Alexander Scott and Douglas Gifford (Edinburgh, 1973), pp.88-100

Riach, Alan, *Hugh MacDiarmid's Epic Poetry* (Edinburgh, 1991)

Ridley, M.R., *Second Thoughts* (London, 1965)

Ritchie, Anna, *Viking Scotland* (London, 1993)

Robberstad, Knut, 'Udal Law', in *Shetland and the Outside World 1469-1969*, ed. Donald J. Withrington (Oxford, 1983), pp.49-68

Roberts, J. Graeme, 'Tradition and Pattern in the Short Stories of George Mackay Brown', in *Literature of the North*, ed. David Hewitt and Michael Spiller (Aberdeen, 1985), pp.176-88

Roesdahl, Else, *The Vikings*, trans. Susan M. Margeson and Kirsten Williams (Harmondsworth, 1991)

Rush, Christopher, *Into the Ebb* (Aberdeen, 1989)

Saddlemeyer, Ann, 'The Cult of the Celt: Pan-Celticism in the Nineties', in *The World of W.B. Yeats: Essays in Perspective*, ed. Ann Saddlemeyer and Robin Skelton (Dublin, 1965), pp.19-21

Schach, Paul, *Icelandic Sagas*, Twayne's World Authors Series 717 (Boston, 1984)

Schei, Liv Kjørsvik, and Gunnie Moberg, *The Orkney Story*, 2nd. edn. (London, 1987)

——, *The Shetland Story* (London, 1988)

Schoene, Berthold, *The Making of Orcadia: Narrative Identity in the Prose Work of George Mackay Brown*, Anglo-American Studies 6 (Frankfurt am Main, 1995)

Schofield, Jack, Review of David Lindsay's *A Voyage to Arcturus*, *Studies in Scottish Literature* 10 (1972), 59-61

Scott, Alexander, Review of Alan Bold, *Hugh MacDiarmid: The Terrible Crystal*, *Scottish Review* 32 (1983), 34

——, Reviews of Eric Linklater, *The Ultimate Viking*, and Naomi Mitchison, *The Land the Ravens Found*, *Saltire Review* 3:8 (1956), 66

Seaton, Ethel, *Literary Relations of England and Scandinavia in the Seventeenth Century* (Oxford, 1935)

Sellin, Bernard, 'David Lindsay: Scotland and the Northern Connection', in *Studies in Scottish Fiction: Twentieth Century*, Scottish Studies Vol.10, ed. Joachim Schwend and Horst Drescher (Frankfurt am Main, 1990), pp.67-82

——, *The Life and Works of David Lindsay*, trans. Kenneth Gunnell (Cambridge, 1981)

Sharp, Elizabeth A., (ed.) *Lyra Celtica: An Anthology of Representative Celtic Poetry* (Edinburgh, 1896)

——, *William Sharp (Fiona Macleod): A Memoir Compiled by his Wife*, 2nd. edn., 2 vols (London, 1912)

Sigman, Joseph, 'Adam-Kadmon, Nifl, Muspel, and the Biblical Symbolism of *Sartor Resartus*', *English Literary History* 41 (1974), 233-56

Sigmundsson, Svavar, 'A Critical Review of the Work of Jakob Jakobsen and Hugh Marwick', in *The Northern and Western Isles in the Viking World*, ed. Alexander Fenton and Hermann Pálsson (Edinburgh, 1984), pp.280-91

Simpson, John, 'Scott and Old Norse Literature', in *Scott Bicentenary Essays*, ed. Alan Bell (London & Edinburgh, 1973), pp.300-13

Smith, Brian, 'The Development of the Spoken and Written Shetland Dialect: A Historian's View', in *Shetland's Northern Links: Language and History*, ed. Doreen Waugh (Lerwick, 1996), pp.31-44

——, 'Shetland in Saga-Time: Rereading the *Orkneyinga Saga'*, *Northern Studies* 25 (1988), 21-41

——, 'Stony Limits: the Grieves in Whalsay, 1933-1942' in *MacDiarmid in Shetland*, ed. Laurence Graham and Brian Smith (Lerwick, 1992), pp.42-72

Smith, Janet Adam, *John Buchan* (London, 1965)

——, *John Buchan and his World* (London, 1979)

Smyth, Alfred P., *Warlords and Holy Men: Scotland AD 80-1000*, The New History of Scotland, Vol.I (London, 1984)

Snyder, Edward D., *The Celtic Revival in English Literature 1760-1800* (Gloucester, Mass., 1965)

——, 'The Wild Irish: A Study of Some English Satires Against the Irish, Scots, and Welsh', *Modern Philology* 17 No.12 (April 1920), 147-85

Stafford, David, 'John Buchan's Tales of Espionage: A Popular Archive of British History', *Canadian Journal of History* 18:1 (1983), 1-21

Stafford, Fiona, *The Sublime Savage: A Study of James Macpherson and the Poems of Ossian* (Edinburgh, 1988)

Stefánsson, Stefán, Review (in Icelandic) of Eric Linklater's *The Men of Ness*, *Eimreiðin* 39:4 (1933), 455-56

Stenberg, Theodore T., 'Blake's Indebtedness to the Eddas', *Modern Language Review* 18 (1923) 204-06

Stephens, Thomas, *The Literature of the Kymry* (Llandovery, 1849)

Stevenson, Ronald, 'MacDiarmid's Muses', in *The Age of MacDiarmid*, ed. P.H. Scott and A.C. Davis (Edinburgh, 1980), pp.163-69

Taylor, A.B., 'Shetland Place-Names in the Sagas', in *The Viking Congress Lerwick 1950*, ed. W. Douglas Simpson (London & Edinburgh, 1954), pp.112-29

Tennyson, Lord Alfred, *The Voyage of Maeldune* (London, 1892)

Thomsen, Grímur, 'On the Character of the Old Northern Poetry' (1867), rpt. and ed. Edward J. Cowan and Hermann Pálsson, Studia Islandica 31 (1972), 45-105

Thomson, Derick S., (ed.) *The Companion to Gaelic Scotland* (Oxford, 1983)

——, *The Gaelic Sources of Macpherson's Ossian* (Edinburgh & London, 1952)

Thomson, William P.L., *History of Orkney* (Edinburgh, 1987)

Thorkelin, G.J., 'An Essay on the Slave Trade', (London, 1788)

——, (trans.) *Fragments of English and Irish History in the Ninth and Tenth Century* (London, 1788)

Thorpe, Benjamin, *Northern Mythology*, 3 vols (London, 1851)

Townsend, J.A.B., 'The Viking Society 1892-1967', *Saga-Book* 17 (1966-69), 102-115

Turville-Petre, E.O.G., *Myth and Religion of the North* (New York, 1964)

Usborne, Richard, *Clubland Heroes* (London, 1953)

Van Hamel, A.G., 'Óðinn Hanging on the Tree', *Acta Philologica Scandinavica* 7 (1932-33), 260-88

Visiak, E.H., see Pick, J.B.

Waddell, L.A., *The British Edda* (London, 1930)

Wainwright, F.T., (ed.) *The Northern Isles* (Edinburgh & London, 1962)

Waring, Walter, *Thomas Carlyle*, Twayne's English Authors 238 (Boston, 1978)

Watson, Roderick, *The Literature of Scotland* (London, 1984)

Wawn, Andrew, *The Anglo Man: Þorleifur Repp, Philology and Nineteenth-Century Britain*, Studia Islandica 49 (Reykjavik, 1991)

——, 'The Cult of "Stalwart Frith-thjof" in Victorian Britain', in *Northern Antiquity: The Post-Medieval Reception of Edda and Saga*, ed. Andrew Wawn (London, 1994), pp.211-54.

——, '*Gunnlaugs saga Ormstunga* and the Theatre Royal, Edinburgh 1812: Melodrama, Mineralogy and Sir George Mackenzie', *Scandinavica* 21 (1982), 139-51

——, 'Shrieks at the Stones: The Vikings, the Orkneys and the Scottish Enlightenment', in *The Viking Age in Caithness, Orkney and the North Atlantic*, ed. Colleen E. Batey, Judith Jesch and Christopher D. Morris (Edinburgh, 1993), pp.408-22.

West, Herbert Faulkner, *A Modern Conquistador: Robert Bontine Cunninghame Graham. His Life and Works* (London, 1932)

Wheaton, Henry, *History of the Northmen* (London, 1831)

White Jr., George Leroy, *Scandinavian Themes in American Fiction* (Philadelphia, 1937)

Whitney, Lois, 'English Primitivistic Theories of Epic Origins', *Modern Philology* 21 (1924), 337-78

Wilson, Colin, see Pick, J.B.

Wilson, David M., 'The Norsemen', in *Who are the Scots?*, ed. Gordon Menzies (London, 1971), pp.103-13

Wittig, Kurt, *The Scottish Tradition in Literature* (Edinburgh & London, 1958)

Wolfe, Gary K., *David Lindsay*, Starmont Reader's Guide 9 (Washington, 1982)

Young, Douglas F., *Beyond the Sunset: A Study of James Leslie Mitchell (Lewis Grassic Gibbon)* (Aberdeen, 1973)

IV: CORRESPONDENCE

Letter to author from Marjorie Linklater, 24.11.87

Letter to author from George Mackay Brown, 30.12.87

Letter to author from Naomi Mitchison, undated, but postmarked 18.8.88

INDEX

For general themes and major works, see chapter sub-headings in the Contents.

'Darraðarljóð', 18, 180, 185
Darwin, Charles, 38
Dasent, Sir G. W., 25, 28, 38
Dennison, W. Traill, 183, 185
Douglas, David, 25, 28
Douglas, David C., 233
Drummond, James, 25
Dryden, John, 17, 42
Dufferin, Lord, 25
Dunbar, William, 11
Dunnett, Dorothy, 5
Edda, The Poetic, 1, 26, 114, 126
Edda, The Prose (Younger), 1, 3, 25, 26,
    98-99, 100, 104, 135, 138, 139,
    141, 181
Eddison, E.R., 207
Edinburgh Magazine, The, 19
Edinburgh Review, The, 45
Edwards, Paul, 258
Egil's Saga, 2, 22, 145, 146, 203, 207,
    209, 228;
    Egil Skallagrimsson, 120
Einar Wry-Mouth, Earl of Orkney,
    271, 272, 275
Eirik's Saga, 23, 59-60, 61, 112, 214-6;
    Eirik the Red, 60-1, 111, 113
Elphinstone, Margaret, 5
Emerson, Ralph Waldo, 38
Erskine, Ruaridh, 45, 46
Eyrbyggja Saga, 20, 22, 23, 27, 29, 104,
    110
Eyvind (Melbrigdason), 229, 256
Fenrir, (On myth.) 162, 192, 253
Fisher, Joseph, 43
Fraser's Magazine, 28
Frazer, Sir James, 28, 145
Freyr, (ON god) 138
Galt, John, 3, 19, 29
Ganga-Rolf, of Normandy, 233
Garborg, Arne, 97
Gathorne-Hardy, G.M., 62, 164
Gerald Cambrensis, 42
Gibbon, Lewis Grassic, 3, 48, **53-64**,
    70, 205, 216, 272
Gimli, (ON myth.) 190

Gisli's Saga, 120
Gobineau, Count Joseph, 38
Gosse, Edmund, 26
Goudie, Gilbert, 28
Graham, John J., 186-7
Graham, R.B. Cunninghame, 3, 27
Gray, Joseph, 186
Gray, Thomas, 2, 3, 17, 18, 30, 185,
    249
Greenlanders' Saga, The, 59-60, 61,
    112, 214-6
Gregory, Lady Isabella, 204
Grettir's Saga, 2, 29, 94, 120, 135, 145,
    203, 207, 208-9, 221, 228
Grieve, C.M., see MacDiarmid,
    Hugh
Grundtvig, Nicolai, 40
Gunn, Neil M., 3, 46, 47, 48, 49, 50,
    57, **65-92**, 105, 156, 189, 205, 211,
    280
Haggard, H. Rider, 2, 26, 27, 29, 188,
    207
Hakon, King of Norway, 7, 19, 27,
    179
Hakon (Paulsson), Earl of Orkney,
    262-3, 264, 266, 267, 268, 269, 270
Harald Finehair, K. of Norway, 179,
    187, 207
Harald Hardrada, 7, 120, 159, 160-1
Harold (Godwinsson), K. of
    England, 7
Hastings, Battle of, 7, 233
Hávamál, The, 21, 114, 126
Hayton, Sian, 5
Head, Sir Edmund, 189
Heard, Gerald, 168
Heath-Slayings, Story of the, 127
Heimskringla, 2, 3, 21, 22, 24, 26, 30,
    104, 164, 193
Henderson, Ebenezer, 22, 25
Henderson, George, 45
Herbert, William, 94
Herder, Johann G., 204
Hjaltalín, Jón, 28
Hogg, James, 3, 23, 29, 134